WOODSTOCK

an inside look at the movie that shook up the world and defined a generation

Interviews and Recollections

WOODSTOCK

an inside look at the movie that shook up the world and defined a generation

Interviews and Recollections

Dale Bell foreword by Martin Scorsese

RARE BIRD

This is a Genuine Barnacle Book

A Barnacle Book | Rare Bird Books
453 South Spring Street, Suite 302
Los Angeles, CA 90013
rarebirdbooks.com

FIRST PAPERBACK EDITION

For more information, address:
A Barnacle Book | Rare Bird Books Subsidiary Rights Department
453 South Spring Street, Suite 302
Los Angeles, CA 90013

Printed in the United States

10 9 8 7 6 5 4 3 2 1

Publisher's Cataloging-in-Publication Data

Names: Bell, Dale, 1938–, author.
Title: Woodstock: An Inside Look at the Movie that Shook Up the World
and Defined a Generation / Dale Bell.
Description: First Hardcover Edition | A Barnacle Book | New York, NY;
Los Angeles, CA: Rare Bird Books, 2019.
Identifiers: ISBN 9781644280409
Subjects: LCSH Woodstock (Motion picture)—Pictorial works. | Woodstock
Festival (1969: Bethel, NY)—Pictorial works.
| BISAC PHOTOGRAPHY / Photoessays & Documentaries | PHOTOGRA-
PHY / Subjects & Themes / Celebrations & Events
| PERFORMING ARTS / Film / Genres / Documentary
Classification: LCC PN1997 .W64 2019 | DDC 791.43/72—dc23

DEDICATION

This book is dedicated to three people:

BOB MAURICE

Producer of Woodstock, whose relentless efforts to preserve our
artistic integrity were unsurpassed;

TOM TAGGART

the mythical "Port-O-San Man"
whose worldly compassion for the kids at the Festival and in Vietnam
symbolized precisely why we fought for artistic integrity so vehemently in the
first place;

and

MAX YASGUR

a farmer whose generational understanding provided Woodstock
Ventures a happening space.

ELEN ORSON

Editorial Assistant

WOODSTOCK CREDIT LIST 1970

A FILM BY MICHAEL WADLEIGH

directed by MICHAEL WADLEIGH

produced by BOB MAURICE

editor and assistant director
T SCHOONMAKER

associate producer
DALE BELL

photographed by
MICHAEL WADLEIGH
DAVID MYERS
RICHARD PEARCE
DON LENZER
AL WERTHEIMER

sound & music & assistant to the director
LARRY JOHNSON

music advisor/coordinator
ERIC BLACKSTEAD

sound recordist
LEE OSBORNE

music mixer
DAN WALLIN

editor & assistant director
MARTIN SCORSESE

editors
STAN WARNOW
YEU-BUN YEE
JERE HUGGINS

production managers
SONYA POLONKSY
LEWIS TEAGUE

location unit supervisor
JOHN BINDER

production secretary
HANNAH HEMPSTEAD

location technical supervisor
MARTIN ANDREWS

location music engineers
BILL HANLEY
ED KRAMER
LEE OSBORNE

dubbing supervisor
GRAHAM LEE MAHIN

film coordinator in Hollywood
FRED TALMAGE

music assistant
DANNY TURBEVILLE

additional photography
MICHAEL MARGETTS
ED LYNCH
CHUCK LEVY
TED CHURCHILL
RICHARD CHEW
BOB DANNEMAN
STAN WARNOW
HART PERRY

documentary sound
LARRY JOHNSON
BRUCE PERLMAN
CHARLIE PITTS
CHARLES GROSSBECK
JOE LOUW
MALCOLM HART

assistant editors
BETTINA KUGEL HIRSCH
MIRIAM EGER
BOB ALVAREZ
PHYLLIS ALTENHAUS
MUFFIE MEYER
TED DUFFIELD
ED CARIATI
WINSTON TUCKER
ANGELA KIRBY
MIRRA BANK
BARNEY EDMONDS
LANA JOKEL
BILL LIPSKY
JANET LAURETANO
SUSAN STEINBERG
ANITA THATCHER
JIM STARK

production assistants
ED GEORGE
CHARLES CIRIGLIANO
KEN GLAZEBROOK
AL ZAYAT
ALICE MARKS
ANTHONY SANTACROCE
JON BOORSTIN

thanks to—on location:
FERN MC BRIDE
ALEX BROOKS
HAROLD SMITH
PETER BARTON
RIC BERGER
SUSAN BERGER
RENEE WADLEIGH
GINNY DUNN
ELEN ORSON
SHARON BINDER
ANNE BELL
JEANNE FIELD
CATHY HILLER
MAGGIE KOVEN
FELICITY LYNCH
ROBERT SOLOMON
JUDY UNDERHILL
VALERIE PERLMAN
NONI WATERS

VALERIE SANTIAGO
STEVE KRAFT
JOHN MORRIS
STEVE COHEN
CHIP MONCK
CHRIS LANGHART
HUGH ROMNEY
TOM LAW
KEN BABBS
THE HOG FARM
THE MERRY PRANKSTERS
SIDNEY WESTERFELD
MAX YASGUR

thanks to—at home:
BILL GRAHAM
BILL HILLIKER
JOYCE FRESH
BEAU GILL
CHUCK HIRSCH
PETE, GLORIA & HERMAN
NORBERT & VIC
BOB ROIZMAN
MARILYN SILVERBERG
DULCINDA

processing lab in New York City
J&D LABS

opticals
CINEMA RESEARCH CORP
PACIFIC TITLE & ART
NATIONAL SCREEN
KEM CORPORATION
ÉCLAIR CORPORATION
CAMERA MART
HANLEY SOUND

titles
CHARLES CIRIGLIANO
color by TECHNICOLOR

"Going Up Country"
sung by Canned Heat
The Song "Woodstock"
written by Joni Mitchell

CONTENTS

FOREWORD

MARTIN SCORSESE: ON WOODSTOCK

WOODSTOCK OBVIOUSLY EMERGED FROM its historical moment. And one of the things about that moment was that everyone was waiting for a big, defining event that would counteract all the awful things that had happened. There was the music. There was the idea of rejecting the rest of the world and living in a natural state. There was the drug culture. There was the political stance against the government, specifically its policy in Vietnam. And they all came together in this moment. It's interesting that people called it "the Woodstock Nation," because that's what people wanted—to be separate, to have their own community. And for three days, they had it. When I look back at the second half of the 1960s, I realize it is the only time I have ever heard people talk about love in serious terms, as a force to combat greed, hate, and violence.

What does it symbolize today? What will it symbolize for future generations? Well, what does the Paris Commune symbolize today? What do the New York draft riots symbolize today? They're events from a more distant past, but it's the same past that Woodstock is now receding into. What it symbolizes is that things can happen, incredible events that are the product of many particular elements converging at a particular moment. And those events can't be repeated—look at Woodstock II. But the fact that something new did happen on a grand scale, something that felt like nothing else that had ever happened before, means that something entirely new can happen again, in a way that we can't predict.

INTRODUCTION

DALE BELL, ASSOCIATE PRODUCER OF THE FILM WOODSTOCK

IT SEEMS LIKE YESTERDAY. A group of "long-haired freaks," clad in bell-bottom jeans and tattered hair-bands, some sporting cowboy hats, invade the Warner Bros.'s lot in Burbank, California, in the early winter of 1970. Tumbleweeds dance in the Santa Ana winds among the vacant sound stages. Tall grass forces its way through the empty tarmac. It looks like *The Day the Earth Stood Still*. Or is it Stanley Kramer's *On the Beach*? We say to each other, "is this the Hollywood we've all dreamed of?"

Only a handful of security people greet us, wondering who we are. Where did we come from? What are we doing on their premises?! And WHAT, they demand, is that weird gear we're trucking onto their lot? Whutt're editing tables? We know fillum, they say. (A western twang to our New York ears.) Fillum editing machines always go up and down! Not sideways! Ribbing each other at our expense, they tease, "Your long hair is going to get caught in the reels of fillum! Maybe you'd better wear hairnets!"

From their offices above and around us, Fred Weintraub, Producer; John Calley, Worldwide Production Chief; and Ted Ashley, Chairman, must have been looking on, bemused. Back in New York City, the chairman of Atlantic Records, Ahmet Ertegun, might have been smiling like the Cheshire cat. The boss of all of them, silver-haired and silver-tongued Steve Ross, might have been clapping his hands in glee.

Not one of them knew then that our "hippie movie," *Woodstock*, would pay their salaries, keep their children in school, allow them to take their vacations, and enrich their stockholders much less that it would finance the rebirth of the once-mighty Warner Bros., revolutionizing the music business at the same time.

Nor did anyone know how our movie would affect the drug culture, the war in Vietnam, the civil rights struggles in the South, or the aftermath of Kent State. How many times since have writers, musicians, commentators, comedians, and politicians invoked the event they experienced only on film, in vain or in glory?

A scant four months earlier—August 15, 16, and 17, 1969, the jubilant days that now live for generations—half a million people had forged a pilgrimage to a tiny spot in New York State. We had trekked along with the largest, most highly sophisticated documentary film unit ever assembled to record it all. No precedent to guide our efforts. The presence of drugs was a certainty. The crowd could become uncontrollable. Pandemonium? Nirvana? Madness? Peace and love? Mayhem?

As each performing group of musicians found their way to the front of the vast platform to face their daunting audience of loyal, peaceful fans, we filmmakers huddled on the lip of the stage, making plans. Film loads were calculated, camera positions assigned, songs from the set selected, style was discussed.

But we were fearful that our fifteen cameramen would run out of precious film if the helicopters couldn't land with our mandatory cargo; we were entirely without financial means, just enough to purchase raw stock. Everything else was a house of cards built on promise and speculation and many gut feelings. (**As late as two weeks before the festival, in early August, no one was preparing to make the movie!**) Somehow we had assembled this massive crew and a complete kit of the best equipment available in the space of six days. Without funding. And now here we were. In IT.

Bonded together by camaraderie and adrenaline, we fought off claustrophobia, fear, heat, hunger, and sleep. Working from plywood sawhorse tables underneath the massive stage, deprived of food and water, covered with mud and rain, risking electrocution in the windy thunderstorms of Saturday, virtually sleepless for three nights, we moved synchronously through our paces, like a well-trained army.

Runners assigned to each of the six onstage cameramen gathered like ball boys in tournament tennis, ready to leap forward when a cameraman needed help or a new roll of film. Loaders beneath the stage, their sweating arms immersed in black film-changing bags, loaded and unloaded magazines tirelessly in ankle-deep mud, knowing that one scratch on the emulsion of one film roll could ruin a good day's—or night's—work!

During daylight hours, when we could maneuver among the throng of half a million people, we tried to determine the kinds of stories we would be able to cover before nightfall, for everyone knew that the documentary sequences would be equally as important as the music. We were mindful to keep our eyes out for spontaneous situations and *to film what interested us, to turn off when we lost interest.*

Never before (and need I say, never since, despite so many attempts at imitation!) had such advanced technology been married so dynamically, so swiftly, so harmoniously to a vision we filmmakers had developed independently in the tumultuous cauldron of the 1960s. Over the course of a short but turbulent journey, we were thrown together—total strangers and life-long friends—to pool our collective experiences, our skills, our wisdom, and our vision, to create for future generations a single, revolutionary memoir. As none of us could truly assess its impact before the movie was released, we were unaware that we were creating a symbol for an age. But driven by the desire to get it right, we managed to record *live on film* for posterity the most successful documentary the world has ever known…an icon of this century, *Woodstock.*

I always considered myself the least likely person to be at White Lake, New York, that August of 1969. Because my head had always been saturated with Broadway melodies interlaced with Bach, Beethoven, and Brahms, and sometimes Chopin, there was no place for Baez, Butterfield, or—*what was that name?*—Sly and the Family Stone.

I was busy raising my family—three small sons: Jonathan, David, and Andrew—with my wife Anne in a Victorian three-story gingerbread house on the banks of the Hudson River facing the vast Tappan Zee. Had we inherited the mantle of revolution from former owner Betty Friedan, whose *The Feminine Mystique* called for a changed role for women, and had been written in our bedroom only six years earlier? We had just returned from spending a year in Washington, where I was part of the press corps in public television. This assignment brought me in touch with President Lyndon Johnson, cabinet members, and the likes of Ralph Nader. I counted myself a member of the Establishment. I was by no means a "long hair," and I had few friends who were. Most of them were more than a little intimidating to me.

In 1965, I had hired Michael Wadleigh and John Binder, fresh out of NYU Film School, and had given them their first official jobs. They had long hair and iconoclastic minds. But because they were so good, and so different in personality from other crews who were walking the halls of educational television in New York in 1965, they quickly received calls from other producers.

Soon, Mike and John were working regularly, traveling the world, meeting other camera crews like themselves, picking up on new technologies. Natural light, *cinéma vérité*, adopted by handheld cameras being designed in France and Germany; these new cameras could revolutionize traditional thirty-five-millimeter news-gathering. So aware were Mike and John of the importance of harnessing these innovations in cameras, recorders, and postproduction gear that they visited engineers and factories in France, Switzerland, and Germany, and explored applications of the equipment to new concepts in filmmaking.

They weren't alone. Others of us, pioneering in educational television, found ourselves more advanced than commercial networks in our urgency to marry "live" satellite broadcasts with energetically "talking heads," each ready to dissect the latest State of the Union address, for example. Yet our burgeoning medium was still searching for a message.

In 1966, adhering to the Aristotelian unities of time, place, and action, I devised a program that would be filmed within a twenty-four-hour day, by thirteen cameramen located in ten different spots between San Diego and London, as though it was *live on film*. On this project, I brought together Mike (by then "Wads" to my "Ding") and David Myers, the legendary cameraman from the Bay Area who would become our collective mentor.

Yet Mike and John Binder remained close friends who brought their families and friends to our house on the river. Gradually, in the winter and spring of 1969, I found myself anticipating unemployment for the first time since I had been married. Mike and John invited me to work out of their offices on upper Broadway until I could find something permanent.

It was there that I came in contact with a whole new breed of long-haired, ingenious, funny, inventive, passionate, brilliant, and sometimes weird people who were to change my life completely. Among them was the very youthful Larry Johnson, almost an alter-ego of Michael, whose spiritual sense of the powerful music of his generation might have surpassed even his technical ability to record it and deliver it purely to another medium.

Our encounters were tentative at first, but suspicion quickly gave way to mutual respect and appreciation. There was no way to ignore those infectious minds, the sense of camaraderie, the philosophical dichotomy, the sluice of energy that coursed up and down Manhattan. After all, we were filmmakers, above and underground, destined to take on the world. By virtue of the extraordinary variety of our work, we were fast becoming the eyes and ears of the thinking, caring populace in the United States and abroad. Our portable cameras had catapulted us to the front lines. Our responsibility was to tell it like it was. And so we were uniquely poised to leap into action when the festival happened.

From the moment the film opened in March 1970, a scant eight months after the incredible experience on Max Yasgur's farm, I knew that someday, somehow, our story had to be told. Soon after I returned home on the Hudson River, I was deluged with requests to talk about my experiences. So as not to forget too much, I took some elaborate notes, gave several talks to students, and recorded the lectures so that at least my family and I would have them for posterity.

Even today, when people discover that I helped to make this movie, I'm asked, *What was it like?* My experience was just one of many. I cannot pretend to know how it affected those who were friends first, employees second, and extended family forever. Far be it from me to try to verbalize or homogenize their experiences. Nor should I. Far better for me to ask them to talk for themselves.

It was on this supposition that I asked them all to help in the production of this reunion on paper. Each of the eighty-some people we brought to the site has a story to tell: how they got there, what they expected, what they encountered, how it affected them. Couple those on-site with dozens more people in editing rooms that stretched from New York to Hollywood, and the extended family expands logarithmically. We would work together, eat together, marry and live together, and finally, we would grow into maturity, which is exactly where you find all of us right now, talking about our children and grandchildren. We've had reunions, gathering together with our families on the anniversary days in mid-August. How many other film crews in the history of the cinema have kept in touch for thirty years?

But this reunion is different. It permits us to tell our story as filmmakers, not the story of the festival itself, which has already been analyzed and spun to a fare-thee-well.

What I have assembled through this effort are recollections that may have remained private to them for all these years. Some were there at the very beginning, before there was even a mention of a Woodstock festival, before the KEM (or the Keller, as it was first called) was invented, before Merv Griffin assumed an unwitting role as "Godfather" of the multiple-screen concept that later led to our ability to create a kalidescopic movie. Some joined the production after the event, still others were added during the final days of postproduction.

Most of us were unaware of the attempts by other filmmakers to secure the rights to film the festival. My recent conversations with Ahmet Ertegun, Chairman and Founder of Atlantic Records, and with Porter Bibb, then working as a producer on behalf of Al and David Maysles, have yielded very curious results, told here for the first time. All of us seemed to be like ships passing in the night, unaware of the others' activities until now. Unraveling our little history still holds a great deal of fascination.

I wrote the following letter to our "extended family" in June 1998:

I need your help. I see this as a chance to preserve our story—how each of us contributed individually to the collective whole.

Since the initial release of the movie and the accompanying magazine articles, this is the first opportunity I know of where those of us who made the film can actually tell our own stories—and right some wrongs in the process! To me, that is an important distinction, one which should make this book interesting to a film audience as well as to readers more interested in our imprint on the world's culture.

I have always been impressed with the impact *Woodstock* has had on the fabric of America, but it has not, in my opinion, been limited to a sociological blot. Rather, I believe we affected how a generation was perceived; how music was written, recorded, marketed, and how it gave birth to the music industry we know today; …how electronic and digital innovations developed from our extraordinary marriage of vision and new technology; how the production of sound for movies, including Dolby, THX, and surround, evolved through techniques we invented; how nonlinear editing grew from our use of multiple-image KEMs; how performers were billed, marketed, and sent around the world on tours that had no precedent prior to our movie; how movie marketing to young people was transformed once we had drawn a new audience into the movie theaters; how our movie gave birth to MTV, *Saturday Night Live,* or how the establishment embraced and co-opted our revolutionary images, in spite of our efforts to deny them access; and, basically, how we long-hairs managed to astound the world with an historic icon, born in synchronicity. Nothing could have been accomplished had it not been for this totally unique synthesis. You may have your own views of these manifestations; I want to try to get them out of you.

Witnessing the remixing of the *Director's Cut* just five years ago reassured me that together we have created a monument to film history that remains as fresh and dynamic today as when it was first released almost thirty years ago.

These are our stories, mingled with perceptions from some of the performers and others whose work contributed to the success of the movie. In keeping with the tenor of our original times, I think of this project as a cinéma vérité book. the movie itself, this is also a *multiple-image* book. As a *bookmaker*, then, I have tried to minimize my intrusion into the content of others, as though I were a *filmmaker*, allowing objectivity and individual storytelling to emerge.

As a result of this *Rashomon* experiment, you may be reading sections of our history through different eyes; thus, some repetition may be evident. I hope you can tolerate an occasional *overlap*. Think of it as a *double exposure* or a *long dissolve*. You may also perceive some *instant replay, slo-mo*, and *stop-motion animation*. Allow your memory to collect this accumulated experience a piece—and a personality—at a time. The truth about this movie, *which almost didn't get made*, emerges.

By pulling all of our collective experiences together, I hope that those of us who may have caused pain to others in the odyssey of making this film will be shown compassion and forgiveness. It's not an excuse to be lured by a mysterious siren, but we were alive in extraordinarily tumultuous times, with a responsibility as documentarians to record them. We might have thought we were exempt from normal society—"The Untouchables." Maybe we had to believe we were in order to succeed at our craft. But it was an illusion that would haunt some of us the rest of our lives.

Dale Bell
Grand View on Hudson
New York
and
Mission Hills, California
June 1999

PART I

A CINEMATIC VISION ABORNING

MERV GRIFFIN

THE FREEING OF AMERICA

(WE REFER TO MERV Griffin as the "Godfather of *Woodstock*," for his innovative assignments to the Wadleigh film team provided them an experimental laboratory for new cinematic technique.)

MERV: What can I tell you about *Woodstock*?

DALE: Tell me what you remember.

MERV: Is Michael Wadleigh still alive?

DALE: Very much so. *And* in New Hampshire. And sends his best.

MERV: Oh, my God. Give him my love.

DALE: I will.

MERV: He was such a different kind of guy, for a photographer at that time—a film photographer. He was very kind of aesthetic. Almost fragile, but you realized there was a genius there behind that camera.

DALE: You're absolutely right.

MERV: I think the first thing Michael did—when we flew together in that DC-3 airplane I chartered out of New Jersey, that was to do—I did *Sidewalks of New York, Sidewalks of New England*, a Thanksgiving Day show with the kids at my farm—is that all I did on the Sidewalk things?

DALE: In Providence, you did Aretha Franklin's concert.

MERV: Yes, and then we did that baggage sequence with Paul Revere and the Raiders at the Boston airport. And I did a couple of songs—we were using the turning of the leaves of New England as background because it was so spectacular and so colorful.

DALE: What do you remember about this merry gang of filmmakers?

MERV: There was some innovation they had in shooting—it was very much cinéma vérité. I mean Michael was afraid of nothing camerawise. He wasn't locked into the moves of the day. In other words, he was very adventuresome behind that camera. I remember we did "Quiet Nights" on a rocky beach where I was walking the rocks, you know, in a kind of cold weather outfit, doing (singing)...."Quiet nights and the quiet stars...", which had been prerecorded by the orchestra and I was singing it live. He was the most awesome photographer.

DALE: Well, he was. Unfortunately he's stopped doing it, the damned fool.

MERV: Has he stopped?

DALE: Yeah. He's writing and he's producing CD-ROMs and he's written screenplays, but he has not been a cinematographer virtually since *Woodstock*. No, in 1975 we did something together.

MERV: I just recall the time I think he mortgaged his house, his family, his wife's ballet shoes—everything—to do *Woodstock*.

DALE: What did you think about the movie?

MERV: It was fabulous. There never has been a gathering like that. Oh, there've been gatherings—but not with that spirit—I mean it was the first. To have a memory like that recorded of the first of anything is wonderful.

DALE: What impact did it have?

MERV: It was tremendous. And of course that was the decade everything—every institution—broke down. It was the freeing of America, good or bad. It just took away the reins that were on everybody and the framework that was around everything you did.

My show was a great platform for all the people who protested everything. The show was on nighttime in New York and other major cities, Metromedia. Jane Fonda couldn't get on any television show except mine. And the reason she could get on mine was because we were syndicated, so there was nobody who could say, "Merv, you can't have her on." But she was persona non grata on the networks, as was Mohammed Ali. He was not allowed on. All the civil protests came on my show. The Mailers...and on the other hand, we gave equal time to the Buckleys and everybody else.

But my platform was the source of speaking out in America and they couldn't stop me. I had on the first protest against—by a world-famous person—against the Vietnam war. Lord Bertrand Russell, who later ran the Vietnam War Crimes Trial in Sweden. Bob Consodine, who was the front page writer of the then *Journal-American of New York* wrote that "Merv Griffin should be taken off the air for what he's done." And his son was my cameraman, Barry, on the show. And he wrote this piece and I answered him. He said, "We're in wartime and Merv Griffin puts on a protest against America." And I said, "We're not in wartime, what are you talking about? It's a police action, no war has been declared."

DALE: How do you feel about that today, Merv Griffin?

MERV: I feel good about it. It was a contribution. I was the only one ever allowed to go to Alcatraz to tape the Indians, which I did, when they took over Alcatraz. My philosophy of the show was that there were many voices speaking in America, not all of them do you agree with, but you should hear them. They should have some place to speak. Of course, it was misused too. *The New York Daily News* would run out and cover what they called a "major protest" and there would be four wackos standing on a corner with some signs. But they would build it up like it was something.

And then one night, a whole black organization took over my show. They rose up out of the audience. They contacted every pressman in New York and told them it was going to happen, but they didn't tell me. With these high African whistles! But they picked the wrong show. It was during the Vietnam War, and I stopped—I let the cameras go. And I said, "Okay. Who's your spokesman and now what are you protesting?" And they said there weren't enough black jazz musicians in my orchestra. And I said, "There are four. What are you talking about? It's a quarter of the orchestra." I said, "You picked the wrong place and the wrong cause. Do you know what's going on in the world?" So that kind of made their thing poop out.

Michael, he was a part of that too. He photographed the happening of the youth and their music.

DALE: Every one of us was doing this…in New York City in the 1960s.

MERV: My God, well all of it was happening on my show. Remember the famous one that made the front pages? When the kid—Abbie Hoffman—from the Chicago Seven came on my show and he was wearing what CBS said (by that time I left syndication and had been on CBS two years)—he was wearing the [American] flag. They said you cannot wear a flag as a piece of clothing. And so they prodded him out of the show with an electric prod and just left me talking to a black screen. And then when I did the commercial, Roy Rogers and Dale Evans came up in the same shirts for Ford Motor Company! Bob Woods from CBS almost had a heart attack.

MICHAEL WADLEIGH

TRIUMPH OF THE WILL

(INTERVIEW WITH MICHAEL WADLEIGH, director of *Woodstock*, on the Warner Bros.' lot in Burbank, California, spring 1994, while completing the remixing of the soundtrack and adding some forty minutes to the original length of three hours, four minutes for the definitive version the *Director's Cut*.)

DALE: Did you have any idea back then that it was going to be anything more than a concert, that it would be this big thing we call Woodstock and have a different connotation?

MICHAEL: Absolutely. I mean, you gotta remember that Woodstock started out as a village that was famous as a radical gathering place. That in 1919 in the village of Woodstock, the American Communist Party was started. In the 1920s, all sorts of radicals came up there—socialists and everything else. In the 1950s, Allen Ginsberg went there. In the 1960s, Bob Dylan, Joan Baez, everybody else. So we really had a sense that we were a continuation of the traditions of that village in making the festival. So, we thought we were onto something big. And then, of course, when we got that beautiful farm from Max Yasgur with pastures, and lake, and bird stands, and everything, we thought, "Well, this is a place where people are going to want to come." And, sure enough, a half million people got there, and 3 million tried to get there. That's what the cops said on the roads.

DALE: At the time, though, were you so busy working that you couldn't absorb this, or was it pretty clear right as it was happening?

MICHAEL: I think it was pretty clear right as it was happening. Because 500,000 people you don't overlook. And then also, as a kind of barometer, when we saw the *New York Times* headline—well, for two days running, we got full-width banner headlines for the *New York Times*. So, we thought, *Well, we're going to really be something.*

Everyone thinks of it as sort of the seminal event of the 1960s generation, indeed. We're called The Woodstock Generation after the festival. But the other interesting thing is that it's like *The Canterbury Tales*, or *The Pilgrim's Progress*. It's really a timeless idea where you see kids streaming out of the cities that are so dirty and complex and pollution-ridden and crime-ridden, coming to the countryside. You know, back to the land, back to the garden, to sort of this pristine natural setting that has the lakes and trees and so on, and the innocence of nature. And then you see the sort of cathedral erected in nature, where the wooden stage goes up, where the choirs will come to sing, where the priests will give the sermons, where the jugglers and the clowns will perform.

So, I guess really the responsibility of the documentary may be that it might turn into something of a more timeless nature where the general human condition—where war and peace and generation gap, and human rights, and so on, our relationship with the Earth—can all be looked at within a kind of metaphorical context or construct called Woodstock.

DALE: Having been there yourself and experienced the whole thing—literally from start to finish—are there things that the movie doesn't capture? I mean, what does the movie capture and what did you have to be there to kind of be a part of?

MICHAEL: Well, even there, I think the reason for the film's length was that when Thelma [Schoonmaker], Marty [Scorsese], and others and I were editing the film, we never thought we were "editing a film." We thought we were editing an experience, that we wanted to "take you there," you know? So that part of the POV that you might miss if it were a brief film, and part of the experience, would be the length of it. So, we thought that we really needed a long film to make it more like the surrogate experience. But, for us, of course, who were there, the thing that isn't shown is the arduousnes of making the movie. Just the sheer ability to stay awake for four days in a row. You know, I took speed. Most of my crew did, just to keep focused. We certainly didn't have any marijuana or beer or anything like that. We would have all gone to sleep and zonked out instantly. So in a way, we couldn't be quite as free to enjoy the event since we were working.

DALE: When you look back at it now, are there images that only come into focus twenty-five years later?

MICHAEL: Well, the thing that I also keep remembering, maybe because I'm embroiled in it now, are certain performances. Like Jimi Hendrix doing the "Star-Spangled Banner." I can transport myself back there to see that man play as if it's [happening] like today. I'm not talking about the film. But he was such an incredible musician and had such a oneness about his guitar and his body. It was virtually like he took his own guts and strung them in place of the strings—really playing his own body. I've often thought of that, and, of course, thought of him, as maybe an example of the kind of loss we all feel for the idealism of the 1960s, which seems to have all vanished.

DALE: Overall, this whole picture—how do you describe it now to people who weren't there?

MICHAEL: Well, as Jerry Garcia says in the movie—it was a biblical, epical, unbelievable scene. And it truly was biblical and epical. You had your masses, you had all your essential body functions from eating and drinking, to taking a dump, to what have you. You had your music, you had your entertainment, you had your jugglers, clowns, priests, and everything else going on there. So, I think more and more people are describing Woodstock as an epic. You know, as the sort of left-wing version of *Triumph of the Will*. That it's just one of those larger-than-life experiences, and it really was.

DALE: You kind of got thrust into being the guy who did *Woodstock*…

MICHAEL: But then I would point out to you that, as television journalists, as movie journalists, we have tremendous responsibility. We, collectively, are the most powerful media that this planet has and we're so influential. Take drugs, for example. The film seems to be arguing for drugs. And here, twenty-five years later, we have this disastrous, horrendous problem with hard drugs. So, in a way, you have to look at what you did then, look at the situation today, and say, "Well—did I do the right thing?"

As you know there is a famous song in there by Woody Guthrie's son—Woody Guthrie being one of the most famous of all time social commentators and songwriters—well, his son Arlo sings, "Coming into Los Angeleeeeeze, bringing in a couple of kees, don't touch my bag if you please, Mr. Customs man." It seems to be arguing for drugs.

Well, it's my own personal opinion that you should divide soft drugs from hard drugs. But it's also my own opinion, along with Gabriella Marchesa and many other Nobel laureates, that this policy of the continued illegalization of drugs is simply not working. That we should be dealing with drugs, not as a matter of criminalness, but as a matter of sickness and disease. In fact, the criminalization of it simply keeps the problem going. It makes it huge business. It makes people kill people and damage them and beat them up in order to steal money so they can support their habit. Is this sort of soft approach on drugs the right thing to do?

DALE: Responsibility for The Woodstock Generation?

MICHAEL: Well, I was raised by two very good parents who instilled in me the fact that you were supposed to step up to the plate and put your ego aside. I'm trying, and I hope I'm doing it now, articulating concerns that a lot of people had.

Part of the richness I think people ignore about Woodstock is the richness of alternatives. After all, in America, one of the big things we're supposed to be is the land of individuals. Which means individual opinion, alternatives, you know. Well, I think what Woodstock symbolizes is counterculture, alternative culture, alternative points of view, alternative lifestyles, questioning everything.

The biggest realization—it wasn't so much a look back as a look at a timeless situation. Country Joe's song wasn't really about the Vietnam War, it's about all wars; Joan Baez's song about Joe Hill is about all organizers; "Freedom" and "Handsome Johnny," songs that Richie Havens sings; "Summertime Blues," that there ain't no cure for them because your congressman won't get you a job, and on and on— they're all metaphors. They work today every bit as well as they did yesterday.

DALE: Has it sunk in these years later any deeper, or is it pretty much the same?

MICHAEL: Absolutely. I suppose it went through four basic phases. First was the excitement of becoming partners with the guys who were putting this thing on. Wow! We're going to do this event. Then the depressive feeling that it would never happen, that we couldn't get the political clearances, that it would just be a great idea that never was. Third, then, the exhilaration of it actually happening and then beyond our wildest dreams with all these people coming. Then fourth, the horrible responsibility which turned into a nightmare of actually getting the film made.

When the rain happened, there were power surges in the electricity, then it knocked out the motors on eight cameras that I had—I mean, they were just fried. So, I lived in terror that I actually wouldn't have the equipment to finish the piece.

And, indeed, when Jimi Hendrix plays the last piece of music, we were down to three cameras. That was it.

And then, of course, you move into the post-coital things of—we made it through *that*, now let's sit down and see what we've got. Working with Thelma Schoonmaker, who I think is the greatest editor that's ever lived, working with her to put the film together on something that's got to be one of the most ambitious films ever made, even to this day—ambitious in terms of its editing—after all, we shot 160 hours. The finished film is four hours long, but with the multiple images, we used ten hours of film. And sixteen to one, as you know, that's not much of a ratio.

Then it came out and we won the Academy Award. We became the highest-grossing documentary of all time. That was great. And then the downside of it was, for me—my personality—in a way, I got too much credit. You know, my partners who put on the event were sort of forgotten, and the guy who made the movie, which now became the event for millions of people around the world, had to become a spokesman for it. And, after a while, especially after the 1960s ended, and the whole country turned to the right, people would literally call me in the middle of the night and ask, "What does it all mean? Where are we going?" And I'd say, "Fuck. Hell if I know—give me a break."

Q: You kind of got thrust into being the guy who did Woodstock…

MICHAEL: But then I would point out to you that as television journalists, as movie journalists, we have tremendous responsibility. We, collectively, are the most powerful media that this planet has, and we're so influential. So, therefore, our work, whether I'm giving an interview to you—whether you're making a documentary or whether I am—I think it has tremendous impact on people. As role models, as surrogate experiencers, as experiences people would like to have—if you say that this is the most famous documentary of all time, then shit— the filmmaker has to say, well, did I do the right thing.

Take drugs for example. As you know there's a famous song in there by Woody Guthrie's son—Woody Guthrie being one of the most famous of all time social commentators and song writers—well his son, Ario, sings "Coming into Los Angeleeeze, bringing in a couple of kees, don't touch my bag if you please, Mr. Customs man." It seems to be arguing for drugs.

And here, twenty-five years later, we have this disastrous, horrendous problem with hard drugs. Well, it's my own personal opinion that you should divide soft drugs from hard drugs. But' it's also my own opinion, along with Gabriella Marchesa and many other Nobel laureates, that this policy of the continued illegalization of drugs is simply not working. That we should be dealing with drugs, not as a matter of criminalness, but as a matter of sickness and disease. In fact, the criminalization of it simply keeps the problem going. It makes it huge business. It makes people kill people and damage them and beat them up in order to steal money so they can support their habit. So in a way, you have to look at what you did then, look at the situation today and say, well—did I do the right thing? Is this sort of soft approach on drugs the right thing to do?

Q: Responsibility for the Woodstock generation?

MICHAEL: Well, at fourteen years old I had the nickname Silver Tongue of because I was a super debator and I was interested in a political career. In the Youth in Government in Ohio, I was governor of the state for the day and things like that. So I'd always been a big mouth and I had been a writer and that sort of thing. But the responsibility part of it—that wasn't really welcome. But I was raised by two very good parents who instilled in me the fact that you were supposed to step up to the plate and put your ego aside. And I'm trying and I hope I'm it doing now, articulating concerns that a lot of people had.

Part of the richness I think people ignore about *Woodstock* is the richness of alternatives. After all, in America, one of the big things we're supposed to be is the land of individuals. Which means individual opinion, alternatives, you know. Well I think what *Woodstock* symbolizes is counterculture, alternative culture, alternative points of view, alternative lifestyles. Question Everything. And I thought that that pretty much summed up the attitude that you should never nail down your ideology. You should always remain flexible. You should always listen to the other person's point of view. Always have possibilities open to you.

The biggest realization—it wasn't so much a look back as a look at a timeless situation. Country Joe's song wasn't really about the Vietnam War, it's about all wars. Joan Baez' song about Joe Hill is about all organizers. "Freedom" and "Handsome Johnny," songs that Richie Havens sings; "Summertime Blues" that there ain't no cure for them because your congressman won't get you a job—and on and on, they're all metaphors. They work today every bit as well as they worked yesterday.

MARTIN ANDREWS

WOODSTOCK, THE WEIRD WOMBAT

(MARTY BEGAN WITH MIKE Wadleigh's and John Binder's company, Paradigm Films, as a technical wizard, a function he performed on the movie.)

THERE'S NO DOUBT THAT *Woodstock* was the weird wombat wrenched from the womb of Merv Griffin's *Sidewalks of New England* TV special.

First, that special was a real special. It wasn't just the usual abortion of a "package" stitched together by some schmuck who managed to assemble available talent with a Union crew in some production facility by dealing with "the usual suspects" (lawyers, agents, and other assorted hacks).

Like *Woodstock* (peace, music, multi-image location documentary), *Sidewalks* had a conceptual conception: get Merv out of the studio and integrate his regulars (Arthur Treacher, etc.) with others on location in New England to follow the changing fall foliage. Merv cajoled local-color jokes from Jud Strunk in Vermont. A brilliant Agnes de Mille dance rendition of the Lizzie Borden story was staged in a graveyard for the highbrow audience. Paul Revere and the Raiders provided some Yankee rock and roll on top of the Prudential Building in Boston for the hipsters. There was Aretha Franklin for the Black and Gospel audiences. For general interest, there was the dynamic staging of a Gilbert and Sullivan's piece with soloists and choruses on different balconies of buildings in Gloucester, Massachusetts.

In turn, *Sidewalks of New England* grew out of the previous year's successful *On the Sidewalks of New York*, which was a similar concept shot by Wadleigh at outdoor metropolitan locations.

The technological innovations of *Woodstock* sprang or evolved from technological innovations in those *Sidewalks* shows. Taking a massive video camera out of the studio had probably only been done previously in circumstances where the camera was dollied out of the studio door no farther than its umbilical cord would allow.

Wadleigh has a wonderful story about how one of those enormously heavy (and expensive) Norelco cameras managed to get dropped off one of New York's bridges! In spite of this and, I'm sure, other blunders, the decision was made to stay with the more innovative (and less expensive) nonunion crew. Understandably, they also decided to drop the TV cameras—not off more bridges, but as the recording medium of the subsequent *Sidewalks of New England* show!

Wadleigh chose to use the newly developed Éclair NPR sixteen-millimeter film camera for several reasons. His NPR was the only camera to have survived the documentary he did in the Hindu Kush. Its quick-change magazine minimized the exposure to airborne dust, sand, and moisture (rain, snow, humidity), and reduced film-change time.

These sixteen-millimeter cameras weighed about twenty pounds and were ergonomically suited to handheld operation in standing, sitting, crouching, and even prone positions. Wadleigh would start a shot standing, and as he crouched down (human boom shot), he would press his eye on the 360-degree orientable viewfinder (literally keeping in touch with the viewing image) and with his "eye contact," force the viewfinder around as its relationship to the camera changed.

He, I, and others were left-eyed and were enabled by the design of the camera to read the F-stop and focus numbers with the right eye. This was important, because these "wild-eyed hippie filmmakers" had the audacity to change focus and zoom while hand-holding and walking around with these NPRs! Wadleigh's right eye was bad enough that, although he could see the F and focus numbers, he couldn't read them. Thus, he had special rings and other accessories made up, which he sold to others at cost. I believe that those with the worst eyesight make the best camera operators because, in life, they are looking harder to compensate for their deficiency. (Producers: hire cameramen who wear glasses!)

These cameras had a minimal noise level at one meter and needed no blimp because the motor's drive shaft directly turned the shutter, registration pin, and wedge-shaped claw. The mirror shutter (variable from five to 180 degrees) ran on a shaft below the aperture and cut the frame side to side, enabling horizontal pans with less strobe. The reflex viewing area in the ground glass showed what was just outside the film area engraving so we could compose better as well as keep the mics out of shot. The rotating turrets enabled us to quickly remove the zoom lens and go to the five point nine wide-angle lens while still shooting (losing only a few frames in the rack-over). This liberated us from follow-focusing and increased our mobility.

It is impossible to overstate the effect that this camera design had on the rock and roll razzle-dazzle style that persists to this day. This style has been hyped beyond absurdity by MTV with its mandated quick cutting. Such hype has negated the incredible mobility and fluidity we achieved with the technology on the *Sidewalks* show, and later at Woodstock.

The technology alone did not create this style. We did. The old, Mafia-tainted, father/son I.A. gang could not have done it. It would never have occurred to them even to take a camera off the tripod. They had nothing but loudly voiced contempt for those of us who did. It's amusing to see movies—even today—where a hippie type is seen hand-holding a camera. It is always characterized by ludicrously spastic camera-shaking. Our footage was solid, or Merv would have had us fired instantly.

The relationship between film equipment and the culture that produced it is noteworthy. The German Arris are precision tanks that can be dropped or even thrown on the floor (*mea culpa*) and still function. The French Éclairs and Beaulieus are high-tech marvels. The Swiss Bolexes are fussy, fingernail-breaking wind-up watches. The Japanese Doiflexes were knock-off rip-offs. The American BNCs and Panaflexes are reliable beasts that require a curious array of ancillary equipment (dollies, cranes, camera cars, "weightless" rigs) and an army of Union personnel to operate them.

HARK, HARK, THE DOGS BARK; THE HIPPIES ARE COMING TO TOWN

Only the young, "uninitiated" hippies could have discovered the capabilities of these technologies. And we were naive enough to actually make use of them. Who were we? We were baby boomers, white, middle-class, male, and well-educated (I went from Allen Stevenson to Promfret to the University of Pennsylvania, where I earned a Masters not just in film but also in the more amorphous Mass Communications). I hope that Dale Bell (Exeter/Princeton) will coerce educational information from other contributers. It will probably be the first time that they have professionally exposed themselves to an industry that is actively hostile to such information.

There is a certain justification for this. Those crusty old veterans somehow entered the business and survived years of working for free or in the Union matrix and have learned that one must constantly come up with unique solutions to unique problems. Pure fantasy must be turned into gut-wrenching reality. There is no such thing as the impossible. We come up with solutions to these unique problems with our only concerns being how much it will cost and how long it will take. The last thing an old vet wants to deal with is some wise-assed kid with a degree who is maimed by concern over the conflicts between various Eisensteinian montage techniques when in fact the kid's job is to get cars parked or to schlep equipment.

We were young and typically rebellious, from our Oedipal conflict with fathers wanting us to "grow up and get a job" to society at large. We, in our naiveté, knew it all. We knew that it was time to "get real" with integration. We saw through the sham and lies fed to us by our government about Vietnam. We were rebels with a cause, backed by a phenomenally dynamic, revolutionary, and compelling music scene augmented by the adventure of mind-expanding and life-enhancing (we thought) drugs.

We not so much "dropped out" as were locked out by the Union. We "tuned in" to what was going down by reading I. F. Stone, getting together and sharing the messages in our new music. We had long hair, funny clothes, and were acutely aware of (hip to) the difference between the bold, adventurous us (hippies) and the status quo gang. We were free radicals who had discovered our own unified field of peace, drugs, and music in a world gone mad with greed, ignorance, and stupidity.

We weren't rocket scientists (it was only a month before Woodstock that NASA landed mankind on the moon and Ted Kennedy landed Mary Jo Kopechne in the waters off Chappaquiddick). But we did have the new technology—Éclair NPR, lavaliers, shotgun mics—that could broadcast the sync signal via cordless transmitter to Nagra recorders. At the time my three favorite (perfect) pieces of technology were the Nagra recorder, the Beachcraft Bonanza airplane in which my cousin Buckminster Fuller flew me over the lakes and islands of Maine, and the British Leyland double-decker bus in which David Meyers, Larry Johnson, and a bunch of crazies traveled through England with me and my English bride, Lizzie, on our honeymoon (just after Woodstock). Anyone out there want to edit 50,000 feet of honeymoon footage?

I learned how to use this new technology by hands-on experience. When I got a gig I would have the equipment delivered to my apartment where my friends (who were my crew) and I would load the camera and recorder with "short ends": Some were as much as 400 feet to compensate us for jobs on which we knew we were going to get "stiffed." We would then get high in one way or another and film our whacked-out antics in the most bizarre and innovative ways our addled minds could devise. It was this sort of innovation that got us to *Woodstock*.

An example: Charlie Peck, who I met on *Sidewalks of New England*, the Big B (who wasn't a part of the Wadleigh team, but should have been), Charlie's wife Jane, Lizzie, and I had a film package delivered to Charlie's apartment in Greenwich Village. Charlie and the Big B were going to the Midwest to make a documentary about the filming of *Cold Turkey*, a story about a whole town that gave up smoking. Charlie and B were afraid they would be persecuted for the length of their hair. After we were pretty ripped on food, booze, and so on, Lizzie started to cut B's wild mane while I recorded sound and Charlie covered the action with the Éclair. B and I were cameramen; Charlie was a soundman. As filmmakers we could interchange functions and were fluent in all film skills. Whatever shape Charlie's adulterated mind was in, his camerawork was flawless. In this case, as a soundman he recognized the feedback noise and consciously shook the camera to augment the shock of it. As spaced out as we were, we were in sync with each other that night. We've got the film to prove it!

After the highly zonked B had flipped out and was losing energy with a bad joke related to Goddard and the *Nouvelle Vague*, and I had just run out of tape, Charlie kept shooting as I put together the world's fastest on-camera Nagra reel change. The Big B made a fairly calm remark about losing sync. I put my headphones over his head, Lizzie stuck the scissors in his mouth, and I jammed the shotgun mic between the headphones and his ear. I then yelled, "Sink or swim!", letting off a savage blast of feedback perceived by the Big B through the phones (and the soundtrack via the mic). This propelled B into renewed paroxysms of insanity, etc., etc., etc. The resulting piece, called *The Haircut*, was coupled, at Martin Scorsese's request, with his thesis film *The Big Shave*, retitled *Shave and a Haircut* and sent off to an Italian film festival where I heard the films were understood neither individually nor collectively by the neorealism critics and audience. I think it was a bit too "neo" for them!

MARTY TO THE RESCUE

How did I get involved with Wadleigh's *Sidewalks of New England* crew? The Éclair, as innovative as it was, was not the piece of perfection that the Nagra was. The Éclair's Achilles' heel was its motors. With the quick magazine changes and fast pace of production the motors kept crapping out and sync could not be maintained between the separate crews needed to provide multi-angle coverage.

What to do? Help! Panic insinuated itself into the equation of filmmakers who were not that far along, in experience, from the always inadequate film-school education. The now-legendary Ted Churchill came up with the solution: me.

Ted told the powers-that-be on *Sidewalks* that he knew sort of an old guy who had worked on a lot of gonzo films and had some power to stare down and humble adversity. In desperation, they bought it—and, while discussing our financial vicissitudes in bed with Lizzie, the call came in telling me to take a cab to La Guardia where there was a ticket in my name. I was to be flown in, picked up by car, and taken to a place on the Penobscot Bay in Maine. My bags are always packed, and I took off with wild enthusiasm to return to the land of my ancestors (signers of the Declaration of Independence, generals under Washington, pre-Colonial governors of Connecticut and Massachusetts, a second secretary of the treasury, and an original Dutch settler of Manhattan).

I got up the next morning and looked out of my motel window. My God! I could actually see Bear Island (Bucky Fuller's side of my family). Nobody seemed to be up. I had no alternative. I stripped off my pajamas, ran buck naked across the lawn, and jumped into my beloved Penobscot. Once past the cardio-vascular shiftover to survival mode, the body glows. When you get out, every follicle of the skin sings with *joie-de-vivre*. When I got out I was confronted by a contingent of clothed strangers led by Ted, who introduced me to them—a barrage of names that I immediately forgot, but eventually came to know as best friends and comrades in combat.

Ted's incessant energy had gotten everyone pumped up to a state of embarrassing veneration for this "old guy" who, in actuality, had just turned twenty-nine. People knew about my connection with Bucky Fuller, and I'd just gotten back from a junket in Kenya.

I was able to solve the sync problem by wiring ten twelve-volt batteries in series and running them through an antique World War II inverter that was controlled by aligning the vibrating fingers of some kind of tuning fork to give sixty-cycle sync. *Voila!* We went to the stronger AC motors, which didn't crap out, and we held sync. I was not only home free, I had validated and perpetuated the veneration bestowed on me. I managed to stay half a step ahead of all the oddball troubleshooting and triage tasks that came my way, but that half step seemed to be all I needed. I was on the team, and what a team it was! What a time it was!

It was Merv's show, *Sidewalks of New England*, that assembled the *Woodstock* crew, shook them down, and enabled them to develop their documentary style with Éclair NPRs, Nagra recorders, wirelesses, lavaliers, and shotgun mics.

After the show was delivered to Merv, members of the crew came by Wadleigh's production office (some armed with their own personal footage) to reedit *Sidewalks*. The music numbers on the KEM in a multi-image format became presentations for soliciting rock and roll work. It was these presentations that got us the *Woodstock* contract. Finally, the money that Wadleigh made from *Sidewalks* enabled him to tough it out on *Woodstock* to the point where Warner Bros. took it over.

Hendrix had his Band of Gypsies; Wadleigh had his big, bad band of jester/ joker/juggler/jongleur/jerk-off/freako/hippie wacko sweethearts. Wadleigh looked like Jesus Christ and the rest of us looked like his peripatetic leper colony. I'm a hard-core Yankee, a real Down-Easter, and I know and love these people. They believe good fences make good neighbors; you mind your business, I'll mind mine. But we shattered our way through every shibboleth. We left a trail of totaled rent-a-cars in our wake. We'd drive across fields, and if we couldn't get around a stone wall we'd go though it. Call Avis, tell 'em to pick up the casualties and send replacements. We had camera dolly races down the serpentine driveway of the most pretentious motel in Sturbridge. We spun them out, we wrecked them, we sent them back to New York, we got replacements the next day. We would blast down the highways at eighty-five miles per hour to make a commercial flight.

Wadleigh just reminded me that these flights had a limit on the size of our equipment cases, but not on their weight. Consequently, large cargo boxes were made up and we packed them so that there were no voids—no empty spaces. Those mothers were stupefyingly heavy—the densest matter in the universe. The airport baggage handlers made no attempt to conceal their contempt for these unwashed, lazy hippies who'd descended on them. They couldn't conceive why we were even at the airport. When they had to deal with our equipment they were instantly flummoxed. They had to get help from people whose job description did not include weight-lifting and baggage-wrangling. We'd be frolicking about—merry pranksters—while they reluctantly banded together, temporarily united in the task of getting rid of us. We left them dazed, discordant, disconsolate—drained.

Ever hear of a carhop? Wadleigh redefined the expression. We were flying down the highway at maximum speed. All of a sudden, Wadleigh, who was driving, turned to whoever was riding shotgun and said, "Here, take the wheel and put me next to those guys!"—in another car to the right of ours! Whereupon he proceeded to wriggle out of his window, claw his way across the roof of the car, get on the roof of the other car and squirm through their window to deposit himself in the laps of his nonplussed but happy-to-see-you ("Hi, Mike, what's up?") colleagues.

Epithets to aphorisms.

We put the local gentry through some changes. In Gloucester, they thought they were ready for us. They weren't. They doubly weren't! They had stretched this huge sign across the main drag. It read, "WELCOME TO GLOUCESTER, MASSACHUSETTS, USA, MERV GRIFFIN & CREW!" Underneath were the signatures of the mayor, the Board of Selectmen, the Library Committee, the postmaster, undertaker, barber, etc., etc. The sign was enormous and was flown way up, maybe six stories high, across their miracle mile pride and joy. Remember, this was in their heyday, when the trawlers in the harbor were depleting their fisheries with impudicity.

The freak crew rolled in at dusk and did a full pub crawl, going through the town's entire supply of Brandy Alexanders, which I had the honor of introducing to my new friends. This drink started out as a curiosity and evolved from a fad into a rite of passage and then into a ritual. The revelry was intense, and the next morning we woke up to the alarming sight of the "& CREW!" crossed out in a sloppy but aggressive manner. It was a clear and conspicuous rejection of the long-haired louts who had ravished their nightspots.

In spite of the bad vibes directed at the crew the night before, the whole town turned out at dawn next day to see Merv. They were…disappointed. And surprised, first not to see Merv who, with Arthur Treacher and the gang, didn't show up till hours later. What they saw instead was this much-reviled crew swinging into action to gussy up their already fair town with bunting and whatnot for a massive Gilbert and Sullivan production number. This involved prepping not just the four or five balconies that were to hold Merv on one and Arthur on another and various choruses on yet others, but also the whole town as the background.

It was a big deal and, maimed as we may have been by our dipsomaniacal carousings, we hit the deck running and blew them away with the intricacy of our preparatory moves. There was no budget for crowd control, so we politely asked people to make room for the power cable we had to run and all the other maneuvers required to do a multi-camera, multi-angle big number, big production shoot. The locals come from good, God-fearing, no-nonsense, straight-backed Yankee Puritan witch-burning stock. They had not appreciated our nocturnal revelry, and naturally assumed that such rowdy misfits couldn't possibly have worked a day in their lives. They had no alternative but to reject this prejudice in response to the quiet but rapid and vigorous machinations they were now witnessing. They may be a proud crowd, and they may be stubborn in their righteousness, but they are not phonies. They are sufficiently secure, in their houseproud way, to suffer the indignity of being wrong.

As the day wore on, Merv & Co. still not having materialized, we got into the rhythm of our "zones" and cranked out the work. The locals got into our numbers and began to anticipate when they might be in our way. As they sensed our rhythm, their avoidance quickened to a shuffle. Expostulations of surprise turned to deferential grunts of embarrassment. The day ground on and our pace never slackened; we were way past what would be a midmorning coffee break; we were cranking, baby, and the body politic was backing off, out of our way and out of the contempt in which they'd initially held us. They were backing off, but they were about to be routed. They had come to see Merv. They were coming to accept us. More than that they were into our activity, they were into us.

They became emboldened and started to praise us. Encouraged by our polite response, they reached further and began to apologize for the lack of civility and hospitality of whoever had altered their banner of welcome. We received this gracefully. They kept talking; we kept working. Apologies for the sign expanded to apologies for prejudging us. Obviously we were no strangers to work. Clearly we enjoyed our work.

I remembered two of the many work-ethic aphorisms carved into the beams of my boathouse in Maine (e.g., "HONOR YOUR WORK AND YOUR WORK WILL HONOR YOU," and "THE REWARD OF GOOD WORK DONE IS MORE GOOD WORK TO DO"). I repeated these to the group that was now following me around. They clucked in approval and all of a sudden we took the quantum leap and they complimented me on my L. L. Bean shoplifting jacket (actually a hunting jacket with ample interior pockets for transporting the tools of my trade). "Oh, yes," I said, and took my first break to show them some of those essentials (light meter, amprobe, wrenches, and so on). They loved it. It became a love fest. They began to admire the interesting clothing and hairstyles of my friends. They expressed awe at the indefatigable pace of our labor and our dedication to our calling. They invited me to their home for dinner. They had a daughter!

The love fest had gotten out of control. They would have been disconsolate had they not been completely blown away by my final pièce de résistance:

"I must gratefully refuse your kind invitation as tonight after we wrap this location I have to get on Merv's private plane and fly off to Providence to shoot Aretha Franklin" (see photo of Marty and DC3 shot by Wadleigh). Had they checked, they would have found out that by this time Merv was even more of a fan of his crew than they were. It was his pleasure not only to spirit us about in his leather-upholstered, private converted DC3 with stocked bar, but also to dine with us at the best restaurants available, enjoy our spontaneity, and even, I have reason to believe, personally foot the extravagant bills generated by these fêtes.

Merv came up the hard way. He ground out a living singing in an endless succession of one-night stands in an indeterminate number of road houses, clubs, and other venues. He made his way into TV and became a dominant presence. The apotheosis, aesthetically, of his TV career was this *Sidewalks of New England* special. The special that actually was special—for him, for us on the crew, and for the audience.

Merv is a very focussed, ambitious, no-nonsense entrepreneur. If at any time he had had reservations about the competence of the work done by any individual or by the crew in general, that would have been it for him (or us). I am personally flattered that he appreciated our work, and I wish him well in his real estate and gaming ventures—he earned it and he deserves his success. I hope he'll invite us all down to one of his joints sometime for a reunion.

It was his show, *Sidewalks of New England*, that assembled the Woodstock crew, shook them down, and enabled them to develop their documentary style with the Eclair NPR, Nagra recorder, wireless, lavalier, and shotgun mikes.

After the show was delivered to Merv, members of the crew came by Wadleigh's production office (some armed with their own personal footage) to reedit *Sidewalks*. The music numbers on the KEM in a multi-image format became presentations for soliciting rock and roll work. It was these presentations that got us the Woodstock contract. Finally, the money that Wadleigh made from *Sidewalks* enabled him to tough it out on Woodstock to the point where Warner Bros. took it over.

CHARLIE PECK

THE SO-CALLED SIXTIES

RACIAL SEGREGATION, ECOLOGICAL DOOMSDAY, mindless suburban sprawl. Assassinations, police riots, decaying inner cities. Lyndon Johnson and his Techno Wonks and their disastrous land war in Asia. And then there was always the bomb...the Hydrogen Bomb. With all this appalling crap so sharply in focus, it was hard not to develop a serious attitude problem. For Christ's sake, there must be some ideals worth considering that haven't been twisted, co-opted, or even completely forgotten about! But what were they? Where were they? Mom used to say, "Charles, you seem to be marching to the beat of a different drummer." Heck, you bet I was!

In his hilarious book about class in America, Paul Fussel concludes with a chapter that deals with the different drummer types. He imagines that each complacent insulated class is in its own private darkened theater comfortably watching a movie that panders to all their cherished attitudes about status, dress, manners, and oh, it's all so reassuring. But a few uneasy, maybe bewildered individuals have seen enough. Quietly they get up and slip out the side door...into the clear light of day. Discarding standard mind-numbing conventions, they are content to go it alone.

In the 1960s these outsiders got to be a lot more visible. They were dropping out in record numbers, finding each other, and beginning to adopt some interesting new values: honesty, peace, mutual respect; odd notions like that.

You rarely saw them down at the corner saloon. You never saw them at a cocktail party. For them, Mother Nature's own marijuana seemed more appropriate. Like, you know...it grows.

They were colorful, persuasive, irreverent, and full of ideas about how to make the planet a lot more livable. The media loved them. And in August 1969 they had a very public party in a farmer's field near Woodstock, New York. By all accounts, it was a huge success.

And, thirty years later, that still has a lot of people having a snit fit, and so they insist that all of this was merely a part of some sort of seamy "drug culture." Too bad. In their knee-jerk rush to sanitize the past, they not only misuse the word "culture" but manage to overlook a far more intriguing phenomenon. There will always be some self-defined individuals who will never be a part of any definable anything. THEY JUST WANT OUT!

They're out there all right, but for the most part, unseen. They like it that way: authors, cabinetmakers, musicians, entrepreneurs, comedy writers, jewelry designers, jugglers, pastry chefs, film editors, genius freelance computer consultants…people who come and go as they please.

Go ahead, call them names if you want. They couldn't care less.

And by the way, remember those oddball Puritans who, for moral and ethical reasons, sailed away from England in their wooden ships—way back in 1620?

All of this is very American. It's a part of what makes us so special.

SEXY MEDIA MACHINES

But our story begins in France. In the mid-1960s the Éclair Company was hard at work developing a revolutionary motion picture camera, the NPR. For the shutter they used the same idea as the German Arris, a rotating mirror. Below and mounted at a cocky angle was the cylindrical battery-powered motor. To replace it all you needed was one tool, a coin. The lens turret featured a new insert-and-twist bayonet mount. This meant that the lens, usually an Angenieux zoom lens, could be replaced in fewer than two seconds, with one hand.

But the best part was the camera's magazine/transport system. The sprockets, pressure plate, and film loops were incorporated into each film magazine. That meant that a fresh roll of 400 feet of raw stock, eleven minutes, could be snapped to the back of the shutter assembly, ready to roll, in less than a second.

And all designed and hand-assembled for one purpose: to try to insert a silent handheld motion picture camera inconspicuously into any interesting real-life situation, anywhere.

And to record the sound along the way, the Éclair was designed to work with another European masterpiece, the Swiss-made Nagra III portable tape recorder. Compact, rugged, precise, it was about the size of five bricks lashed together and almost as heavy. The Swiss Army tape recorder.

The only other time I ever saw equipment like this was aboard a Marine amphibious assault ship. Talk about heavy duty. You could smack the control panel with the butt of your Swiss Army rifle, and nothing would happen. Everything was recessed.

Oh, but when you opened it up and looked inside, the sight of the motors, pulleys, and electronics was breathtaking. Hand-crafted with not a cubic centimeter of space wasted; parallel colored wires, cute little transistors, all carefully arranged and accented with shiny, silvery, perfectly soldered connections. And it was there in all those unseeable, complex electronics that the engineers at Nagra had really done it. The sound it recorded was rich and pure; crystalline highs, gut-punching lows, almost as faithful as any recording studio in its time. And all there in that indestructible portable box.

THE SUSPENSION OF DISBELIEF VS. BELIEF

As it was with many new developments during the turbulent 1960s, the nifty movie equipment from Europe came with a vision, maybe even a responsibility. Innovative technology could and should be used to bring about positive social and political change. By replacing bulky and expensive studio cameras with more advanced portable sixteen-millimeter systems, events could now be documented as they unfolded, in real time. There would be no need to narrate or pontificate. What happened in front of the lens would be powerfully and intimately real. By documenting political campaigns, prisons, mental hospitals, even a war, films could now be made that might move people to do something about society's ills. In their self-satisfied fashion, the French called it cinéma vérité, the true movies.

Vive la différence! A cadre of cinema saboteurs creating a radical subversive film genre.

And the folks over at Éclair had done their job perfectly, because as it is with any artfully conceived and carefully crafted piece of machinery, the Éclair camera could cast a powerful spell.

When young Michael Wadleigh saw it, he was a goner. He left a promising future at Columbia Medical School and…off he went, with his friend John Binder doing the sound, filming a team of mountain climbers up through the snow and ice to 20,000 feet.

According to Michael, "That little 'clair never let me down. Sweet machine. She was a bit hefty but very sweet."

When I saw it for the first time in 1968 at Michael and John's office, Paradigm Films, on Eighty-Sixth Street, my reaction was the same. It was just so SEXY!

"Go ahead, put me on your shoulder. Let's have a little fun, *Chéri*." …Ah, romance. Adventure. CINÉMA VÉRITÉ….

She was French, you know.

But as Michael says, she was a bit hefty. The Éclair NPR weighed twenty-seven pounds, and after holding it on your shoulder for ten minutes or so, your forearm would begin to ache and shake. The image in the viewfinder would start to sway and wobble, and that was that. *Au revoir, Chéri.*

Fortunately there were a few who could get through that. Rock steady.

Do you remember the ninja from James Clavell's book *Shogun*? Those were the guys who could stand on one foot in the freezing rain, perfectly motionless, all night, and then like Spiderman, scale a sheer vertical wall and assassinate somebody.

"Aaaaaaaaaaah…so. You are a most worthy ninja. You understand that the pain exists only in your mind and therefore…does not exist at all." That's what it took! Filming with the NPR required cerebral cortex denial! But once that mind-bender was accomplished, a person could carry that beautiful camera ANYWHERE.

But these handheld camera people had to have much more than that. The new cinéma vérité required that they be creative types as well, athletic artists with an eye for detail, and the best of them had a sympathetic concern about other people's lives. This assured that they were always curious, alert. Very important. There was always the chance that somewhere out there…something might just happen…and not get…DOCUMENTED.

There was no director, no rehearsals, no script. This was THE TRUTH, twenty-four frames a second. Traditional film and television production in those days was like an assembly line, existing for the convenience of corporations and unions. What we were up to was more like team sports. The methods we developed were highly mobile, just camera and sound with someone nearby running interference while reloading the film magazines. And none of those blinding movie lights, just force-process the film; no Winnebegos, no Teamsters, no crafts services, no trucks full of stands, cookies, dots, flags, scrims, gels, sandbags, and 5,000 watt generators. The result was sometimes raw and grainy, but it was always true. True Grit.

We tried to be inconspicuous, staying ahead of the action; relaxed, silent, moving; just going with the flow. ANYWHERE.

One producer from NET, Mort Silverstein, didn't even bother leaving his motel room. He just sent us out there to do our DOCUMENTING.

Here's an example that would come later from the *Woodstock* movie.

One of the cameramen at Woodstock was David Myers. At fifty-five years of age, he was by far the oldest member of the film crew and a past master at this "going with the flow ANYWHERE" stuff.

And for some reason he walked right past the rock stars, right past the flower children, and discovered an average American, the Port-O-San man, busily servicing the public toilets. I can still see David, turning to his soundman and shrugging. "What the hell, let's do it." LET'S DOCUMENT!

Could Dan Rather or anyone from the networks have done this? The very idea is laughable.

But at Woodstock, David and his soundman treat the Port-O-San man with respect. They are patient, just having a chat, rolling all the time. There is no interview ("If you were a twee, what kind of twee would you be?"). And pretty soon the guy relaxes and comes up with his own touching irony. He has a son fighting in the war we are all railing against (who knows, that son might be dead as he speaks) and he has another son right there at the festival shouting, "Gimme an F, U, C, K...be the first one on your block to have your boy come home in a box."

Whew.... Most of us who have seen the movie remember this moment; a perceptive and thoughtful man caught up in an all-too-familiar 1960s dilemma. He shared a bit of himself that day, and we love him.

But I'm getting ahead of myself. Let's begin again.

TOO MUCH THE MAGIC BUS

It was 1968. I was twenty-six years old and living in New York City when my pal Chuck Levey came to me with exciting news. Chuck was a terrific still photographer who had found about the Éclair NPR and the verité film style from Messrs. Binder and Wadleigh. And after I checked it out, I knew exactly what to do. I gave notice at my comfortable job at the Channel 13 Art Department, and... off I went.

Ah...Adventure, Romance, CINÉMA VÉRITÉ...

Well, maybe not so verité. John and Michael had convinced Merv Griffin and his producer, Bob Shanks, that Paradigm Films could apply its free-wheeling film-making style to an upcoming star-studded Thanksgiving TV special. What a stretch! America's adorable daytime talk show host and assorted glitzy showfolk on the road with a bunch of radical film freaks. But it just so happened that behind that boyish, affable charm, Mr. Griffin was a bit of an adventurer. He was interested in getting out of his hot, overlit television studio and finding something over the horizon, filming musical performances in various locations with multiple cameras.

And for this, Merv had the perfect vehicle, an airplane that still enjoys a long and glorious history of being able to go ANYWHERE, the venerable DC 3. All of us hippie filmmakers took one look at this gleaming silver antique, and just piled right in and...off we went. There were eight of us, all in our mid-twenties, and all charged up with a curious, freaky esprit de corps.

The journey was boisterous and arduous and led by our own dynamo mojo, Michael Wadleigh, ninja *ne plus ultra*. Enigmatic, quiet by nature, built like a wide receiver and with piercing blue eyes, Michael radiated an intense yet benevolent authority, which on this trip demanded that everyone involved find the freedom to EXPLORE.

And explore we did. We had to. Filming with multiple cameras like this had never been tried before, so we had to sort of make it up as we went along, and if confusion, doubt, or exhaustion intruded...well, just check out the intrepid Mr. Wadleigh: calm, focused, alert, just going with the flow.

He demonstrated some Newtonian physics for us one morning by sliding off the tailgate of an accelerating station wagon onto a runway at Logan Airport in Boston. And as he went skidding and bouncing along the concrete, we all shared one vivid, horrifying reality check. If anything should ever happen to Michael... THE EXPLORING...would be all over.

Shit.

But of course nothing would ever happen to Michael. He was like a Terminator. No problemo. After completing his interesting little slide for life, he just got up and got back in the car, his striped sport shirt in shreds, and...off we went.

"Where to, Michael?"

The question needed no answer. By this time we were moving fast forward with our own hippie gusto, perfecting sync sound, three camera, handheld shooting in the wilderness. At first there were problems keeping all three cameras in sync.

Technical note: Keeping three cameras running at exactly the same speed was difficult in the days before crystal controlled motors. So our whiz kid, Marty Andrews, devised a power source driven by ten car batteries and a special transformer called an inverter, delivering 120 volt/60 cycle power to the alternating current motors of the three NPRs. Same alternating current, same camera speed.

Once everything was all in sync, the exploration continued. It was challenging because Maestro Wadleigh was always busy choreographing some new multi-camera ballet, shooting from cars, boats, and helicopters. Our irrepressible soundman Larry Johnson called it "The Hully Gully," and Michael's vision soon had the three cameramen (Michael, Chuck Levey, and Ted Churchill) literally running circles around the flat, formal, proscenium look of the day.

We finished the shooting in about four weeks. Damn it! We were having so much fun! But…I had helped to slay the multi-camera-sync-in-the-wilderness beast. I had earned a seat at the Paradigm roundtable. I was at the wheel, as we headed back to Camelot at an average speed of eighty-five miles on the Massachusetts Turnpike. After all, there was so much more to DOCUMENT.

THE QUEST OF SIR MARTIN

It was a typical early morning on the Merv trip. All us bell-bottomed long hairs in some faraway motel parking lot, sipping coffee, when into our midst walked the latest addition to our crew, Martin Lord Andrews VII, sporting an iridescent orange jumpsuit. We all looked at each other and just knew…this wild ride was about to become a lot more…uh, experimental.

Technically, things had gotten a little out of hand, and Marty had come prepared. Circuit tester, ammeter, metric alien wrenches, epoxy, dental tools, soldering tools, jeweler's tools, fuses, plugs, adapters, connectors, and something called a space blanket all lovingly organized in nesting fishing tackle boxes. He had adapted the L. L. Bean duck hunting, fly fishing thing to our go-for-broke production style and always seemed to be nearby reaching into his field jacket to produce an extra core, sync cable, 85 ND#3 lens filter, a Q-Tip.

And the odd thing was you couldn't tell how old he was. This was partly due to his voice. As coxswain for the University of Pennsylvania crew team, he had blown out some of his vocal cords. Now he spoke in a lilting baritone croak. But it wasn't just the voice, Marty had an honest, worldly, preoccupied eccentricity that is usually associated with a long and full life. Man, he was so weird, he didn't even have long hair.

We had all read and talked about becoming so-called filmmakers. Marty seemed to be the real deal. So when we got back to New York, his place on Fifteenth Street became our after-hours experimental film salon.

Far from the *Chitty Chitty Bang Bang* world, our own home-movie Merlin was in there kicking down the doors of perception. Marty's experimental films were weird, shocking, and sometimes funny, like his short film *Banana Head*, a story about smuggling contraband hallucinogenic fruit.

The hall running the length of his apartment was impassable. It was crammed full of projectors, all types; sixteen millimeters, eight millimeters, Super 8, slide projectors; all aimed at a rear projection screen in the doorway to his cozy living room. There were two cats, three beautiful aquariums, a lava lamp, and a refrigerator full of sparkling French apple wine. Of course the whole place was wired for sound, speakers everywhere. The walls were covered with photos, memorabilia, interesting paintings and tapestries, and the windows were all covered up too, because Marty…was seriously…INTO FILM.

And his skill and enthusiasm were so infectious that right away Ted Churchill, Larry Johnson, and I got out our eight-millimeter cameras and we were GETTING INTO FILM.

Raw stock? We pre-fogged it. We post-fogged it. We froze it. We baked it. Once we fucked up fifty feet of Kodachrome so bad, the emulsion fell off at Kodak's processing plant in Fairlawn, New Jersey.

Oops. Sorry.

Double exposures? Hell, quadruple exposures. Get ready for this, guys! I ran the same piece of film through my little eight-millimeter camera twenty-two times, shooting out the front of the Flushing Line train. Grand Central-Shea Stadium, Shea Stadium-Grand Central. Back and forth, all night. FAR OUT, CHARLIE. The result was like driving through an exploding supernova.

Ted Churchill really GOT INTO single framing. On a crisp autumn afternoon he would take his Bolex out for a stroll, clicking one frame of film every two or three seconds. Of course, as we sat in Marty's permanently darkened living room and watched, at twenty-four frames a second, Ted's wanderings got sped up… like up to about a hundred miles. But…uh oh…wait…he's stopped…at…a… STOP SIGN …and…Ohhhhhhh, wwwwowwww…he's GETTING INTO the stop sign. He's exploring the stop sign, one frame at a time. He's GETTING INTO the word STOP, the letterforms. He's GETTING INTO the octagonal geometry of the stop sign, and pretty soon he's got that inanimate symbol of authority pulsating, vibrating, spinning out of control until you couldn't even tell if it was a stop sign or a kaleidoscope any more. My God! Teddy must have been there all afternoon! You could tell, because in the last four or five seconds of this masterpiece, he began to lose the light. Evening arrived. The city lights began to sparkle. Fade to black. Marty and I were floored. BRAVO, Teddy, BRAVO.

Then the phone rang. It was Larry up at Paradigm. "Get up here right away. The KEM is here."

THREE SCREENS

And that's the way it was. All of us downtown at Marty's GETTING INTO IT. John and Michael smiling approvingly at our antics while going out and spending their own money in the real world, keeping Paradigm Films on the cutting edge.

They had moved their office into a bright, spacious place overlooking Broadway on the Upper West Side. It was late in the evening when we arrived. And there it was, direct from Germany, the biggest, most advanced, most expensive film editing console in the world. We couldn't get close to it because there were three or four technicians making it work with American electricity.

So we returned the next morning, bright and early, Chuck, Larry, Marty, and myself. We couldn't wait to GET INTO this Teutonic beauty. We brought with us all the crazy footage we could find, like my green and red high contrast shot from the front of the roller coaster ride at Coney Island. And we needed a lot of footage too because the KEM had three screens, three big screens. Anyone familiar with Rube Goldberg's Moviola can imagine our excitement. No more clattering, chattering antique with that dinky screen and always tearing up the sprocket holes. The KEM used rotating prisms and had a terrific sound system. And that meant... ROCK AND ROLL!

Three screens, two screens, one screen, BLAST OFF! Hendrix, Doors, Beatles, we transformed that luxurious editing console into our own funky, three-screen, music-driven, multiple-image theater. And once we got it all going, there were so many MORE POSSIBILITIES. Beautiful sometimes literal associations presented themselves. Mirror images, repeat images, curious juxtapositions, reality dissolving into a wild light show. Someone put together a beautiful three-screen version of Aretha Franklin's performance from the Merv show. The splicing and fooling around went on for days, weeks.

We were having so much fun that it took me a while to notice that Michael was becoming a lot more enigmatic than usual. As it turned out, he was busy planning the ultimate handheld multiple-camera-in-the-wilderness documentary ever. Someone had decided to organize an outdoor arts and crafts and music festival near an upstate village named Woodstock, and Michael Wadleigh was exploring again.

GOOD VIBRATIONS

Financial backing? There wasn't any. But there was The Spirit: youthful, fresh, audacious, and cocky. It made some folks uncomfortable, but it was our Spirit, and we loved it. There, I've gone and said it, Love.

We loved our sexy machines. We loved each other. We loved challenges, exploring, being alive in the world. We loved our Rock and Roll music, the best background music any generation ever had. We loved our pioneering cinéma vérité. We thought it was important.

Naturally Michael was able to attract a lot of talented people. Seasoned producer-types like Dale Bell and Bob Maurice came along to take care of business and logistics. Besides Chuck Levey and Ted Churchill, other great cameramen, David Myers, Don Lenzer, Ed Lynch, and Dick Pearce, came along, and they had The Spirit too. Day by day, more and more young, talented film people, like Martin Scorsese, Thelma Schoonmaker, and Marty Andrews became involved with The Spirit.

And in spite of financial and logistical obstacles, the film crew of about eighty went up to Woodstock and returned with 350,000 feet of history…with hardly a slate in it! No problem. The Spirit and a lot of money from Warner Bros. got it in sync right away. Did I say Warner Bros.?

Apparently there were kindred spirits out there in Tinseltown too.

Far out!

We all enjoyed the day-long, night-long three-screen screenings. What a party! And then as the final editing process approached, the whole thing packed up and went to Hollywood. But those of us left behind still had The Spirit.

LEWIS
TEAGUE

THE ORIGINAL BOB MAURICE

(LEWIS BECAME OUR ADVANCE man in Hollywood prior to our move in December 1969.)

BOB AND I WERE fast friends in high school in North Tarrytown, in Westchester County, New York. The first time I ever got drunk was when I was fourteen when I drank a quart of Gin with Bob on the HS bleachers before a football game. We shared many adventures, including being chased by the police in stolen cars. He was sixteen years old and went to jail for that. Since I was only fifteen, I went to a youth detention home. When I turned seventeen, I quit high school and joined the Army. I lost touch with Bob for three years.

When I got out of the Army and decided to go back to school, I somehow tracked Bob down and was shocked at what I found.

In North Tarrytown, Bob lived in a tiny walkup apartment with his French Canadian blue-collar parents. It seemed that every time I visited them, everyone was screaming and Bob was destroying his collection of Jazz LPs by smashing them, throwing them, or stomping on them. He was an extraordinary jazz buff, constantly replacing his collection only to destroy it again.

When I looked him up after the Army I expected to find the same guy; blue collar, uneducated, and having skirmishes with the law. Instead I found a guy who had already been in City College for several years, and was passionate about books and learning. He hadn't discarded the blue-collar aspect of his personality, only added to it. He continued to pay his way through college by working construction. He became a professional student, eventually going to college for about nine years. I don't know if he ever earned his baccalaureate, but he certainly became one of the most well-read and knowledgeable people I've ever encountered.

But when it came time to produce *Woodstock*, Bob credited his years on the construction site with giving him the skills he needed. "Working construction.

Two guys want to dump their wheelbarrow of bricks in the same spot. The problem is solved by assuming an aggressive stance and saying, 'Hey! Fuck you! That's my spot!' Dealing with the studios is a lot like that," he said.

He had the charm and intelligence to make that kind of toughness work.

Bob Maurice hired me to work on *Woodstock*. Even though I had known Michael Wadleigh for some time, and had in fact introduced the two of them, I had known Bob since childhood. So when he needed someone on the west coast to be an advance man, I'm the one he called.

He needed someone to find work space for the huge postproduction crew that was already at work editing the film in New York. As it was a nonunion production, Bob wanted to stay away from the studio. They also needed housing for the crew, and in the spirit of the time, it was decided that some sort of communal arrangement would be most satisfactory. (And less expensive).

It wasn't difficult to find three houses, on Franklin, Genesee, and Orlando, that would rent to us. The hard part was finding and setting up editing space that would fulfill our needs. We needed half a dozen editing rooms to accommodate the new KEM flatbed editing machines, plus rooms for assistants, space for sound editors, a screening room, and offices for Bob, Mike, and Dale, etc.

Working with several realtors, I found space on Yucca and Vine that seemed to fit the bill in terms of space and price. Of course, we needed to do extensive electrical rewiring. The most interesting challenge was setting up a screening room where we could screen the work print. We needed to run five sixteen-millimeter projectors in sync with the sound track.

It's my opinion that the experience of screening the work print was far more exciting than seeing the finished film. The visual area in front of us was apparently larger. It was rougher and more dynamic. The quality of the work prints was better than the final film, which had to go many generations before it reached the screen. And it was definitely louder and longer.

Once Mike and Bob arrived from New York most of my job was finished. I had made many of the initial contacts with the optical labs, but when Dale Bell arrived, he took over. I stayed on as a glorified production assistant helping out Bob where I could, and watched the film come together. We all knew we were working on something important. The end of the year, not to mention decade, was approaching and all the magazines were declaring Woodstock one of the defining moments of the 1960s.

Mike had extraordinary charisma. He was very bright, supremely confident, and a gifted craftsman. He was very focused, seemed to have unlimited energy, and had a vision.

Several years earlier, I had been visiting Mike in an editing room in New York where he was cutting a documentary about Aretha Franklin. He wanted to show me the new Keller Editing Machine he was working on that allowed him to view three shots in synch with one soundtrack. Since the performance sequences had been filmed with multiple cameras, it helped him to make his cuts from camera to camera.

It was very exciting to watch the multiple images of Aretha singing her heart out. "I'd like to make a concert film and edit it on this machine," Mike said. "And I'd optically marry the images into a triptych."

I agreed that it would be very exciting. "And you know," Mike said. "*Monterey Pop* made a lot of money."

At the time I was working as an associate producer on *Loving*, a feature film that Columbia was financing, so I guess Mike thought I knew how to produce. He asked if I was interested in producing his concert film. I was, and for a while we made several attempts to either produce our own concert or get the rights to film existing concerts.

At some point along the way, I needed to take a salaried job and suggested Bob Maurice to fill my shoes as producer. I had already introduced Bob and Mike in 1967 when I was running an experimental theater in Los Angeles called the Cinematheque-16. Mike had been impressed and wanted to finance a larger multi-media theater. I brought in Bob, my childhood friend, as my partner. When the multi-media concept didn't seem to be going anywhere, I went off to work as associate producer on *Loving*.

So that's how Bob Maurice took on the job of producer on *Woodstock*.

Warner Bros., the studio, was trying to get Mike Wadleigh, the visionary filmmaker, to buckle under its authority. Bob rightly assumed that his role was to run interference for Mike with the studio so his vision could reach the screen. Having known him since high school, it was amusing to see him handle the studio.

The film turned out to be a greater phenomenon than anyone could have predicted, and Bob, as did many others, rose to the occcasion.

SONYA POLONSKY

ONE PERSPECTIVE ON THOSE EARLY DAYS

(SONYA POLONSKY BEGAN AT Paradigm Films and continued on the movie as production manager.)

DALE: When did you begin at Paradigm?

SONYA: I began in February of whatever year it was. I was never sure if it was 1968 or 1969, but it was the winter before the summer of Woodstock. So was Woodstock in 1969? It was February of 1969, I had worked in book publishing and I wanted to change my job. I needed to make a living. I knew Bob Maurice, who had recently connected with a small film company called Paradigm Film. I knew Bob Maurice from City College. He introduced me to Bob Juliana, who had left Teletape to form a company with Mike Wadleigh and John Binder, called Paradigm Film.

Mike and John had done a lot of documentaries for Teletape. I think Teletape owned them. Teletape produced *Sesame Street* initially in that studio on Eighty-First Street and Broadway. Bob Juliana became the administrative head; John and Mike were the production team. Thelma Schoonmaker—I don't know if she was a part of the company—worked all the time for them, editing everything they did. They had certain regular jobs that they had done for Teletape, and I think they took them over as their own. I'm not sure how that worked. One of them was the *Merv Griffin Show* and/or interviews with him on a personal level. Another one that they were in the midst of when I first arrived, there was a series of spots for the Ringling Brothers, Barnum and Bailey Circus. Why you laughing?

DALE: I didn't know anything about this.

SONYA: I believe John Binder directed them and Thelma was cutting them and they were fabulous. There were trapeze artists. They were great. They had several other long-lerm contracts that they did year after year. A young woman named Pat

Sandalay was a kind of line producer for their jobs. I believed they were still backed by Teletape as an independent company, but I'm not sure. I know that when we were working on Woodstock the final break with Teletape came. We were working in offices that were leased to Teletape. That were given to Paradigm through their connection with Teletape. The reason we all had to move out in the middle of the night to Chuck Hirsch's studio was because of some breach with Teletape that finally happened later.

DALE: So you joined them to do what?

SONYA: I joined them to be a secretary. I was thinking of leaving book publishing and knew Bob Maurice, who was heading up a distribution arm of this new young company, and he said, "Why don't you come and see Bob Juliana the administrator because we need a receptionist who also can do petty cash and typing." I said fine; I had been working in book publishing as a reader and a secretary. So they hired me. So I went to work there.

DALE: Who were some of the other people who were there at the time?

SONYA: Well, at the time, Bob Maurice, who was my original connection from City College, was running the distribution arm of this very young company. Jeanne Field was his assistant. She had arrived there I believed shortly before I did. She was not that old there and the distribution company as a whole was new, but they did have films. They had, I think, two or three films by Jim McBride, *My Girlfriend's Wedding*, and *David Holtzman's Diary*. They also had [David Loeb Weiss's] *No Vietnamese Ever Called Me Nigger*, which I believe there was some legal hassle with.

Thelma Schoonmaker was always there cutting things. Martin Scorsese was affiliated with them and was around. He would come sometimes and show films of people he had discovered. Also, he would bring his friends, The Ace Trucking Co., sometimes. They were a comedy group. A bizarre sort of hippie comedy group.

DALE: From downtown somewhere?

SONYA: They were his friends and he would get a huge kick out of them. I know that he and Thelma and Mike and John all knew one another from NYU. I was always hearing about Lewis Teague, who was also in that class, but he was in California at that time on a fellowship. Louis was an absentee member of this NYU class that was so brilliant.

Because, what I was learning when I worked there that there was all these connections and connections and connections. That had to do with their former life.

DALE: Tell me more about NYU. Who else was in this class?

SONYA: Jim McBride was in it...

DALE: Chuck Hirsch, Brian De Palma??

SONYA: No, none of them. Brian went to Columbia; they were separate, but they all knew each other by then. Brian and Marty became friends independently. But it did not have to do with school. It might of had to do with Bob DeNiro, but I'm not sure. Bob DeNiro did not go to NYU.

DALE: The first movie that Marty did, called *Who's That Knocking at My Door?*, was that a part of that distribution?

SONYA: Yes it was. That was my first day on my new job.

DALE: Tell me.

SONYA: I got this job as a secretary and Bob Maurice said to me, "Come in Wednesday," I think. He said, "Don't come to the office, come to the New Yorker Theater. We have to look at a movie." I was thrilled because my first day at a new job at 9:30 in the morning I was going to look at a movie. The movie was *Who's That Knocking*, and Dan Talbot, at that point, owned the New Yorker and he was not yet a distribution company. So, probably Bob was showing it there just to have a place to show it. That was a big thrill and I remember, at that point—

DALE: Who's in the movie?

SONYA: Harvey Keitel. Harvey Keitel was in the movie and—

DALE: Bob DeNiro was not.

SONYA: No, Bob was not in that movie. They had already inserted a sex scene for distribution. Because some company was distributing it and said they couldn't unless they had a sex scene. So, they put in this sex scene that was shot someplace else with different people or something. I didn't know that, I just thought it was a part of the movie. Mostly, what I remember from the movie is I remember it was black and white and I remember a montage from the end—there was a montage and they played that rock and roll song from the 1950s, "Who's That Knocking," and I have a picture in my mind of Harvey in close-up, sort of stroking a crucifix in the church. And, it's the climatic scene in the movie where all of his obsessions come together.

Actually, what had happened was that some weeks before that or during the time that Bob Juliana was interviewing me, there was a screening on the afternoon at Movielab of one of their sixteen-millimeter films. It was one of the Jim McBride movies, which they were screening for distribution. I went there in the afternoon and I remember we were all sitting there and I remember Pat Sandalay, who was this very tall blond, with very long hair and big glasses, was seating in front of me and she looked very elegant. Everybody was very nice and we were all sitting there and chatting and somebody said, "Well, who brought the film?" and everybody kept saying, "Who brought the film?" and they suddenly discovered that nobody had brought the film, because they each thought somebody else had!

That thrilled me because I came from this very straight book-publishing world where people were very respectable and older. Here I was in this crazy world where everybody was sitting waiting for the film, and they were all geniuses, and somehow nobody brought the film and everybody laughed about it. I just thought it was terrific.

That was before I started working there, but my first day on the job was looking at *Who's That Knocking*, and I don't remember why and I don't remember much about starting there. I remember my desk in the front of a big room and I remember going up in the elevator that was run by this very old black guy named Pete. I remember getting coffee at Charlemagne Deli downstairs. I remember the big windows that were there and that it was on Eighty-First and Broadway.

There were other people who hung around; they had a lot of friends who they allowed to use the equipment when it wasn't in use. One of them was notably Peter Barton. And Peter had made two films that were prizewinning, one was called *Riff*, which I went to a screening of. It was about a Latino boy who lived on the East Side of Manhattan, uptown I guess in Harlem or on the fringes of it and who climbed a lot. He was always climbing. The film was in black and white. It had no sync sound and it won a lot of awards and *Riff* became sort of famous. It was about a boy who came from a bad background who had possibilities of getting out.

He made another one called *Alfred* about an old bum, again black, who poked around in the garbage at the Safeway, which was on Ninety-First and Broadway. Alfred was on welfare and gave away all his welfare checks to hookers. He was a very sweet old man. He gave away his checks to these women; he just thought they were wonderful. These whores on upper Broadway would take all his money and he would walk around with a shopping bag and look in the garbage. So, Peter made a film about him, too.

These people that he made films about—Alfred and Riff—used to hang around the film company. I remember one day, I was sitting in my little receptionist desk in the big room and somebody came to see someone. I can't remember who, but Alfred was sitting there in the waiting area. The room was very big and sunny. The relatively straight person was sitting there, too.

We had this huge garbage can in the corner. Like a tin drum, that we just threw garbage in. I looked up and Alfred was sort of bent over it, looking for cigarette butts and his jacket was split in the back and his pants were split and his rear end was showing. And I remember thinking I didn't know what to say. I thought, *I don't want to call attention to this, but what if this person, who's sitting there waiting, looks up and sees Alfred's bare butt sticking out?* It passed, but that's sort of the kind of thing that I remember.

At that time, first Mike had shot a big budget industrial, for Jam Handy, which was the publicity and industrial shooting arm of General Motors. They did a thirty-five-millimeter industrial that involved Panavision, anamorphic lenses, and three screens, which Thelma cut on the KEM, I think partly to experiment with techniques, but also they delivered the industrial that Jam Handy wanted. While Thelma was finishing cutting that, I think she made occasional trips to Detroit.

Mike went off with the Paul Petzoldt National Outdoor Leadership School and shot an expedition with Charles Grossbeck—the mountain climber turned soundman. And while they were away Thelma was cutting the Jam Handy show and then I think from that they started shipping dailies back from Wyoming and she was syncing dailies. That's when I started learning editing, because I'd be working from nine to six, at my desk, and then I would go in and sit with her and she would teach how to sync up dailies. I had no idea of what I was doing; I liked it though.

DALE: What do you remember as the first time you heard about this Woodstock festival?

SONYA: I remember that at a certain point everything changed around. It must have been late spring, early summer. A new company was formed with Mike Wadleigh, Bob Maurice, Thelma, and me because they needed another officer. Larry Johnson, who I didn't mention, was around all the time during the Teletape Paradigm days. He was basically Mike's all-over assistant and kind of fair-haired boy.

DALE: All of a sudden, you found yourself then involved in this project.

SONYA: I was still the secretary and I was sort of involved. And I knew that they formed this company and they were trying to sell the movie. But I wasn't really involved in any decision-making way. I was just there to answer the phones, do the bills, order equipment.

I had to call around and get the lenses. I didn't even know what a projector was. I remember when I first went to work there and I had to call and order equipment, for small jobs, and Bob Juliana was still there. I would say to him, "Bob, what's an Éclair?" and he'd say, "Well it's this crust that has custard and cream in it and chocolate on it..." I would say, "okay...", but that was the extent of my knowledge. I had to try and get a synchronous motor and I didn't know what sync was.

John Binder, at one point, which I don't remember well, tried very hard to explain to me the workings of the Nagra and of sync. He gave me a comprehensive film school lesson in one hour. Which totally bewildered me. All it made me feel was that cameras and recorders were just too difficult for me, I would stick to something I knew.

So, when I saw Thelma working on the editing machine, which seemed relatively simple compared to other machines, where I could see the story, I thought if I have a future here that's where it is. Also, because she herself made things seem more accessible to me...

When you [Dale] arrived to work on *Woodstock*, you were another part of that group of people that everybody knew, that I didn't know, like Fern McBride. Fern appeared when we went to the site, because you hired her as a location manager. There were all these friends and connections, like Marty and his connections, that were always appearing.

The main thing I remember from that whole experience was that you could think that you knew everything that was going on, but in the meantime some whole other thing was going on.

A lot of it had to do I believe with Mike's personality. He was able to keep a great many balls in the air at once and he was also capable of extreme secrecy. So, he would only tell people what they needed to know. Bob was also extremely secretive. Probably he got along very well with Mike, in ways that nobody else could ever get along with either of them, because they were both quite secretive and both quite smart.

PART II

A FESTIVAL IS HATCHED

AHMET ERTEGUN

A LITTLE SECRET

(AHMET ERTEGUN IS CO-CHAIRMAN and co-CEO of The Atlantic Group, celebrating its fiftieth anniversary in 1998. Ahmet founded the company Atlantic Records so that he could devote his life to listening and loving music.)

DALE: How did Atlantic first get involved with the *Woodstock* project?

AHMET: I was approached by Paul Marshall, who is a lawyer who represented the promoters of the Woodstock concert. Of course, at that time, nobody knew that it was going to be such a momentous occasion. It was just another rock and roll event, similar to what they did in Monterey and so forth. I thought there were going to be at least three Atlantic acts on the program. This was six months at least before the concert—maybe February or March 1969. And I thought that if I recorded the concert, I might be able to get permission from one or two of the acts. I wasn't sure, but I thought I might have three live albums. So we made a deal for 75,000 dollars.

DALE: With the promoters?

AHMET: I made the deal with Paul Marshall. He sold me the rights to record the concert for records and he proposed to me—asked me if I would be interested in the movie rights. And I said what movie rights? No, I'm not interested in the movie rights. So then he couldn't sell it to anybody. So he came back to me and said, look—you've got 75,000 dollars committed—give me another 25,000 dollars and I'll throw in the movie rights. I said okay.

DALE: Wow.

AHMET: I had no idea that it would mean anything, but I thought, well, I'll have some footage of three of my acts. I thought maybe Zeppelin would be on that thing—I don't remember which acts they were, but I knew that Crosby, Stills & Nash would be on it.

DALE: And you had just signed them.

AHMET: Yes. We already had a record out. I didn't go to the concert.

DALE: Did you send somebody?

AHMET: Yes, but you know something? We didn't have the responsibility of recording it. For that money, they were supposed to record the concert—the promoters—and shoot the movie. They kept the rights of making the record and the movie. Of course, after what happened happened—and this became such a huge thing, which nobody expected—we knew as the thing approached that a lot of people were going to this because it was such a big bill.

I was now down to having only one act in the show. We signed Melanie a few years after that. We made some records with her. But nobody else.

DALE: Did you have anything to do with bringing Warner Bros. in?

AHMET: You must realize that I had sold my company already to Warner /7 Arts. About the time of the Woodstock concert, Warner /7 Arts was bought by Kinney Corporation and when I told them we had the movie rights to Woodstock, they were beside themselves and proceeded to work on developing the movie.

DALE: At the time Steve Ross was there with Ted Ashley after Ross and his funeral-parlor/parking lot/cleaning seivices/car rental conglomerate bought Ashley Talent Agency in 1967.

AHMET: Yes, Steve Ross and Ted Ashley were partners in Kinney. You know, Fred Weintraub only got the rights because I bought the rights.

DALE: I can't get over it. For $25,000. When you saw the movie, what was your impression?

AHMET: I thought it was terrific. I mean it was a terrific event and I'm glad that they filmed it because otherwise it would have all been people telling what it was like. In the film, you can see what it was like.

DALE: What impact did the movie have on your artists?

AHMET: Well, all those who were there were delighted that they were there because it was such a historical event in rock and roll. It was such a spontaneous thing that nobody engineered. I think it was a highlight of the end of the 1960s. A high point—a happening—an event that really was symbolic of the feelings of all the things that had happened before that. You know, Haight Ashbury, Flower Power, and all of that. It had all of it going on—sex, drugs, and rock and roll.

DALE: What do you think the Woodstock factor is in our culture today?

AHMET: I think that now, young kids just think of it as a great moment that they missed. Those who were there, those who lived it at that time, are nostalgic about those times, the music of the 1960s, the whole revolution of the young people. It was a culturally significant event.

DALE: Do you see positives that came out of that Woodstock event?

AHMET: Did you go to the twenty-fifth anniversary concert?

DALE: No, I did not. I tried to see film of it, I know the film has not yet been released. I talked to people that were there, so I have a little sense of it.

AHMET: It's not the same thing. It's just like some of those historic Rolling Stones concerts, Altamont and so on—you can't recreate that.

DALE: Describe for me what is the power of music as represented by Woodstock.

AHMET: How would you characterize the Woodstock factor, is that what you mean?

DALE: When somebody asked him in the middle of the movie, "Why are all these people here?" Mike Lang said, "Well, it's the music and it's the lyric." Music has an incredible power and I thought you might characterize it in some way.

AHMET: It's more than just the music. I think people went there expecting to spend three days just in continuous music and hanging out and being with other people who loved this and it was like a spontaneous gathering of people who shared a new point of view about life. It was the culmination of the 1960's revolution in music. And the antiauthoritarian, antiestablishment feeling that pervaded throughout the young people at that time. I think the song…"By the Time I Get to Woodstock…"

DALE: …by Joni Mitchell.

AHMET: Yes, Joni Mitchell—that Crosby, Stills & Nash recorded, I think that symbolizes more than any other the feeling of Woodstock.

MIKE LANG

IT'S THE MUSIC

(MICHAEL LANG WAS THE on-site festival executive producer. Mike had responded to John Roberts's advertisement: Young Men with Limited Capital Seek Adventure. I interviewed Mike in his offices on Broome Street in SoHo, New York, after not having seen him for many years.)

DALE: Think about the movie. Who else was involved in pitching you for rights to make the film? Give me a little timeline.

MIKE: It didn't really happen that way, nobody pitched us, at all. The only person who ever proposed, to my recollection, the idea of doing a film was Al and David (Maysles). And that was sometime in May or June of 1969. We tried to sell it to several studios, nobody "got it" at all.

DALE: This was in the spring, though.

MIKE: Yes.

DALE: March 1969?

MIKE: That's kind of early on for us, it was much later than that. This was probably April or May, May or June, that we talked with Al. We had made some initial sort of approaches around that same time, around May, to some companies. Before that it was just such a mad scramble to put the thing together that nobody was thinking film at all. We didn't even think film until May.

DALE: You're kidding!

MIKE: No.

DALE: I thought that people like Eric Blackstead [who would produce the two Woodstock record albums for Atlantic] and Bob Maurice [*Woodstock* producer] were probing all over you guys...

MIKE: Not at all.

DALE: …and that there was a bid out for, anybody could have the rights if they had a million bucks.

MIKE: That was much later on that we were looking for someone to come in and do it. We spoke with…my initial interest was in the Maysles to do it. And I had spoken with them.

DALE: With Porter Bibb [the Maysles's brothers' producer].

MIKE: With Porter and with Al and David. And we sort of went casting around for it, and then forgot about it for awhile. And then, Artie Kornfeld [one of the Woodstock Ventures partners] really made the contact with Freddie Weintraub at Warners. Last minute. Once this excitement started to get generated I guess Freddie came in. I don't really remember how Michael and Bob got involved, at that point. The reason that we didn't have the Maysles I believe is that we couldn't put the funding in place in time.

DALE: And they didn't have any money.

MIKE: And they didn't have any money.

DALE: We didn't have any money.

MIKE: You didn't have any money, I know, but you had volunteered to come in and shoot anyway. And it just happened that Artie made this Warners deal the day before.

DALE: But now give me a timeline for that.

MIKE: That was literally Thursday.

DALE: Thursday before music began on Friday.

MIKE: Yeah. Yeah. Thursday, I believe it was Thursday that Artie called me in the morning and said, "Warners is in." And you guys were already committed to coming in that day or the next day.

DALE: So we had 22,000 dollars in the bank by the time we started. That's, I don't know, either more guts than the Maysles had…

MIKE: It was, definitely.

DALE: …but it was probably more money than they had…

MIKE: I think so. I had hired Michael Margetts and his partner, remember those guys? [These were two British cameramen who began filming on site long before we got there.]

DALE: That was the smartest…Give me his name again.

MIKE: Margetts.

DALE: Brilliant. And he had come up a week…

MIKE: Two weeks. I brought them up two weeks before. I just thought, y'know, let's catch this. No matter what happens, if there is going to be a film, this is stuff we're gonna need, so. And they were great! They were terrific. They just came, and they were everywhere. And, the next thing I knew, you guys showed up.

DALE: Came up on Saturday, left somebody behind (John Binder and Ed Lynch), started on Sunday plotting, Monday my first, the train, the caravan began on Monday morning. So we had, by the time Thursday came around, we had eighty people. And I had all the cameras I could possibly get out of New York, and no raw stock. All the people and no stock. So I'm going over to wring Kodak's neck.

MIKE: Yep [laughs]. Right.

DALE: …for fucking that whole thing up, but…

MIKE: So that's, uh, and then we, I guess we had a brief talk about what to cover, and how to cover and which acts to cover.

DALE: Do you remember my asking on the lip of the stage that, I don't think you were there, actually, I think Chip was there, and Steve Cohen was there, I looked at the front of the stage and said...

MIKE: …"we need a platform."

DALE: We can't I mean, I looked at Wads, and said, "Wads, it's gotta be this high."

MIKE: Yeah, I was there.

DALE: That was the best thing that you guys did for us.

MIKE: Yeah, I remember that. It was kind of a high stage.

DALE: It was either that or our cameramen would have to work from stilts!

MIKE: Yeah, exactly.

DALE: We sensed even though we were there, and possession was nine-tenths of the law, in that Friday-Saturday-Sunday era that there was a real evolution of change in the feeling that all of you guys had about us.

MIKE: Mmmm.

DALE: When we arrived, we felt these guys are giving us shit. Thank you, we had the platform. But we're not getting anything else, all that food's over there and we're starving, we're going to save their ass, they don't recognize it yet. They've got water, we've got nothing. They're eating over here, we're getting B12 shots, they've got places to sleep, we're on the plywood, what was going on? Was it like, "Leave these film guys alone"?

MIKE: No, what was going on was there was so much on our plate to finish that to add one more thing on the back of the crews or anybody else was an impossibility. I mean, as you know we didn't finish the gates, even, or the fences. There was just so much infrastructure that had to be in place, from plumbing to toilets to God knows what. And don't forget we built that site in three and a half weeks, that nobody had the room for anything else. So it was just, "Let them fend for themselves, we can't really pay any attention to this," other than the essentials. And that's really the attitude, it was…I wouldn't say it was an annoyance, to have the crews up there, but it was just another thing to worry about. And we had so much to worry about.

DALE: The attitude seemed to change. On Saturday…

MIKE: Yeah. Well…

DALE: …when all of a sudden, something happened. Somebody came over from the Green Room, such as it was, the arched green room, with FOOD! Now do you remember that, did you instigate that?

MIKE: I remember, it was just a function of that, it was sort of in the formula at one point, you know, this is something that we have to deal with when we get to it. And that's when they got to it. Things were sort of in gear and rolling, so people could think a little bit broader about responsibilities.

DALE: But that was the time when we said, "I think they realize we're here…" By that time, I mean it being Saturday, we knew on stage that there was going to be a deal. Somebody was going to finance it.

MIKE: The deal was in place by then; actually, the deal was in place by Friday. But it had nothing to do with that, really; that was nobody's consideration. It was just, things loosened up enough to pay attention, I think. I remember Artie trying to get the artists to sign releases [laughs] on the way to the stage. Because that's how much we eliminated the possibility of film happening. We hadn't even discussed those rights with the artists beforehand. So we said, "Let's see what, you know, let's get as much as we can on the way in, 'cause it's gonna be harder on the way out, after the fact."

DALE: So as it turned out…you didn't get anybody, did you?

MIKE: I think we got a few people to agree, yes, during the weekend. Albert Grossman of course would not, before he had a chance to think about it and put his two cents into everything. But I think my recollection is that Artie got several people to sign agreements to be filmed. And I think that…actually, I think that more than several, I think quite a few. At least to be filmed. The ones that we didn't get, I guess we filmed anyway, but it was important to us, not that we made a deal with them, for what the rights would cost or anything else, but just they agreed to let the cameras roll. Artie can give you, I hope, some detail on that [chuckles].

DALE: Well, John says that he may even have copies of the original contract that Artie had spelled out with Freddie, that had been one of these things that there's a signature on the bottom, that required Woodstock Ventures to deliver X, Y, and Z; I mean it was a preposterous list of impossible things… [Mike is saying "yeah; right; uh huh" through all this] that could never be delivered at that moment, you know.

Was there a point in here while we were on stage, while we were at the festival when you felt a turning point as it related to us directly? I mean, during the rain, or at some other point, and you said, "My God, I hope they're shooting this, or I wonder or…"

MIKE: Yeah, Friday, I mean when we saw the thing start to take form, I remember thinking how glad I was that finally there were people here who were going to document this, because we realized that this was much bigger and much more significant than anyone thought it was going to be.

DALE: So it did, I mean at times you were being interviewed by this guy, and by my dear friend Greg Jackson, who I brought up to the site; he did the "Why Do You Think These People Are Here?"—that wonderful inane question. [Lang giggles]…"Aw, it's the music."

MIKE: I think it was, "What do these musicians have?" right?…

DALE: Yeah, it's called…

MIKE: …"Music." [Laughs]

JOHN MORRIS

A NERVOUS BREAKDOWN?

(JOHN MORRIS WAS THE Festival Location Coordinator and one of the "Voices" on the albums.)

Dear Tenacious Dale,

My relationship with the movie began when you, Wadleigh, and Maurice all showed up the day or two days before, and all I remember is guys in funny cowboy hats, an orchestra ramp for shooting in front of the stage....

And then during the festival my amazement that everyone worked so well with us and with the artists.

We started out with a "no one onstage" policy that as I remember was loosened up as you proved you knew how to work with the artists and with the crews. As I remember Jim Marshall negotiated a deal to control all the press people to keep them off the stage in exchange for him being the only one allowed to shoot onstage.

I remember Renee Wadleigh was something beautiful to look at from my perspective through all the rain, mud, and problems. Also Wads, you, and Larry, whom I must have had in my field of vision for three days.

The most memorable incidents are signing the deal for *Woodstock* upstage with Freddie Weintraub after the festival had begun, and realizing what a limb Bob and Michael, in fact all of you had climbed out on with no net.

The main remembrance, however, is as close to a nervous breakdown as I have ever been in my fifty-nine years.

The tornado storm that came up on Cocker's set, watching the towers sway in the wind, knowing that there were 300-pounds follow-spots not chained to the towers, being told that 1. Baez was having a miscarriage, 2. Anne, my wife, had fallen and broken her ankle, 3. Cadogan, my dog, was lost and there was a guy with a gun in the audience; all the while the storm grew, we were clearing the stage, trying to get people away from the towers, and we had to cut the power.

Standing onstage with the mike shocking my hand, trying to be calm, and there was Wadleigh on his knees shooting and being some strange connection to reality which is 180 degrees from what it should have been. None of the rumors were true, but all hell was breaking loose and this guy was recording IT.

IT was something in a very strange way that was like a copper wire as earth, a ground, and it got me through.

All in all the friendships that were so instant with you. Wads, Bob, and Larry carry on to today. We have a line that can be a phone call or just an understanding that we fought that battle together and survived. It's still very strong in our memories but it was a battle we all went through and the respect lasts to this day.

Other film-related remembrances:

Seeing the synced sixteen-millimeter projectors in the studio across from Zabars. All the camera angles, only a few weeks after the event. What brilliance, what a flashback so quickly.

Dubbing an announcement on the way to or from Japan in LA. I had never done that before and it was another reunion.

Seeing the team that had fought the battle and feeling all those feelings.

Strange it is that those same people have been at crossroads through the years. Were it not for you and your lovely Anne, I would have never lived in Snedens Landing.

Wadleigh being there too working on George [Washington] until he disappeared again, as he had done previously when I was living in London.

Larry [Johnson], when I came here, being an advisor and friend after twenty years.

Bob [Maurice] in Santa Fe, a new friendship because he wanted nothing to do with it all. Just an antique dealer, bookstore owner whom I knew from another life, on the condition that when I got calls or did interviews I never mentioned where or who he was now.

The overall reaction I have (which keeps getting reinforced by occasional clips of the film on TV) is that people who met in August of 1969 who, although they don't stay in constant touch, could eat dinner for seven consecutive days and have a great time, based on respect, intellect, and a joy of life.

Best,

John

PORTER BIBB

A FOOL'S ERRAND?

(PORTER WAS THE PRODUCER for the Maysles Brothers film company. They almost snared the rights to film the festival, but the deck was stacked against them.)

DALE: This is Porter Bibb and it is Sunday the tenth of January. Where should we start, I'd like to start…can we start with *Out of Africa*?

PORTER: Ted Ashley was the chairman of Warner Bros. at the time. And Ted had signed onto the concept *Out of Africa*. The rights were owned at that time by Peter Beard, the photographer, and a close friend of mine. He had based his concept of *Out of Africa* on a melange of historical and fictional and real-life elements that would have been a very interesting film, had it ever got made. I had written a first-draft screenplay and we had also talked, incestuous though it may be, to Ahmet Ertegun about having the Stones do the soundtrack for this movie.

Ashley, unbeknownst to us, was in the midst of a very bitter divorce and as a result wanted to go to Africa. We thought it was a sign of positive progress on our part in moving the project forward that he said, "Lets go see where you're gonna shoot this."

DALE: Mmm [laugh].

PORTER: But, what he was really doing was getting out of the country during the thick of his divorce.

DALE: Right.

PORTER: We did, subsequently, journey to Africa with him and toured all of the major Dinesen high spots from her book. We came back and found that the project absolutely had died while we were away. And Ashley was in the process of being removed but it hadn't happened yet. We saw that his power was going.

Ahmet backed off of the project for whatever reason and we put the whole thing, ourselves, on the back burner.

DALE: So, then, how did Woodstock enter into this?

PORTER: Well, it was through those connections that the Maysles and I had. The Maysles were not part of the Beard project.

DALE: Right, understand.

PORTER: But, I was working with them on other documentaries and we conceived the idea of doing a rock concert. Actually, it was an interesting idea. We were going to follow the Rolling Stones on a tour of Russia.

And Woodstock just emerged as an event. We thought we would do a split-screen version of the Stones, showing them in the United States and in Russia, and contrast the performances and the audience. Because the only time the Stones had appeared in Eastern Europe had been in Poland a few years earlier where they had huge riots and the police had got the water cannons out to put the kids down.

So we thought there was a potential for conflict and an interesting subject for a documentary. We were looking at music and through the relationship that I'd developed with Amhet and with Ashley, so we gravitated to Warner's for the money.

DALE: Now, did you know at the time, that you were talking to Ahmet, that Ahmet had the film rights?

PORTER: No, we did not.

We had, before we approached Ahmet, we had had some preliminary talks with the Woodstock principles. Namely, with Mike Lang.

We were, at that time, the Maysles and I, were basically covering a lot of different ground and not always attending meetings or meeting people together. It was a very fluid situation. And I do not mean to suggest, in any way, shape, or form, off the record, that there was any dissension.

We were just scrambling.

The way documentary production companies do when they don't have a project.

DALE: Right! [laugh]

PORTER: And [laugh] so I met many, many times with Mike Lang and the Johns [Roberts and Morris] and Artie [Kornfeld] and David [Maysles of the two brothers, Al and David], also, had separate meetings with some of the same people at different times…

I can't tell you exactly what was going on because it was fast and furious and what I…my role was principally the producer's role to kind of make sure that there was an economic viability here. And Al and David were focusing more on the event and the acts, and getting the acts, first of all, signed up, which is something that the Woodstock principles were in the process of doing and we were doing a parallel effort.

I felt that that was a fool's errand, because dealing with rock and roll acts that had not even committed to perform at a concert…

DALE: Sort of the cart before the horse…

PORTER: Cart before the horse. But David was extremely good at that end of the business, having spent twenty years or more as a documentarian and always aware of getting the rights before he shot.

And so, a major effort was undertaken there, and we spent a lot of time with Ahmet, and the answer, bluntly, is that it was never revealed to us that Ahmet had the rights.

DALE: Were you ever negotiating with Paul Marshall?

PORTER: Yes.

DALE: Okay. And Paul Marshall never told you that he had sold the music rights to Ahmet Ertegun?

PORTER: Never told us.

DALE: And he never told you that he then offered the film rights to Ahmet?

PORTER: No.

DALE: And that Ahmet had turned him down?

PORTER: No.

DALE: Keep going.

PORTER: Nope, we were. I would say we, 'cause I want to speak for Al, and David can't speak for himself, but I was never aware of that I had, as I said, a business, an economic responsibility as the Maysles's partner, and they had the creative responsibility. And they saw a groundbreaking opportunity to make a major theatrical rock film. I saw the economics being covered by the profit of a soundtrack album.

DALE: Well now, you started negotiating, you negotiated, then, with Ted, having just played with him for *Out of Africa*.

PORTER: And it was a very friendly and enthusiastic, it was very much parallel. And Ted Ashley is a former agent and one of the most voluble, amiable, and smooth comfort, confident, Egyptian…

DALE: [laughs]

PORTER: …characters I have ever met in my life. And just as Peter Beard and I were absolutely certain that *Out of Africa* was going to happen, at Warner Bros. we had a high level of comfort that, despite the fact that we were never even shown a piece of paper, Warner Bros. was ultimately going to fund a *Woodstock* project. And on the blind faith that documentarians…

DALE: [laughs]

PORTER: …must live by, we just plowed forward and did what we were supposed to be doing as filmmakers. That is lining up schedules, people, talent, and to the extent of Al's and David's going up to the site, as Woodstock was beginning to break ground and become a reality…

DALE: When did they go up, do you remember?

PORTER: Several times in the month before the concert.

DALE: So, in July, did they go to Woodstock itself or to the news site or what?

PORTER: Oh, and they retained, there was an English crew up there that you may…

DALE: Michael Margetts.

PORTER: Yes, and they retained them to shoot some footage, and we began to build a modest file on the emergence of Woodstock. Perfectly candidly, I was so consumed with trying to get a business deal together that I was paying very little attention to them. They would just say, "We're going up to the country," and they would be gone. And I would be in some meeting—I'm trying to think of where I met Lang. Down in the village somewhere.

DALE: Yeah.

PORTER: And Paul Marshall and going back and forth between the Woodstock people and the Warner Bros. people. And as the event became more and more likely to happen, and more and more benchmarks were overcome in terms of the size, the scope of the event. The ticket sales, as you know, were originally conceived of as a for-profit paid admission venture.

DALE: Right.

PORTER: But the papers were running…I'm sure you've got the files of the *New York Post* and all the other papers [laugh], even the *New York Times*. Almost on an every other day basis there was news about what was going on with this thing. And we were living by the headlines while we were dealing with the people that we thought were the right people to be dealing with.

DALE: Right.

PORTER: It became very nervous-making because as we got closer and closer to D-day, because Maysles films, as a business, did not have great resources. And we were starting to line up a very sizable commitment in terms of crew and equipment and could hardly have covered that if we couldn't cut a deal with somebody.

DALE: Sure.

PORTER: At one point we were offered the opportunity to be hired for contract filmmakers by the Woodstock principles. And that was not appealing to any of us.

DALE: You mean by John Roberts.

PORTER: Yes. The Maysles said no, they had to be in control and didn't want to be just per-diem filmmakers shooting the thing.

I recollect there was the possibility that there was going to be live or taped television coverage, as well. That was a possibility. I can't remember where the source was, but that made some of us and the money—because we were looking for independent money as well—very nervous if they thought what we were going to do was not exclusive.

So I stayed focused on Warner Bros. and my recollections are not precise in terms of the day-to-day evolution of that dialogue, but I would come back after every meeting with Ashley and the business affairs guys and report that we're going to do it with Warner Bros. and they're going to put the money up about two or three days before the event opened. I think it opened on a Friday, didn't it…

DALE: Yes.

PORTER: I had this question put to me by Ted: "What if it rains? You'll have a completion bond." And I came back and I said, this is insane, my answer to Ashley was if it rains, you're made, we're made—we've got a whale of a film.

DALE: [laugh]

PORTER: But, I spent at least forty-eight hours calling London and elsewhere trying to find out if we could [both laugh] get a completion bond on this very bizarre [Dale laughs] event. And that really was a fool's errand, but I made...

DALE: This was Lloyd's of London you're talking about...

PORTER: Well, Lloyd's was one, I think Film Finance was in business at that point as a bonding agent. I was calling every entertainment law firm I could think of on both coasts and in London trying to find somebody to come up with a completion bond. So I could go back to Warner Bros. and pick up what I thought was to be their check. What it was was the most graceful, diplomatic, and conclusive way to say NO from Warner's, but I didn't catch on to that.

DALE: And you're saying...just think calendar-wise for a second. You're saying this happened in the week prior...

PORTER: In the week. In the week prior to the event, by the best of my recollections.

DALE: Do you remember when you went to Wadleigh offices and what you saw and what your response was?

PORTER: Well, I would come back a little earlier. I think David and Al came first to Mike. I don't know who contacted whom.

DALE: Let me flash a little bit at you...Were you not, or were the Maysles also at that time not already in the process of filming the Stones as part of *Gimme Shelter*?

PORTER: No.

DALE: That was to come later?

PORTER: That came afterward. That was a specific reaction to having lost out on *Woodstock*. The Madison Square Garden thing didn't happen until Thanksgiving, after the August Woodstock.

DALE: That's right, you're right. Okay.

PORTER: No, once we lost out on *Woodstock* we went into a full-court press to try to recoup something. And our relationships with the Stones were fairly good. And since they were not at Woodstock, we convinced them that we should be doing some kind of filming.

DALE: Okay. So Al and David went up to Wadleigh...

PORTER: Well, I came up there and I was as dazzled as they were by what this split-screen, multi-screen demonstration. But I had a couple of creative egos, the likes of which I couldn't exaggerate in the Maysles brothers and I let them work out the relationship. Try to work it out. And I just was happy to have anybody of Mike Wadleigh's caliber as part of the project.

DALE: You realize, that after seeing that their participation was not going to exist, that we could, what should I say, do it all ourselves?

PORTER: Right.

DALE: When you realized that, or when they realized that, or the three of you, how would you characterize that?

PORTER: Frankly, that was not an issue. The money, the *sine qua non* of our involvement was...I mean, that would be the focal point and the highest priority of Al and David, but to me, it's who had the money. Who's going to do the deal? [laugh]

DALE: Um-hmm.

PORTER: And make the film. And I just thought, not presumptuously, that we were going to get the money and work something out with Mike.

DALE: Isn't it strange that when Mike and all of us decided to go ahead we had 23,000 dollars in the bank, period?

PORTER: That's 23,000 dollars more than Maysles films had.

DALE: Period.

PORTER: We always heard, and this may be something you've heard from other Mayslesians. We always heard that the Wadleigh team was able to pull it off because Mike got some kind of a second mortgage or a mortgage on a house that he had recently bought in the Village.

DALE: Not so. [To my knowledge.]

PORTER: Not so?

DALE: Not so. I mean I went to the...I tell you, on the Saturday that we went up to the site and it was the first time we went and that was the Saturday before the Friday...

PORTER: Right.

DALE: He had 10,000 dollars in the bank, and we looked at each other and I said Michael, we cannot do this on only 10,000 dollars. We need more than that and we went to a guy by the name, whom you know very well, probably, Danny Fales.

PORTER: Sure.

DALE: Who was then at Time-Life Alcoa and Wadleigh had just finished shooting, *30 Days to Survival,* in the Wind River range of Wyoming. And they were to pay him in two weeks 15,000 dollars or something. And I went to Danny on Monday morning and I said "Danny, I don't know what I have to do to put my hands around your neck, but I need that check today." And damn if we didn't get 13,000 of the 15,000 dollars...

PORTER: That's fabulous. I, no, I didn't know any of that.

DALE: In one day.

PORTER: And when I said Maysles didn't have a nickel in the bank we had a pretty good business. It was certainly a growing concern that we had a lot of receivables, but as you know, from your background and experience, the documentary producers are last people to get paid in any list and just cobbling together the money to buy the film, not to mention that it didn't ever occur to me that I couldn't have the money to pay the crew, but, needless to say, we didn't get it, because when I came up empty on the completion bond concept, I went back and realized then how stupid and how foolish I was to be deterred by Ashley in wasting time in going and looking, and events had gotten ahead of all of that on your end and Al and David, I guess, were firming up their feelings about the new technology that Wadleigh was introducing and it just became obvious that it wasn't going to happen on our end.

DALE: What is amazing, I'm still talking in that week before...

PORTER: Yes, yes...

DALE: On Monday night. Well, I never slept from Sunday through Friday, well, actually, I never slept that whole week, literally. I mean, I may have gotten an hour and an hour and an hour, but never, you know, anything. Because, I was looking at preview reels from camera men who had been asked by Al and David to shoot for them. Who now heard that we were going to do it who wanted to work with us.

So they'd come in at midnight and show me an hour reel, or something. You know, mean, it was that crazy.

PORTER: Well, and it was crazy on our end in a very negative and depressed way. We were obliged to unhook all of these people that we'd lined up. Because we really believed, up until that last week, I did anyway. I can't speak for Al or David, but I really thought that we were going to pull it off. And the whole Wadleigh-Maysles confrontation was something that really wasn't even a factor in my thinking because I wanted as much talent as I could get out of the venture and I said, we'll shoot, work it out later.

DALE: Um-hmm.

PORTER: It probably would have felt destructed after *Woodstock* if we had worked together because Al and David just are not capable of that kind of compromise.

DALE: Nor is Wadleigh or any of us.

PORTER: No.

DALE: I mean it just would not have worked at all.

PORTER: Yeah.

DALE: I mean in hindsight, in retrospect. There's a part of me is saying this is the movie that almost never got made at all.

PORTER: Right. And I'm, I think that's almost the title, because it was within a hair's breadth of never happening.

DALE: Warner's was out. Did Ted Ashley know that his, let's say, subordinate, or at least a guy on his own level, but his colleague, Ahmet Ertegun, had the movie rights?

PORTER: I have no idea about that and just to position Ted and Ahmet, it's my understanding from having known both of those guys reasonably well that they probably, with hindsight, probably were talking a half a dozen times a day about this project, without my knowledge.

DALE: Um-hmm.

PORTER: I mean, Ahmet loves to play the Sphinx when you sit in front of him and you're trying to cut a deal.

DALE: Right.

PORTER: And just smiles that Cheshire smile and, but. Ahmet, I dealt with him years before, well not that many years before. But I had a number of run-ins with Ahmet. Always liked him, but I found it almost impossible to out-negotiate him.

And Ashley is, of course, he was just the master. It would be extraordinary if the two of them didn't know everything about this project. They were treating it as a bunch of flower kids coming in with a wild idea.

DALE: Now there you were in the middle of that. But if Ahmet had told Ashley that he, Ahmet, had bought the movie rights from the producers through attorney, Paul Marshall, then Ashley would have been—as chairman of Warner Bros., which had acquired under Steve Ross, Atlantic—Ashley would have been derelict in his responsibility to his shareholders if he had not engaged someone to shoot the movie!

PORTER: I don't think, no, not necessarily, I think that..

DALE: Because what else would Ahmet's 25,000 dollars outlay for the movie rights have represented?

PORTER: Well, what you say is rational, but it's irrational in the sense of a major Hollywood studio. I mean, how many documentaries have you ever seen a studio produce? None. It would not be feasible or even realistic for Ashley to think that Warner could make this movie. He wouldn't know how to begin. And nobody on the production side, I think John Calley was then running the production side. They wouldn't know where to turn.

DALE: But, if they had not, I mean if somebody totally unrelated as it turns out it turned out to be Wadleigh, but if somebody totally unrelated shot the movie, what would Ahmet do, say, "We have the movie rights. I bought them for twenty-five thousand dollars?"

PORTER: Well, [laugh] what did happen? I don't know.

DALE: "Sorry, you can't shoot these?"

PORTER: I mean, no, what happened, what did Ahmet say after Woodstock, when you guys showed up with the negatives?

DALE: Well, you know, I can't answer because I was not involved in that. But then Warner's had to, and they did come to us on Saturday of the festival, and it was a deal that we heard of, when we were on the site, through Bob Maurice, but I mean then Artie Kornfeld says that he contacted Freddie Weintraub who went to Ted Ashley who then sent Arthur Barron up on the site—on Friday to be, you know, a consultant. And Arthur's rhetoric was that "these guys are the most disorganized bunch of long-haired hippie freaks I've ever seen."

PORTER: [laugh]

DALE: And told Ashley to pull out.

PORTER: Well, see, this is news to me, but I'm not surprised by any of it. I thought, we all thought, we were pretty damned sophisticated [both laugh] in 1969. I thought I'd been a lot, seen a lot, couldn't have any wool pulled over my eyes.

DALE: [laugh]

PORTER: That's why I stayed in the movie business for another ten or twelve years because of that innocence. Nothing that happened in Woodstock is unusual in the normal course of theatrical moviemaking. It was unique to us because documentaries really suffer mainly on the economic side, but generally have a very clear vision of what you're going to do and you don't have to go through the imagination to do it. And you know, youth is a wonderful rationalization for [laugh] lack of knowledge.

I envy you for all of those things.

DALE: On August 15, 16, and 17, where did you find yourself? Friday, the first day of the festival, where were you?

PORTER: That morning, I was driving up to Woodstock, with six or seven other people, not the Maysles. I don't think they went.

DALE: No.

PORTER: I could not miss it. And I just hitched on, I don't know, I think there might have been some people from the *New York Post* or some group of media people going up. And I ended trudging most of the way. I think we were stopped on the Thruway in the middle of the afternoon and walked into Woodstock, like most other people, and I found a bunch of friendly faces backstage. I mean, I knew dozens and dozens of the music people, the managers. And I saw the many people we had been talking to on the Wadleigh crew who were going to work for me. And I don't know who specifically invited me backstage, but I spent the entire concert through Sunday backstage. And, as I said before, loading magazines from time to time, besides taking pictures. Then I lost my camera in the mud.

DALE: Oh, God.

PORTER: But I ended up hitching a ride on one of the helicopters at the end of the thing and got out of Woodstock via chopper.

DALE: Fascinating.

PORTER: And I'm sitting there. I have to tell you. I am a former journalist. I've worked for Newsweek before I got into the documentary business and I'm such an observer, maybe even a voyeur, that I had no feeling of loss or regret or competition. I was so consumed by what was unfolding in front of everybody in that field that it was really forty-eight hours after that. Monday-Tuesday I got together, again, with the Maysles in New York, and I said, "I cannot allow us to fail the way we failed. It was probably my fault because I didn't get the money, but we are going to something that is equal or better than *Woodstock*." And from that moment on, the whole *Gimme Shelter* saga began.

DALE: Um. Um. Um.

PORTER: But, while I was up in Woodstock, I knew we were participating utterly, in its way, in an historic [both laugh], and I was consumed by it. And dazzled…
DALE: Yeah.

PORTER: …At the way Wadleigh was running the show. Maurice, you, too. I was not very friendly to Bob, because we were the head to head competing producers, but I really admired what he was up against and how he was handling everything.

DALE: We decided on that Saturday before. And you know, there's a snap of Bob and me and Mike leaning up against a New York State Thruway police car. Henry Diltz took the picture. We just looked at each other and said, "Damn it, guys. We can do this." And we looked and stared and said, "Okay, this is what we have to do." And like generals in the army, we put it together between Sunday and Thursday.

PORTER: Yeah. Well, you guys made history, too, from the film side. About *Woodstock*, it blew me away. You may remember, I came over frequently during the postproduction process…

DALE: Right.

PORTER: And I saw what was taking shape. It was film history.

JOHN ROBERTS

REMINISCENCES

(JOHN ROBERTS FINANCED THE Woodstock Music and Art Fair through his Woodstock Ventures company.)

July 4, 1969, America's 193rd anniversary. I'm sitting in my apartment on East Eighty-Fifth street in New York City wondering what everybody else is feeling so good about. Out the window I can see fireworks over the East River, but they give me no pleasure. I'm twenty-four years old and the possessor of a rapidly dwindling unearned fortune.

Earlier that year I had chosen to finance and produce a rock festival in Woodstock, New York. As the expression goes, it seemed like a good idea at the time, and for a while it had been a lark. Ticket sales were brisk. The acts were falling into line, and it had seemed like an easy way to make money, have fun, and "do something meaningful" with my life. There had been that little problem with the site in Woodstock, what with the landlord deciding not to rent it to us, but in early April we had found another site about fifty miles away in Walkill, New York. We had gotten our approvals from the town fathers and begun to build the festival. In June it all came unglued. The town got nervous about all the long hairs and the strange smoky smells that seemed to follow them everywhere. They moved to revoke our permits, and notwithstanding our strenuous efforts, that movement had been successful. On July 3 they booted us out.

So Janis, Jimi, and Creedence were booked to play at a festival that no longer existed. Some 80,000 tickets at fourteen dollars a pop had been sold, and about 500,000 dollars worth of work had been done to prepare a site we no longer could use. I was not merry.

History records that Max Yasgur, a dairy farmer in Bethel, New York, picked up the phone that weekend and saved our bacon by offering us his land and political protection. The next six weeks were the most frenzied of my life and the most expensive. By August 1, we had sold another 20,000 tickets, but we had also spent another million bucks moving and rebuilding the festival. On average about 25,000 dollars a day was flowing out of my coffers, so I was not feeling particularly flush on August 3 when Bob Maurice called me to talk about the movie.

We had always thought it would be a nice idea to make a movie about the festival, but it had never been a front-burner item. When you spend your days thinking about Port-O-Sans, traffic jams, food concessions, fencing, security, and the 10,000 minutiae of production, moviemaking seems kind of ethereal and unreal. Like everyone else in our group I had seen Monterey Pop and been excited by its energy and spirit but I also knew that documentaries were not moneymaking enterprises. To my mind a movie about Woodstock would be more of a keepsake, a filmed record of what I did last summer, and not a venture to charm my increasingly restive banker.

Over the course of the spring and summer we had gone to several meetings with filmmakers like Pennebaker and the Maysles brothers, and they had all expressed interest in making our movie. But talks had languished and then died when it became clear that we would have to finance their efforts ourselves. Bob Maurice and Mike Wadleigh had been latecomers to this process. I had seen some of Wadleigh's work and thought it to be original and clever, but nothing I had seen altered my fundamental view that financing a documentary was a sane use of my vanishing resources.

Sunday, August 3, 1969, was turning into another typical day at the office. Negotiations with our food concessionaire were turning ugly and it was starting to look like we would have to rebuild their kiosks to their specifications or they would take their hot dogs elsewhere. Given that the festival was scheduled to open in twelve days this was a powerful argument on their part. We were out of leverage.

Around noon I decided to take a break and go someplace where the phones wouldn't ring with Woodstock problems. I walked down to my dad's apartment in midtown. He was out so I flipped on a ball game and made myself at home. The phone rang. It was Bob Maurice. "How did you track me down, Bob?" "I called every Roberts in the book with a nice address," he said. I should have been more impressed with his ingenuity and determination than I was. Mostly, I was tired and pissed. "Well, you found me," I said, "what's on your mind?" "About ninety grand," he said, "that's what it will take for you to own this movie." I lectured him patiently on the economics of documentaries, concluding with a polite but firm refusal. "You'll have to get it somewhere else, Bob, I'm pretty much tapped."

In the context of so many bad decisions that summer this one looms large. *Woodstock* the movie became the highest grossing documentary of all time with revenues exceeding 100 million dollars worldwide. The soundtrack albums sold over 6 million units also grossing in excess of 100 million dollars.

A week later one of my partners made a deal with Warner Bros. for the 90,000 dollars. When the smoke cleared they owned ninety percent of everything, and we got ten percent of the profits from the film and about one-half of one percent of the albums. Even those drastically reduced percentages were enough to bail us out of debt when the show lost 1,600,000 thousand dollars and ten years later we could count ourselves slightly in the black.

It is difficult for me to take ownership of the movie in the modern psychobabble sense of the word. Of course, the festival fathered the film, so I have some causality, but still, it always seemed beyond my control or authorship. That weekend in August was such chaos. I barely remember the moviemakers, and they never showed up at the crumbling headquarters office from which we ran the logisitics, or from which they ran us. It is indicative of the power of film that people would occasionally ask me in future years if I actually attended the festival, since they couldn't remember seeing me in the movie. I remember thinking about the film sometime that weekend, but my thoughts ran to whether there was film in the cameras and whether they could shoot in the rain.

After the festival I became aware that indeed a film had been shot and the instantly historic nature of the festival invested the movie with considerable potential. But we had other fish frying…clean up, lawsuits, partnership problems, an aftermath that consumed the better part of the next year. There was some legal wrangling with Warner over providing artist releases and occasional panicked phone calls from Sid Kiwitt telling me that Bob was threatening to burn the film if he didn't get his way, but as for the quality or nature of the actual product I was pretty much in the dark.

When it was released the following March, I was astounded. For one thing it was a technological marvel pulsating with ingenuity and energy. For another it was the first real look I'd had at what I'd wrought. Mostly, it was hugely entertaining, joyous, and honest. I looked around for ways to take ownership, but couldn't find any. I consoled myself with a river of royalties.

In my mind the Woodstock festivals of 1969 and 1994 were quite similar. Every generation needs a small taste of anarchy, and the Woodstocks provided it. The movie caught that and much more. What was riveting about that era was the duality of society. While half a million youngsters were at Woodstock that weekend, an equal number were slogging through the jungles of Vietnam. While the late 1960s were considered the high-water mark of liberalsim in America, in 1968 we elected Richard Nixon and ushered in almost twenty-four years of unbroken Republican leadership in the White House. Society divided itself politically and temperamentally into over 1930s and under 1930s, anti-war and patriotic (it would take a few years before most people came to understand that anti-war sentiments or civil disobedience were not necessarily unpatriotic stances), long hair and short, pot smokers and liquor users, hip and square, part of the solution or part of the problem. It was not a time of gray complexity.

Woodstock celebrated one side of that equation and it's all there in the movie. An entire generation of Americans sat in dark theaters and thought, "That's just like me and, man, there are a lot of us out there who feel and think about things the same way." As such the movie was an empowering and validating document. But Wadleigh's achievement was even more impressive. His movie also dignified people on the other side of the equation...the man who spoke so movingly of his son in Vietnam, the Port-O-San worker, Max Yasgur, all these people were treated with dignity and respect, in essence building a bridge between generations and stressing our shared yearnings. It was a noble film.

PART III

A FUSION OF VISION AND TECHNOLOGY

DALE BELL

TRIPPING NORTH

SIX OF US IN a car, driving north out of New York City on the Thruway. The time? Early morning, Saturday, August 9, 1969. We are heading for a destination far distant: a tiny town called White Lake. As we speed along the Hudson River, then veer into the Catskills, none of us is aware at the time that this odyssey we are embarking upon will one day catapult all of us, for different reasons, into the record books of filmmaking. Truly, we are on a trip with a destination into the unknown, somewhere a synthesis between vision and technology. Or perhaps, a potential catastrophe of huge proportions.

We are a raggle-taggle bunch…Larry Johnson, a world-class swimmer from Florida with an uncanny ear for sound and music, the very, very youngest of us all; Thelma Schoonmaker, a prematurely gray, brilliant film editor and old-movie buff from New Jersey who types at speeds in excess of a hundred words per minute; John Binder, a rambling storyteller from York, Pennsylvania, college-mate, soundman, and original partner with Michael Wadleigh; Michael Wadleigh, high-school debater and Columbia University medical student dropout from Ohio turned cameraman with eyes in the back of his head, ears to match, and stamina extraordinary; Ed Lynch, a cameraman friend of Michael's whom I had scarcely met; and me, a public television producer, very short of hair, brought up in eastern establishment schools, sprinkled with itinerant trips to Wyoming and Paris, now living on the shores of the Hudson River in a grand old Victorian house with my wife and three young sons.

In another car were Bob Maurice, perennial philosophy/religion student at CCNY, construction worker, our chief negotiator; Eric Blackstead, Cornell graduate, music and performer guru; Jeanne Field, who had recently joined Bob in the distribution business; and Sonya Polonsky, colleague of Bob's from CCNY, who was working in production in Michael and John's company, Paradigm Films.

For months, we had loosely speculated that we might make this trip. In the city, led by Bob Maurice, a new soon-to-be-partner of Michael's, we had attempted some negotiations with another group of people—the promoters, who were going to put on a music festival—the biggest of its kind, ever. Bigger even than Monterey Pop, they said. Bigger than the most recent Atlanta raceway concert. They had rented a farm in Woodstock, New York, as a staging area, but local townspeople had objected so violently to the possible presence of a lot of long-haired hippie freaks that the promoters were forced, at the very last minute, to move their venue. Announcements on the radio scant weeks away were describing the new site, telling listeners that three days of peace and music, craft bazaars, and swimming were now going to take place at the destination for which we were now headed... White Lake. All for eighteen dollars, they promised; tickets would be required for admission. Fences would surround the perimeter, the announcements warned. No one would get in for nothing.

But why us? Our negotiations with the promoters had broken off about a month ago, and a new group of filmmakers, Al and David Maysles, veteran cinéma vérité producers, had entered the fray. They had told the promoters that the 500,000 dollars of rights payment they were demanding as a hedge against ticket sales was unrealistic, but that they would film it, in the style of Monterey Pop, and share the proceeds with the promoters. The essence of a new deal.

Then something strange happened. The Maysles, in this very small town of Manhattan, called to ask us whether they and we could join forces in the making of the film. At first, we didn't quite know what to make of this request. After all, we knew how we wanted to go about making the film, even then. We were documentarians, after all, brought up in New York City in the 1960s. No better cauldron existed for those of us concerned about social causes, the state of the world, the war on the other side of the globe. We were as Saint-Exupéry had described us in *Night Flight*—a camaraderie built on danger and the threat of imminent death. In New York City, one could aspire for no higher honor than that of filmmaker. Now was our time. If the Maysles couldn't get it together...

I am getting ahead of the story. Michael Wadleigh and his original partner, John Binder, had approached me in 1965, looking for work. I was then a producer at National Educational Television. Michael would shoot camera, John would take sound: a two-man team, they pitched. If we didn't like the dailies, they said, we wouldn't have to pay them! So, being frugal, I gave them their very first job: we were going to film the first reunion of the Communist party USA in many years. And because we feared that we might not be granted easy access to the get-together, Michael had ingeniously designed a forerunner to the Steadicam: a rig with an aluminum backplate, one welded pipe extending the length of his back, pin-hinged to another pipe which held the Éclair camera by its handle comfortably over his right shoulder, leaving his hands entirely free when the seat belt was fastened snugly about his waist. With a little stroke of black magic marker over the red signal light he could walk about with the lens wide open, and film everything he faced, without appearing to do so. I was astonished at his aplomb and his ingenuity. Of course, the Communist folks stopped us, but not until we had succeeded in a walk-about which captured the B-Roll we needed for this upcoming NET documentary.

But as luck—or perhaps politics—would have it, NET then canceled the documetary. We had shot for two days, fused our personalities, were rejected by a higher Kafkaesque authority, but the three of us were united for ever. All we needed was another project.

The Vanishing American Newspaper, written by producer John O'Toole, filled the void just a few weeks later and brought us together again. A Chicago commuter train that did not stop where it was supposed to almost killed all three of us on the first shoot day, but we survived to spend eight weeks on the road together. Bound by Michael's plug-into-the-cigarette-lighter ice-cream-maker, all four of us were diabolically linked.

I would leave film production sporadically at NET to produce live, interconnected events:

Control room live television became my forte, and in 1967, I even applied it to film. My subject was the tobacco industry. "A day in the life of…" It was to be "live on film" later to be edited for all the inherent contrast we could muster. A precursor to *48 Hours*! I teamed Michael and David Myers, my mentor cameraman from Mill Valley, together in San Diego. Ironically, they had never met before. The resulting film, *The Smoking Spiral,* which intercut all the poignant paradoxes of the smoking controversy, set the industry and Congress on its ear, so to speak.

On one of their European jaunts, Michael and John discovered a German electronic designer who had created a flat-bed editing table called the KEM. Playing sixteen-millimeter and/or thirty-five-millimeter film on cores through viewfinders and sound playback amplifiers, it revolutionized traditional film editing technology and concepts. One six-plate machine would enable the editor to combine two sound tracks to one picture. A larger, more formidable eight-plate permitted the editor to weave one track to three pictures, or two tracks to two pictures, or three tracks to one picture. Everything was completely interchangable.

Each of us in our own way was searching for that elusive answer to how to display, or exhibit, that reality which the world generated daily. We had pursued different technologies toward the same end: how to find the truth about what we saw, and how to allow—nay, encourage—the cameras to tell the story without the intervention of an outside figure. Immediacy was one essential component. We had taken to heart that Lerner and Lowe adage: "Don't talk at all. Show me!" Let the person in front of the camera show it. In its humor, its poignancy, its diversity. For us, I think, it was somewhat akin to pointillism, where each little bit in and of itself was not truly significant but when put together and juxtaposed with each other, a sense of reality became visible from the dots once you withdrew and created a little perspective.

The first KEM to visit the US had arrived several weeks earlier and was available to assist Thelma ("T") in her test edit of two songs, the first of which was called "R.E.S.P.E.C.T." Michael and two other cameramen had filmed in Providence with Aretha Franklin. The *Merv Griffin Show* received their single-image edited version of the shoot for which they had contracted, but Michael had double-printed the negative. He put the three strands in the hands of Thelma, who proceeded to fashion the very first multiple image rendition of a motion picture sequence since Abel Gance had succeeded so well with the silent *Napoleon* in the 1920s (even taking *The Thomas Crown Affair* and *Le Mans* into consideration). Just two weeks ago, then, if you came to our offices at Eighty-First Street and Broadway on the second floor, and went into the shiny white-walled screening room, you were treated to a singularly memorable event.

First, you had to stand. No seats. And not simply one traditional projector in a booth. Behind you on pedestals were three Grafflex projectors, all plugged into a single multiple electrical box, which also received the cord from a MagnaTech playback machine. Four synchronous machines united by a common switch. When the lights were dimmed in the room, and the four-way switch was thrown, a single, traditional image popped on to the shiny wall at the other end of the room. The other two projectors were running black leader in sync, lingering behind the center projector until they played their role in this daring exhibition. Then, on a word from the very formidable Aretha on the wall, two images appeared side by side. And, of course, on a subsequent music change, three images overwhelmed the viewer by their dynamic presence. Music bounced from stereo speakers on the two far walls, all designed by Michael's peach-fuzzed, ever-gregarious sound wizard, Larry Johnson.

The impact in that darkened room was truly overwhelming. Though the songs only lasted for a few minutes, it seemed as though you were suspended in eternity, so powerful was the experience. Sensory overload! At the end of Aretha's "We Shall Overcome" a la Wads and Thelma, you were very sorry you were only white. Already we had a "pilot" and the Maysles, in asking us to join them in making the *Woodstock* film—whatever it was going to be—had heard the rumors of the three-image film reverberating on the street, so to speak. Ultimately, when they saw this "pilot," they were blown away.

Now (back to the story), here we were together again in the car: Those who knew how to shoot events with multiple cameras, as though live on film, harnessed with others who had the ability to record and edit those resulting multiple images and sounds into one coherent overall film, were now speeding northway on the Thruway, aiming for Max Yasgur's bowl-like farm, a two-hour drive from the city, passing hitchhiking long-hairs with backpacks and guitars.

Michael had just returned from Wyoming days earlier where he had been filming a thirty-day survival course for young people in the wildly rugged Wind River Range. It would later be titled *30 Days to Survival*. Another film he had shot several months earlier high in the Himalayas was now being edited by Thelma, under the working title of *Once Before I Die*, a man's fulfillment of a life-long quest to climb to 19,000 feet. Michael had carried his camera and sound gear himself to this altitude, without oxygen. It had never been done before. Now off his ice-cream fix, no one questioned his toughness.

As we approached the farm, all of us began talking animatedly about what we might encounter, which groups might be performing, how to handle the shooting of the music and the recording of the sound on multiple tracks, how to get behind the music to film the people who would be arriving. Our Saint-Exupéry camaraderie was evolving. None of us had seen the site. We had no idea what we would encounter, for we had only had the briefest of phone conversations with the promoters who were in New York City and who had not yet visited the site themselves! And one of us in that car was even asking: Who was The Who? or Sha-Na-Na, or Jimi Hendrix? (That was me, but I could hum Verdi!) What was this reality? How to grab it?

Understand the technology and, in our case, push it beyond where it had ever been. Long before computers, we were the walking software. In cinematic sense, we were pioneers, heading where we knew not, but filled with the sense of the possible. We were not saying to oursleves this is the kind of film we are going to make; rather, we were saying that it might be possible to make it this way. We had no idea of what we were going to do once we had shot it. Postproduction was on the other side of the planet, far from our consideration.

But slow down, here is our exit off the Thruway. Several miles away, we would set our eyes on the farm with its sloping bowl leading to the stage, or so we heard.

Boy, these roads were narrow! Barely two cars could squeeze by. What would happen when more cars arrived up here? Rumor had it that maybe 50,000 people would show up for the three days. No one knew. (I wondered whether the promoters were aware that a recent concert at a racetrack in Atlanta had attracted one hundred fifty thousand people!!! Could that happen here??)

And then we were at the actual site, driving along a farm road, looking down a glen toward a mass of long-hairs scurrying about, one on a motorcycle, bounding over hills and through tall fields of grasses. Long hair. With many curls. Could he be Mike Lang? Yes, someone said. Maybe one hundred men and women were working on the construction of the stage, right at the base of this bowl. Plywood had been built around it to protect it from the audience. Chain-link fence was on its way up. Yes, it would surround the site, we were told, but we remained skeptical.

We looked at their stage, listened to the carpenters and designers. Conferring with Wads, I asked that they create a lip on the edge of the stage, with back to the audience, just at the right height so that a cameraman, standing on this extended platform, could place his bent elbow on the stage proper to use it for support. Beneath the stage, with layers of more plywood, I asked that they create a large, crude table where the assistants who would be changing magazines for the Éclair's would be able to work. Plywood would be needed in some of the towers, too, so that tripods could be hoisted up and fixed for the longer shots of stage and audience. Our sleeping quarters, such as they might be, would be under the stage or the trucks, again on four-by-eight plywood, on the dirt. We would bring sleeping bags, I said, lying through my teeth! Who had money for sleeping bags? Who had money?

We discussed the kinds of lights they would be using to illuminate the performers, the sound system, and how we could tie into it to make multiple track recordings. Where were the various activities going to be held? Where was the food, the toilets, the medical facilities? How many people were they expecting? How were they going to arrive? How about the performers…how were they going to get into the area, if the roads were clogged? There will be helicopters, John Morris said. (He was one of the promoters/producers.) Food and water and performers would all come in with the choppers. Like Vietnam, someone muttered!

We must have sounded as though we could do it, even though we had no idea that it truly might be possible. Instinct was taking over, not practicality. All we did was ask questions and listen to responses.

But something was happening. The more we talked, gave advice, argued, probed with the promoters who, at first would have nothing to do with us, the more we began to realize that we were capable of pulling this off.

We looked around. It would take a massive effort. It would require untold amounts of gear, of people, of vehicles, of food (for the promoters were telling us that they would have their own hands full trying to supply their own people with enough food when the 50,000 people arrived). We needed an army.

It would demand extraordinary coordination and cooperation among us as filmmakers. If the Maysles were thinking in terms of two "divisions," we reasoned, maybe we should, too. One group would be in charge of the concert filming, another of the nonconcert, or documentary portions. Wads and Larry would deal with the picture and sound of the concert; Thelma would act as asistant director. John and I would deal with the documentary portions, and I would be responsible for getting the people and the gear. Bob would negotiate and try to insulate us.

In the grass overlooking the stage, where none of the promoters could overhear us, we began to plot, among the echoes of the hammering and the boom of the loudspeakers ordering the winches to build the towers. One critical question remained: were the promoters going to get the site prepared well enough in advance so there would be something to film? They only had five days before the first music was to begin and there was lots to do. Or would the whole project be a bust?

But, we looked at each other, that meant that we, too, only had five days! I remember surveying the tiny roads one more time before I said that if we were going to do it at all, we would have to bring everyone up by Thursday afternoon at the very latest. We could not count on working at night for there wouldn't be any light except very close to the stage.

We first talked concert. It would take six cameras, six cameramen, six loaders to change magazines, six assistants to take the loaded or unloaded magazines to the cameramen, and six notetakers, each keeping meticulous track of what their person was shooting, with which roll, at what time, with which type of raw stock. The loaders would work under the stage, standing on plywood, their hands never leaving their black changing bags. They would have to get a head start on the cameramen so that they could then keep up. An estimated total of twenty-four people to shoot the music, if they were only filming over eight-to-ten-hour days. But what would happen when the music began at noon and ran until the next dawn?

If there were six cameramen, we would need six 110-volt sync motors and a couple of spares, so count eight at least. Where would we find them? Where would we find eight Éclairs? Most cameramen would have one, but some might not. Everyone had to shoot with the same kind of equipment, at minimum.

How could we keep track of sync? If each cameraman started at different times, how would we ever know how to track it? I suggested that we find a digital clock, luminous, which we would mount on stage at the back. Each time a cameraman started to shoot, he would catch the clock first, then keep rolling. This would at least give us a starting point. Could we slate each cameraman? It would be the job of the assistants or the notetakers. They would have to prepare in advance a series of labels that would be color-coded to each DP. Each notetaker needed a color-coded clipboard with preprinted grids to fill in information. This would help us enormously. Where would we get the people? Who would we need? Only the best, we reasoned. Since I had given much NET (National Educational Television) work to many of the best DPs in New York and Los Angeles, we ran a list that included Richard Pearce, David Myers, Chuck Levey, Ted Churchill, Ed Lynch, Fred Underhill, Don Lenzer, among others. Where would we find enough assistants, and then the other people?

How could we get them here between Monday and Thursday afternoon? Could we pay them? What? How many people would we need on the documentary side? John Binder and I calculated three teams of camera-sound each, hopefully on motorcylces so they could get about in the crowds. After all, if there were going to be 50,000 people milling around, it was going to be very crowded on this little farm. Each of the teams would have to carry walkie-talkies, all on the same channels so that we, at home base central nearby the stage, could communicate with all of them at one time, as though we were live, again. We would establish some sort of communication with the promoters, keeping up with their activities so that we could route one documentary team to cover a "breaking story." How were we going to charge batteries? Where would our power come from? Would the promoters permit us to tap their lines even while they would not get us food?

How could we make the film if we didn't have footage of the building of the stage? Who were those two Brits (Mike and Michael!) who had been shooting here for the last three weeks? Could we buy some of their footage and include it our own film? We would have to leave someone here this Saturday to fulfill that adage that "possession is nine-tenths of the law." John would remain behind with Ed Lynch. John was garrulous, assimilated information and personality quickly, and was not threatening. He could get on with the people while the rest of us tried to sort out how to go about pulling all of this off.

By the time we had finished calculating, it looked as though we needed about fifteen people with cameras, an equal number of bonafide assistant camerapeople, about ten people on sound, six of them to work with the promoters on the concert sound, and another four to work on the documentary side. We would need about twenty other assistants who would help to keep track of what was going on. Some people would have to sleep while others worked. Maybe we really needed five more assistant camerapeople and another ten assistants? Thelma, Michael, and Larry would deal with the music, aided by Eric Blackstead, who knew many of the musicians and managers. And perhaps more importantly, he knew the music: he knew how the performers played their sets, which piece came up first, which performer had the lead and when it was transfered to another player, how long each piece would run, all of this very valuable information for those of us trying to plot out how to cover the music. (Eric would later produce both records.)

A new, young feature director we knew in New York, Martin Scorsese, who had just completed *Who's That Knocking at My Door?*, with Harvey Keitel, would assistant direct with Thelma on the concert stage. They would be connected by headsets to the camera people, finding out what each person was shooting, so they could coordinate shots as live television directors would do in a control room environment. Wads would always take the number one position, down front and in the center at six o'clock, picking up the lead performer. Dick Pearce (if we could find him and if he was available!) would be upstage at about eleven o'clock. Don Lenzer at one o'clock. The two of them could also get good audience shots through the performers. Chuck Levey would be at four o'clock. Fred Underhill at eight o'clock. Stan Warnow would be in one of the towers and Hart Perry would be in another, providing us with wide shots of the stage and audience.

David Myers and Al Wertheimer would be the lead documentary people.

After Bob Maurice and Sonya finished their session with the promoters on site, we left that evening to return to New York City where we would confer again. On the way back, we talked more about what we would have to do. Suddenly we determined we had not counted on one element—the raw stock. How much would we need? How much did we have on hand? What would it cost? Who had that much? Would Kodak? We calculated again: there were going to be three days of peace and music, as advertised! How many cameramen would be shooting the concert? Six! How many songs would we shoot? How long were the songs? How many of the acts would appear in daylight? How many at night? What kind of night stock would we need? Kodak was selling two kinds. How much should we push the ASA of the stock? We couldn't determine any of that without knowing how much light the promoters were going to give us onstage. And particularly, how much white light? For if all they had on hand were a lot of blue and red gels, we would never see a performer's face clearly, and the whole night shooting would be eliminated. If the raw stock could not register the talent, and the film could not be made except with daylight acts, then the promoters would not ever recoup any of the money the film might eventually make. So, we reasoned, there was a direct tie-in: light with profit. We would be able to argue that point tomorrow, we thought.

But if there were going to be twenty-six groups, and we wanted to film one song from each of them, it would take twenty-six times one eleven-minute roll times the number of cameramen shooting at that time. And if we wanted to shoot more of, say, "Pinball Wizard," the section from The Who's already-famous "Tommy" opera, and that piece ran for twenty-five minutes, we just increased logrithmically the requirement for raw stock by two and a half times!

Then what about the documentary portions? Many of us thought the motivations of the people, the lifestyle, the individual stories, the lay of the land at the festival, and any other activities, might be even more valuable than some of the music. What would happen if someone was killed? Or if someone gave birth? It was possible, after all, for there were going to be 50,000 people, we heard! According to the radio advertisements, this festival was to be a statement to the world about the Vietnam War and about drugs as well. Hundreds of acres, a craft show, places for children to play, swimming, an art fair. It was to be more than music. As true documentarians, we had to listen to what they were saying and try to incorporate it into the overall film. Our role was not to comment on the action, except perhaps through how we eventually structured the film to tell the story. Our job was to get the best coverage we could under the conditions, with the people we could amass in this short space of time. And money!

Already, in our minds at least, we were calculating the postproduction and beginning to worry about it. We had talked of color-coding, of organizing so that the syncing up would be made easier. How would we ever get these multiple images onto one screen? Michael, Thelma, Larry, and I were always searching for a new paradigm. Live on film, to the extent possible. Simultaneity. How could we convey to an audience the explosive variety of activities happening live and simultaneously without invoking multiple images as appropriate? We couldn't release the film with three projectors, or six, or could we? Those answers would have to wait.

Where were we going to get the money for something like this? How would we get the permission from the groups to be able to film them? Would we need releases from the people who would be gathered there, or would the fact that we were filming constitute a release in fact? Was there a precedent?

How would we get food in? From where? The raw stock, how much? How much money did we have in the bank? How to rent the gear? If we told the rental houses what we were doing, they would never let us have it. If they asked for money up front, how could we triage the money we had? What was more important, the gear, the people, or the raw stock?

At 7:00 a.m., on the second floor of our offices at Eighty-First Street and Broadway, on the following Sunday morning now five days away from the moment we would have to start filming the concert, we met and made plans.

Wads had $10,000 in the bank. Immediately, Bob and I would try to get money in from Michael's last film in Wyoming. That might add another $10,000. Most would have to go for raw stock, for without it, the whole effort would be lost. We might have to save some for film supplies, like audio tape, gaffer tape, etc.

We drew up a final list of people, with alternates. They were scattered all over the country, but I had my trusty phone book connecting me to them. We would—I would—tell every cameraman that we would guarantee them a day's pay at $125, the then-going-rate. If the project went beyond that their time would be on "spec"—they might get paid and they might not. Because I had done business with most of the people on other projects, and given them days and weeks filled with work, this could be construed as "give back" time for them. My word had to be trusted. Those of us in the room would work on "spec" with the prospect of rewards later if we were successful in finding more money.

I would also have to find the gear. Because I had been renting so much gear in the last five years from camera houses in New York City—Ferco, Camera Mart, Laumic, General Camera—my name was relatively trusted there, too. Perhaps I could tell everyone that I was only renting for a one-day shoot, which was going to occur on Friday? I would have the gear back to them by Monday, I could assure them. But I would also have to pick up the gear early, so that I could get it to White Lake early enough to be useful. But I couldn't tell them about the actual site for they would be fearful that their insurance might not cover loss or damage. They could hear the radio adverts just like everyone else! This was a strange form of trust in which I was basically telling a little white lie, for White Lake! It bothered me, but I saw no way out of the dilemma. We would charge the gear—not pay cash, take the insurance coverage just in case something might happen to it, and then pray.

But how would David Myers get from San Francisco to New York? David would have to charge the plane fare on his own card. Preposterous! No one would ever agree to such terms, not even David.

By this time, we had determined that we probably needed an enormous amount of raw stock…enough to be able to shoot for 175 hours between now and next Sunday night when the festival would end, if they held to their schedule. One hundred seventy-five hours translates into 375,000 feet of sixteen-millimeter film or more than 900 individual rolls of film, some of which had to be accessible for daytime use, the remainder for night time. With thirty rolls to the case, we would need thirty cases, which also occupied a huge space, easily the inside area of a large-panel truck. How to get it to the stage? In only four days? Where to store it safely from other people and the elements? If it got too hot, the emulsion would melt as I had experienced in Venezuela several years earlier!

When Wads returned to the site on Monday, he would take the twenty-five rolls remaining in the icebox from pevious shoots. I would purchase some more from whatever sources I could uncover, including Kodak up on York Avenue. We decided we would not purchase the full amount until we saw how we were shooting on the site, but I would ask Kodak first thing Monday to set aside several batches of what we needed. Wednesday would probably be the final judgment day for purchasing. I would send the raw stock up with whomever was going on Tuesday, and so forth. Wads and I would confer by phone when he arrived on the site. We had a plan. We would spend everything Wads had in the bank. Bob Maurice, who was also helping Wads maximize some of his films through distribution, would continue the negotiations with the promoters with Eric Blackstead's assistance. Bob would also try to find big money from studio financiers. I would remain in the office day and night until everyone was on the site on Thursday. Sonya Polonsky, who had been working as a production manager for Paradigm Films and already knew many of the people we would be working with, would organize. Thelma, Larry, and Marty Scorsese would get to the site as quickly as I could find cars, other people, and gear.

We realized that no one had ever done this kind of film before. Fewer than twenty-four hours earlier, reality had been a figment of our imagination. Until we had scouted, we knew nothing and feared everything. But contact with the site, the people, and assessing the conditions gave each of us a deeper sense of confidence which we then passed on to each other by our very energy. One step at a time. It was truly an extraordinary feeling we were building among us. We felt we could conquer anything. If only Bob could make a decent deal with the promoters and their producers on-site, we might have a slightly easier time when we finally got settled.

I looked around the room. None of us were over thirty years old. Whoops, that's not exactly right. I was. I was thirty-one, married with three young boys, the oldest of whom wanted to come with me to the site if I went! But I was the only one in a "traditonal" relationship. And oh, yes, Michael was only a year younger than I was. But everyone else? Larry still had peach fuzz on his upper lip, didn't he? Was he twenty?

Maybe Bob was my age, too. I didn't know him very well. He was very philosophical, contemplative, and always muttering under his long hair and bushy beard while he climbed the rafters like an Indian on a construction site. "Gotta clear out my head," he would say, as he paced back and forth ten feet above the floor. He had a devilish sense of humor and a wonderful twinkle in his eye as he contemplated the ramifications of each of his actions. "I could drop a keg of nails on them from here!" he would conjecture, much to all of our amusement—and distraction!

We knew we did not want to produce "news coverage." Let the news teams do that! We wanted to produce something which would last, which would be different, and which would truly represent the seminal role that the combination of music and lyrics played in the life of the generation of the 1960s. Chaos. Assassinations. Malcolm X. JFK. MLK. RFK. Their names and initials reeled off as a litany of torment amid turbulent civil rights struggles.

Beatings. Dogs. Water hoses. Fires on crosses. Open marriage concepts. The increasingly hostile generation gap. Drugs, beards, and long-hairs. Killing and maiming in jungles halfway around the globe, matched only by burnings and shootings in our own south. Political upheavals at home. Wars on poverty. Gender wars as women sought their legitmate civil rights. Chicago riots and brutality. Ralph Nader taking on the monolithic multinational corporations in David-Goliath fashion. And men on the moon? Huge chasms yawing between government and the people, gaps of faith and trust.

And yet we were politically active then. Anything was possible. Hadn't Neil Armstrong taken "one small step for mankind" less than a month ago? One person could make a difference. We were doing for our country just as we had been mandated by JFK to do on that cold, windy January morning on the Capitol steps at the beginning of our decade. What was its reality? Could this festival become our symbol?

Now we actually might be on the threshhold of accomplishing something significant on our own, without being told what to do. Could we truly defy our traditional authority figures and become independent? How, we constantly asked ourselves, could we produce a film for a general audience—not simply for a music-infected group of long-haired hippie freaks? That would be preaching to the choir! Was it because all of us had already been brought up on "educational television" that we felt the need to appeal just as our own television programs had been doing? Was it because each of us, in our own personal way, had literally or symbolically "been shot at by sheriffs" in Mississippi while investigating what we perceived to be injustices with the food stamp programs? Was it because we had attempted in our previous work to try to uncover the truth, or the injustice, as we saw it, and to reveal that "people story" to millions in their living rooms? Was it because we were constantly trying to be objective in our filmmaking?

Wads packed his camera. Larry and Thelma would join him and together, they would go back up to White Lake to join John Binder and Ed Lynch, who were already there. Once Wads arrived on the site, we would communicate by phone.

Bob got on the phone with the promoters and the potential financiers, probing, cajoling, fighting, selling, holding back. His extraordinary effort at corraling this herd of cats was to prove we were not foolish.

Sonya and I set up one office with two desks and three phones. For the next four days, I ate and slept in that office, getting only a very few hours of sleep as she and I assembled the people and the gear, handling the logistics of moving this little band into the Catskills, working the time zones.

David Myers did pay for his own ticket and was in White Lake by Tuesday night, from San Francisco.

Dick Pearce had contracted to film with another producer that week, but when I located him in Hartford, I promised to find his producer another cameraman so that he, Dick, would be free to join us. I gave away one of the cameramen, Joe Consentino, from the Maysles team, who called me asking to work on our project. I told him I couldn't take him to White Lake but that I could get him this job in Hartford! He accepted, and Dick drove across Connecticut into the Catskills. He arrived aboard his motorcycle on Wednesday. He would join Wads on stage and provide extraordinary footage out into the crowd.

I tried Don Lenzer at the Chelsea Hotel where he always lived. They said he was shooting on the west coast. Did they have the number? Yes, and they gave it to me. I reached Don in Los Angeles, convinced him to get on a plane that would arrive at JFK about the same time as David Myers would land from San Francisco. I sent Danny Turbeville, a cohort of Eric's, out to the airport to pick up both of them and drive them to White Lake with their gear. They never saw the city.

Don had recommended that I hire a cameraman friend of his from Seattle, Dick Chew. When I reached Dick, he told me he was getting married that Saturday. I asked him if he could postpone the wedding, come to New York, and help us film this concert. Within three hours, he was paying his own way on an airplane for only 125 dollars guaranteed for the first day—his ex-wedding day! Could we please get him a camera? Goodbye wedding; hello, Woodstock!

Al Wertheimer, a Bob Drew-trained verité cameraman I had heard about in the city, would also drive from New York with his converted Auricon camera. Because he was not slated to shoot any of the concert, I approved his unique gear.

Jack Willis kindly declined my offer to be a soundman and always regretted it.

Other people who had been contacted by the Maysles called, eager to work. Even in the middle of the night, they would want to come by to show me their reels. One cameraman showed me a piece he had filmed with Joan Baez. It shuddered and shook; it was not at all what Wads and I expected from handheld cameramen. I rejected him as I did others for fear of muddying the waters.

Ferco, Laumic, and Camera Mart believed my story about the one-day gear rental that had to be picked up on Tuesday, or Wednesday, or Thursday, as the case might be. And Oh, Yes, it would be returned on the following Monday afternoon. No, I could not tell them where their gear was going. I had to scrounge to find 110-volt motors and four magazines for every Éclair. Why did I need a 25–250-millimeter lens? Why did I need three 5.9-millimeter lenses? What was this project I was filming? I began running into myself at some of these houses: when Camera Mart didn't have something I needed, I would quickly call a second place and order the piece. Bob Roizman at Camera Mart would then call me back, asking why I was renting from the very same place he was calling to fill my order! Although I never checked, I am sure I had all the available cameras, lenses, magazines, and motors in New York City that weekend.

Our messenger service had allocated some dozen motorcycle messengers to us on a full-time basis so that I could pick up gear as quickly as we were ordering it. Later, as the *New York Times* began reporting huge traffic jams on the way to the festival, I became fearful that my cover might be blown, but it was only on Tuesday after the festival, when all the gear was returned, that I divulged what had actually happened!

Joe Louw, who had taken those historic *LIFE* Magazine pictures of three men on a motel balcony pointing to an adjacent building while they huddled over the slain MLK in Memphis, drove up to White Lake to do sound and take stills.

Cousin to Buckminster Fuller, Marty Andrews, an engineering wizard who had been working with Wads and John, made it on one of the early treks, for he had to design and build all the electronics.

My wife, Anne, was able to get her mother to stay with our kids, so she filled our VW bus with food, blankets, and other people—and not our oldest son, Jonathan, much to his dismay—and became one of the chief notetakers on the lip of the stage. She was joined by Jeanne Field, helping Larry, by Fern McBride from NET, by Cathy Hiller assisting her soon-to-be-husband Stan Warnow, and by Renee Wadleigh, helping Michael.

Marty Scorsese was in one of the early trucks, transporting gear and headsets. He traveled north with Ted Churchill, one of our marvelous cameramen.

Many others joined the team, some of whom I did not know until they walked through the door to the office with a recommendation from someone else. (Others I met for the first time when they presented their bills back in New York!) They were hired on the spot. For nothing. If I didn't know them, Sonya no doubt did. I'm not sure I ever put either of the two phones down in those four days.

Because so many people were working on spec, I wanted to be sure they had decent accomodations while they were in White Lake. In one phone call, I reserved the Minnie's Sands Motel (Or was it the Silver Spur?) ten miles away, figuring that our guys could get there late at night. They quoted me $6,000 for all the rooms during the several days I estimated. And while some of the arriving crew left their clothes at the hotel, no one ever got back to the hotel during the festival. Exhausted and filthy, those who had been foolish enough to avail themselves of this facility had to return on Monday or Tuesday to pick up what they had left behind. They were the very last to arrive back in New York!

At dawn on Tuesday morning, I prepared my first budget to share with Bob. Both of us wanted to know how much we were extended just in case none of the negotiations proved fruitful, or if they did, what we would have to recoup from first monies in. I worked over two samples: one based on only paying every cameraman the $125 for the first day, and a second considering full payment over the length of time they were in New York and/or at the site. In both cases, I did not cost out the expense of processing and printing all the film; I counted simply the purchase of the unexposed raw stock.

As part of my estimate, I included a $5,000 premium for insurance; as it turned out after several calls to brokers in town, no one would insure the project. It was far too risky. When I rented the gear from camera houses, I agreed to pay additionally for the insurance coverage, anticipating a rejection from brokers. But if we lost any of the gear, or damaged it, we could still be held liable, in spite of the extra coverage.

When I showed Bob the higher figure of $125,000 for the four full days we rightfully were obligated for, he blanched. We had put together only $23,000 from fees due Wads; all the rest was on the come, so to speak. At four in the morning, we simply glared silently at each other. We—he—had to find the money.

As Bob was barking around New York for the financing, I called my father. His boss, Jules Winarick, owned the Concord Hotel at Kiamesha Lake not far from White Lake in the Catskills. On several occasions, Jules had kindly extended his hospitality to our family so that we could visit for a weekend of fun, games, food, and frolic with my father. To repay his courtesy, I thought he could put up the $125,000, gain some publicity, and have something to talk about for the rest of his life. With permission from Bob, I asked my Dad to talk with Jules about the opportunity. Alas, Jules declined. Later, during one of our New York screenings, he and my Dad came by to acknowledge how dumb he had been to the offer.

More than a year later, while I was talking with Paramount about another project (John Knowles's *A Separate Peace*), Sam Jaffee, president of the studio, came into Warren Lieberfarb's office to tell me that he, too, had been offered rights to the movie for an inital investment of $55,000. Like possibly many other studio heads at the time, he regretted that he had not accepted. Jules Winarick had company.

What remains fascinating to me is the fact that no one knew that Ahmet Ertegun had already agreed to purchase the rights to the movie from Paul Marshall, attorney representing the festival producers, for $25,000. Equally astounding is that Ted Ashley, Chairman of Warner Bros., knowing that Atlantic, a subsidiary of Warners, controlled the movie and record situation from the very beginning, would allow it to slip away, out of his grasp!

Anticipating the likelihood that we might all be sleeping out, Bob Maurice had purchased sixty sleeping bags and tied them to the roof of the panel truck he had rented. At the first sign of rain in New York City that night, he had driven the truck up onto the sidewalk underneath his friend's New Yorker Theater marquee. After the rain stopped, he returned to Eighty-Eighth Street and Broadway to start the drive north to White Lake in the middle of the night. Of course, the only sleeping bags remaining were those he had secured inside the van! He drove the van down to the office, picked up the Xerox machine and some extra extension cord, and headed north. The copy machine would enable us to distribute song sheets and schedules to individual cameramen and their assistants.

And the *New York Times* kept writing, while radio announcers kept talking: "The New York State Thruway is closed!" Television stations, hiring helicopters, kept sending images of very clogged exits from New York City as seemingly the whole of New York State converged on Max Yasgur's farm. Eventually, we were to learn that the 50,000 estimators had failed to add a zero! It was staggering!

The raw stock? I warned Kodak on Monday morning, first call. I told them we would be ordering about 150,000 to 200,000 feet of film on Tuesday and a like amount on Wednesday. Wads and I had not yet determined how to divide the types of emulsions we would require: one for daylight, another for night. On Tuesday, Kodak said they had thirty cases of the assorted emulsion numbers (7242 and 7245) we required. I told them a truck would pick it up on Wednesday morning. Yes, we knew we would have to pay cash. We knew of the 2% discount for paying cash. It would be just under 18,000 dollars. Fine, Mr. Bell, just send your truck over and everything will be ready.

On Wednesday afternoon, our truck arrived at the Kodak York Avenue pickup station. I got a phone call from my messenger. Kodak had set aside three cases, not thirty! I screamed! They, too, had failed to add a zero! What to do now? No one had ever purchased thirty cases at one time before, they said! Nine hundred magazines??? They didn't have thirty cases in New York!!!

I was in a cold sweat. Everyone was in the process of finding their way to White Lake. Already some twenty people were on site with twenty more to head up on Wednesday. Twenty would follow on Thursday morning, bringing our total to more than sixty, all of whom were willing to do this gig on "spec," mind you! And now, no raw stock to put into the cameras!!!

Even before the music began, we were about to be blown out of the water!

Break it down into pieces, I said to myself. Don't panic. Take small steps. How much do you have in New York? I asked Kodak. They said they could find another ten cases by tomorrow. Maybe a hundred thousand feet. In Rochester, I asked? In Washington? In Chicago? In Los Angeles? They would call back. Meanwhile, I sent the truck with the three cases up to White Lake along with a couple more sleeping bags and snacks and drinks.

Between that Wednesday morning and Friday afternoon, I did nothing but scour all over the East Coast for raw stock. I bought from rental houses. Kodak found cases in Rochester and Chicago. I found some in Los Angeles, which had to be shipped into Kennedy airport. From there, it had to be transhipped to LaGuardia, where my messenger service, Coleman Younger, also working on spec, would take it off the airplane and transport it to the Marine Air Terminal where it would board a small aircraft bound for Monticello, New York.

Several cases actually took a wrong turn and ended up in Liberty, New York. I couldn't find them for hours! They had to be shipped back to the Marine Terminal before it could be bicycled to Monticello. Another batch was shipped to Monticello, the proper destination, but no one unloaded it. Hours later, it arrived in Rochester, the home of Eastman Kodak, via Albany! Every case would have to land in Monticello, from where it would then have to be airlifted, case by case, until Saturday afternoon when most of the last batch arrived with Bob Maurice, on those very same helicopters which were depositing the talent at the Woodstock stage. Remember the choppers in the background, on the soundtracks? It may sound like Vietnam, but that's raw stock they're transporting! Not just food and talent.

At one point, before the imports arrived, Michael and the crew were down to their last case, and it was only Friday! Ding, he said to me, what are we going to do? The music was going to begin that afternoon! Wads, I said, we had proceeded on faith—blind faith—to this point. All the people who were coming to help us were flying on trust. We had to extend ourselves just a little bit more, and pray.

By Friday afternoon, the first helicopter shipment landed on the big hill behind the stage. The festival producers brought it down to the film team huddled on plywood under one of the trailers to the side of the stage. We had achieved a modicum of cooperation!

I was able to leave New York City Friday afternoon, laden down with food stuffs I had purchased on upper Broadway. My tiny VW beetle made it to White Lake by about nine at night. Walking another hour after my battery died, I arrived on stage just as Joan Baez was singing "Swing Low, Sweet Chariot," haloed in a mild drizzle. It was appropriate. I found Anne and we all hugged. Looking out toward the audience, I could see the outline of the huge towers set against the dark blue sky. From their tops beamed down gelled spot lights. A garland of lights was draped loosely between the two towers near the top, providing scant illumination over the crowd. A haze of what I could only identify as possible marijuana smoke gathered where we were, in the bowl of the natural amphitheater. Never having been around that kind of smoke before, I could only surmise, but I was told that I had guessed right!

Beneath Joan Baez's a capella rendition of "Swing Low" I could hear a low, constant rumble of noise indicating that, just on the other side of the tall fence separating the audience from the stage, tens of thousands of people were milling around. The initial experience was indescribable.

Whenever the electrical wires connecting the cameramen to 110-volt AC power grazed the puddles on stage, one or another of the guys would let out a yelp because of the little shock that pulsated through their headsets. Later, when we were syncing the dailies, these little synchronous movements would aid the assistant editors in establishing a common point!

Near the stage, we had established headquarters in the back of a trailer. There was our trusty Xerox copier and telephone. Beneath the trailer lay the four-by-eight plywood slabs which would serve as our beds. As I went down to inspect our home away from home, the phone rang. At the end of Baez's set in the middle of these half million people, here was the guy we had hired to show the Aretha Franklin film to the performers, should they want to see what we were intending to do with the film! He wanted to know: "Where was everyone?"

(As part of our plot to win over the performers, we had trucked our three projectors and our demo, pilot film of Aretha singing "R.E.S.P.E.C.T!" and

"We Shall Overcome!" to the local Holiday Inn in Liberty, New York. We were paying this one guy fifty dollars per day to stand by, ready to "sell" a group on our concept. Now, at midnight, he was calling to demand double time for his efforts! I asked him how many people had seen the films far. None, he responded. If we let him come to the site, we wouldn't have to pay him double time, he offered. He wanted to be where the action was! As it turned out, over the three days of peace and music, Aretha never showed her face on film even though her presence was felt everywhere on stage and in the mind's eyes of our cameramen!)

Finally, Friday night came to a close on Saturday morning. Gathering around me, crew members asked what they were to do now. I suggested that they go back to the hotel. After all, I was still relatively clean and rested after my six-hour drive to the site. We could have scrambled eggs and bacon the next morning, I dreamed. As I was starting to try to arrange carpools, I looked around. Any movement at all seemed hopeless. I asked how many could sleep on the ground around the trailer. Some hands went up and they began to disperse. A few people took the handful of sleeping bags and laid them out within the entrance to the trailer to deter potential thieves who would have to walk over them to get to our stashed gear. Anne and I felt we could be comfortable on our mattress inside our blue and white VW van.

Two crew members had motorcycles. They were confident they could return to the motel and be back at the site by 9:00 a.m. At two in the morning, they departed, carrying their camera, sound gear, and raw stock, so they could begin filming in the morning on the way in. At seven o'clock in the morning, I picked up the phone in the trailer. It was the two guys. They had just arrived—at the hotel! It had taken them five hours to go four miles! I postponed their arrival back at the site. Two hours later, I called to wake them up. At 10:00 a.m. they started back; at 1:00 p.m. one of them arrived. They had run out of gas, he claimed. From one farmer, they cajoled some gas, but could not use it until they found some oil to mix with it from another farmer. Then, they got stuck in the mud. The second guy walked in an hour and a half later. The music had began at noon....

Saturday, I sent two people back to my own VW with the keys. Their instructions were to try to get it started and bring it back, but if they couldn't, they were to fetch all the food for the crew. Three hours later, they returned with the VW and food, a great relief for our crew who had virtually nothing to eat. From New York City, I had rejected an idea that I bring along a hundred hot dogs; those wieners would have been winners right now!

Over the next two days, I monitored the progress of each case of the raw stock from its various starting points across the country. By Sunday, it had all arrived. And so had the rain, the mud, the B12 shots, and finally, some juicy steaks from the festival producers. Bob must have made a deal!

On Saturday night, Wads and I wanted to get a helicopter shot with the stage, the supertroopers beaming down, the car headlights, and the glowing campfires on the periphery of the audience pit. Late that afternoon, the last arriving helicopter (with more of our raw stock on board, thankfully!) said they could be at our beck and call. The eager-to-please pilot said he could take us up for his standard rate of $200 per hour—money that we didn't have, of course! No matter. Wait, I said. Down the hill, I found David Myers back at the stage. He located his camera and gave it to his assistant, who was instructed to change lenses, load the magazines, and meet us at the helicopter field in half an hour. We checked our watches, cross-checked our destination with him, and climbed the hill. After half an hour had passed, we couldn't find the guy. David and I criss-crossed the field over the next two hours, one of us constantly returning to the pilot to hold him in place.

Look at the movie. If we had been able to corral the assistant, the camera, and the pilot at one place, the shot would have been in the film. But we couldn't and like so many other efforts those days, this one got away.

JEANNE FIELD

"ARE YOU WOODSTOCK EXPERIENCED?"

(JEANNE JOINED PARADIGM DISTRIBUTION before coming to the Woodstock site as an assistant.)

In early summer 1969, a rock concert was announced. I was in the East Side Book Store across from my apartment at 16 St. Marks Place and there was a poster with a bird on a guitar and it was called the Woodstock Festival. Woodstock first came into my consciousness as an art community north of New York City and the home of Bob Dylan where he recuperated from an almost-death experience in a motorcycle crash. As he improved he started playing music with a group called The Band and introduced them to his record label, Columbia, who brought out Music From Big Pink. The Band was going to be at the festival and maybe Dylan would be too. There were a lot of bands listed on the poster I'd barely heard of but some names stuck out bigtime: Janis Joplin and the Holding Company, Jefferson Airplane, The Who, Jimi Hendrix, Ravi Shankar, Joan Baez. But who'd heard of Melanie or Jeff something or other? Arlo Guthrie was coming and he was Woodstock incarnate.

Michael Wadleigh owned a VW bus, perfect for this kind of weekend. I began to lobby my new boyfriend, Larry Johnson, to go talk to Wadleigh about going to the festival in August. Camp out, get high, hear music, all near Woodstock. Larry said Wads was into it, so I bought four tickets for Mike, Renee (his wife), Larry, and me. Great!

I was a recent hire at Paradigm Films. I'd met Bob Maurice in 1968 at a screening of an independent film and kept running into him at other screenings. Bob had been charged with starting a distribution arm of Paradigm Films and was a regular on the independent film screening circuit. Bob was a pretty distinctive looking man even by New York City late 1960s standards. Usually dressed in skinny jeans and T-shirt, his most distinctive feature was his enormous head with his large glasses, brooding brows, and helmet-like long hair.

Raised poor, he put himself through college working heavy construction in New York City and his physique and carriage still spoke of those days. He could have a hilarious way of speaking, making up voices and laughing at his own jokes, then he would become absolutely serious. Given his druthers he would have stayed home and read medieval history but here he was trying to carve out a niche in a peculiar and difficult business, art house cinema distribution. He loved to discourse for hours on movies, history, art, drinking, and carousing.

Bob knew that I had worked at Janus Films, the premiere company distributing the world's best auteur films, and was now doing freelance projects. He asked if I wanted a steady job and at first, I said no. Michael Mann, the film director, who at the time was studying at the London School of Film, was a college friend of mine and he and French film student Elio Zarmati had succeeded in getting a sixteen-millimeter film crew into the Sorbonne. This was in the fall following the 1968 student uprising in Paris and I was able to sell the resulting film to NBC.

Sometime at the end of the year, I did begin to interview with film companies like Mike Shea's and the Maysles brothers. Porter Bibb was working for Al and David and I admired their films like *Salesman* and Porter offered me a job but was not impressed when I said I could start the end of January after spending a few weeks skiing in Aspen. He told me to forget it. So, in February, I called up Bob and said if he was still serious, I'd start at Paradigm.

I met with John Binder (who tells me all these years later that he was impressed by my smile, my short skirt, and my pretty legs. Ah, well) and Michael Wadleigh, who had no objection, and they were in fact delighted when I showed them the 5,000-name mailing list I had "liberated" at Janus. So I joined Bob and his girlfriend, Joyce Fresh, in the distribution wing of the company.

Paradigm made a lot of documentary films but also supported the filmmakers who were beginning to graduate from NYU, and the list of films we distributed started here. Wads, John, and their friend/editor Thelma Schoonmaker went through the NYU Masters film program and they also taught film there.

The first feature Haig Manoogian supported, *Who's That Knocking*, was directed by Marty Scorsese and shot by Wadleigh, sound by John. We also distributed Marty's short films *Murray, Is That You?* and *The Big Shave*. Jim McBride was also doing films with these guys, *David Holzman's Diary*, which broke the line between fictional and documentary filmmaking, and *My Girlfriend's Wedding*.

This last was in its final editing stages at Paradigm and became my first big project. We crashed and burned. No one was interested in this English girl, Jimmy's lover, who was loaded half the time, who had to get married to some Yippie in order to stay in the country, and also had to go to Brooklyn to get an abortion from Dr. Adams, the best answer to unwanted pregnancy this side of Puerto Rico.

We had much better luck with *No Vietnamese Ever Called Me Nigger,* a searing look at the treatment returning black vets were getting in the US. David Loeb Weiss was the director and John Binder edited and oversaw the production, which included several passionate, in-depth interviews with young black vets and the march from Harlem to the UN Plaza where Martin Luther King urged the civil rights movement and the anti-war movement to get together. This film got a lot of attention from film festivals, film societies, libraries, the coffee houses that were doing friendly outreach to young draftees, college union theaters, and of all places, IBM, which bought several prints in an attempt to bring their employees out of the 1950s.

Other filmmakers whose films we took on were Les Blank, Paul Bartell, Jeremy Paul Kagan. Brian De Palma and Chuck Hirsch had an office down a few blocks on Broadway and had just made *Greetings* with Robert De Niro and this film was a breakout success for another small company. I was also writing a film column for an underground newspaper, *Culture Hero*, run by the Canadian conceptual artist Les Levine.

Following my article on the Puerto Rican cinemas in East Harlem, I did the first-ever print interview with Marty Scorsese. It was conducted in our favorite uptown Italian restaurant, Tony's, on Seventy-Ninth Street, and covered Marty's insistence that to be a film director you began by calling yourself a director. He knew from the start that if he filmed the neighborhoods and people he had known all his life, he would be successful.

Marty had become a frequent film editor at Paradigm where his two-fisted editing style earned him the moniker The Sicilian Butcher.

Other filmmakers Bob and I were setting up relationships with were San Francisco experimentalists Bruce Baillie, Scott Bartlett, and Bruce Connor. Then the Woodstock machine began to rumble.

The Promoters of the festival put the word out that they wanted a film made. Leacock/Pennebaker, Maysles, Paradigm all made presentations. Michael and John had recently purchased an eight-plate KEM editing machine from Germany with three picture heads and had done an Aretha Franklin film for Merv Griffin. Turning part of the office into a big screening room, we all pitched in to run the resulting extravaganza, the likes of which had not been seen since Abel Gance's

Napoleon. Aretha hit the high notes in five moving images and you couldn't help but get up and dance. When David Maysles saw it he punched out Wads, knowing he'd been bested by a junior. Larry jumped in and shoved his fellow soundman down the stairs to Broadway. Paradigm had the gig.

Another media event took place that July in Central Park. As a small lunar landing module settled onto the face of the moon, CBS, ABC, and NBC broadcast those first steps on huge outdoor screens set up in Sheeps Meadow. Larry and I spent the night cruising the crowd sharing the amazement at this moment. The US was on the moon but it was still in Vietnam so overall, we had a guarded opinion of the government's accomplishment.

These days were a big turning point in my life. In truth, the one real reason I had joined Paradigm is that I had learned while I was at Janus that I didn't want to sell movies, I wanted to make them. Woodstock was my chance.

I went to Bob and told him. He said no way. He said I had to continue covering distribution for him because he was going to be a producer on Woodstock and Joyce had just been diagnosed with a brain tumor. These were difficult times for Bob but it established a real bond between him and Michael. Wads had gone through three years of med school at Columbia University and was very astute scientifically. He became a strong ballast for Bob and they found a solid friendship during these days. Bob wanted to count on me too, and he could, up to a point. My own ambition, my stubbornness, prevailed. He would not work it out with me to do both distribution and production. He said it was all or nothing. I did what I had to do.

On Thursday, the day before the music started, I rode up to Bethel (the new festival site which had been hurriedly found and built when the original Woodstock site had been nixed by the nearby neighbors) with Van Schley, a friend of Larry's and mine, and Eddie Kramer, music producer for Jimi Hendrix and the guy the promoters had hired to do the on-site recording. The roads were by this time gridlocked and impassable. Eddie slept through Van's hell-bent driving on the shoulder of the road, and drooled all over my shoulder. Thank god for Eddie Kramer though, he was the reason we were shepherded over back roads to Yasgur's farm by one of the organizing team (and one of the most important people at the festival, since he mixed and recorded every moment of music that was played).

We arrived in the middle of the night and the place looked like a construction site. The stage was barely finished. The movable sections that would have allowed one band to set up while the other played were nowhere near finished and never would be. Wads was on stage in his reservation hat and light meter working with Chip Monck to get his readings. The grip truck was parked in back of the stage and the camera magazine loading pit was being constructed underneath the stage. The indispensable Marty Andrews used his genius to create an electrical patch board out of two by fours so that all the cameramen could be connected via headsets and their equipment run on AC instead of batteries. The place was electric.

That night was the only one we made it to our motel, The Silver Spur, which we renamed the Silver Sperm. I have no idea where it was or is. My sense of geography that is usually akin to Sacagawea's was out of whack. They led, I followed.

Back again at the stage in the morning, I was assigned to Dick Pearce, a New York documentary cameraman from Kentucky. A calm professional, he in turn was assigned to Stage Left, on the stage. I pulled cable, kept him in fresh Éclair magazines, listened on the headset for any directions from Marty Scorsese or Thelma Schoonmaker, scavenged food, provided a backrest and other novice filmie jobs. And I was on the stage or on the film platform four feet just below the front of the stage for the next three days and nights.

I remember so clearly the beginning. John Morris convinced Richie Havens he had to be the first one. They led him over from the performers area, tables and chairs covered by a large white silk, across the bridge that connected to the stage that looked out on a sea of hundreds of thousands of people. It was so exciting. It was my first film.

My high was interrupted by Steve Cohen, the stage manager, who came over to me and said, "Who the fuck are you and what are you doing on my stage? You belong down there," pointing at the platform. Dick kept on shooting Richie, and I told Steve we were there to stay. You can actually see this event in the movie in the wide shot during Richie's first song (not in the videotape though because of course they've reformatted it for your TV).

I have to admit that a lot of these three days are a blur. It's hard to say what I remember from the experience and what I saw later on film. The music was loud, the hours long, the sleep almost nonexistent. The crew slept on the ground under the grip truck and with an evening of music ending early morning, most sleep was caught sometime during a day that was hot, muggy, and noisy. And we had it good. You've all seen what the people on the other side of the fence put up with. The music was great and also some of it was terrible.

The musicians were under huge stress from the interminable waiting-to-go-on, from the heat and storms, from the overwhelming crowds, and some of them definitely welcomed the offer in postproduction to overdub their vocals. High points for me were Richie H., his passionate singing, his smiling broadly with no teeth; Joe Cocker air guitaring and delivering "With a Little Help from My Friends"; The Who, with Pete crowning Abbie Hoffman over the head when he tried to grab the mike; Arlo, funny and relaxed, talking to the crowd; Santana, an unknown San Francisco band, holding AC equipment in the rainstorm, realizing we were all lightning rods; Sly and the Family Stone singing "Higher, Higher" with everyone on their feet screaming with them; CSNY warming the stage when we were all shivering in the wet coldness at 4:00 a.m. Sunday morning; Paul Butterfield Blues Band coming on at 5:00 a.m. and getting an exhausted crowd moving again; The Band, playing but insisting that they would walk if they saw a camera or its operator, which meant we all had to peak over the stage lip; Janis's performance, though not one of her best, still gutsball; Grace Slick looking like she had just stepped out of a penthouse suite; Jimi noodling for an hour before hitting on his stirring war motif "Star-Spangled Banner."

I didn't see all the food and crafts booths, the camps and lake, the people wandering. Because of the crowd and my assigned job, I stuck close to homebase. Maybe I missed the real deal, but this was work and I was making a first film, and boy, was I serious.

Back in New York, things got into high gear. We celebrated with champagne when a Warner Bros.'s check in the amount of $100,000 arrived. Thank god because Woodstock had been paid for with the line of credit established by Paradigm with its equipment suppliers and Kodak. The low-key office became a beehive with three shifts of editors syncing the hundreds of thousands of feet of film.

I was dying to join them but Bob prevailed here. I continued my distribution duties but my heart was elsewhere. Larry Johnson was the assistant director and head of sound and was working long hours. I began to work with him after I put in the time for Bob, watching and learning as he inserted "Wooden Ships" and edited the lyrical opening section of the film.

Paradigm had now become Wadleigh/Maurice Productions as John had decided to devote himself to his writing and Michael needed full-time allies. One of the perks of being part of the company was attention from the managers and bands who had been in the festival. Many of them came by the office to see their footage and give comments on which piece they preferred. CSNY, Joe Cocker, Alvin Lee came over.

Other perks were great seats at Steve Paul's Scene for the Jerry Lee Lewis show.

Then, a few weeks after the festival, The Stones came to town, playing several days at Madison Square Garden. Bob Maurice was able to get access-all-area passes for us to see them. I was hanging around the backstage door to collect mine when Al Maysles pulled up in his camera van. I went over to see if I could help him and he gave me his tripod and said to set it up in front of Mick Jagger's microphone. I did that, telling the security guard I had to stay there to make sure it wasn't moved. Al came in, set his trombone-looking camera onto it, and still I stayed. I saw the concert from this vantage point until the crowd surged and Al and I had to be pulled over the stage to avoid the crush.

This was the beginning of *Gimme Shelter*, the antithesis of *Woodstock*. Whereas the Woodstock Festival was the last blast of flower power, the free concert at Altamont would be it's last gasp. Woodstock was a coming together, a party where I felt there were a lot of people out there like me, people who wanted to find a way of living that was loose, loving, and trusting, finding a way to go back to the land. Against that was murder in the concert crowd and later, the Maysles being stomped by some of the Angels viewing their violent footage. The Outlaws ruled rock and roll. It was a sobering December event which brought the 1960s to an end.

When it was announced that Warner Bros. was moving a crew to LA for the rest of postproduction, once again I went to Bob. He would not hear of my going. So I quit my distribution gig and went with Larry as his girlfriend, bringing our cat, Woodstock, along. This move pushed me into a realm of tension that began to seep into the production in several areas.

It's not news that when something big is happening, people's egos get bruised and they begin to change. Bob was under immense pressure. He had never produced before, but he was loyal to Michael and he was smart and tough. He wrote me off and I was not usually welcome in the Yucca Street office. This was okay because Larry was doing most of his work at the Record Plant logging tracks, mixing down and I was able to continue working with him.

I lived at the Orlando Ave. house with Wads, Dale, Yeu-Bun Yee, and Thelma and on occasion made sure they had dinner waiting and the house in order (this meant making sure the packing crates that served as furniture were cleaned once a week). Bob seldom visited there and less after he caromed into our driveway and ran over Woodstock the cat. Bob and I eventually called a truce when he and I agreed that we wouldn't backbite each other in favor of the health of the production.

Once the mix began at Warner Bros., the mission was almost complete. Everyone knew that this unknown company with an unknown director (a line that circulated was "Michael always has been famous, just nobody knew it but him") had pulled off something great. But the Suits at the studio were still riding the crew hard and it came down to some creative decisions that Wadleigh and team were not willing to give up. One night we were working late on the lot and Larry told me to go over to the security guard and talk to him. I can usually talk to a post so this was not a problem for me. I kept him talking for about twenty minutes and while we chatted, people who will remain nameless walked the film soundtrack out of the vault and into three car trunks. I said goodnight and we were out of there. A day later, every time we left the lot, our car was searched. But the plot worked. WB was over the barrel and Wads won his way.

With the film finished, it was on its way to screenings at the Cannes Film Festival, Tokyo, London, etc. Larry and I eschewed all of these. We were working. Crosby, Stills, Nash & Young invited us to tour with them and make a documentary film. Larry brought along cameraman David Myers whose Port-O-San man interview remains one of the highlights of the film. David became an important mentor for me as I continued to learn filmmaking.

We returned from that tour and rented an isolated, back-to-the-land Topanga house owned by Jim Morrison, who was on his way to Paris from where he never returned. The tour had taken a toll on CSNY, who broke up at the end of the year, but the footage became part of *Journey Through the Past*, a film directed by Neil Young, which Larry and I worked on at Neil's ranch in Woodside, California.

Warner Bros. sent a limo to Topanga to pick us up when Larry was nominated for an Academy Award for Best Sound but it was the year that Patton swept and he and Thelma, who was nominated for editing, lost. The film won for Best Documentary and remains one of the most financially successful films ever made.

I thought, how easy, work on a first film and it wins the Academy Award. Two years later, *Marjoe* won the Award for Best Documentary and Larry, Dave Myers, John Binder, and I had worked on that. Easy.

I have continued to work in the film and video business, weathering many changes in my personal life and seeing the sort of movies Hollywood likes to make become ones I don't rush to see. Not easy.

Since *Woodstock* and *Marjoe*, I've never again worked on a movie that won an Academy Award, but I cherish the experiences and the people I've met doing the films and videos I have done. John Binder and I got married a few years ago.

We're still in touch with Michael. Larry Johnson is a close friend. Dale Bell is too. Paradigm and *Woodstock* changed my life and to this day I have conversations with new acquaintances who love to hear this story.

OUR ARSENAL

THE DEFINITIVE LIST

9	Éclair NPR cameras
11	Éclair constant speed motors
10	Éclair variable speed motors
1	Converted Auricon 16 mm camera
5	9.5 to 95 zoom lenses
3	Bolex cameras
3	Arri S cameras, constant and variable speed motors
4	5.7 lenses
2	5.9 lenses
1	300 mm Kilfit lens
1	25 to 250 mm zoom lens
	Assorted Bolex and Arri lenses
40	Packets of lens tissue
45	85 filters, gel type
11	Spectra Pro lighteners
6	Minolta spot meters
4	Wadleigh designed body braces (pre-Steadicam)
1	Myers body brace
1	Tripod with spreader
15	Battery belts

50	Camera magazines for the Éclairs
25	Changing bags
7	Nagra tape recorders
6	ATNs for the Nagras
11	Dozen D-cell batteries
6	804 Sennheiser microphones with windscreens
5	404 Sennheiser microphones with windscreens
8	Headsets
5	PRO-A headsets
6	Walkie-Talkies
10	Talex two-way headsets
	Repair kits and tools
350,000	Raw stock, 60% in #7725, 40% in #7242
10	Rolls infrared film that never arrived
30	Rolls of raw stock delivered to the office two days after the festival!
400	Rolls of 131 3M 1/4" audio tape
48	Empty take-up 1/4" reels
102	Rolls of gaffer tape
6,000 ft.	Electrical wiring
100	Cube taps
1	Lowell light kit with 18 bulbs
60	Rolls of thirty-five-millimeter tungsten-balanced still film
10	Still cameras
3	Grafflex projectors
3	Projector stands
	Aretha Franklin, James Brown, and Paul Revere Films
1	Dual 1012 turntable
1	JBL amplifier

2	Speakers
1	Slide projector
	Sync cables, camera cables, power cables, mike cables, phone cables
8	Cars
5	Motorcycles
1	Helicopter
3	Tents
12	Sleeping bags
1	Coffee machine with coffee
	Blankets
	Bars of Soap
	Water containers
	Cold chests
	Cooking utensils
	Flashlights
	Disposible raincoats and umbrellas for the cameras
	Rain boots
	First aid supplies
	Vaccines
	Speed
3	Boxes of NoDoze
2	Bottles of champagne
1	Bottle of rum
400	Frankfurters
75	Chickens cut, cooked, and wrapped, then forgotten at the motel
	Egg and tuna salad sandwiches
4	Vans
1	Copy machine

2	Telephones
1	Typewriter
1	Folding table
6	Folding chairs
	Stationery supplies, pencils, marking pens, assorted music albums of those performers on stage
1	Record player

JOHN BINDER

HOW I GOT TO WOODSTOCK

(JOHN WAS MIKE WADLEIGH's original partner in Paradigm Films.)

I was in a cottage at Montauk on the tip of Long Island where I had gone with my wife Sharon and my son Josh. I wanted to clear my head and write for a while. I was tired of documentary films, and of living in my partner's shadow. I wanted to go my own way.

Wadleigh called me one morning. I knew he was putting together this operation to film a music festival up in New York state. He'd been thinking about a music film for a while, perhaps on Gospel Music or one of the 1950s rock and roll revivals that were appearing. We had just terminated a partnership called Paradigm Films, which we had formed five years earlier out of film school at NYU.

We had started as a cinéma vérité team. Michael on camera, me doing sound, making our decisions together. He was very bold and dynamic. He made things happen. I was moody and thoughtful. Without me to caution and council him he would have probably gone over a cliff. Without him I would never have had the adventure of those years.

Our combination had worked well from the beginning. We worked hard for four or five years and got as close as brothers. As partners and brothers do, we accumulated a list of irritations and offenses against each other over time. Larry Johnson joined us eventually and replaced me working in the field with Michael. That helped, but eventually we offended each other in irreparable ways. We broke off our partnership. The breakup occurred just as Michael started negotiations to do this film.

Dealing with Warner Bros. is not something he had done before, especially as he scrambled to amass sixty people and equipment with 24,000 dollars in the bank and some credit at the camera rental houses. He came and talked to me about reconsidering, and helping him produce the film. I knew it was another long-term commitment. It was his "thing," not mine. I was determined. I heartlessly turned him down and headed for the beach.

I'd been away in Montauk for several days when he called. He said he really just needed someone to go to the festival site and hold down the fort until he could get there. He said Bob Maurice, who had agreed to produce, and Dale Bell, the associate producer, and Larry Johnson were all maxed out in the city and couldn't possibly leave.

As usual he talked me into it. I would not otherwise have gone to Bethel, New York.

A list of unusually talented people had worked with us at Paradigm over the years. It was this gang that Michael called upon to shoot *Woodstock*.

Dale Bell, working with producer John O'Toole, had given us our first professional job at public television station WNET in New York. It was to be a documentary on the "American Communist Party." We hadn't shot much before the powers at WNET got cold feet and O'Toole had to come up with a safer subject. We criss-crossed the country shooting lots of film on the subject of *The Vanishing American (hometown) Newspaper*. We were neophytes when we started, but by the time we finished that shoot, we had become pretty good at our jobs.

Thelma Schoonmaker worked for a documentary producer in the city and she hired us a few times, then she started working with us on our projects. Scorcese joined us as an editor often, and also Jim McBride. Thelma edited Marty's first feature, *Who's That Knocking*, which we shot for him. Michael collaborated on McBride and Kit Carson's influential *David Holtzman's Diary*. We all worked together for free on anti-war films when Vietnam heated up, and so on.

Nobody was in the union. The union wouldn't have us. Everyone of us knew how to do more than one job on a film production. Everyone could shoot a camera, record sound, edit film, some, of course, better than others, but crosstraining and free substitutions were the norm, flexibility the principle. For example, Bob Maurice had come to Paradigm to start our distribution arm when Michael pressed him into service as producer of *Woodstock*. Working with Bob in distribution was Jeanne Field, who worked on *Woodstock* as a camera assistant.

So, we didn't have any permanent configuration at Paradigm. When we needed extra cameras or more people for bigger jobs, we hired them from our expanding pool of acquaintances, or we joined them on their projects. We were like musicians who come together to work on various gigs but don't form a permanent band. Whoever we didn't know from NYU we met this way, including David Myers, Ed Lynch, Chuck Levy and Charlie Peck, Marty Andrews, Richard Pearce, Ted Churchill, Peter Barton...

Michael was more of a leader than a boss. When he picked up his camera and started moving, everybody grabbed their gear and went to work. Aside from coordination and support, nobody needed much palaver.

It is significant that we had all worked in this semi-independent way because it formed the ethos that made filming possible under the impossible conditions that were to come.

The first event of my *Woodstock* experience occurred as I was driving up the New York Thruway. A State Trooper pulled me over. He was a big country boy. I still remember his huge hands and feet. He asked where I was going. I told him to the music festival at Bethel. I had longish hair. He took a step back and ordered me out of the car. He'd been briefed "There's gonna be a lot of you people coming up here." He made me open the trunk of the car. There was a cardboard box in the trunk. It held a motorcycle rack that you could bolt to the bumper. Some kind of red packing grease had soaked through and stained the outside of the box. When the big trooper saw those red stains, he touched the butt of his pistol with his hand. "What's in the box?" I told him it was a motorcycle rack. "What's that red stuff. Blood?" He wasn't kidding. "You wouldn't have a body in there?" I laughed, uneasy with his paranoia. He kept his eye on me as he reached inside the box half-expecting to discover human body parts. When he touched the iron motorcycle rack instead, he looked disappointed. He kept me long enough to run a check on my license. I told him I was going to work on a movie. He asked what movie stars I knew. I told him that we'd filmed John Wayne once. It changed his whole attitude. I often thought of him later and wondered how he felt when the rest began arriving and closed the Thruway with the biggest traffic jam the world had ever seen.

Wadleigh had told me to look up a guy named Michael Lang, an organizer of the festival, when I got to the site. I found him in his headquarters in an old frame farmhouse on Yasgur's farm. People were coming and going. Phones were ringing. Michael was on one of them. I looked around the place. Someone opened the door of an old stove in the kitchen to check on a cookie sheet piled with marijuana leaves that she was quick-drying in the oven. Music was playing loud. There was record or tape change and I heard Joe Cocker for the first time in my life. I had to ask who he was. As I remember, everyone stopped what they were doing. They ignored the phones for a while and listened. This English guy was not background music.

There were two people there already filming when I arrived, two British guys, the Two Michaels (was everyone at Woodstock named Michael?). Michael Lang had hired or cajoled them into documenting what was going on at least until

Wadleigh's crew arrived. Michael Margetts, the cameraman, had been a fashion photographer in "swinging" London and dropped out from what he described as a highly paid rat race. "I have a rule. I only turn my camera on when I see something that turns me on, and I turn it off when it doesn't excite me. I don't film anything out of obligation."

I didn't contribute all that much to the making of the film. But I think I made one important contribution. When the other camera and sound teams started showing up and asking what was the plan—Wadleigh wasn't there yet, he was still negotiating with Warner execs in New York—I just passed on British Michael's philosophy. Film what turns you on and stop filming when it turns you off. That may not sound like a plan, but it was ideal for *Woodstock*.

Later, a consultant for Warners showed up, an old school documentarian. Wadleigh was busy, so he foisted the guy off on me, told me to reassure him. I failed. The consultant called Warners and advised them to back out. It was a hopeless situation, he said. There was chaos here and we didn't have any organization at all. He couldn't understand that ours was the perfect response to an uncontrollable situation. He missed the main point of Woodstock and of the 1960s altogether.

There was a lot of anxiety as the flow of people kept increasing and reports proliferated that the dogged roads made escape impossible. It scared me. I was talking to someone who noticed my anxiety. "What's bothering you, man?" I said this was getting to a bad situation. I, like a lot of people, feared catastrophe. The hippie carpenter I was talking to surveyed the scene. "Anything you can do about it, man?" Obviously there wasn't. He added, "Then why worry about it?" And after that I didn't. I think everyone there went through the same anxiety I did, and most of them surrendered to the situation.

A few moments that moved me most never ended up on film. It was before our crew arrived. I visited the Hog Farmers's settlement on a hill at the edge of the woods away from the big natural amphitheater where the audience would settle in. I'd been to other communes previously but Wavy Gravy's "Hog Farmers" were legendary. They had a field kitchen set up and had begun to feed the ever-increasing masses from huge amounts of tasteless but nourishing brown rice and raw vegetables. I sat down in a circle of young people and asked them about life in a commune. Because they were eating, food became the topic of the conversation. They sang the praises of veggies and brown rice for a moment, dogmatically, but then someone mentioned meat. Guilty grins appeared on their faces and in lowered tones, they all confessed to missing animal flesh in their diet. One of the girls elicited jealous giggles as she described in juicy detail a recent adventure of slipping away from the group in some town they'd paused in recently and making her way stealthily to a hamburger stand and devouring a double cheeseburger. These were just teenagers. A reverent hush fell over them, and for a long moment they savored in their minds memories of forbidden flesh.

Later I was sitting in a teepee as the sun went down and darkness replaced it. Five or six of us sat in a circle, almost completely silent, passing a joint, exchanging glances, approving smiles, thinking our private thoughts. When the light was completely gone someone stood up and stepped out into the night. The others followed, me behind them. There were lights coming up the hill which turned out to be a caravan of buses. The "Merry Pranksters" arrived. I had heard nobody signal their arrival, yet everyone materialized from the woods, from tents and teepees, and all in silence. I had the distinct impression that communication had become telepathic. The Pranksters spilled out of their buses. The Hog Farmers greeted them with hugs, kisses, and laughter. It was a meeting of the tribes, or as close to it as white dropouts could get. Ken Babbs of the Pranksters and Wavy Gravy stood in the headlights of the lead bus and tossed the I-Ching to predict the fate of the festival. The results of the coin tosses were read aloud from the book. The omens were good. Everyone drifted off again to their respective nests. I felt that I had glimpsed something that now is ridiculed if it's mentioned at all. It was the other side of the American soul, the opposite of individualism, the Indian side, the yearning to belong to the whole tribe.

A much different moment I witnessed came on Sunday morning, the weekend of the performances, after the night of the big rainstorms immortalized in the movie. People were padding around in inches of water. Everything was wet. There was a meeting of the festival honchos behind the stage a few yards from the main power box. All the electricity had been shut off the night before in the storm so people wouldn't get electrocuted. Lang and Kornfeld, Chip Monck, John Morris, and Steve Cohen were huddled discussing the danger of turning on the power that could electrocute God knows how many people who were standing in all that water. Somebody said it could be like dropping the hair dryer in the bathtub for thousands of people. Nobody wanted to pull that switch. Some were saying that they had to call it quits, declare the festival over, too much risk turning on that power. In the midst of all this, somebody—I think it was Steve Cohen, but I'm not certain anymore—quietly broke off from the group, sloshed over to the power box, opened it, reached in, and pulled the master switch. The power came on harmlessly. The festival continued. Only that small circle of men knew what a disaster Woodstock could have been.

We had a semitrailer sinking off angle in the mud behind the stage with our equipment in it. I was walking through the dark at night and I came across a little cabal of guys in a circle plotting something. I heard a familiar voice prompting the others to come with him to rip off our truck. I ran off into the dark and got two guys on our crew, Charlie Grossbeck and Fred Underhill. We dashed to the truck. Abbie and his guys were already climbing inside. One of the women on our crew was trying to stop them. We jumped up and managed to run off all but Abbie and a cocky-looking sidekick who had a very expensive lens in his hand. Grossbeck had already relieved Abbie of whatever he was stealing, but his friend would not let go of the lens. Abbie said, "Let us have it, man. It's Warner Bros.'s stuff. We'll give it to Newsreel." I explained that Wadleigh had rented all this stuff and the insurance company had canceled his insurance since it was an official disaster area. Warners had nothing to do with it. Abbie bought that but his friend didn't, and we were very close to a fight. Abbie stepped between us. "Hey, man," he said, "Are you gonna be the first guy to throw a punch at Woodstock?" He grinned, took the lens from his buddy, and gave it back. Later that night Abbie and the rest of the Lower East Side boys stormed the stage while The Who was playing. They were going to take over and politicize this thing. Abbie jumped up onto the stage right in front of Peter Townshend, who clobbered him over the head with his solid-body guitar. Abbie fell backward off the stage. He didn't get to disarm Townshend as glibly as he had disarmed me.

The shooting of the film was an ordeal for everyone, as it was for the audience who endured the rain, the mud, the hunger, the lines to the portable toilets. We were zombies by the end. Someone had passed some coke around the night before and those who used it were revived for a while but then they crashed and fell out under the camera truck or the stage and it was pointless to wake them. A few hardy souls remained alive to film Jimi Hendrix when he came on with his "Band Of Gypsies" at eight o'clock Monday morning. Jimi was high and searching for something elusive on his guitar. He would start and stop. He'd whisper to his band. They would try again. He wasn't satisfied. The crowd had dwindled to a fraction of the night before. Those that were paying attention at all were shouting out for old favorites. Jimi didn't yield to them. He stepped to the mike and muttered something about trying to "find something here" and then he kept noodling and searching. This must have taken half an hour. I was standing behind Wadleigh on the ledge where he was shooting just below center stage. Hendrix was just a few feet away. He was riveting even if there seemed no rhyme or reason to his musical fumbling. It seemed that he was hopelessly lost in space, would never get it together. What a shame, I thought. The legacy of heroin, I presumed, but I presumed too much. Suddenly he found it. The volume increased, slashing notes and exploding chords ripped into the exhausted, hungover, mud-sodden silence of Max Yasgur's farm. Jimi's guitar conjured up every tortured blooddripping experience of 1960s America. I don't know how Wadleigh kept shooting. It raised the hair on your neck. Energy shot up your spine. The Kundelini energy that all those fire-breathing hippie-yogis were trying raise in that session that appears now in the film was raised at that moment by Jimi's guitar spitting out the most angry and ecstatic "Star-Spangled Banner." I, for one, wept and it still raises a tear when I recall it today.

I didn't work on the film after the shooting phase. I did keep an office near the editing rooms. I was privileged to sit through the hours of assembled footage, about two days' worth, as I recall, of showing the work of all the cameras with six synchronized projectors simultaneously. It's too bad that film could not have been magically preserved, too, before it got shaped into the film we see today.

Anyway, during this time I kept in touch with the gang that was cutting it. It may have been after everyone had packed up and gone to Hollywood to finish it when I got a call from Thelma Schoonmaker. She wanted to tell me something funny that had just happened to her. There had been a great deal of Sturm und Drang among the Warner Bros. executives about what kind of rating this film was going to get. They had to leave in the nude bathing stuff, it was already a famous part of the festival from magazine pictures and such. Thelma had become embroiled in these considerations. It was feared that they might get an X-rating from Mr. Valenti's censors and lose a lot of money. (What must have scared them most was some footage of a young man walking along, alone, amid a number of naked people fresh from the lake. I had seen this guy in person when I was with Ed Lynch as he filmed the skinny dippers. We saw him twice, in fact hours apart. He was hard to miss and impossible to forget because both times, as he strolled nonchalantly along with the crowd, he had an erection that he made no effort to disguise.) Eventually, the guardians of our innocence and the censor board came to an agreement. A marketing fellow called from Warners. I picture him with a cigar in his mouth and gruff impatient voice. He was a man of few words. He said decisively, "Thelma [cigar chomp chomp], one hard-on and you get an X."

THELMA SCHOONMAKER

WHERE ARE MARTY'S CUFF LINKS?

(PRIOR TO HER ROLE as supervising editor, Thelma Schoonmaker acted as assistant director, with Larry Johnson and Martin Scorsese, at the festival).

THELMA: You do have the story about Marty [Scorsese] and his cuff links?

DALE: No.

THELMA: Oh. Well, we all thought when we went up there, we were going to stay in a motel. We had booked a motel, the Silver something or other.

DALE: The Silver Spur, which was renamed the Silver Sperm.

THELMA: By us, you mean.

DALE: Yes.

THELMA: Anyway, so we thought we were going to stay in a motel, and after shooting during the day we would go back there at night. So people brought suitcases thinking that would be the way it was, but of course, once we got there, there was no way for us to get out of the festival grounds. The roads were jammed or blocked off. Scorsese had actually brought his cuff links, thinking maybe we would go out to dinner at night and he wanted to be properly dressed. He wasn't wearing jeans. I was, but he was not. I mean, nobody had any idea what we were going to find up there. But at one point there was one little tent that we had—has anyone talked about this?

DALE: No. Go ahead.

THELMA: Well, I don't know where we got this tent, whether one of our multitudinous crew had brought it with them, but it was used mainly by Wadleigh. I think I slept in it briefly for a couple of hours, but at one point, Marty, for whom sleeping in a tent on the ground was as far from his idea of what one did in life as could be. He tried to get a few hours of sleep. Having grown up on the

Lower East Side, he didn't like trees particularly or grass and here he was in the midst of this mudswamp and water running down through the middle of the tent—and suddenly the tent collapsed on him and we actually have footage of him flailing around inside.

But it was something that reminded me. Oh, the ticks! I remember feeling ticks in my hair. We would just put our heads down on the bare ground (or mud) to try and sleep and then I found a tick in my hair. Oh, my God, it was a nightmare.

Occasionally someone would come up with a hot dog—I don't know where they came from—and stick it in your mouth as you were trying frantically to get a freshly loaded magazine from some poor bastard who was underneath the stage—and how many people were down there?

DALE: We had at least half a dozen people who were underneath there at all times.

THELMA: Who were doing nothing but load film. Pregnant women…

DALE: Right. Whoever we could recruit. And then there were the runners who would take the film from under the stage to the lip of the stage, and/or hold cable for the camera guys above.

THELMA: And then there was the whole episode of the great thought that we would be able to do concerted camera moves. All the cameramen had headsets on and Wadleigh and Scorsese were trying to come up with ideas for everybody moving in at the same time, which we thought would be wonderful in multiple image. Or backing away at the same time or tilting up at the same idea.

We had grand ideas of how that was all going to work, but, well! It just turned out that because of either the dampness or so much electricity up on stage, everyone would get these screaming, high-pitched squeals going through their headsets and you would see cameramen all across the stage ripping their headsets off. And finally we just gave up and told everybody do whatever they do. So nobody was really planning anything. We were just relying heavily on the cameramen to do what was right. And of course, in the case of Wadleigh, he was thinking out concerted camera moves, like moving in at the beginning of a certain lyric in the songs that he knew very well. And Dick Pearce in the back was doing some fantastic stuff. But we just had to wing it and hope that we were going to get what we needed. There was no way to know. We had high hopes for concerted camera moves when we went up to Woodstock, particularly because of the multiple image idea, but there was just no way to do it.

SONYA POLONSKY

THE ROAD TO THE SILVER SPERM

DALE: Do you remember first going up to the site on Saturday before?

SONYA: Yes. Before the festival started I went up there one day with Bob. You might have been there, but I remember going up with Bob. Or, maybe everybody was doing something different. Maybe you were there and I was just tagging along after Bob or something. I just remember having to follow Bob around and we talked to Michael Lang. We hung around the trailers. They were building things. Nobody was there yet; it was just Woodstock Ventures. We talked to a publicity lady.

It was more like an "arrangements" visit. It had been settled. Or, we thought it was settled and then it wasn't settled. Is that possible?

DALE: Absolutely.

SONYA: I just remember these little spots. But, I remember the two or three weeks before, when we were doing preproduction and you were making deals with people, and everybody had a different deal. But, the next time I went was with Jeannie.

DALE: You didn't go up on Saturday before?

SONYA: No. I was left in the office. I just remember staying around until three o'clock in the morning every night and coming in around seven or eight in the morning, into the office. I remember having the worst sore throat of my life. It must've been mononucleosis, but I didn't know what it was; I kept smoking.

It didn't go away and later when I was up at the site my sore throat went away, but my foot swelled. Which made my experience slightly different from other people's because I went to the clinic.

I remember we went up there Thursday; we slept in the parking lot and I remember waking up from a sound sleep with rain falling on us. We were lying in the dirt. I don't remember what we did, I think it [turned into a] sunny day later. I don't remember when we got the Silver Sperm, but I remember the sign went on and off. Do you remember the Silver Sperm ranch?

MARTIN ANDREWS

AH, WOODSTOCK!

I HAVE JUST THROWN out about sixty pounds of paper rummaging through my four-banger filing cabinet looking for a copy of the bill I wrote for my work on *Woodstock*. I itemized everything I did. It took more than a day to construct. It looked like a Chinese restaurant menu. I waited until the Warner Bros. deal was a *fait accompli* and then socked it to them. Nobody complained. I believe I was the highest paid technician on the job as a result of this waiting and itemizing. What a tool to jog my memory after thirty years. I can't find the bill. I have a perfect memory—it just doesn't last very long…

Memory is a curious thing. It's like a path through the woods: the more you travel down it, the easier it is to see. It doesn't even have to be true. A lie told enough times becomes the memory—the truth. For example, at Woodstock I remember crouching down (a classic "Marty work position") working on something when I felt a sharp jabbing pain in my right arm. This was no mosquito: this was serious! Not being able to drop my work, I looked around to see this guy withdrawing a hypodermic needle from my arm. He was naked from the waist up except for a makeshift white headband with a funky red cross smeared on the front in lipstick. I could tell from the disheveled hair and twisted grin that he was "one of us" and probably stoned. He said, "It's cool, man! They told me to give B12 to the crew— you are on the crew, aren't you?" Now, I don't know whether this memory is true or not. Maybe it doesn't matter, as it sums up the chaos and craziness of the event. It's the truth of Dr. Hunter Thompson and Gonzo journalism—which I love. But I love the actual truth (whatever that is) even more, because it is so frequently more astonishing—mind-blowing—than fiction.

Another clear memory that may or may not be true has to do with *Woodstock*'s famous fornication scene. I had field-stripped Ted Churchill's NPR in the equipment truck when I heard this couple discussing where they were going to "get it on." I couldn't abandon my project, find a camera, load it, get a charged battery and follow them. They would have been lost in the crowd before I got it together. So I was delighted when destiny threw my friend and hero, David Myers, my way. He came into the truck wiping his noble brow in the heat of exhaustion, and was about to recount the vicissitudes of his immediate past when I cut him off, saying, "Pardon me, David, but you see that couple? They were just outside the door talking about where they could go to fuck." One of the most endearing and exciting human qualities is to be ready—ready for anything. David was as ready to fly across an ocean and go to my wedding and honeymoon as he was to forget his fatigue and pursue the aspiring fornicators! He was out of the truck like a shot and the shots he got were perfect in showing what was going down without being so pornographic as to be unusable. In retrospect, I wonder whether any of this happened. I don't even know for sure that it was David who shot that scene.

One scene I do know David shot was the famous Port-O-San sequence. It is legendary and is why he is as much of a titan of the documentary world as the likes of the great Robert Flaherty. Like a chess master, David can instantaneously run down the available options (scenarios), position himself in the right place with the right angle, focal length, and focus to visually tell the story best. He knows that shots have to have a payoff. But he is a greedy, avaricious son-of-a-gun (aesthetically), and is able, like no other, to pile payoff upon payoff until the story is totally told and the audience is in a state of delirium.

He did this at my wedding in London's Ealing Abbey. He got me and Lizzie with my bride's three brothers in the choir, the priest wrapped up the service, David and Larry Johnson (his best boy/soundman) walking backward down the aisle, tracking us all the way and showing most of the huge family crowd as a moving background. As Lizzie and I reached the entrance to the building, David stepped aside to let us go out and racked over to the 5.7 lens (infinite focus) with the eighty-five daylight filter. He was behind us as we went down the steps and had a spontaneous smooch. That would seem to be the perfect payoff: but not for David. He had a shot of the double-decker bus (our honeymoon vehicle) and its driver in view. He started to go for the driver, Rick (who was awarded Best Bus Driver in London the year before). All of a sudden, out of the gaggle of Fleet Street reporters and cameramen comes this aggressive, obnoxious still photographer with a fully decked-out Speed Graphic Large Format (Intimidator) camera. This guy is shouting at me and Lizzie to stop kissing at the top of the stairs and do it down by the pool of gongoozling reporters at the bottom of the steps. David sizes up the situation (still rolling), moves in on this abrasive, cockney-accented East End yobbo and interviews him! "How long have you been doing this kind of work?" "'Bout thirty-seven years, mate." "I'll bet you've seen some strange ones." "Right, mate. Hey, bride and groom, do that down here!" "How does this wedding rate?" "Not bad with the double-decker bus and all the hipsters!" Pay-off number two. Payoff number three came as David panned over to our bus driver and asked him what he thought it was going to be like driving a bunch of American hippies around England for a month. All this in one shot! He and Larry did a complete sound, motion picture from altar to altercation to honeymoon in one bloody shot!

The Port-O-San scene in *Woodstock* was the same thing. David doesn't just passively record what's happening. He covers the cleaning man's professionalism in doing his job. Asks a series of leading questions involving the man's work, establishes a comfortable rapport. He compliments the man on his work—a courtesy which elicits the information that the man has a kid at Woodstock and another flying choppers in 'Nam. Just as the man leaves frame and the shot has been paid off, a freak exits another Port-O-San unit with a dope pipe in his mouth. He offers it to David, who declines (incidentally, I should have mentioned already that I do not remember crew members ingesting dope while at work. As rebellious as we were, we knew that dope and work don't mix). Back to Port-O-San, with David now engaging the hippie "customer" we find him quickly establishing a rapport with someone who is clearly incoherent. David prods just enough to stay alive. Then we get another payoff: the subject asks David the name of the film he's making. David avoids the long *Woodstock* option, quips "Port-O-San," and then pans over to a unit with the word "PORT-O-SAN" proudly filling the frame. Payoff exponential/extraordinaire! David, you are the best—an inspiration to all of us.

THE CALL TO ARMS

The Woodstock festival had been hyped all summer long on the radio. I don't enjoy being in crowds, so I had no intention of going. I remember the call from Wadleigh, which ended with his asking me to bring all the film in my fridge ("the project was somewhat underfunded"). I grabbed all the Background-X (ASA 10), Tri-X, and assorted cans of color, gathered up my location toolkit, and was on my way. It was a few days before showtime, so we had no trouble getting there. As much as I wanted to shoot, Wadleigh told me that I was to be location technical director.

I didn't know what that meant but it sounded pretty important. The job defined itself as we went along. Basically I was grip, gaffer, triage agent, and general recourse of last resort for cameramen who still hadn't been around that much. One of the first things I had to deal with was to create a platform for the crew to shoot from in front of the stage. It was still early enough to get scaffolding, which worked perfectly. I pride myself on not over-ordering stuff that never gets used. My intuition is located somewhere in my viscera. I instinctively know how much film or tape I have remaining. I can rewind a cassette tape and stop it exactly where I want to be. This time I did order extra scaffolding—just in case.

The "just in case" immediately became apparent after I had assembled our shooting runway. Where was the press going to be? The "extra" scaffolding was used up for them so that they would not interfere with "our" space. My gut instincts had proved infallible again.

Talk to me, Marty!

I suppose that, beyond general exhaustion, the most stressful number I did at Woodstock was to literally cobble together a two-way telex-type system so that the stage cameramen could talk to each other and Marty Scorsese could cue them as to what to shoot. There were wild fantasies about the cameramen dancing together (three steps to the left, two to the right, pause a beat, three to the left; bossa nova, tango, merengue, cha-cha-cha). Others didn't want to be encumbered by such a system. I put the project not just on the back burner but actually off the stove until people figured out what they wanted. I had other urgent things to do. This is what I mean by triage. As the most urgent tasks were completed, the demand for a communication system increased. As showtime approached the demands went from urgent to insistent. "Talk to me, Marty! What's happening with the (communications) system?" I had to do something, or tell them to shove it. Shove it disappeared as an option. I talked to Dale Bell.

It was Dale who introduced me to Lee Osborne, who took me to the legendary Bill Hanley. Bill's a dyed-in-the-wool Yankee from Boston. "What do YOU need?" "Well, I'd like..." "No, what do you...NEED?" "Okay, I need eight headsets with attached microphones, an amplifier, and an eight-channel distribution board." "Lee, give him six headsets and an amp. He'll have to work out the distribution himself. I can't give him a whole mixing console. It's too much. He doesn't need it." He was right. All I really needed was a distribution system for audio. It would be similar to power distribution, which I deal with on the mega level. What I required was pissant level—I'd just have to make my own. We were less than an hour from showtime. What to do? "Talk to me, Marty! Where's the system?!"

Necessity can be a mother, all right. Coupled with urgency, the options get narrowed in a hurry. When the festival people built the barrier wall to keep the hordes off the stage, they pile-drove two-by-eight-inch boards vertically into the ground and evened off the top with a chain saw. I grabbed about a one-foot length of top board off the ground and hustled a handful of nails from a stage carpenter. The layout was simple: six channels into the amp, six out to the headsets. I just had to cobble it together. I thought of connecting all the incoming cables and all the outgoing cables together, but such a Marloilla is notoriously unreliable. "Marty! How long? Talk to me!" Murphy's Law was running rampant. I had to go with the "nail board," not high tech but strong as an Arri. No need to solder them now. The mechanical connection of wire to nail is all that counts. Final sound check for stage is going on overhead. Bang, bang with the hammer; wrap, wrap with the wire. Cameramen's eyes on me, burning into my hunched-over back. Bang, bang, wrap, wrap. "Talk to me, Marty…" Richie Havens and his drummer are coming out…Hook up the amp to the board. Thump, thump, thump. I can hear Richie's foot thumping out the rhythm on the stage right over my head. "TALK to me, Marty!" Plug in the amp —thank God—transistors—no warm-up time. "TALK TO ME!!" "Okay, guys, go!" It was on—up and running! Richie's yelling "freedom" over and over, unaware of its special meaning for me.

The system worked great— except I don't think they really made much use of it to coordinate their shots. It was one of those ideas that are good conceptually, but, in reality, the cameramen were too busy riding out their own shots to be bothered with the nuisance. I guess Marty Scorsese used the system to cue them as to which numbers to shoot. It was really more of a rallying point, a catalyst, a flash point, a defining rig that if done would justify us hippies working the job; a validation of the producers having selected the Wadleigh team over better-known competitors.

The rest is history. We went, we did it, we changed the world! The communication system was located at the base of the scaffolding I'd rigged for the press. It worked beautifully until some bimbo dropped a clipboard on it. Oh, well. It wasn't hard to rewire, and the repair gave me the chance to solder the connections. I also elevated it and covered it up from the onslaught of further clipboards and—as it turned out—the rain! Repair time: fifteen minutes. People were into the goings-on. I don't think anyone noticed it was out. At least there was no more "talk to me, Marty!" They were able to talk to each other instead.

SHENANIGAN SLATING

We spent quite an amount of time trying to figure out an easy, foolproof system for slating our takes. We thought of having a big clock with a second hand right in the back of the stage. We abandoned this idea when we realized that the soundmen would have to read off the time on the track and then hand-slate the takes. Finally we just went with the hand slates and whatever system the camera/sound team was used to. Larry Johnson and David Myers had little, preprinted notebooks with roll numbers. Larry would write what the scene was—if he could. He did that on the thousands of feet of my honeymoon footage that he shot, with Jeannie Field doing the paperwork. I still haven't had the money or the time to edit *The Honeymoon*, but I still have the notebooks, and it seems like a good system. Better than just shooting the Éclair's frame fogs and audio bloops.

One thing we did on my wedding film, and on other projects where I was cameraman, was to perfect the art of the creative or organic slate. This would generally take the form of hitting the subject (Dick Cavett, *inter alia*) with the shotgun mike. We would also write a scene number on a matchbook held close to the wide-angle lens. Hapless editors (including Wes Craven, on my skiing flick) had to match the sound and picture of striking a match. I don't know how much of this shenanigan slating was done at Woodstock, but I would love to see it all put together on a reel!

After the film was shot and various friends, girlfriends of friends, etc. were syncing up the *Woodstock* footage, I came by and was horrified to see them doing it in real time on the KEM machines. They were just sitting around watching the footage! Yikes! These hippies! I showed them how to use synchronizers and squawk boxes. You can also loop the extra film or mag track in the synchronizer and feed fill into whichever runs out first to speed things up.

I wasn't able to be there for the actual assembling of the first KEM machines, but I did receive the panicked call: "Help, everything's in German!" I reacted as my kids do now to computers: "Don't worry, the Germans are no fools, everything's got to be foolproof. Just stick the modules together and see what plugs fit into each other." This advice seemed to work.

We never really solved the projection problem on the East Coast. It was possible to run the projectors in sync, but it was a bitch to load them with everything lined up properly. My old Kalart Victor had a wonderful access and visibility of the gate. To sync them would have involved attaching AC sync motors to a rotating inching knob (sort of a power take-off on them). They didn't go for this—but I wished they had. It was a great projector, and served me well for over twenty years—ah, the insanity it put up against my screen and other people's walls! You could bypass the sound head and just project the picture. This also meant you could load and unload the projector in mid-reel. Real time- and energy-savers.

I haven't kept up with what's out there now in the way of projectors. I've had a Siemens Interlock for the last ten years. I suspect the technology hasn't advanced at all since *Woodstock*.

Some of my memories are involved with rain—and mud. I was there when the rain started. Wadleigh was freaking out because he was basically financing everything personally with the *Sidewalks* money. He said, "I'm wiped out; it's all over." I said, "Come on, Michael, this will just make it more interesting."

As the drama increased and lifted the burden off his shoulders, it landed on mine. It devolved to me to clean things out and keep them working. In one of two sessions of sleep in four days (each session fewer than three hours), someone found me sleeping in a river under the equipment truck. He woke me up with the alarming news that both of Wadleigh's lenses had condensation in them. I got to the stage just in time to prevent a catastrophe. Someone had a sun gun only inches away from the lenses. I grabbed the lenses and ran off to hide and go back to sleep with the precious glass snuggled in my armpits. The only way to get rid of the condensation was to warm the lenses up slowly. Had that sun gun done its thing, the glass would literally have exploded from differential expansion. Come to think of it, I must ask Wadleigh what he did without his special lenses. I hope he, too, seized the opportunity to take a nap.

I wish I could have found that bill that I wrote, because it spelled out the entirety of my complicity with *Woodstock*. I was burned out from another job and arrived on the scene pretty wasted just to begin with. There are many memory paths I haven't trodden due to raising three sons, living hand-to-mouth, and looking forward to new work rather than back in my wake. I look forward to seeing what my wonderful buddies come up with as their memories.

CHUCK LEVEY

THE PERFECT JOB

(CHUCK WAS ONE OF the many members of the New York University "Mafia" who brought their talents to the movie. Chuck was primarily a stage cameraman who would be the only person on the original team to duplicate his role in the summer of 1998, the nostalgic tour in A Day in the Garden.)

In the 1960s, Mike Wadleigh and John Binder had a film company, Paradigm Films. It was the hub for a number of people who were interested in film. Not movies, not commercials...film.

At that time I was an assistant art director working at Public Television in NYC. Much of the stuff that I was involved in was On-Air Promotion, graphic design, photography, animation, live film.

At the time Mike, John, and I were married to women who were dancers. They were all members of the Paul Taylor Dance company. We also lived within two or three blocks of each other. We had kids the same age who all played together. That's how I got to know Mike.

I quit my job at Channel 13 in order that I might get more involved in film, as a cameraman. Paradigm hired me to work on some projects. Among others, a groundbreaking Merv Griffin TV special, during which many of the multi-camera location techniques later to be used at Woodstock were figured out. The crew that worked on this shoot, Mike, John, Marty Andrews, Larry Johnson, Charlie Peck, Ted Churchill, and myself, went on to get the *Woodstock* film done.

In July 1969, my then wife and I bought two tickets to go to the Woodstock Music and Art Fair. At the same time, Wadleigh and the group at Paradigm were putting together a package in order to get the job of filming the concert. In that package was film that I as well as others had worked on.

In the beginning of August, I was in Philadelphia working on some forgotten project when I got the word that Mike had gotten the gig and I was asked to work on it. Maybe it was you, Dale, who called. I don't remember. WHO KNEW!

It seemed like a great job, a perfect job for a twenty-eight-year-old film hippie. Where are those tickets now?

I was originally supposed to be shooting MOS (Mit Out Sound) with a Bolex. At that time I did not own an Éclair NPR or anything else. When I got to the stage area, however, I was handed a rented NPR, assigned a soundman (Tom Cohen), and told to shoot whatever I wanted to. Setting up, people arriving, anything that set the stage for the coming concert (I had arrived three days before the concert was to start).

On Friday morning—maybe it was Thursday, the day before the concert started, I'm not sure—the first day of the concert, before I left to go shoot at the Hog Farm, I went up on the as yet unfinished stage and looked out and saw a hayfield being cut. Upon returning some hours later I went back up on stage and saw something entirely different. PEOPLE!!! Everywhere. It was staggering. And it was only early afternoon. Something was happening and I was there with a camera. The PERFECT JOB!!!

That afternoon (or the next afternoon) the performances started. Technically the only way for multiple cameras to stay in sync, at the time, was to have AC motors on the cameras and a sixty-cycle tone on the track. To help in lining up the picture and sound (post) I remember trying to get a shot of my watch at the head of each roll shot on stage. Not always (rarely) possible, especially at night. I seem to remember that as each camera roll went on the camera, the assistant wrote the time of day, or night, and the performer on the tape that was wrapped around the magazine. That tape then went on the can as the film was unloaded after it was shot. Also on that piece of tape was the cameraman's name, roll number, etc…TIME CODE!

Santana was the first of the big groups to perform Saturday. The plan for shooting performance was simple. Mike had only assigned us rough positions, zones, to shoot from. That was his only direction. Ride it out. Let it rip. Don't worry about the holes in the stage.

Marty Scorsese…I barely knew him. He was trying to do his thing from stage left. He was screaming into the "not so-clearcom" trying to tell me (and I guess other cameramen) what to do. Of course, he couldn't see what I was seeing and because of his chatter I couldn't hear the music so I looked at Marty and took off my headset. The beauty of Mike's plan was to hire people who could do it on their own. On or off the stage. Do the right thing.

It rained. Nobody left. Maybe they couldn't. Mud. So I got my camera, switched from the AC motor to the constant speed battery-powered motor with sync cable, for documentary use, and went out into audience/crowd not knowing what to expect. Everyone was going "with the flow." Mud, use it. Sliding contests happened. The incredible good feelings were not dampened. Being on the stage was, of course, a lot of fun. But, being a documentary cameraman, I was most comfortable "out there." I was "out there."

During the filming of the event I had no idea of how the world was viewing it all. Macrovision. Being in the middle of it all I couldn't see out. The eye of the storm. I don't remember caring. I was having the time of my life. Given the choice, I wouldn't have been anywhere else, doing anything else. Our time had come. I guess that this, later on, would be the only disappointment of Woodstock; our time came and went. What we did there was record a point in time. For years things were either BW or AW (BC, AD) for me. Some things still are. BW I got married, had kids. AW I got divorced.

I've since remarried and had more kids. AW. Life is not linear.

Jimi Hendrix came and went. After his "Star-Spangled Banner" was garbage, a sea of garbage. It smelled bad. I didn't think of it as meaningful then but in retrospect maybe I should have. I wanted to go. Get my kids and take a shower. I'm not sure of the order. It was over.

I got my kids, presently in their thirties and just fine, one granddaughter, had my shower, and went home. The film went to the lab, J&D Lab. By the way, Joe David, whose lab it was, and who timed all the workprint, is in his late eighties and still alive. He now helps his son and grandson at J&D Lab, still in Manhattan although now at 27 East Twenty-First Street. They don't do film anymore. Only tape stuff. I see them fairly often.

When the film came back from the lab, we were all invited up to see it whenever we wanted. Although the shooting was over, I still felt very much a part of the family. Often I helped editors to sync up dailies. I might remember something that could be helpful. Peter Townshend, for example, was easy because of his trademark windmill arm movement ending on the strings of his guitar. The film was being cut on the brand new KEM three head flatbed editing table. Once one camera was synced up, other members of The Who, or whatever group, lining up became easier to deal with because there were visual as well as audio cues. Other cameramen helped with their footage as well.

The first cut that I saw was five screens. Five projectors for picture and a sixth for magtrack. Was this ever done before? I don't know. It was rough but it was mighty effective. It was very long. Only people who worked on the film, friends, wives, etc. were there. Somewhere between five and seven stoned hours went by before Jimi Hendrix reappeared.

The heaps of garbage didn't come back until at age fifty-seven I saw the film once again. My eight-year-old son wanted to know what all that stuff was.

When the film went to LA to be finished, I definitely felt left behind. Many of us on the shooting crew did get together from time to time. But I could not wait for the film to be done and everyone would come back.

I said that this was the perfect job. But it was much more than that. Yes, I was paid to be there, as was eveyone else. The film was a great success. Artistically and commercially. I was and am very glad, proud to have been a part of it. It was a once-in-a-lifetime thing. The fact that it was filmed makes it real for those who were not there. No one can say "it can't be." A point in time. A family. History.

As I told you. This has been more difficult than I would have thought. The other night I had a dream. I was at an event much like Woodstock. Only it was an event celebrating the movie. Crowds were watching not only the movie but what seemed to be home movies of everyone who was involved in the making of the movie. In the home movies that I was seeing were all the members of my family, past and present. All younger. It couldn't be. Weird. Thank you, Dale. I'll send the therapy bills to you.

Woodstock was one of the greatest documentaries ever. I felt as though I was at the French (why French?) Revolution when it all started, and I had a camera (my camera was French). I doubt that any of us knew at the time the extent of what we had become involved in.

I'm not sure what, if any, effect it had on the way documentaries that followed were made. Clearly, it wasn't the first cinéma vérité film ever shot. It wasn't the last. IT WAS THE BIGGEST AND THE BEST!

Remember, originally the idea was to make a concert film, a great concert film of a great concert, BUT 500,000 (by the way, in speaking last week, August 1999, with a cop in Bethel who worked security in 1969, he told me how estimates were made back then. The estimates made from helicopters by the state police did not include people in the wooded areas. There were lots of trees. The Bethel cop placed his guess at more like 900,000 not including those stuck out on the roads. That additional would probably make it one million at least) people showed up. Therein lay the genius of Mike Wadleigh. Rather than have cameras with fixed positions, on cranes, dollies, etc., it was set up to be shot as a documentary. SERENDIPITY? LUCK? What's the difference? We were ready.

Charlie Peck and I had already been good friends and remained so. He couldn't go to Woodstock because he was working on another project at the time. After *Woodstock* we formed Charlie Company. Together we got projects to do and tried to do them in the "Paradigm/*Woodstock*" tradition. We even did a three-screen, handheld promo piece for IBM. Shot with an NPR and cut on a KEM.

Years went by. Many of them. Charlie now works in computer design. I see him often. Even more lately because of your project.

I remained a cameraman. I still am. Officially I'm called a DP with a local six hundred card. But I'm a cameraman still. I've tried to stay with documentary even though it's gotten harder to earn a living with it. I've had some success shooting documentary style' commercials and sometimes it's OK. I think that the reason they pay so well is so you'll take it seriously.

This may sound odd but I never really promoted myself as one of the *Woodstock* cameramen. I don't know why. Only in the past few weeks have I even thought much about that because of Steve at Kodak and Dale of *Woodstock*. Now there seems to be more interest in me because of 1969 than I can remember. Last week I was back up in Bethel heading up the team that shot the Day in the Garden concert for Kodak. As I was introduced as one of the original cameramen I was greeted with awe. Amazing. Maybe because I'm still alive, I don't know. Obviously, I was the oldest on the crew. When we wrapped crew members told me how "honored" they were to meet and to work with me. Truly amazing! But not bad! Of course, I'd hire them all again in a second.

ARLO GUTHRIE

BEYOND "CATCHING THE FUZZ"

(SON OF THE LEGENDARY folk musician Woodie Guthrie, Arlo's initial on-film perceptions about the status of the New York Thruway and its police force have since been dwarfed by his view of what the festival and the movie symbolize. The second part of his conversation closes the book.)

DALE: Did you expect to be filmed when you arrived up there, or did you have any idea at all when you got to Woodstock in 1969?

ARLO: As far as my memory goes, I had no idea that they were either recording for audio or film anything that was going on there. I don't remember seeing any cameras or recording equipment, and so I was surprised like a lot of other people when there was talk of a movie coming out, or a record.

DALE: And do you remember…your story conforms to several others, I have to tell you, do you remember what your reaction was when first you saw yourself in the movie?

ARLO: No. I never went to a screening.

DALE: And so, when did you first see it?

ARLO: Probably on home video or something.

DALE: You didn't go to a theater?

ARLO: Right, I never saw *Woodstock* in a theater. Still to this day.

DALE: And when you saw yourself and you saw yourself in the context of the festival, what did you think?

ARLO: I wished I would have known [laughs] that we were doing a film, I would have been a little better prepared. *Woodstock* was a double-edged sword for me on the one hand; it was one of those moments that we all knew was historic at the time that it was going on.

On the other hand, I had got there, at least as far as my memory goes, the day before I was supposed to play. And so, I was indulging in all the things that were going on there. I think I had to play on the first day, because I was one of the few people who was able to get in or something like that, and I really wasn't ready to perform in front of anyone [laughs]. And I was too young to realize that I could have said "No!" when they asked me. Realizing that there would be millions of people who would see me throughout the decades now, I sort of regret not doing that, looking at what was one of the most wonderful and at the same time one of the most ridiculous moments of my life [laughs].

DALE: Your story is a little bit similar to Country Joe. He had just come up for the ride. He wasn't going to be playing for two days. Just wanted to sit on the edge of the stage and watch everybody else.

ARLO: Right! Right! That's what we were doing. And we were all hanging out and goofing off and having a great time, and I was perfectly willing to forgo any of the pleasures of performing until after I was done playing. Or, I was going to forgo the pleasures of goofing off before performing until after I was done. Which is what you always do. But in this one particular instance I was sort of caught off guard, and had to think of things to say that were, at least for the performance, were worthy of being at least paid attention to. And I was lucky to get that far.

DALE: Have people come up to you and said, "Well, the New York Thruway is closed"?

ARLO: For the last thirty years!

DALE: Right! And "what do you think about the fuzz?"

ARLO: That's right! [laughs] My kids still get a kick out of that!

DALE: Well, I mean, they are lines that are eminently quotable, I think.

ARLO: Well, that's what I'm saying, I could have thought of probably some lines that would have been a little more sort of nobler in the mind…you know? But what are you going to do? It's done now, and I'm refusing to regret a single moment of it.

DALE: That's the right attitude, I think….

ARLO: It was the last great moment when we were all in the same boat. It was after that we all decided it would be better off to be in separate boats, so that we could get our act together or reevaluate our own uniqueness, or any of the fancy words they use today; but that was the last time we were all in the same boat. Didn't matter if you were black, white, yellow, red, or tan; didn't matter if you were man, woman, clothed, naked, rich, poor, this or that, everybody was in the same boat at Woodstock.

And the fact that we all not only got along, but had a hell of a party, disproved beyond a shadow of a doubt the theories put forth by the same idiots who proposed the Domino Theory: who told us that if we didn't go over to Vietnam, there were going to be Chinese Communists in New Jersey within two weeks. As if they could have found their way around New Jersey! And we were told by these same people that if those hippies get in control of things, there's going to be stealing, and murder, and injustice, and the American way of life is going to fall apart.

And everybody bought into it! And all of a sudden, when you have half a million, that's the least number by the way, you have a half a million people all not only getting along, but getting along under the worst conditions imaginable, and everybody going home smiling anyway, this is not just historic—this is of Biblical proportion. And I don't mean that lightly, I think there was a great spirit that moved everything, at that time, and really not only protected us but gave us the right attitude to deal with it.

I'm so pleased to have been a part of that; yeah it would have been nice to have been able to have been more eloquent, you know, or something like that; or take advantage of the moment; but I've had years to do that now, so I'm not complaining too much.

DALE: How has it your appearance in the movie affected your career?

ARLO: Well, I think anyone who played at Woodstock and who had some memorable moment, whether it was musical, or lyrical, or visual, or verbal, whatever it was, attained a status within the American culture, actually in the sort of global culture, that was beyond anything we ever dreamed of being. I still don't need reservations in restaurants in Italy, or India or wherever, simply because I was at Woodstock. Which is, you know...I'll take it.

STAN WARNOW

HAPLESS DOCUMENTARY CAMERAMAN

(STAN IS THE ONLY member of the team who brought the twin talents of both cameraman and editor—besides Michael Wadleigh—to the movie. The second part of his piece can be found in "Post.")

August 1994. I'm sitting in a field on what used to be Max Yasgur's farm in White Lake, New York, site of the original Woodstock festival. And as it was twenty-five years ago, there is music being performed on a stage, and an audience spread out along the hill that forms a natural amphitheater with a makeshift stage below. But unlike twenty-five years ago, it is a small audience, just a few thousand. The reason is that the official Woodstock II festival is being held at another site, about eighty miles to the Northeast, and that's where the crowds are. But that doesn't interest me, for my memories are here. Twenty-five years ago I was more of a kid than an adult (still am in some ways), but now I am here with my own kids. They have heard about Woodstock for years, and I wanted them to get a chance to experience something of what the original was about, and this is the place for that, far from the computerized corporate theme park that is Woodstock II. But while I am physically here in 1994, part of me is far, far away in another time and place entirely.

Winter 1969…and the times were still changing. I was living in a walk-up apartment in downtown Manhattan and was enmeshed in all that the 1960s meant in New York. So it was only natural that I was a regular reader of the *Village Voice* and sometime during that late winter or early spring, I began to see weekly ads for an "Aquarian Exposition…Three Days of Peace and Music…The Woodstock Festival." They were going to hold it in Woodstock, New York; I had actually been to a small music festival there the previous summer and had a great time. But the musicians at that festival were local and unknown, at least to me…and the festival these ads were touting seemed too good to be true—the ad listed practically every major band...including The Band, Hendrix, the Who, the Jefferson Airplane, Grateful Dead, Iron Butterfly, Joan Baez, and on and on. I remember thinking that the major omission seemed to be The Doors and Bob Dylan (which remains a consummate irony for me in that the festival that really did define a generation was named after the town where Dylan lived at the time). Because of all the big names listed in the ad I thought that Woodstock could be "this year's Monterey Pop," the festival and subsequent film that had made a big impression on me. Of course, Woodstock the event and the film turned out to be just a little more important.

That spring turned into the summer of 1969...and oh, what a summer it was... the war in Vietnam raged on, men walked on the moon, and then came Woodstock. I had rented a house for the month of August in Roxbury, a remote rural town in the Northern Catskills with my then fianceé, now ex-wife, Cathy Hiller (but that's another story). This was a very conscious back-to-the-land type of venture (going up the country)! By this time it had become even more apparent that the Woodstock festival was going to be a major event. I had decided that unless I was going to be able to work on the film of the festival, I would not go, as I sensed the crowds were going to be overwhelming. But it was unclear just a few weeks before who was going to make the film, but finally I heard that Mike Wadleigh had gotten the nod. I knew Mike from NYU and immediately got in touch, and much to my delight, was told they could use me as a cameraman.

Almost everything about Woodstock became memorable, and our trip there was no exception. Cathy and I started out on Thursday, August 14, at dawn. I'm a car buff to this day, and at that time I owned one of my all time favorites, a British built Mini Cooper 1275S, a performance-enhanced version of the innovative sedan that had the look of the kind of car that forty clowns would climb out of at the circus, with its tiny ten-inch wheels and odd square shape. But that odd-looking assemblage was actually a brilliant engineering breakthrough, which brought the word "mini" (as in miniskirt) into the English language. And it was a barrel of fun to drive.

The route that made the most sense from where we were was almost exclusively twisty back roads, which of course didn't disappoint me in the least. I was tearing along at somewhat over the speed limit when disaster struck. A deer bounded across the road just as I came around a bend and though I was almost successful in my heroic attempt to swerve and avoid it, the car sideswiped the deer, was thrown into a skid, and we hit the guardrail. We were Okay, but the car was totaled, the deer was dead, and we were stranded. We walked to a remote house, phoned the

State Police (who graciously drove us back to town!), and thus began a day-long odyssey to get to the festival. First we took a bus to Kingston, New York, renting a car, and driving to the site at White Lake, New York—an inauspicious way to begin what would become perhaps the most memorable three days of my life.

When we arrived at the festival, the site was a center of feverish activity. A few thousand attendees had arrived already, but movement around the area was still reasonably unfettered, and I got a chance to get the lay of the land. Fortunately, I knew a lot of the people who were working on the film either from film school or previous working situations. On Friday morning there were production meetings and camera assignments were determined. Not being acrophobic I volunteered to man a camera on a stage left tower for the first afternoon's performance and thus Cathy and I had a panoramic view of that historic first afternoon. As I was shooting coverage of the vast human mosaic visible from the tower I began to realize that this had become more than this year's Monterey Pop and was some kind of cultural landmark and turning point. It's hard to remember now, but at that time young people with long hair and countercultural (for lack of a better word) lifestyles were still considered a fringe minority. Suddenly, here was a manifestation of the fact that this was no longer the case, that by sheer weight of numbers we had entered the mainstream…a fact that was to become a decidedly mixed blessing.

As that Friday afternoon continued, reports of clogged roads and hippies swarming over the countryside began to filter back to those of us actually at the festival, along with the ever increasing presence of helicopters flying bands and supplies in and out. As twilight turned into night, I made my way down the tower to shoot more close-up footage of the performances. A last minute addition to the stage had been built—a catwalk suspended about three or four feet just in front of the apron of the stage allowing for terrific low camera angles of the performers— and I spent parts of all three nights shooting MOS footage from there as well as wandering around backstage looking for opportune moments to shoot when there was enough ambient light. And of course I was able to soak up some great performances in the process.

There was a lot more to the festival than musical performances. For one thing there was waiting between performances for bands to set up. It must have been during one of these waits that we met a stage crew member who went only by the name of Muskrat. If memory serves, he was an itinerant carpenter, a true 1960s person who lived day to day, without an official identity (social security number, bank account, etc.). He had signed on to help build the stage and then had become part of the stage crew. Over the three days we had several recurring discussions about the festival, life, love, politics, and philosophy in general. Unfortunately the almost thirty intervening years between then and now have obscured any but the most general recollections of the content of those dialogues, but aside from the people working on the film, he's the only person I met at the festival whose name has stuck with me through the years. The concert went on into the predawn hours, and I don't believe I got any sleep at all that first night.

During the day on Saturday, I shot a lot of footage out in the crowds surrounding the stage, both audience and general activity around the festival site. Already having done a fair amount of editing, when I began to shoot audience reaction shots, I quickly realized that it would be helpful in postproduction if the editors actually knew what groups were playing and what they were playing. I began scribbling the names of the groups and the selection (if it came over the PA) as the announcements were made. I would then shoot ID slates either before or after the particular selection. Though at the time I could not know that I would be lucky enough to be editing some of the very footage I was shooting, the knowledge of which groups were playing and what they were playing turned out to be a valuable resource later on.

Walking around the outer areas of the festival with a shoulder mounted Arri 16S was a fascinating experience. In addition to photographing activities far from the center of the action, people would come up to me and ask about why I was shooting and I would get a wide range of responses when I told them it was for the official festival documentary. There were a fair number of negative responses, along the lines of "you're ripping off our culture," and probably an equal number of "far out...right on...where's it gonna be shown" type of comments. But it was later that day, in the backstage area, that I had my one close encounter with what could have been a really ugly situation.

As I was returning to the backstage area to replace my exposed film magazines with new ones, I saw a Hell's Angel type on a Harley trying to force his way past the security detail at the gate to the restricted backstage area. The people manning that particular gate were not security guards, just festival staff who were controlling the crowds. He was threatening to run them down, his gripe being what made those people in the backstage area so damn special that he couldn't go in there and look around. The bike's engine was running and he was inching it forward trying to force his way into the backstage area. The security people were blocking his way, but I could see the situation was coming to a boil. Had I had film in the camera I would have been shooting away, but for the moment all I could do was observe. Not surprisingly, the guy was probably stoned on something, or some combination of things. It looked to me like things were about to get physical.

Usually I'm a quiet, nonconfrontational type of person, so maybe it was the spirit of the whole festival (peace and love!) converging on me at that moment, but before I quite realized what I was doing, I heard myself joining this very heated discussion. Like a fool, I started reasoning with this guy. I pointed out that there had been no violence at all at the festival, and surely he didn't want to be the one to bring it all crashing down. I told him that everyone who was backstage was there because they were trying to do their jobs. Surely he could understand that... He had a job, didn't he? I pointed out that if there were no reserved areas all of the several hundred thousand people who were there could converge on the stage at will, that the bands couldn't set up or get in and out, or get on stage to perform, and there would be no festival. I remember that I kept coming back to the fact that I was simply there doing my job. Somehow, against all odds, my reasoning finally got to him. I believe we all shook hands and he finally backed up and backed off, and everyone else heaved a huge sigh of relief. And hey, I felt really good about myself. Exhilarated, I went back, picked up some fresh magazines, and headed back out to shoot some more, my only regret being that I had missed getting footage of a dramatic moment...but who can say how it would have turned out had I had film in the camera (ENRAGED BIKER RUNS DOWN HAPLESS DOCUMENTARY CAMERAMAN!).

By Saturday afternoon it had become clear to everyone in our little corner of the world and in the country as a whole that the festival had become an historic event. TV crews were all over the place and we were hearing that the story was front-page news across the nation. I'm sure it wasn't at the time, but for me, the events of the festival are blurred together from about Saturday afternoon on... all that remains are fleeting images remembered as if from a dream...Crosby, Stills & Nash mesmerizing the crowd...the Jefferson Airplane at dawn on Sunday morning...overwhelming fatigue after two nights without sleep...the legendary rainstorm...The Who with Pete Townshend and his disintegrating guitar... Hendrix ripping through his psychedelic take on the "Star-Spangled Banner"... and then Monday morning with the site looking like the remnants of a Civil War battlefield, except the bodies were sleeping instead of dead.

It was a wrap...except that it was really just beginning, but I couldn't know that then. After three days of living in some 1960s Shangri-la, the real world began to reassert itself. Giving some other crew members a lift, we drove to New York City Monday night (I remember being stopped and hassled on the Palisades Parkway by a New Jersey State Trooper who clearly was hoping for a pot bust, but I guess we didn't give him probable cause, though if he had been telepathic we would have been in big trouble). I turned in the rented car, took care of some odds and ends in the city, borrowed a car from my stepfather, and we headed back to the Catskills to finish up our month in the country.

ELEN ORSON

SUMMERTIME BLUES

(ELEN ORSON WAS SIXTEEN, maybe the youngest assistant in all of New York, when she joined the staff as an assistant editor; but later she found herself "drafted" into the "army" as an onstage camera assistant. The second part of her piece can be found in "Post.")

It was late July of 1969. I found out through friends that a company uptown needed to hire an assistant editor, and I was looking for work, so I called for an interview.

The day I trekked to Wadleigh-Maurice, I was nervous. Their studio was all the way up Broadway, farther uptown than most film companies, really far from the labs and studios of the Midtown "Film Ghetto." I could assume that this place would be stuffy and uptight, so I did something civilized with my hair and dressed respectfully, fidgeting with my skirt on the uptown bus as I rehearsed my résumé in my head. They were looking for an assistant to "sync the dailies" on a film about a wilderness survival school in the Grand Tetons. I could do that, I was confident, even though I had heard that it was shot entirely without clapsticks.

But the moment I walked into the studio something seemed, well…a bit odd. I had heard that this company made educational films. But this didn't look like a scholarly place, not at all. There were long-haired hippies. There were women here, working. Editing was one job in the business where women were actually accepted in the work force, but here there were so many! And young! Doing everything, not just editorial. And the place was a buzzing beehive of activity.

My interview would be with a man named Dale Bell. The door to the editing room was open, and I could see him, sitting there, expecting me. I walked in, shook his hand, and then caught a glimpse of the editing machine behind him, this astounding tank of a contraption that looked like a NASA control room console. This was a Keller, later known as a KEM, and virtually no one in America had ever seen one before. I forgot my lines. I just said something like, "Hi. What the fuck is

THAT?" and then lost myself in studying its rollers, screens, and plates. I think he liked that, and I think that's why he gave me the job...

Days later, I started working on the dailies, syncing the picture to the sound by eye. The film was indeed shot without slates, since the film crew had to follow these kids through the woods and over mosquito-infested streams in the mountains, and there was no way to stop for anything like a clapper, or any other conventional form of sync reference. How was I to know when there was supposed to be picture to go with the continuous rolling sound?

Lucky for me the soundman had contrived a gizmo which would make life easier for me. After the shoot, in the transfer from 1/4" tape to sixteen-millimeter mag track, he had rigged a Bic pen over the mag, connected to a meter somehow, and every time the meter detected the radio signal of the camera's sync motor in the recording, the line would move from one side to another. Pretty infuckengenious. This way I could at least get into the ballpark, "eyeball" the picture into sync, and proceed happily on my way through the reams of film.

But now I had this new job, and although I needed the money, it was summer vacation time and I had been making other plans. Since early summer, New York FM radio had been running ads for a wonderful festival that would take place in Woodstock, upstate New York, in August. This was going to be the largest confluence of rock culture ever held. I wanted to go in the worst way. I had even begun hinting to my parents that I might be "attending a three-day music festival," something like the Newport Folk Festival. But this film was my new priority, so taking off now would be out of the question. Bummer...

During this time I was sixteen and I was still in high school. I worked on films during summer breaks, and at night during the school year. I commuted into the City from New Jersey in my school uniform, and changed at the bus station for work.

Two years before, when I was fourteen, a whirl of political activity swept the planet and I dove headfirst into it. My friends were hanging around in the park but I had other ideas. Through my older sister Janice, I became involved with a documentary film company in SoHo. They let us work with them though we had no formal skills, because we had a willingness to learn and we would work for free. We were documenting the student demonstrations and upheavals of 1968; through these experiences I learned to load a camera in a riot, and record sound while being tear-gassed, and edit for three days with no sleep.

This led to actual jobs, for money, later on with a company in Midtown Manhattan.

Bouncing between school and work, from 1967 to 1969 I didn't sleep much. But people sensed that I really wanted to make films, and they were happy to teach me. I became the Resident Hippie Chick. And I gained a variety of skills, from camera to editing to bookkeeping. Today such a level of independence at that age is practically unheard of, but this was the 1960s and I was a youth. Looking back, I doubt there would have been any way of stopping me.

THE YOUTH MOVEMENT AND THE DISASSEMBLY OF THE STATUS QUO

There is a quote going around that "if you can remember the 1960s you weren't there," which means you were perhaps among the timid who did not inhale or lose your mind in those crazy days. Or it meant that you were on the other side, a lock-jawed mallet-headed member of the Establishment.

In the late 1960s, all you needed was love and a pair of bell-bottoms and the urge to try anything new, and that was your ticket to the other side of the establishment fence. And rock music, loud rock music, was the language, the inspirational prayer, the very embodiment of the young counterculture psyche. It formed a perfect loop and so it's hard to say whether we wrote the words or the words wrote us. The lyrics united us, reminded us, helped us along. And drove our parents crazy.

Perhaps it's also true that if you need an explanation of the 1960s, you won't understand anyway. To us, the youth, most of our parents and their values were hopelessly outdated. They were still stuck in WWII regimented thinking after twenty-five years, and they were absolutely dedicated to the preservation of the status quo. They would say, "Those darn kids don't appreciate the sacrifices we made for them!" And we'd say, "No, thanks." We wanted all Cold War hostility to stop so we could get on with life, liberty, the pursuit of happiness, and justice for all, which had been promised but remained undelivered. We had been raised on the high moral ground. And Superman, and Roy Rogers. We had been raised to look for the bad guys.

John Kennedy had given us dreams of journeying to outer space in rockets, and instead, the government was shipping us off in truckloads to Vietnam, and chucking us in front of live ammo in somebody else's war. After some ten years of this, to believe in the righteousness of the Vietnam War seemed ridiculous and immoral. We were no closer to peace; just the opposite. And our parents kept bugging the boys to cut their hair and register for the draft, because it was the right thing to do. If your country calls, you don't question it.

War, status symbols, racial bigotry, suburbia, plastic values and the whole system had to go. It Had To Go. Anyone over thirty was not to be trusted. We picked up our knap-sacks and split. We wore flowery exotic clothing and grew our hair long, so as not to be confused with anyone even vaguely associated with the Army. We sat in, tuned in, turned on, took it to the streets, put it on the line, put it up against the wall...or wherever else "it" needed to go.

This wasn't only happening in America. Versions of the same scenario were happening all around the world, and this made us feel incredibly strong; we were sure the world was ours and we were going to change things, at last.

The 1960s should be called the beginning of a Restoration period. This movement included restoration of decaying neighborhoods; healthy eating; spiritual consciousness and humanistic values, free speech and art forms. The ball started rolling then, even if it took three more decades to accomplish some of these repairs.

Documentary film was an art form that had been heading for oblivion in the late 1960s. The market for documentaries had crumbled from its once-thriving status in the 1940s. But now the political urge to change the world and to show others the truth found perfect expression in documentary film making. Such incredible events were going on all around us!

If you were talented and fortunate, your films would appear and win prizes at some international festivals, and you might even make back the negative cost. But for the average young filmmaker in the 1960s, if you wanted to make a documentary, it meant that you had to beg money, be a true believer, work "independent." You had no health insurance unless you lived off your grandmother's trust fund or you borrowed from your parents (More rounds of "Cut your hair!" "Why don't you get a real job?"). Or generally, you were late with the rent. Your teeth needed care in the worst way.

Later, TV was to provide a huge market for documentaries, which would save the documentary industry. But that was later. Much later. In the 1960s, TV presented fluffy variety shows and spy sit-coms, and most theaters only ran Hollywood feature films. There was nowhere to show your film for money. In the 1960s, you had to be nuts to want to pursue the documentary end of the business.

I was admittedly nuts at the time.

BEING THE YOUNGEST MEMBER OF THE CREW

As I settled in at Wadleigh-Maurice, the reason for the buzz around the office soon became clear. The producers were working on a deal to film Woodstock Festival. It was iffy because the financing wasn't in place and the concert site itself kept moving around. They were trying to get a handle on how to pull a huge crew together on spec, and everyone knows you never work on spec, or shell out your own money. Not on a documentary. You could get reamed. I started to pick up on the rumors in the wind: They were going to film it, somehow.

But this would be a cruel joke: here I am working for the same company filming the Festival, and I'm assigned to a different project. (One that they were scrambling to get finished in case the other deal came through.) And then in the week before the Festival, a decision was made to start filming, and a recon crew left for the site. My little heart sank, and I went back to my dailies while all around me, World War III broke out.

But on Thursday I got a call from Thelma Schoonmaker, who had gone upstate. "Elen," she said, "It looks like we're going to need all hands on deck. We need anyone who can help to come up here. You'll get paid for the weekend, don't worry, but we'll work that out later. Can you come up?"

Can You Come Up? Words of Magic. A dream come true. Yes, I'll come up!

That night I told my mother that I had a job for the weekend filming the same festival I had wanted to attend. She had seen the news reports of hoards of people heading for New York State from everywhere, and was not sure I'd be ok. "But we're not camping out, like the crowd, Mom, we have hotel rooms." And when she realized I would be in the company of Adult Professionals, she gave permission. I had spoken to some friends who were driving up that night and I could hitch a ride with them. I packed hurriedly and sped off to meet them in New York.

We drove up the Thruway, and the traffic got thicker and thicker. I remember nodding off in the back seat, and waking up to glimpses of people, and more people, and more people walking past the crawling cars. My friends were able to drop me off at the Silver Spur Dude ranch, my hotel, and they left me with the phone number at their hotel. They said, "Call us and we'll give you a ride home." But of course I didn't see them again till we were all back in New York. And they were never able to get back to their hotel anyway.

In the morning I met up with the other crew members. Some were familiar faces from the studio in the City. Many were not. We wolfed down breakfast and then were ferried over to the festival site. It was the last I would see of my lovely little hotel room, although I didn't know that, but somehow I knew to take my bag and bedroll along just in case.

This was the opening day and workers at the site were literally running to finish in time for the late-afternoon start-up. The production assistants were gathered up backstage, in the area that was reserved for the film crew. Coordinators with clipboards buzzed around. They had to shout over the noise of hammers and saws; carpenters were still building the rotating stage platform! We were asked who could do what, and then were assigned to various tasks. I raised my hand when they said "Does anyone know how to load magazines?" and suddenly I was on the camera crew.

Underneath the stage, we set up plywood tables and began preparing the artillery for the coming battle. But I had never loaded an Éclair magazine before, I had only worked with Arriflexes. No one had time to teach me the fine points, and this was very critical stuff, so I was reassigned to a cameraman as his assistant and runner.

The air was thick with preshow jitters. I shook hands with my cameraman, Ted Churchill, and he looked over his shoulder at the coordinator, sort of to say "You must be kidding! This five foot three teenage girl is my assistant?!" I asked him to have complete confidence in me, or something like that I was at least able to convince him that I had cut my teeth in the Chicago Riots and I could think on my feet. But I think what won him over in the end was not the way I could wrap cable, but that I could give a really good backrub, and that's important to someone who has held twenty-five pounds of steel on his shoulder for ten hours straight.

Ted Churchill and I, we were a team. He was given a camera position high atop one of the lighting towers, where a platform had been set up for us to shoot. One of the first scenes of performance would ultimately be ours, a pullback from Ritchie Havens on the stage to the great sea of people.

We had four magazines, and it was my job to go down and get more film when the first two mags were shot. That would give me about twenty-two minutes to make it through the crowd, drop off, pick up two more magazines, and hustle my butt back up the tower. I had brought a shoulder bag which was just large enough to hold two magazines, and I could sling it over my back and hoist myself up the scaffolding, a good sixty feet of climbing. Don't look down. Don't look down. I am not afraid of heights, but I'm terrifically afraid of falling. However I did this all afternoon, through the beginning hours of the concert. The crowd got thicker and thicker until there was no path left to get to the backstage gate. I had to just tip-toe over and through the solid mass of people, laying on their blankets and grooving to the music. Faces became familiar...jog right at the blue blanket, hop over the cooler...wow, they're still kissing...

As night approached, a drizzling summer rain began to fall, and they called us down from the tower and repositioned us on the stage. The performances were happening in a steadier fashion now, whereas the afternoon had been a little shaky with many long gaps between acts.

Ted would give me a warning that he was about to run out of film, or I would be standing behind him watching the meter and I would warn him. I waited for the click-chunk-whir sound, that meant the last frames had traveled through the gate. Ted would whip off the mag, I would thrust a new one into his hand, he'd slap it on, I'd take the spent one, mark it, and stand by again.

So close to all that fine music...the rest of the evening was a blur of satisfying mental bliss, gauzy around the edges. The mist made everything softer and we settled into a work groove, while the rain gently fell, creating the first installment of muddy mud. We had to stop several times while filming, because the humidity made the film emulsion swell, and the film jammed in the gate. Whip off the mag, clean the gate, slap the mag back on.

The day-by-day details of the weekend are well documented elsewhere. When I close my eyes and think about it, I see moments, brilliant flashes and swirls of color: Joe Cocker's shirt, Janis Joplin's velvet tunic, the purple light in Sly Stone's hair. Green hills and black clouds; everything feeling muddy and damp. I can smell the mix of film emulsion, cow, and trampled alfalfa. And people, people moving everywhere, smiling muddy half-naked happy people. I remember keeping track of what we were doing—not just the film crew, but the crowd, and the performers; Were we eating, resting, waiting, swimming naked in the lake, going to the Port-O-San? Was it time to go to the medic tent? Find our shoes? (Hope that they've dried...) Get ready for more music? I had an extremely fine vantage point for it all.

All of us on the film crew became participants in the Festival, not just *voyeurs*. Can it be that the performers took it up just a notch further, flashed their pearly whites a little more, strutted their colors finer, because of the big round camera lens not three feet away? I hope so, if everyone got a better show out of it.

I remember moments where the NBC and ABC news crews came to the edge of the stage and did their thing: man with a mike and a video cameraman, trying to summarize the event. We looked at them with more than a little pity. They would not be eating Hog Farm food, or singing along with the songs because they did not know the words. Straight. Kind of cute, in a Lawrence Welk sort of way. Hopelessly disengaged.

I remember the Big Storm. That's me in a huge close-up, my long hair whipping with the wind, on stage in the scene where the storm's hitting. I was holding the AC line to the camera in my hands, looking up at the HUGE black clouds and little spurts of lightning, wondering if we'd all be fried on the stage. Ted was doing a three hundred and sixty degrees pan of the melee when they were about to cut the power, and he caught me in frame as he came around, and held on the shot. Thanks, Ted.

I remember sitting out the Storm after they cut the power, under the stage with my blanket over my head, a strange calm break in the busy-ness of the previous two days. Then Marty and another crew member came along and asked if I had extra blanket, and we all sat there for a while. Just taking it all in, calmly, like we were on a park bench or something. I remember being tired with every muscle hurting…I remember the ride back home in a VW van with a lady from the crew (Anne Bell). I remember the overwhelming sadness that it all had to end, this giddy, silly, wonderful display of the strength of our…oneness.

MICHAEL SHRIEVE

AS A STREET GANG, OUR WEAPON WAS MUSIC

(IF ELEN ORSON DEMONSTRATED that youth counts, listen to Rock and Roll Hall-of-Famer Michael Shrieve, who caused an overnight sensation with his drum solo on "Soul Sacrifice" with Carlos Santana's band.)

DALE: You were the youngest person on that stage at Woodstock. What did you see when you went out there for the first time and what did it feel like?

MIKE: Well, yes, I was young. I had turned nineteen a month prior in July, so I was young. But everything felt in place for me. I remember thinking when walking up toward the stage at Woodstock that it was like standing on the beach and looking at the ocean. And there were people as far as you could see until the horizon. It was nothing like anything I'd seen before. It was a fantastic feeling actually. It felt really good to see all the people. There was a lot of talk prior to being there and that first step onto the stage so everybody was filled with anticipation.

DALE: When did you get there, to the site?

MIKE: I believe it was Saturday. We had been slaying in Woodstock. In fact we were living in a rented house. We had been there for several weeks to a month. Santana had their first album out, that had been on the road for a long time in the States and we were taking a break. We were relatively unknown outside of California. We were quite popular in California, but we were playing with all the big groups and a lot of the big festivals, the Atlanta Pop Festival and the Texas Festival and playing with—so we were very familiar with the groups—The Dead and The Airplane and Janis Joplin and a bunch of R&B groups we were touring with as well, who happened to be on these bills.

So we were in Woodstock and we were in a place and jamming and living there. And a week prior to the concert, there was a lot of talk and then some days before on the news, they started showing the reports and photos of all the cars coming on the interstate. And as time got closer to the concert you saw that something extraordinary was going on.

There were a lot of festivals in those days, so I wasn't jaded, but it was another festival. Then you began to see that something else was happening beyond anybody's control. When they closed down the interstate, you knew that something was really going on. We were glad to have been in Woodstock already. But then we soon found out that the way we were gonna have to get to the site was by helicopter. And so it was all very exciting. We did fly in on a helicopter and it was an incredible sight to see.

DALE: Now describe that from the air.

MIKE: Well the interstate was closed and there were cars parked out as far as you could see. Also I think that it's important to recognize—I'm sure a lot of people have explained the mindset at this time. People wanted to change the world and the music and the culture was the vehicle that people wanted to change things with. So to see the interstate closed and then to fly over the site and see all the people was absolutely incredible. And you realize that this hippie thing had gotten to this point. You felt like it was really peaking and that something was seriously going on now. It was all exhilarating. It wasn't something that you felt afraid of. You felt a part of something larger than yourself. As a nineteen-year-old kid, I honestly didn't feel afraid to—first of all the band was very much a unified force and we do what we'd do everywhere else. But the feeling was extraordinary of seeing the massive people gathered together.

DALE: Mike, what led you to be a drummer. What was the path that you took as a young person, to end up in Carlos Santana's band?

MIKE: The story of how I got in Santana is a story worth telling. It's a classic rock and roll story. Should I tell it?

DALE: Go ahead.

MIKE: I was living in the Bay Area. I was a young drummer, very much into jazz and R&B and not so much into rock and roll as a drummer.

DALE: Where did you get that from. Was it from it from your parents, or from environment, or a combination?

MIKE: Yeah, there was a lot of music around the house. My father listened to a lot of jazz when I was growing up. And the house was filled with music. And then, I don't know. I just started picking music up that I liked. And I started playing drums in the eighth grade and then got really serious through high school and practiced a lot and got into stuff.

Obviously, the Beatles were happening and this was the beginning of the San Francisco scene. Jefferson Airplane, The Grateful Dead and these kind of groups were playing around and I was very young, but they would come and play down the peninsula, the Palo Alto area.

I lived in Redwood City, but I would go see those groups whenever I could. I was critical of music at the time, in terms of listening to what I liked and what I wanted to play, but I was very much a sixteen-year-old who was interested in the scene and what was happening.

Jefferson Airplane played once in Palo Alto and I remember going and thinking—looking at Jack Cassidy and Yorma—how does one get like that? What do you do to become that? There's such a great distance from where I am and where they are. Not particularly that I wanted to be them. But the way they dressed and the way that they appeared to be was such a great distance from where I was. I was curious.

So I started playing around and I got pretty serious about it. I started going to the Fillmore up in San Francisco and seeing such great music. I mean Cream and Yardbirds. And Yardbirds with Jeff Beck and Eric Clapton and Miles Davis and B.B. King and Ray Charles and Charles Lloyd. A lot of good stuff going on. And Michael Bloomfield was the guitar god at the time. And there was a concert going on there called Super Session. With Michael Bloomfield and Steven Stills and Al Cooper. And for some reason I started calling my friends. I was still living with my folks, and I said let's go see if we can sit in, which was absolutely absurd. I don't know why, but I thought about it that it was even possible. But everybody said no. Everybody said that's crazy. And I decided that I would go by myself, just so that I could say that at least I tried.

So I borrowed my father's car and I went up and made my way up to the front of the stage and pulled on Michael Bloomfield's pant legs and said, "Could I sit in?" And I figured that he'd kick me in the face and say, "Get out of here, kid."

DALE: Right! Kicking sand on the skinny kid on the beach?

MIKE: Absolutely. He was the deal. And the shocking thing was he said well, what do you play. I said, drums. He said, Well the drummer's a really nice guy. And I don't even remember who was playing drums. Let me go ask him. And at the point, panic set in and I thought oh my God, I was doing this to say that I tried.

And next thing I know he said, Yeah. It's okay. And I actually sat in at the Fillmore, which was the Mecca. This was the place that every musician wanted to play. So here I was sitting in with these guys that were great to me.

DALE: Who was playing with you?

MIKE: Broomfield and Stills and Al Cooper was over there playing the organ, but I must say in all honesty, I don't remember one second of being on that stage. That's how frightened I was. But it passed. It ended I was backstage afterward and now here I am backstage at the Fillmore, so I'm really cool. And Stan Markem and David Brown. Stan Markem was the manager of Santana at that time. And David Brown, the bass player.

They came up to me and said "We heard you play and you sound really nice and we're thinking about getting another drummer. We have a band called Santana." I was very familiar with the band, in fact I had seen them with my brother at a church dance in Redwood City and said, I really wanna play with these guys. And I had seen them around. They were already playing the Fillmore. Well, I didn't hear from them. I saw them once play at a high school in our area and I went backstage and said hello. Met the other guys.

A year passed and I was hustling recording studio time at a local studio in San Mateo, California, for my own band. It was kind of a fusiony group. I had my father's car again. I would go to the studio often to try to hustle time and I was doing some recording. And as I was walking in the door, the drummer in Santana was literally walking out. They had just had a big fight a big falling out. And they were recording their first album for CBS and Clive Davis. So there was a bad vibe around the room.

But a couple other guys remembered me and recognized me from that night and said, You wanna jam? So it was a year later and we're jamming in the studio and we played all night long. And at the end of the evening, it was late in the morning at this point. They took me in a room and they said, "Would you like to be in the band?" And it was just like that.

They literally followed me home to my parents house in my car. I woke my folks up. I said, "See ya later. This is where I get off." I packed some things and I got in the car with all of them and drove up to the Mission District in San Francisco and I slept on the couch. And I'll say one thing, same thing I said at the speech at the Hall of Fame was, although it was a time of peace and love and hippies everywhere, I soon found out that this band was not so much about peace and love.

It was more like a street gang. And its weapon was music.

I was very young and very white and here I was living with a black militant, a Mexican, a Nicaraguan, a Puerto Rican, one other guy from down the peninsula, Greg Rawley. So things started happening fast from there.

DALE: You were, at that point, seventeen?

MIKE: I was about to be eighteen. We played the Fillmore and people booed when they first saw me, because they were a popular band and they missed the other drummer, until after I did a drum solo. And they gave me a nice ovation. Shortly after warming up at gigs, we went into the studio and recorded the first album. And then hit the road. So Woodstock was a part of that.

DALE: You went on the stage when at Woodstock. Go back to there now.

MIKE: It was Saturday. On that day it was Canned Heat and Credence and The Dead, Janis Joplin, Jefferson Airplane, The Who. John Sebastian played as well.

I'm not sure of what the scheduling was supposed to be. We were there hanging around backstage and something happened. They said, "You're going on now, instead of two or three hours later down in the afternoon."

DALE: Were you at all aware at the time that there were film cameras up there? And was there discussion?

MIKE: Yes, there was discussion, but it was very much a different time then, than it is now in regard to cameras and consciousness of that sort of thing. We were musicians. And we were the kind of musicians that Clive Davis would come in the studio and we'd kick him out. Billboard—we'd throw away, and so we were very much, as a group, just into the music. And into being a unified force for the music. Not even at a cosmic level, but just more of a street level.

We were very aware that there was cameras. There was a lot of photographers and there was—It's not the sort of thing that you go and check your hair for. We must've been nervous, but as a group we played to each other. We didn't see ourselves so much as performers, but as musicians. And I think part of the strength of us being in a situation like that.

We were an unknown band. Bill Graham got us on the bill. If it wasn't for Bill, we'd never been on there. I believe we got paid five hundred dollars to do the gig. Just sort of token money to get on the bill. So yes, we were aware that there were cameras and it was being filmed. Of course, nobody realized the outcome of that.

DALE: When was the first time that you saw yourself in the film?

MIKE: I recall that we were in New York. We had a day off and *Woodstock* was showing. So as a group, we went to see the movie. We had heard nothing about it, except that we were in it. We were waiting in line like everybody else and the prior showing before was coming out and we saw that people were pointing at us and looking at us and everything else. We weren't famous yet or anything. We were a working band with a record out and working really hard.

We went in to see the movie and there we were sitting together. It was unbelievable. It was an unbelievable experience for me personally. Seeing myself split on screen into six times or whatever it was. I didn't know whether to shrink down in my chair or stand up and say that's me, that's me! It was unbelievable and they picked the best piece, I mean "Soul Sacrifice." We had a tough time that day, because it was hard staying in tune. There was a lot of problems with the sound and I believe that, that might have been the only good piece of music that we played that day.

DALE: That's indeed possible, you know. A lot of this was checker boarding and taking our chances and we would film several pieces.

MIKE: Right.

DALE: But our advance guys—Eric Blackstead, Danny Turbeville—would say, This one is a really hot one. And the configuration of the musicians is such that they'll be doing this and that and, I've seen it before. So that we'd have a little bit of advance knowledge. But it could also be that two cameras ran out of film, or something else on another piece.

MIKE: Right. Like I said, seeing myself split up on screen during the drum solo was real something. To see yourself in a big movie theater playing a drum solo. Parts of it that I, even today, I cringe when I got so soft and when I left space in it. And then I'm thinking, "Come on! There's over half a million people, keep the beat going!" I was more kind of into this jazz thing and all this and that. But after the performance, even at the movie theater, the theater burst into applause. It was the most unbelievable experience for us to see that. It goes without saying that clip changed our lives.

DALE: Do you recall what Carlos's reaction was?

MIKE: I don't recall specifically, but I know that Carlos was having a difficult time staying tune that day. It shows on the film a lot of things about Carlos. It shows his intensity and his passion and his urgency. He was also really stoned as well.

He was doing his best to stay in tune. As he says now, he was saying, "Lord, please just keep me in tune."

I think everybody in the band was completely amazed at seeing themselves on the big screen, for one. And that the performance came off as something really very special. It captured the band—I mean it was great at the concert. Wow. We were a perfect group for that day. We were a perfect group for that festival. We were tribal. Rock and roll is one thing. There was a lot of great acts there. But we were really tribal and it just works for that many people. It still works, but that sound was very effective.

DALE: You say that clip changed—What did it change?

MIKE: First of all, it broke us as a band internationally. My first clue of that was one our first trips over to Europe and Montreux Festival. And I took a walk to the local train station to pick up some magazines, cause I was always a magazine freak. And I walked in and I see this magazine called *Rock & Pop* and I'm on the cover. And it's a big picture of me from Woodstock. I had never, of course, been on the cover of a magazine before, or anything like that. Reviews were coming out and I guess the record was out. Or the film was out, of course. It just broke us everywhere and Santana took off after that film happened.

The effect on me long term, now that I have lived—I'm gonna be fifty in July—so I can look at it now in different stages of my life and my own reaction to *Woodstock* and other people's reaction to *Woodstock*....A place where you can deal with it in a certain way.

For years, I tried to beat it. I tried to do stuff and do other bands and do solo records and just think well, I'm known for *Woodstock*, but I've got to be known for other things as well.

I remember when I was about thirty-five, I was living in New York and walking down Fifth Avenue and somebody said, "Hey Mike Shrieve! Man I just loved your solo in *Woodstock*!" Which is something, of course, I'd be rich if I had a dollar for everyone in my life that I heard that. And the guy looked at me for awhile and said, "Look man, what's happened? You've gotten older!" And I was thirty-five and it really upset me.

And I just thought, Is this what I'm gonna be trapped as? Known as the drummer from the *Woodstock* movie all my life? It really upset me. What I realize now is that the concert meant so much to so many people. To them personally. I meant so much to so many young people who have told me that "We saw you there with all those guys. All those heavy hitters and you were our age. And you didn't seem to be any older than us and you inspired me to play the drums and it just goes on and on." And you can't fight it.

Finally you just have to be gracious enough to say, "I'm grateful I was there." It was a wonderful day. It broke the band. There's nothing that I'm gonna do in my life that is more momentous than Woodstock. I may do better work. I may play better drums. I may record better solos. None of it matters. It does matter, but it doesn't matter in the big scheme of things.

Woodstock is what people know me for. So it's had an incredible effect on my life. I can go anywhere in the world and meet people and everybody knows that drum solo in Woodstock. So I finally have arrived at a place where I feel glad that I'm still making music and I'm creative and I'm not dead. I have a fertile mind and I'm active and everything else. It's taken me awhile to get there.

DALE: Is there something called the Woodstock Effect? How do you see it and how does it radiate today, if it does?

MIKE: The Woodstock Effect? There's different ways you can look at these things. One, you could be bitter, which I was on the road to being. There was a period when I saw some other guys—peers of mine, some big name drummers, like Mitch Mitchell and Ginger Baker and some people like that—really got bitter and angry.

Things change and so do the guitar players. Jimi is a myth and Eric is a myth. Carlos is incredibly famous everywhere around the world. And so there's a lot of musicians that felt like they got ripped off or they didn't get their due and became very bitter and I just made a decision that I did not wanna grow to be old and bitter when life has been wonderful really, if you take a look at it and just say, "Geez, did I expect this?"

Just keep going and remember the reasons that you started doing music initially, because you love the music. So just be grateful. Don't be bitter.

DALE: What is the power of music to a society? How do you see that? What is its role?

MIKE: There's no getting around the fact that the power of music is great and, truly, I think that music has the power to heal. I believe to change, to take hate out of people's hearts and contribute, in a way, to turning negative situations into positive situations.

The power of music is like no other power. What I call it is invisible architecture. Music is invisible, but you—What other forms are there that effect you so much emotionally that as soon as you walk into it, you can't see it, you can't touch it, you can't smell it, or anything. But it creates this place. Depending on what the music is, it can transport you into different areas emotionally. It can change your life.

Whether it's the blues or whether it's something like a concerto or a beautiful lamenting Spanish piece, or classical music or drums from around the world. It can be, on one hand, an immensely unifying experience with a lot of people, or it can be the most personal experience one could ever have.

Its role in society? That's a tough question, and I think everybody would have a different answer unto what should be the role of music in society.

And that would be the same question as well, "What is the role of art in society?" You see it manifest in many different ways. Some artists and musicians believe that art should be a mirror of what is happening in society. So a lot of music in the 1960s was like that. It really tapped into what was going on. What was the pervasive feeling about what's about to happen? There was a feeling in the air that the times were changing. A lot of people were changing internally.

Now, you have that with hip hop and rap music. What they're saying is "We're talking about what's going on." Other people would say, this is negative. They would say, This is what's going on.

Every musician and every artist has their own personal approach to it. I think if you see the power of music then you have a responsibility to use the music in a way that is uplifting and unifying. That's just the way that I feel about it. If you realize the power of it, then I think that you would want to do that.

But there are great musicians throughout history from Stravinsky, to Beethoven, to Jazz musicians, who just do the music that they have inside them. They're not thinking in terms of the effect on society or anything else. So there you go.

DALE: There you go. Thank you.

AL WERTHEIMER

IT SOUNDS LIKE AN ADVENTURE

(AL's ENGAGING PERSONALITY AND cinema style allowed him to film some of the most memorable documentary pieces in the movie, an honor he shares with David Myers. Al and David were also our oldest cameramen/directors. Both began as still men.)

DALE: So June, July 1969, you just finished working with Robert Drew?

AL: Well, no, Drew was out of business at this point, I mean I was with Drew from 1960 to about 1962. They were developing the equipment in order to separate themselves from the soundman; in other words, getting rid of that umbilical cord. Working with Mitch Bogdonovitch, Ricky Leacock and Don Allen Pennebaker. Mostly Pennebaker's ideas. And it had its ups and downs but: the name of the game was "how do we get (cinema) photographers, and filmmakers, to be as free as *Life Magazine* photographers?"

You separated the soundman from the camera man. And the harder job was really for the soundman, to get good sound. The soundman was the one who was supposed to be in on the scene, very close to the subject, so that you would get the sound you wanted and not a whole lot of background sound.

The cameraman could reach out, with a long lens, and operate between twelve and 120 millimeters; and he could go past crowds. But the soundman couldn't.

You know every time there is a technology shift from what was basically using tripod studio camera-type thinking, to portability, to make it more like still photography, where the still photographer was free to come and go, free to climb up on the ladder...Film hasn't quite gotten there yet.

I firmly believe that the more uncomfortable the still and film cameramen and technicians are, the closer they may be getting to the truth. The darker the scene, but still readable in terms of film, the more the people will be acting more natural to their personality rather than posing for the camera. So you know this is maybe why you get close to the truth in dark bars. And people tend to be more themselves.

And that was part of what I was hoping to get into to seek out the truth. Well the truth is relative; it is relative to what your state of mind is at a given point in time, what your background is; how, later on, your truth as a cameraman is going to be fitted in with all the other truths of the film director and the editor, and in the end your truth becomes part of the blend of their truth. And then the question is, how do you take an event that's three days long, with all kinds of feelings, and then eventually make it into a two, three, or four-hour film, which is an abstraction, and two-dimensional magic-act of what the reality was?

So there you are, Dale, you're calling me up and you're saying, "Al, can you spend three days up here at this bungalow, at the Silver Spur at White Lake?" I keep thinking about Woodstock and yet it didn't occur at Woodstock. So…

DALE: What were you doing then?

AL: I was tinkering around with trying to put together a film that I shot on John F. Kennedy, and somewhere along the line you called me, and I asked myself, well, who's Dale Bell?

DALE: Where did I get your name from?

AL: Well you might have gotten it from Channel 13…'cause I had some credits on that beats the hell out of me what the jobs were now. Oh. David Wolper had a whole lot of my footage for a film called *The Making of the President*, the Ted White stuff, cause I had back in 1960 I said to myself, "I'm gonna try to do a one-man point of view of an American Presidential campaign." And at that time Paul Shutza goaded me into saying, "Come on, Al, get off your ass! Come on the road. I'll get you into the camera car." So instead of shooting stills, I grabbed a hold of a Bolex, the first camera I got a hold of. And then I had access to an Arriflex. And we went on the road, with Kennedy, and then later somehow I was able to get myself with Nixon. And we went down to Texas and North Carolina and so on. And here I had about eight thousand feet of film, on Kennedy, everywhere including Hyannisport, the night of the election return. And also Nixon traveling mostly through the South. All that sort of got me going into the direction of film, from stills. And this is how I got involved with Bob Drew and got to know Leacock and Pennebaker and eventually wound up with Grenada Television…

Then you got a hold of me. And I said, "Well, this sounds like an adventure, I don't know any of these guys, I don't know Mike Wadleigh, I don't know Dale

Bell, but it sounds good, and I hope they can pay my fee..." And it was a modest fee. I won't get into the nitpick but the bottom line was, it sounded like an interesting thing. Song, music, lots of young people, it's Upstate New York, I got into a car and next thing I know I was at a bungalow...

DALE: Do you remember what day you went up and who you drove with?

AL: I think I drove alone.

DALE: Did you have a soundman with you?

AL: No, but I was given a soundman by the name of Pitts.

DALE: Charlie Pitts.

Al: After the first day, I lost Charlie Pitts. He disappeared on me. He decided to take his clothes off and go swimming. I needed a soundman so I got a young college kid, no training whatsoever, who wanted to be a filmmaker; I said "You see, this is a stick mike. With a Sennheiser...it was a long one."

DALE: Shotgun?

AL: No a shotgun was always an Electrovoice, but it was something like an 804. And said, "Try not to jiggle it. Try to hold it fairly steady. And when you turn the sound on, here's how you do sync, you push the button and if you can't push the button turn to me and slap the mike with your finger and that'll be our sync mark. We gotta do something. And then just follow me. Just be there. And then when you see me settle in on something, try to get the mike in as close as you can, without getting in the way. And just make sure that you're not on 'Test', you're on 'Record.'"

So then the question was, "What do I do up there?"...it felt like an adventure was about to begin.

DALE: Did you and Wadleigh ever have any kind of a conference about what this film was really going to be about? What your sort of 'assignment' was, what his vision was? Were you on the grass, outside the stage...

Al: No, the only thing I could remember about Wadleigh was that he had very long hair, looked like Jesus Christ or images of what Jesus supposedly looked like, and he looked at me and I had fairly short hair.

And I remember we were already at the site...Somehow I had gotten my car parked, at the site, and yet I remember doing these young kids. [In the movie, we refer to them as "The Kids By The Side of the Road."] I must have walked from there, back out on the road. But at any rate, in this van which we used as a…place…all the camera people, Ted Churchill and…we sort of picked our spot, we were trying to get our little space. "This is mine. I'm gonna leave my extra magazines here, my extra batteries there,…don't touch it!" Y'know? And we sort of hoped that everybody would respect that And most of the guys were working with Éclairs, I wasn't. I was working with an Auricon.

DALE: But also, you were not assigned to the stage…

AL: Mike said to me "Al, you look like you could fit in in town. Go see what you can find in town." And I said, "What do I shoot?" And he says, "Well, you figure out what to shoot. Whatever interests you. Stick with it, y'know?"

So, he didn't want to give instructions. He was not about to tell me that when I get to town I'm gonna find such-and-such and do such-and-such. So I said, "all right…" So that's when Pitts was still with me.

DALE: Well, did you feel this was off-putting? Was this the kind of instruction you could deal with?

AL: No, I felt that since I ultimately wanted to be a director myself, this gave me the chance to direct my own little scene. How it was going to be edited later, I don't know, I didn't know what to expect. And sometimes, if you don't expect anything, and you stay loose and hopefully, if your equipment's working and everybody's awake and you don't lose your soundman, and you don't get muscle-bound, things will develop. Just keep your ears and eyes open.

So you go in there and you find that this little town is being drained of all its gasoline. There's nothing left in the gas pumps. And then like a herd of locusts… the stores have been cleaned out, then next thing you know you get some older people, uh, who were complaining about how these hippies don't appreciate what our boys in Vietnam are going through, and you've got this whole argument about the pro and the anti-Vietnam old people.

Meantime, you'd have some long-haired kids going into the store and this is all kind of taking place on the sidewalk. And then the young people would get involved in a discussion with the old folks, and you're just kind of seeing the points of view develop, and you can't preconceive this. The dialogue is too good; it would be very hard to script.

And I remember what Drew once told Abbot Mills, he said "Look: for God's sakes, stay on their faces! I don't care if they're hitting a hammer or they're putting something in a bag. Show me what their emotions are like while they're hitting the hammer." So I said to myself, "All right Al, slow down, don't be jerky, don't go back and forth, stay with the face. See the reaction. Then go, slowly spin over and see if you can get the person who's talking. And try not to zoom in, focus, zoom back, try to be smooth, you know?"

So what happens is, you've kind of got one eye through the camera lens, watching your story; and in the meantime your other eye is open, looking for things coming into the scene. So that you can prepare yourself to move off that to something else.

So typically, when you do still photography, you close one eye, you have the other eye open, and the only thing you see is in the viewer of the still camera. But in film, you sort of have to be aware of what's coming in. For all you know, there's a herd of people coming across the street.

So originally, when I first got into films, I thought a three-second take was long. I thought a one-minute take was exceedingly long. Then I started working for Bob Drew, and they went through ten-minute rolls. Never stopped the camera. So then I said, "Well. Ok. Never stop the camera. That way, at least, you might get a nice chunk of material."

DALE: Tick off for me…What did you shoot? What do you remember you shooting?

AL: Well, I shot the scene in town…around the grocery store, the gas station, if it's still in the film. I shot the kids on the side of the road; one said she's gotta go to Guatemala or something and he was talking, it was sort of a philosophical discussion about this young couple and she had just come back from somewhere but was going somewhere and somehow it sounded like she was going to South America.

DALE: In the editing we would refer to: these are "The Two Kids By The Side Of The Road."

AL: Is that what it is? Well they were "Two Kids By The Side Of The Road." And that's one of my shots.

DALE: Did you do the one with the…

AL: With the farmer and the uh..?

DALE: Repairing under the car?

AL: Yeah…uh…"…It's a shitty mess! I can't get the cows milked…" And then the girls would be asking the farmers wife for a favor to call so-and-so…That's all my footage.

DALE: "Shitty Mess!"

AL: We just decided: have the camera rolling, walk in, and say "what's going on here?" And then he's able to just give his opinion...y'know, "...how can they just leave cars like that?"

DALE: "Six Ice Cubes Out of the Bag." Was that yours too, you know the guy, somebody comes in, they want to buy six ice cubes out of the bag....

AL: From the farmer....

DALE: Or from the store owner.

AL: I don't know about that, if it was in town it was probably mine. But the other thing is the lake, you know, all the stuff around the lake, where I finally got myself a boat and went out into the lake. And shot from a rowboat people swimming, with the tents on the shore.

And then there was some mounted police I recall, going through. And I said, "Uh-oh. Here comes the confrontation, I smell pot everywhere." You know, pot was in the air. And no, everybody was being very considerate, and everybody kind of properly closed their eyes and there was no confrontation. And that's when I lost Charlie. After that scene, I followed a bunch of nude guys on the road, and I came back and I found myself my new soundman, trained him a little bit. And there were these two nudes and I followed them from the rear, and then I sort of stopped and got into an interview with them.

And then ultimately I did wind up on stage. With...who's the guy who's things were flaring? This was at night...

DALE: This was Roger Daltrey?

AL: Sly and the Family Stone. Now I don't recall that whole "Star-Spangled Banner" business... I mean, everything sort of blended together. I mean, Charlie and I were still talking and we wanted to go back to the car which was parked now at some kind of information booth...

DALE: Did you do "The Woman in the Information Booth"?

AL: Yeah, she's going, she's kind of panicking and she's looking for her sister?

DALE: Right, her sister, they've gotta go to court on Monday?

AL: That's right, that's right, yeah, that's my stuff.

DALE: What was going on in your head when she's spouting all this stuff off?

AL: Well she's telling a story. We're all telling stories. I'm telling a story. Her story was one of, she's looking for somebody in these three, four, hundred thousand people and she can't find her, and she might be on, might be on Lysergic Acid or something. There was a lot of that going on, and my concern was "What am I getting in the frame?" And as long as it's interesting, hold it.

So when I went to the Information area, I was concerned about "How do I make a little scene out of this?" There are a lot of different faces, a lot of young faces, there are some concerned people, some people are slightly panicky, some people have lost their shoes, somebody's telling a story, they're each telling each other. And just hold the camera steady as Bob Drew would say. Stay on the faces and let the people tell their story.

And then when it starts getting a little bit slow, move off to somebody else who's telling a story. And if it gets boring, stop and go somewhere else. And so you get the establishing shot and you go in and the rest of it would be a bunch of faces. And then you'd see these helicopters coming in and you'd say "How Bizarre!" I mean, you've got Marine helicopters, and you've got Hippies, and they're not supposed to be in the same scene together, but how come they're here and how come the Media's now here? And then you find out that the road is closed and... What was his name? The news guy, one of the...

So now it became a media event. It no longer was the individual stories, of these people.

I remember when we first went there, there was a fence. And then all of a sudden the fence came down. And then, I mean, how were you going to hold off these hundreds of thousands of people from not coming in? You might as well be generous and let them in because you would have had a riot on your hands if you tried to take them out.

And then of course, the rain. The Rain. The rain was really a main character in this event. And I was so tired at night and then there's a point where you don't give a rap.

DALE: Where were you sleeping?

AL: I was sleeping in the car that I had rented to bring up. And Charlie Pitts was also sleeping in the car. And then the next thing you knew, other people were trying to get into the car. And you're saying to yourself, "Now why do I want all these...I know it's love, and uh, love and peace. But I don't know any of these guys...and I've got a lot of fancy equipment here and it's my livelihood, and it's

MY car, and what are they doing sleeping on the hood? And sleeping on top of the car?" And after a while I said, "I don't care."

And so I must have gone to sleep, and dawn came, and I remember hearing these coke bottles and Pepsi bottles clinking, clinking, so now I was back in business, and photographing. I found my soundman again, and I see these guys doing sort of a Jamaica, what do you call, when you go like this and you try to go below the stick…?

DALE: The bar…well, you're not talking about the rain sequence?

AL: Yeah, the rain sequence, so I started shooting that and they started to slide, and they start to do a…

DALE: There was a…

AL: Well, it was like a spontaneous happening in the mud, everybody was getting…

DALE: Were you afraid yourself, I mean, of the rain or anything else like that?

AL: No. No. I mean the thing was, they were involved, you see once you get involved, once people are involved, they've got enough on their mind. And then I started trying to get people sliding into me and it was like a happening. Nobody knew exactly what the next move was, but if you just were patient, it would happen.

DALE: But you were getting mud all over your lens, and…

AL: No not on the lens, I might be getting mud on the camera, but not on the lens. I could care less. Maybe a drop or two of water, and that sort of helps the mood of "Yeah. We're in the rain." But it was sloppy. And you could either complain and bitch about it, or you can enjoy it. And it was like going back to childhood. Mud pies. And sliding. So that's a whole scene that developed, I didn't know whether it would get in, or it wouldn't get in. But it is again something that interested me. I mean here are people taking sticks and bottles, and making music.

DALE: It was as primitive as the first people did with stones and rocks.

Al: Probably.

DALE: What were your travails as a cameraman. Was your equipment breaking down, where were you carrying all your extra gear, your magazines, your film stock?

AL: Well we basically had a truck, a trailer, where you left the excess equipment. I remember it was sort of to the right of the stage, facing the stage. You always hoped that the stuff would be there. I mean, what goes through your mind is,

"There are so many people..." and yet everything was there. Nothing was lost. At least I didn't have that experience. Now, of course, since the equipment belonged to me and it wasn't rented, I tried to keep it as clean as possible. But there's only so many magazines you can carry and still be free...

I think we were carrying around several extra magazines in an old army over-the-shoulder bag so it would be something soft that you could carry and still leave you mobile. I mean, this is getting back to the problem of getting rid of that umbilical cord, between the soundman and you, so that you could each not trip each other up. And my job was to just go out there and hunt for scenes.

And then eventually I wound up on stage and I was doing some shooting, and when I was on stage I was surprised at how close Wadleigh would get in to shoot. I mean, I never saw a guy who would be three feet away from the performers, with a camera and then later on I realized he had a five point seven lens, or a five point nine lens, and there was extreme wide angle. So you know, he'd have that real "in-close" kind of look.

And essentially, that was sort of his main position. Where, when I was filming, I was basically filming as a second or third banana in that group. To help. If anything I would shoot the musicians as they'd go backstage, as they were in the wings. I remember Janis Joplin was running from the front of the stage to the back of the stage. Take a little swig, and then run back out to the front of the stage.

DALE: What was for you the most fascinating, the most intriguing thing that you came away from this experience with?

AL: Well, you get caught up in the event. I mean, first it's a job, then you find out it's a happening. Then you find out "How does a town of this many people come and then eventually disappear?" And then, what is happening with the sea of mud here? I mean this was once a field, and now, it's nothing but mud with things that were of value like blankets and shoes and bags and that are just garbage. But they're not really garbage, they're mixed up in the earth and they can be separated and probably recycled. But nobody's about to do that, you find that..depends on how people think. You find that people whose interest is in farming and getting in and out on a road are more concerned about being proper and orderly, while young people who've got nothing to lose, they don't have a lot of property they say, "Hey, this is wonderful. We're having, uh...it's a happening. It's love and peace."

It's just a question of whose point of view you see this from. And so then you wonder "Well, were these older people young once and would they have done what these young people are doing or is it just the process of aging that you become more conservative and you just don't do these things?"

I just found that the diversity of...there was a lot of "Me! Me! Me!" in a kind of a personalized selfish way, and then there was a lot of giving, where some people were really giving. They were trying to help out people in trouble. And the incongruity of this whole business about helicopters coming in ferrying out people who were sick or pregnant...and the combination of putting together Vietnam veterans with flower children...you know, it just, just, all kind of, is all part of the tapestry.

So you think you have answers and then you find out "Well there are no answers." It's just the various shades of a story. And then of course there is the commercial part of it. There are a bunch of promoters who thought they were going to make quite a bit of money, and have a successful happening or that's the way I perceived it and then some guy like Wadleigh goes and puts whatever he's got on the line, and probably what he doesn't have on the line, and it's like a make-or-break project and all you're gonna wind up [with] is with a lot of reflections of peoples' bodies that are essentially two dimensional interpretations of a three-dimensional world with sound but it's an abstraction.

And that's going to ultimately become something which will have a life of its own. It won't be the reality. And it will be manipulated and depending on who's got the final say on it...And you're part of it. Now you find you're just part of the whole where, when you were doing still photography, you were pretty much in control of what story you were going to do, what point of view you were going to do it at, what you were going to enlarge, and what you were going to show the various magazine editors.

Now, you had to kind of dump your ego and say "Well, I'm part of a team. I don't know what they're going to do with all this stuff. Hopefully I'll get paid for all my trouble. If I don't get paid, maybe my repair bills won't be so high, but even if they are, it'll have been an experience worth being part of." Because it's better than having sat in my livingroom, figuring out what to do with my 1960 Kennedy footage, you know.

And it turned out that it was a turning point in American lifestyle...I mean even today they still say, "Well, you remember *Woodstock*?" You know, *Woodstock* is still in the consciousness, of the psyche of the American public.

DALE: Do you think that we glorified drugs in the course of all of this? Were you filming the drug happening scene up there?

AL: No...That to me was not important, I mean it was there; and there was a certain amount of smoking of marijuana. But, I, I was...I'm was basically a square guy, y'know, I was not into drugs.

Hopefully I can unload this film and turn it over to Mike or you, or somebody and hopefully it'll all...I had no idea, how it all was going to fit together. But you know it's like, you're helping toward, you're putting together two or three or four of the pieces of a jigsaw puzzle. Now once you come back to the city, you're no longer part of the decision-making.

But the strangeness of it all was, is that at one point I owned a Steenbeck. I bought a Steenbeck in 1965 (these are film editing devices, they're flatbeds, they get rid of reels, and so on...). And Wadleigh was looking for KEMs. Which he was bringing in from Europe. These are three-headed machines so that you could do split-screen type editing. And I said I had a Steenbeck and he said "Well, would you rent it to me?" I said, "You want to rent my Steenbeck?" I never rented a Steenbeck in my life. I just used it for my material for Granada Television when I was working for Granada. So having an entrepreneurial business sense I said, "Ok, what do you pay me for it?"

So he was paying me six hundred dollars a month, the whole machine only cost me six thousand dollars. So I said, "Gee whiz. In ten months you have a machine paid for." Big Mistake. The fact that Mike Wadleigh rented my Steenbeck machine was one of the worst things that could have (had) happen to me. Because it set me up for a fall. He paid his bill. The machine ultimately ended up at Chuck Hirsch's after they got kicked out of that other studio that they were operating in. And it stayed there for about four-five months, paid good money, paid my bills. And so now I had my equipment I had myself, I had my Steenbeck operating...I said, "Hey, that's not bad, that's a good way to kind of go through life," and I started thinking about buying and renting equipment. And sure enough, I fell into the trap. By 1972 we had eighteen Steenbecks. Tony Santacroce who worked on the film now was working for me.

There was a shortage of machines, I always had bookings in advance. We would have to sub-lease equipment and that always kept our equipment fully booked. And it all started with Mike Wadleigh. And then before I knew it in 1974 I stopped doing camera work; I was now a full-time machine pusher. I was in the equipment leasing business. And do you know, I stayed with it 'til 1995; and I got worse at it.

And ultimately almost twenty-five years went by and I got suckered in through delusions, self delusions about staying with that idea. Because, it was the worst thing I could have done. Because I essentially stopped doing what I loved to do, which was making films and working behind the camera and even though I was in the Union, I never really, after 1974, got involved in doing any further filming. And it's only now since 1995 that I'm back to, of all things, doing stills! Which was prefilm.

Had it not been for a technological change at the time, to permit the recording of the event, it would have been a different event, on film. It would have been done with tripods, it would have been done in a more formalistic way; there is a certain marriage of technique that goes with the storytelling. Now, we were all experimental in our style, we were sort of go with the flow, attitude; we were able to capture that 'cause the film industry and the dyes and the speed of the film, and the technology of the cameras was such, it permitted us to do it, and getting rid of the umbilical cord...And that added to a certain naturalness, and getting close with medium-wide angle lenses to the subject gave it a kind of a presence that you don't get if you just take a long lens and zoom it out, and, and you don't get that texture. So this film had a certain amount of texture.

In my own case, I was always trying to seek the truth with my camera and tell the story of the truth as I saw it. being naive enough at the time to realize: there is really no truth. The only truth we can do is the outer reflections off surfaces rather than what's going on in people's heads. See the writer can get into somebody's skull; but the photographer has to deal with light and with movement, and with outer reflections. And so therefore we make those things more exciting than they really are when we just look at it. When we're just looking at it, it's one thing, but when you see it through the camera lens, it's another thing. When you look at something...when I look at you, I don't see anything out of focus. You're sharp, the wall is sharp, down there is sharp when I change my focus; but with a camera lens, and certain angles, there's a selective focus, you can play with going from the foreground face to a background face. And then maybe going to a foreground face again. Or hands. And these are tricks of cameras, and tricks of the way lenses see things, and tricks of the way cameramen think.

ANNE BELL

WIVES, SISTERS, AND GIRLFRIENDS

(ANNE WAS ONE OF many wives and girlfriends who accompanied their mates to the site to help out as an "assistant" for three days of peace and music. Luckily, we left our kids at home for the weekend with GranMama.)

Initially, it wasn't that I was a big fan of the music, I didn't know much about it. I was a young mother (twenties-young by today's standards) caring for three little sons and a large old ramshackle Victorian house. I had been an actress in summer stock, and I knew about performance and film from my husband, but I had been too busy to know much about the hippie movement, although it was against the Vietnam war. I had no idea of the adventure that lay ahead of me.

My husband, Dale, asked me to help out with the crew that he was trying to assemble (on spec) to travel up to White Lake and try to film the scheduled music festival. The call went out—all wives, sisters and girlfriends were asked to help.

We packed our new turquoise and white Volkswagen bus with a mattress and blankets, some clothes and food, and the tickets. I started north alone with a map on Thursday. Dale had set up the *Woodstock* shoot and was prepping another (paid) shoot for the following week in Long Island. He could not go with me. He would be flying in film and dropping it from a helicopter during the first days of the festival.

I found my way upstate New York, but several miles from Woodstock, the roads became crowded. I could see long lines of people walking along the road. Then the whole road became full of people. About fifteen people climbed onto the outside of my bus, and at least five stood on the rear bumper (it bent very low on one end and remained that way for the rest of its life). We sold it many years later. To this day I always look at the rear bumper of vintage VW buses hoping to find my old van.

Because I had film crew credentials, I was waved inside the gate bringing my human cargo with me. I was told to drive to the stage and park behind it. That was not difficult because the stage and towers were in the middle of Max Yasgur's vast field and you could see it from any vantage point. The stage crew was hard at work still hammering the stage together while the lighting and sound crews rushed here and there. It suddenly dawned on me that I didn't know anyone, I was alone, in this rapidly growing multitude of people. I had been told to look for Michael Wadleigh and his wife, Renee, but it took quite a while before I found them. After I found them, I never let them out of my sight except to go for food.

I can't remember what I did the first afternoon, but that evening I got hungry, so I ventured out of the stage compound. Everybody seemed to be walking together toward some music which was playing behind the next hill. Someone told me the Hog Farm (see Lisa Law's piece in "AFTER...") was serving food. I remember feeling nervous walking alone in the dark with all these people and not knowing where we were going, but everyone seemed happy and in good spirits.

When I finally got to the top of the hill, I could see long lines of people snaking past tables where people were serving a sort of gruel (some sort of hot vegetable and oats mixture I think). I don't know how I got a bowl and spoon but everyone got fed. People were sitting on the hillsides all around the little valley where the Hog Farm had set up camp. Bonfires were burning and some people had brought assorted instruments and were playing music, while other people danced by the firelight making lively silhouettes against the night sky. Later I found my way back to my VW bus, climbed inside and went to sleep. The next day Mike assembled the crew and work began in earnest.

I had met Mike and Renee when he was filming my three-year old son, David, in a public health spot warning parents to lock up medicines to keep them out of reach of children. Mike, as camera man, invented all sorts of games to keep David interested and performing on cue. Mike was delightful and charismatic. His wife, Renee, a very beautiful dancer, had been recruited as I had, to help on the shoot, and she assisted him hour after hour throughout the weekend. Michael gave me a pad of paper and asked me to keep track of which groups were performing and the titles of the songs that they played. He had a stage crew of cameramen and various helpers. Mike and Renee stood on a dropped ledge that ran across the entire front of the stage. I was placed to his left just in front of the huge battery of sound speakers. Directly below us on the ground was the crowd behind a wooden fence which kept them from overrunning the stage.

That afternoon the first thing that hit me was the SOUND! After three hours of the first performance I felt like I had been through an artillery barrage. It was extraordinary! I was supposed to be writing down the titles of the songs but most of what I could hear of the lyrics was "yah yah yah." It all sort of ran together. Between songs, I leaned back and asked the crowd leaping up on the fence behind me, and someone or other was able to tell me most of what I needed to know. At twilight, I happened to glance up at the hill and was astonished to see that there was a mass of people reaching back to the horizon. I had no idea that so many had arrived. Everyone was leaping and rocking and waving their arms in time to the music. That night I heard Joan Baez sing "Joe Hill"—her voice so crystal-clear, with such depth and purity it took my breath away. That night she was supremely beautiful.

I can't today remember the order in which the bands performed over the next three days, but they were so different, each one very individual. None of us who were there will ever forget Country Joe's cynical and heart-rendering lyrics when he sang "be the first one on the block to get your boy home in a box." Everafter, when I think about any war and blind patriotism, I can hear that song.

When one sat on the edge of the stage as I did most of that weekend, the most extraordinary impression was the outpouring vortex of energy that engulfed us during those eighteen-hour stretches. The bands were giving it everything they had. It was an outpouring of joy, humor, sex, sadness, love, anti-war and most of all—longing for a better world. We were all very awake at that moment. It was as if the rest of the world just stopped and for that weekend we lived only in the present and that present was very ALIVE!

The next morning I was promoted. Michael found out that Eric Blackstead and the sound recording crew were keeping track of songs so I was sent with a few others under the stage and given a lesson in how to load sixteenmillimeter film into magazines for the cameras. It was a leap of faith on their part because if we made mistakes loading we would ruin a take which could not be repeated, and the film was in scarce supply. Dale was still begging and borrowing all the film he could find in NYC because Warner Bros. decided to fund the film when they heard what was happening at Woodstock. We had a film crew of six young cameramen trained in handheld documentary work for the stage. They were all friends of Dale's and Mike's and had come to Woodstock on spec (meaning no guarantee of salary).

I was assigned to assist Don Lenzer who would be shooting up stage right as I remember. His camera was attached to a long cable and he and all the other camera men were completely mobile moving about the stage following the performers. With all six men filming at once in sync, the editors were able to show the performers from all angles on a triple-split screen. My job was to follow him around dragging the cable, and get him newly loaded magazines as he ran out of film. The cable was very long, and I had to carefully coil it at the side of the stage so that I could take off after him without getting tangled, when he moved quickly.

We were in the middle of a performance that Saturday night. My eyes were glued to him anticipating his every move. He had remained fairly stationary for the first half of the performance—then the band began gyrating in a frenzy of motion. Don took off after them and I began feeding him more and more cable. Suddenly I felt a tug behind me. I whirled around and saw that a Swami was sitting crosslegged on top of my coil. He had his eyes closed and was rocking back and forth deep in meditation or something. I rushed back and sort of tilted him to one side while I extracted the cable. He never woke up.

The next group to play was "Mountain." Leslie West, their lead singer, was a huge colossus of a man—hence the nickname. Don was wearing earphones so that he could hear Wadleigh giving stage directions. Suddenly he threw off his earphones and left them dragging by their wire on the stage floor behind him. Someone motioned to me to get the earphones and put them on. I crept out on stage and retrieved them. The order came through quickly "Don't let the earphones touch the stage floor again—they will short out all the others." At this point I moved down stage right crouched in the shadows, reeling out the cable to give Don some play.

The wire that connected the earphones to the cable was fairly long. Mountain began to move—downstage—stomping his foot furiously as he kept time to the music. The spotlights moved with him. Don began to move too—upstage behind him and away from me. The cable whisked across to him until the wire to the earphones was used up. In order not to obstruct the audience's view, I took off the earphones and lay down flat on the stage with my arm fully extended holding those earphones off the floor. Mountain and the spotlight advanced. To my horror he paused about three feet away from my head and began a sort of pounding war dance. The spotlight encircled both of us for the rest of the song. I looked up and saw that he had his head tilted toward the sky and his eyes were on the back of the audience. I couldn't tell if he even knew I was there, but I lay there frozen making sure that the earphones never hit the floor.

I can't remember how late we worked that night but I finally made my way back to my VW van and fell asleep. It was pitch black. Suddenly I was awakened by the sound of people rapping on the windows and shouting and rocking the car. It had started to rain and they wanted to get inside. I didn't understand what was happening and terrified I hid under the blanket until they moved on to the other cars.

In the morning I was sent out of our stage compound with Dick Pearce, a cameraman, and Joe Louw on sound. We were told to mix with the crowd and get them to talk about their feelings and experiences. Everyone was young. All were a little damp and bedraggled after spending the night in the field, but they were mellow and happy. The air was warm and the sun was out. The mud games, and nude swimming, and love making was in full swing. No one was angry. It was a magical land, a garden of eden of sorts (albeit muddy), no disapproval, no sin, no negativism, no power plays—just fun.

After lunch the music started again and we all got back to work. It was fascinating to watch the cameramen work. Wadleigh was all over the performers; like a cobra moving around the lead singers picking up odd angles and extreme close-ups. When The Who were performing, Peter Townshend became annoyed and kicked Wadleigh's camera, causing the eyepiece to smash into his face. Luckily Mike was not hurt badly, but we were all shaken as we watched Townshend stomp and smash his guitar at the finale.

Across the stage behind the performers, Dick Pearce's open eye glinted like a cat's as the lights hit on his face. He seemed to do most of his shooting with both eyes open.

Between sets I took a break to visit the Port-O-San. (Who of us will ever forget the movie's interview with the "Port-O-San Man?") Behind the stage there was still a lot of work going on. Big moving vans with generators and all sorts of supplies were coming and going. There was no line at the toilets because they were for the exclusive use of the performers and stage crews, however, the stench was "out of sight." I had to hold my breath when I entered and hurry. A new band started to play and the sound was terrific. Suddenly, coming from the adjacent Port-O-San I heard someone shrieking and beating on the wall. As soon as I exited I realized what had happened. A truck had backed up against the other Port-O-San door and trapped someone inside. No one could hear them screaming unless you were in the toilet next to them. I found the driver and had the truck moved and out stumbled an hysterical person, lucky not to have been asphyxiated. What a way to go!

That night The Who played until 5:00 a.m.

Sunday was the day of the afternoon storm. We were all on stage when the wind suddenly picked up. This got our attention right away because the lighting towers began to rock. Then the huge tarps that cover the stage began to flap like sails. All of us kept glancing up at the sky but the band played on. After about ten minutes the rain struck hard. Everything was soaked. All the crews were running around trying to cover the speakers and musical equipment. Those who had them donned yellow hooded rain jackets and tried to lash down everything on stage. John Morris took a wet microphone and talked to the crowd trying to discourage anyone from running. He told them to settle down and ride out the storm which they did. He told them we could continue the performance as soon as the rain stopped. The wind and rain lashed down harder, and the crews began moving to find cover—afraid that the light towers might come crashing down on stage. I found myself underneath the stage dragging several cameras and electrical equipment to safety—or so I thought. The rain began to pour down between the cracks in the stage floor. It was then that I noticed I was standing on a snarl of huge (as big as a man's leg) electric cables. I didn't know if all the power was disconnected but at that point I crawled under a moving van that was parked next to the stage. I think someone passed me a baloney sandwich and then I fell asleep from exhaustion until the rain stopped and we all went back to work.

Monday morning the audience was a real mess. Everyone was covered with mud and all their blankets and sleeping gear were soaked. The field smelled like a barnyard. Nevertheless they had bonded the way survivors do, and their smiles were triumphant.

I believe I woke up to the sounds of Jimi Hendrix playing the "Star-Spangled Banner." It was a wild rendition that seemed to embody our feeling of having survived something extraordinary. A communal awakening to the possibilities that we were young and strong and people of good will. That weekend we had come together voicing the desire to create a better world. Peace and Love.

DALE BELL

THE PORT-O-SAN SEQUENCE

SATURDAY AFTERNOON AT THE festival. Headquarters for Wadleigh-Maurice Productions, Ltd. on-site at the festival were located on a couple of pieces of three-quarter plywood under a trailer to the left of the stage as you faced the audience pit.

Inside the trailer was the equipment we had brought to the site: begged, borrowed, actually rented, and none of it stolen! We guarded it almost every minute during waking hours. And at night, if someone had to sleep, they slept at the tail end of the interior of the trailer so that anyone getting in would have to literally trip over them.

Fortunately, our noses reassured us that we were not far from the quantities of Port-O-San toilets, just in case.

David Myers and his soundman, Charlie Pitts, had just returned to our headquarters that Saturday afternoon. As he was getting his gear together, picking up raw stock and audio tape for another run into the crowds, I noticed that a worker had just backed his truck up to the many toilets. He got out of the cab of his Port-O-San truck and moved to the rear to unhook his hose. Through diligent training gained at NET on prior documentary shoots, I always knew it was best to ask permission of someone before you filmed them. It eased the relationship, broke the ice.

I approached him with my hand extended in typical Ivy League fashion. He took his glove off and we shook hands. I told him we were making a film, Would he mind if we filmed him? No, was his reply. I knew we were never going to get a signed release from all those who we had filmed; my action was pure courtesy, an introduction on behalf of all of us to a stranger doing his work.

I backed out of the way to beckon in David and Charlie, who by that time had gotten their stuff together and were ready to shoot. David walked in, the red light on his camera indicating that he had begun to roll. Charlie was at his side with his microphone, alas, not pointed exactly where it should have been. Never at a loss for words, and one of the most innocent and engaging people in the world, David began his conversation with the Port-O-San Man.

Should I say that the rest is history? Almost. As he had done so often before, and as he had always trained the rest of us neophytes, David Myers kept shooting, walking, talking, and moving his camera, in and out, anticipating exactly where the image ought to be to coincide best with the words he was hearing or expected to hear. David, the cameraman with the best ears I had ever seen, delicately followed the unfurling of this little vignette, asking those pointed, double-entendre questions with his wry sense of humor ever so slightly suppressed behind the constant twinkle in his eye. "Getting a little behind, aren't you?" was David's first little question which prompted all the rest of the quintessential sequence.

Now where, I ask you, does David get it from? "Getting a little behind?" Whatever does he mean? Whose behind? Or Who's behind? Is he cleaning up other people's behinds? Is he implying that the Man is getting some? David! Each and everytime we were to view this sequence in the editing room, we had to stop and marvel at the innocence of David's opening inquiry. For how long had he known this man he was talking with? A lifetime, or so it appeared. Both were simply doing the job they came to the site to do: David to document, the Port-a-San Man to clean toilets for the company he worked for in New Jersey.

"No," the Port-O-San Man replies, just as innocently. He doesn't know that the young man behind the camera lens peering out with one eye so he doesn't land in the muck himself is the man who has taught us all how to be documentarians. Eternally youthful at the ripe age of 55, he was older than the man he was following with his camera. Though born in the early outbreak of the First World War in 1914, David was far from a man of war. When it came time for him to serve in World War II, David, this warrior for peace, filed with his draft board as a conscientious objector—in the Second World War, mind you. No one did this then, no one except David. To fulfill his obligation to his country, which as a New Englander, he felt he must, he served as an aide in institutions and hospitals, planted trees in the forest. He did not believe in killing, even for all the reasons millions went into the Second World War.

As though it had been orchestrated, rehearsed, and now reenacted, this *pas de deux*, this duet between David and the Port-O-San Man continued. Uninterrupted by the camera, the Port-O-San Man keeps talking with the inquiring man who wants to know how being here, at this site, plays on the man with the long hose. As the Port-O-San Man moves from one stall to another, David follows diligently, never losing sight of the overall narrative thread of this extraordinary man in his eyepiece.

Recall that not seventy-five feet from these stalls, musicians are on stage, playing to half a million people. Helicopters land on the hill behind, unloading performers with their instruments, raw stock for the camera team, and food and water. On the road behind the stage, a swill of humantide flows up and down hill, on their way from somewhere to somewhere else memorable. Already they are in the history books. The Woodstock generation has survived one night on Max Yasgur's farm. Brought together by the lyrics and the music, they symbolize millions elsewhere who share their perspective and their feelings about a new direction for society. By being peaceful, by recognizing they all are brothers, they send a powerful message to the rest of the world.

The Port-O-San Man finishes his task. It hasn't taken him long. His training dictates that he rinse the seats of the stalls with disinfectant. Armed with a long handle, he brushes the liquid around the toilet seats. Now, they are clean enough for the next customer. He knows he will be back again tomorrow. And then, as though feeling the pulse of this multitude, he pauses and releases this simple sentiment born of the recesses of his soul: "Happy to do this for these kids. I have one here, and one in Vietnam." Did he truly say that, unprompted, untutored? Did we get it right? Did no one write that for him to say?

I'm not sure, even as I write this thirty years after it actually happened and still feel the chill-bumps up my spine as I listen to the Port-O-San Man's pronouncement echo in my mind, whether there is anything more profound in the entire movie. Does it compare to "One small step for man..." or "Ask not what your country can do for you?" or "Can't we all learn just to get along?" Was it to capture this essence that we decided to do the movie in the first place? Or does the Port-O-San Man's humanity justify all the heartache we endured and caused in getting the movie made?

Continue to look at the sequence. The Port-O-San Man moves on out of frame. David allows him to leave gracefully. He is on another tack. Earlier, as he began his conversation with the Port-O-San Man, David must have noticed out of the corner of this eye that someone had actually entered a stall and closed the door. In his mind, had he timed the exit of the Port-O-San Man to coincide with the entrance into his frame of the bearded, scruffy hippie? Where did this guy come from? David's instinct must have prompted his arrival. The latch on his door must have indicated to the Port-O-San Man that the stall was occupied; otherwise, he would have emptied its contents and scoured its seat as he had done with the others which were vacant.

The door opens. The hippie sees David, Charlie, and the camera pointed directly at him. David has been rolling this entire time. What timing! The man offers David a smoke from the bowl he was using inside the stall. He extends his hand to David. With a polite "No, thanks!" David claims he is still working—as indeed he is—for he continues his roll.

"We're making a movie." "Oh, what's its name?" the hippie asks. With the twinkle ever in his eye, David retitles our collective effort: "Port-O-San." "Far out!" responds the man with the bowl of dope as he passes out of frame. Always searching for an end to the story, David pans back over the stalls to come to rest on the Port-O-San sign on one of the stalls.

The sequence probably lasts only a couple of minutes, yet it is pure gold. First it represents a pinnacle of filmmaking, the art of allowing something to happen in the frame which is pro-active: the subject engaged by the audience— the filmmaker—who is intrigued with the process the subject is participating in. Secondly, it signals an admonition to every soundman: watch where your subject is and point the mike in his/her direction always, anticipating where the cameraman is going to go. Focus, in other words. Third, it encourages the camera team to find an interesting subject to begin with. Fourth, to recognize that most subjects, if treated with humility and respect, reveal themselves to a camera more so than they might to their closest family members or friends. A camera in the hands of engaging person can extract elements of the soul of the subject. Watch David's ears listen and lead his movements; though subtle, they are always unveiling something new, while modifying the flow of the material.

When this portrait arrived in the editing room, there never was a question that it would find its way into the documentary portion of the movie, virtually uncut. Yet it almost didn't make it, not because of the content but because of the sound.

Fast-forward to mid-February 1970. The Port-O-San Man takes his turn on the dubbing stage, the place where all the sounds originally recorded on site are processed, enhanced, equalized, tweaked, manipulated, and/or otherwise adjusted and modified to make them snap, crystal clear, out of the speakers. In spite of all the patching of cords, pushing of buttons, sliding of dials, opening and closing of pots, bouncing of VU meters, Dan Wallin working with Larry Johnson on the dubbing board, could not crunch the Port-O-San Man's dialogue, or David's either for that matter, so that it would emit at the same level and timbre and with the same intonation as the sound surrounding it. Time was pressing down on us. We had repatched the board several times to effect adjustments. Nothing seemed to be working.

Wads and I were pacing back and forth on the rug covering the floor of the dubbing stage. The big image was being projected above us. Even at this close proximity to the speakers, we were having extreme difficulty with intelligibility. Neither one of us wanted to lose this powerful piece, this symbol of the universality of humanity. But what to do?

Recalling our use of the bouncing ball over the lyrics in the Country Joe MacDonald F.U.C.K. cheer, I suggested that we use a subtitle to allow the audience to read along while they listened to the words. The combination might make the audience hear better. We looked at each other. If high-fives were invented then, it would have been an appropriate use of at least one. The mixers, the editors, all harkened to the idea. So off it went to the title company, preserved indelibly. Yet this was not to be the last we would hear of or see the Port-O-San Man.

During the screening we had for Warner Bros., where students and "Suits" viewed our efforts for the first time on that Sunday afternoon in March 1970 (see "The Longest Optical" in the "Post" section), another spontaneous event occurred. Just after the Port-O-San Man makes his pronouncement about his son on site and the second son in Vietnam, the students (I didn't see any "Suit" doing this!) leapt to their feet and cheered this man for what he stood for. He became an instant hero, a symbol for all caring individuals.

It was the first of many times this happened.

At the press screening in New York at the Trans-Lux Theater in late March 1970, he appeared in full life, dressed in a suit. A Warner staff person, at my instruction, had located the man (through Fred Dubetski at the Port-O-San company in New Jersey). With his wife and family surrounding him, he made his way into the theater, little knowing what to expect. He had been told simply that he was in the film. Period.

When the moment came for his sequence to appear, I moved from my spot at the back of the theater down the darkened aisle slightly behind him so that I could see his face bathed in the reflected light of the screen. As his story unfolded on the huge screen, I saw him clutch a family member close to him. I also think I saw a tear in his eye. But what remains forever imprinted in my memory is the thunderous cheer that erupted from that packed house as they celebrated his remarks. As we had done months before, this warm crowd enveloped him in their arms, lauding his wisdom and compassion.

At the end of the screening, as the house lights were turned on, he was identified for the rest of the audience. Tom Taggart and his family. He stood proudly to receive their welcome once again.

To this day, wherever I have seen the movie, even in London at Leicester Square, the Port-O-San Man received a standing ovation, so purely does he resonate. Yet sadly, this is not the end of this noble story.

Several months after the movie opened across the country, presumably to similar responses, Warner Bros., Wadleigh-Maurice Productions, Ltd., and exhibitors everywhere were served with a lawsuit pressed by attorneys representing the Port-O-San Man and his family. We were charged with defamation of character, ridicule, libel, and he was seeking damages in the millions for what we had done to him before the world. Of course, we were astonished by his action (it was one of half-dozen suits brought against the film for similar exposure or ridicule or whatever). The suit charged that we had not obtained his permission in writing, that we had filmed him in a demeaning occupation, and that to add insult to injury, we had used subtitles to convey his words, as though he could not talk clearly and be understood.

Our hero had been ensnared by greedy attorneys, perhaps? Apparently, everyone in town knew he worked for the Port-O-San Corporation. His job classification was labeled "sanitary engineer." No one had ever inquired about a job description, not even members of his family. Once the sequence in the film was exhibited across the country and around the world, everyone could fill in their own job description. The secret he had maintained from his family for all those years was now exposed. Apparently, his high-school son was ribbed because of his dad's occupation. He was crestfallen; they were shocked that he performed liposuction on dozens of stalls a day. Friendly attorneys must have advised him to sue us.

The lawsuit eventually brought us all together again, but this time in a courtroom with a jury in place. He was with his family, represented by his attorneys. Warners had its legal team. They had paid to bring those of us in to the trial who had primary responsibility for the piece being in the film. David, Charlie, Wads, Bob, Thelma, and I were there, as I recall. Each of us had a different aspect of the story to tell. The jury was presented with photographs, drawings, and other evidence of what we were about; David and Charlie were asked to wear and carry their official equipment package into the courtroom while the attorneys asked the jury whether they thought our team was making a "homemovie" with this professional-looking gear.

I know I felt very sad at this development. None of us bore any hard feelings toward the Port-O-San Man. We simply regretted that he had felt he wanted to press a lawsuit. We hoped it was contingent and did not cost him any out-of-pocket cash. If my recollection is correct, he was offered an out-of-pocket settlement by Warners which he refused, preferring to take the matter to higher courts. Or did his attorneys get the better of him and his family? In any case, he lost.

Warners had every reason to forcefully resist every suit, for a basic constitutional issue was always at stake: privacy. The basic question: if a person appeared at a public event, was the media required to obtain permission from everyone it photographed or otherwise depicted, or did one's attendance at a public event inherently acknowledge that he was temporarily waiving his rights to privacy?

Several suits were brought by people who thought they had been ridiculed by dint of being included in the movie (the man playing reveille on the bugle from the stage on Sunday morning), or caught unsuspectingly in embarrassing configurations (the man making love in the tall grasses who cocks his hat at a different angle once he has completed his session) were two others, yet none of them won. After all, our fifteen roaming cameras on the site were not the only professional documentarians there for the three days! Check the stock footage logs of the major networks. It was a happening, and things were. Look out!

I—we—regret any inconvenience we caused the Port-O-San Man. To each one of us, he was symbol of compassion and we wish him and his marvelous family well. I trust his son in Vietnam returned home safely, but I frankly do not know.

DAVID MYERS

OUR MENTOR SPEAKS

(DAVE WAS THE YOUNGEST fifty-five-year-old at the site, bar none. His wisdom as a cinéma vérité cameraman was already thoroughly established long before he flew in from Mill Valley on his own dime. With uncanny laconic simplicity, Dave guided all of us through our paces, leading always by example.)

DALE: Do you remember under what conditions you first met Wadleigh?

DAVE: Clearly. We were doing a PBS special on smoking. Were you on that one?

DALE: I was the guy who put you together. We were in San Diego and Wadleigh had heard about you and I had heard about you.

DAVE: Like what?

DALE: You had been working with all sorts of people—it was the NET Al Perlmutter unit I had designed this special about the ironies and paradoxes of the cigarette smoking controversy which would be live on film—everyone had to shoot everything in twenty-four hours and then we would edit it in the editing room and figure it all out. So I needed fourteen people.

DAVE: Fourteen cameramen? I didn't know that.

DALE: And you were in San Diego with Wadleigh. Anyway, what was your first impression of Wadleigh?

DAVE: I'll tell you precisely. It was sort of a campfire situation. It was like we were camping out or something. I remember low light. It must have been in some kind of apartment house or something. I met all these other guys and I said, "Where's Wadleigh?" And they said, "He's busy. He's sequestered." They said you'll meet him after a while. Then finally the door opened and Wadleigh came out or I went in and I saw that this gentleman has got his own agenda. And that time we just barely said hello. And then we went and did it…whatever it was.

DALE: You were following the family of a guy who was dying of emphysema. But one of you was at the Veteran's hospital and one of you was with the family. I think you were with the family. That was the first time that you got together.

DAVE: Actually we didn't see much of each other at the time, of course. And then we didn't meet again until some time later, I think.

DALE: That was done in 1967 and I think the next time may have been when I brought you to New York to do Piri Thomas' book *Down These Mean Streets* with Gordon Parks directing. And we spent that month or so—right after the riots—in 1967 in Harlem. You did that wonderful bug-eyed lens thing with Piri reconstructing what it was like to go cold turkey and battering into walls. One uncut magazine!

DAVE: You supplied a wonderful soundtrack.

DALE: By breathing heavily on the microphone. We were crouched together in a corner.

DAVE: We left the sound on the track because it was so effective.

DALE: Anyway, can you remember where you were when we were doing Woodstock? Where you were when you got the call. What were your impressions at the time?

DAVE: I figured what the hell. I was loose. It was proposed—who called me? Maybe it was Binder, or Wadleigh. It was Wadleigh. And he said it's a loose situation. We'll go and if there's funding and if there's anything worth shooting, we'll shoot it. Otherwise, we'll have an interesting weekend. And it was my first rock and roll concert for that matter. I wasn't into shooting rock and roll at the time.

DALE: Really?

DAVE: No, I had never shot rock and roll at the time—in my memory. I'm so nervous having to admit this. But it sounded like, what the hell. And I liked working with you guys—and you were being honest about it so I thought I'd take a chance too. We, of course, had no idea. I remember going up there and I was either in the same car with, let's see, Lenzer—Lenzer at least and we went to a motel about ten miles away. We left all our gear there, except for the cameras, of course. And we thought we'd be back that night. And that was about four or five days before the concert. We never came back, of course, until we picked things up on the way back to NY. But I did take my two essentials, a toothbrush and a little ground cloth.

DALE: When we talked to you from New York, we had no money. And I think I asked you to put this trip on your card. Do you remember any of that?

DAVE: No.

DALE: I remember telling Wadleigh that we couldn't ask these guys to foot their own expenses—their time, yes—but their airfare? You did, of course.

DAVE: I actually don't remember getting up there. I guess I was in the same car with Lenzer—

DALE: It was probably about Tuesday because I think we called you on Sunday and you got a plane on Monday.

DAVE: And they were just building the stage at that point. I don't think they had the stage up yet.

DALE: If you were to describe what your philosophy of shooting is,—your shooting style—is there any way that you can verbalize that? Give a film audience an impression of your kind of shooting style.

DAVE: Well, I play off the people I'm dealing with. I play off what's happening and how people are reacting. That's a simple description—within the context of what we want...

DALE: I've always described you as having the best ears of any cameraman I've ever met.

DAVE: Well, listening is definitely the centerpiece. That gives me the clues. And I'm surprised that so many photographers don't seem to pick up on that kind of verbal—sound cues—people's behavior. Just the way people talk. The emphasis, the way they use language and communicate is a clue to what's going on.

DALE: Because you listen so well, you can anticipate exactly who in a room or situation was going to speak next or react next.

DAVE: Yes. I go with that I don't know whether it's a talent or something. But I listen carefully. I do the same thing in effect on stage with rock and roll. When the music is good enough that I go with it. But I take the cues from what's going on.

Body language also. I was once offered a job with the big guru of psychological analysis of people by body language. What was his name? Raymond Birdwhistle and he was head of some department at State University of Buffalo. Anyway Gregory Basin and I did a film about a schizophrenic, a schizogenophrenic family and I shot a few hundred feet of a mother and a little boy who were in therapy—had some serious emotional thing—and I didn't know exactly what it was either, and I shot this interview with them. And it wasn't even an interview; it was just sort of watching them together. And I'd go to the child and go to the mother and it turned out, when they showed it to Raymond Birdwhistle, he did a better psychoanalysis of the mother and child from the visual, from the movie footage than her therapist had ever done. And he offered me a job with him and I said I couldn't do it. I was interested in photography.

But there is a certain thing about paying attention. I think it's pretty simple. When you're in the groove on something, you're sort of thinking the way they're thinking…whomever you're dealing with.

DALE: There's a short phrase that you once used as to why you got into motion picture photography after having been a still photographer. Do you remember what that phrase is?

DAVE: Remind me.

DALE: That you couldn't shoot stills fast enough.

DAVE: Hey! That's good. Did I say that? That's good. That's very good. Thank you for returning it to me.

DALE: It's yours. I think I got that thirty years ago.

DAVE: No. What actually happened was that I couldn't—I lost interest in my still photography—things I had set up, I mean, deliberate—even documentary footage. But the things that attracted me on the contact prints, and the things that interested me, were accidental. Somebody going through frame. And I thought, well that looks like movie footage and I think I should be shooting movies.

DALE: When you came to Woodstock, was there any sort of shared vision that you got—was there any sort of exchange about what to do?

DAVE: Not that I recall. I was thinking about that the other day. In fact, I told Michael I was very grateful to you. I said to Michael, I'm very grateful to you that you had that little meeting beforehand. Everyone was sitting there on dry grass, and chatting about who does what. And the first thing he said was, "Go ahead, Dave—do your thing. Go ahead." And I just got up and walked away. I never even knew what planning there was. And it was exactly what I wanted; he must have read my mind.

Because I didn't want to shoot—I didn't have a big urge to shoot rock and roll at that time—in that situation, let's put it that way. I really wanted to go out and see what this interesting and really quite significant mass social situation—what was it all about and what was happening. And I was grateful to Michael for turning me loose. I went back once or twice and shot a little bit on stage, but it really wasn't—it was difficult and it wasn't the way I would like to work where I could wander around. The only way you could cover that stuff was to have a lot of cameras and rather limited individual camera movement. And I just wasn't—it just didn't get me.

DALE: When Wads and I designed this part of it—which was really Sunday morning after being up there on Saturday—we said okay, we need these people to do the docu side, these people to do the music side. You probably got the first call because we knew if we could entice you to get there, other people would follow you.

DAVE: Oh, you're talking about your planning ahead of time.

DALE: Yeah. This was the Sunday before. We were actually doing it on Saturday when we went up there. Maurice was really handling much more of the negotiations with the festival people. And Wads and I were insisting on the lip in front of the stage.

DAVE: Very smart move. I think I must have shot a little rock and roll before that because I thought that was the best move you could make. Good for you. You made, not a runway, but a shooting platform that was completely across the stage, but maybe three or four feet below so you had access.

DALE: You could literally put your elbow on the stage and hold the Éclair and it would be comfortable and you could stay that way for a long time. It wasn't too far down or too high up. We just measured and said, "Make it that high." That was really the one thing that the festival people did for us. They were really frustrated with us. Amplify on this whole notion on this sociological mix of people.

DAVE: I hate the word sociology. I was a sociology major for six months.

DALE: Where did your curiosity take you?

DAVE: My simple thought was to get out there and see who's here and what's happening and start relating to the vibes. It was really my only thought. It was amazing because I must have walked at least five miles lateral distance out around and there were little—actually, the atmosphere in some of those little mini-festivals was actually charming and touching. You know, there were a couple of family groups that camped together and they could hear the music and they would dance there and the little kids would dance. It was a different atmosphere from the happening down there on the big hillside.

DALE: Did you have any sense at the time about how what you were doing would be integrated into the whole?

DAVE: Oh, yes. I thought you needed—I mean, it would be not only desirable editorially, but in terms of the emotion—the complex emotions that everybody was going through. You had to have a lot of elements to work with the music. And I guess I had that in mind.

DALE: Go through what you considered some of your strongest pieces were.

DAVE: Oh, the hairdresser. It was serendipitous, but it wasn't necessarily a strong piece—it was simply happenstance. But, by the way, that piece, that thing I did shooting the couple going up in the tall grass and making out and then getting up, the guy turning his hat around. I was cued into that by a black still photographer—a life photographer—and I don't remember what his name was [Joe Louw who had taken the photographs on the motel balcony in Memphis of the assasination of Martin Luther King]. I had run out of assistants and I was changing my own magazines up in the semi and we're looking out in the back and he said, "look at that guy, I think something's going to happen." And I looked over, and I agreed with him so I just threw the magazine on and began shooting that couple. I shot the whole thing on one magazine—eleven minutes. In the middle of it, they got farther away and I left the camera running and pulled the magazine off and slapped another one on and I changed the lens—there was a long zoom lens on there—and then they went back and finished the deal. At that time, we had this instruction for the lab that said "Save tail" and I wrote it in big letters on the outside of the can. That was the other lawsuit besides Port-O-San. They tried to get me to go to Toronto and I was going to Samoa at the moment so I gave them a little deposition.

DALE: Well, I know that we helped you a lot in the postproduction of that because when we asked the optical house, we asked them to "bracket" it. Shoot it in focus, semi out of focus and more out of focus because we knew that something would happen. And when we looked at the three versions delivered by the optical house, we knew we couldn't use the one that was in focus because we knew we would be sued if we put that out, so the big debate was between Bracket #2 and Bracket #3 and we finally opted for Bracket #3.

DAVE: You did? That's why it was out of focus! You never told me. Do you remember why he sued? He was a hairdresser in Montreal and he thought he would lose his clientele if they found out that he'd been throwing it to a lady. You never heard that? The lawyers told me.

DALE: You worked up at the information booth, didn't you?

DAVE: I think I did. And people on the phone to home and stuff like that.

DALE: What was that like?

DAVE: I thought the phone home were more poignant, more interesting to me. I heard a lot about people losing people.

DALE: You were up in a helicopter. Describe that.

DAVE: Well, it happened that I was very interested to do it because I had walked so much of the terrain and seen all of these groups and I wanted to see the overall. But first I thought I couldn't shoot it because the only access I had to shoot out of the helicopter was like an old GM car with the flip window and I just had to squeeze the lens out that little slot. I couldn't take a door off. So I happened to have a ten-millimeter lens with me, which I never used anymore, but I had it there and so I put that on and I was just able to get it out there and get a clear shot. I hope it was a clear shot at least.

Even though I had walked over so much of the terrain and had see the venue from so many angles already, it was almost breathtaking when you got up there and looked down. And even from altitude I couldn't get the whole thing in one frame. And of course, it's better not to. Coming in over from one quarter or another, coming down in over where the crowd just seems to go on forever and you end up crossing the stage, well that's more impressive—more interesting. Or the other way, coming in from the back.

DALE: You did a real circumference.

DAVE: Yeah, I did a wheel-around.

DALE: Word has it that you elected at the time to take a shower.

DAVE: I grew up around New York. I had heard for years about this famous elegant old resort up in the mountains there. And somebody on the site told me that it was not far away. I guess the chopper pilot. And it crossed my mind that since I had the chopper, I might as well go take a shower. He says, yeah, it's only about ten miles away—I could get you there in five minutes. So I said great. Finished. All we could think of doing were the aerials. And he flew me over and we landed in the middle of this crowd of people at the hotel. I took a shower and had a nap for an hour.

DALE: Describe your recollections of the Port-O-San sequence. You started shooting over his shoulder and your first question to him was...?

DAVE: He was dealing with extraordinary diligence with the problem at hand. He was scrubbing these toilet seats around and around—sloshing disinfectant here and there and just working away and I realized he was a very sincere, honest, dedicated worker. And I said, just as a way to lighten it up a little for my own sake, "You're getting a little behind on your work, aren't you." He says, "Oh, yeah. Gotta keep it nice for the kids. Got a son here and a son in Vietnam..." and it went on from there. I liked him, he was a nice man.

DALE: You had the instinct to stay shooting somehow you knew there was somebody else. Do you remember that?

DAVE: Yeah, one of the other—there was another Port-O-San next to it or something. And we sort of ran out of conversation with Mr. Port-O-San and I was aware of this other Port-O-San building next to it, so I thought I'd drift over there and see what happens. And an honest to God, certified, flipped out character came out—with his eyes crossed and clouds of ganja—and he says, "You want a hit?" And I said, not right now.

DALE: "I'm working," was your line.

DAVE: Yeah, "I'm working." And that made sense to him. If you have to work, Jesus, you have to put it off.

DALE: He held out his pipe to you.

DAVE: Was it a pipe? But he was a classic guy. There were two classics in a row.

DALE: What is amazing is that the Port-O-San Man, every time I saw the movie, whether in this country or London or wherever—this guy always got a standing ovation.

DAVE: Really? Well, I think he deserved it. It wasn't for me, it was for him. He was a good man from a very conventional culture, background, blue collar, working guy, but a good father. And I really didn't want him to be put down for it—I wanted everyone to appreciate him, but have a little fun too.

DALE: A classic piece. Tell me about some of the others. It's Monday morning, you're at the back of the stage with Hendrix.

DAVE: Well, of course, I was completely blown away by Hendrix. It was like the distillation of the music and the whole political—we haven't talked about that—but the whole importance of Woodstock. With McNamara, the emotional part relating to Vietnam and to the division in the country over Vietnam and between the young people who were the idealistic citizens fighting LBJ and the generals.

I mean, they knew it was wrong and they also knew they were in danger, personally. Their lives were in danger, in the sense of disruption at least. And it was completely wrong. Hendrix just made a distillation of the intense emotions that really were at the heart of the Woodstock trip to me. And I think a large percentage of the people there.

At any rate, when he finished, I think they left the tape playing back over the empty stage. I had been watching it from backstage, then I went up on the stage and the last thing you saw of him was that huge crowd there and he was playing, and the next cut is my shot of the sun shining over the stage—it was sort of a visual intensification of that distorted guitar at the end there—and there was an empty stage and only a few scattered people where there had been hundreds of thousands.

And then I went out and photographed people, the few remaining people, the two nuts eating watermelon with a hunting knife, eating in the mud and the girl with the parasol who was just tripped out and walking around in circles with the parasol—and some others, I wish I could remember them all. But it was very interesting to me. I did shoot that with a bug-eyed lens which distorted it, but we all felt distorted. We felt we'd been emotionally put in a different place by the whole experience.

DALE: Did it symbolize anything to you? Tell me where you were in WWII.

DAVE: I was a conscientious objector. I refused to go—I was drafted in New York—and I lived in the East Village and my grandparents were Middle Eastern immigrants who were super patriotic and I said I can't go to war. That's not the way to settle this thing, even though I hate the Nazis. And they said, what's the matter with you? You know better than President Roosevelt? And I said, well, maybe not better, but different. So they gave me a 4F or 4D and I'd just been offered another job, I was working as a photographer in New York, and I'd been offered this job that I wanted to take, but I wanted to know that I could do it and not get drafted out of it. So I went back to them a few weeks later—I had this phony, I think they gave me a minister status—and I said I'm not a minister. And two days later they said, "All right, you asked for it" and they gave me a 4E—a conscientious objector. They shipped me out in a couple of days. And what did I do? I planted a lot of trees, fought some fires, worked in a outhouse, broke up rocks—yeah, I was good at that.

DALE: And so here you were, cleaning up garbage again.

DAVE: I was carried away. I was emotionally transported. I suppose it wasn't much contest as to who the'd have on at the last moment, but it was perfect having Hendrix. I was emotionally affected.

DALE: Something happened that day. Mike Lang said it was the combination of the music and the lyric. How would you put it?

DAVE: It was the intensity of the music. I don't even remember the words. And I felt that Jimi had an extraordinary sense of relating to the audience and carrying them to beyond the point where they were.

DALE: We were documenting, theoretically, what was going on. Were we glorifying what was going on?

DAVE: I'd never use that term. I'd never use that term.

DALE: Did we glamorize, glorify drugs?

DAVE: No way. By the way, I went and cleaned up briefly in the tent in the overdose and it was pitiful. That's all. They were just stupid. Stupid. The interesting people never got in there. This was just a dumb minor contingent. They had nothing to do with the emotional context of the whole festival. The drugs were a minor subtext By the way, this is a good time to say. Were you and I in the same van when we left the site when it was all over?

DALE: No.

DAVE: Well, in all the time I spent around the whole entire area, in and amongst all these groups, I never saw any violence or bad vibes. Nothing going on that was hostile or nasty. And when it was all over and we got our gear together and we were in a van and leaving the site, and you know that's the cold bitch farmer territory. And this van, I think it was a pickup truck, came the other way—with these old local farmers in it—looking really mad and pissed off and they tried to run us off the road as we left the site. And that was the only act of violence that I saw the whole time.

DALE: When the movie was released, what did you hear? What did you feel about its impact on individuals or culture? Did you have any perceptions at the time?

DAVE: No, not really. My attentions were elsewhere at that point. After we went to the opening in New York, and by the way, Mr. Port-O-San (Tom Taggart) came to it and he was very charming and very pleased to be important in it. The whole thing that developed later, where he was induced to sue Warner Bros., was brought about by the Teamster lawyer that got hold of him. He was pretty happy. His wife was unhappy. Because they lived in a conventional suburban track and she told everyone that her husband was a sanitation engineer—so it was a blow to her.

DALE: The first time where he got an ovation was at that screening on the Warners' lot when that bit first appeared.

DAVE: Well, I'm glad. The lawyer's lawyer came out and took me to lunch later and showed me this elegant thing, the Supreme Court heard the case and refused to take it on directly but they sent it back to the district court for jury trial and he had this whole testimony printed out very elegantly. The lawyer was showing it to me while we had lunch and I was just rolling on the floor laughing and he said, "Don't laugh. Don't laugh. If we lose this case, WB will never be able to use real people in a movie again." Did you ever hear that one?

Then afterward, after the second trial with the jury, where I had to appear with my camera and my charming wacko soundman with his black leather shaved head, we got to stand in front of the jury and let them stare at us. The judge said to the jury, "Now ladies and gentlemen, look at these two gentlemen." The argument of the lawyer for Mr. Port-O-San was not that we had made fun of him, but that he was misled—he thought that we were just amateurs shooting for our own amusement. So the judge had us stand up there and he said, "Ladies and gentlemen of the jury, look at these two gentlemen. Do they look like amateurs to you?" Then the Warners guys said, "jeez Dave, Warners is really grateful. You're going to hear from us…."

DALE: Do you have any sense of how the film has affected society?

DAVE: I'm amazed that it hasn't affected society more than it has. Society has gone in a negative direction. At that time you had a large faction of the population, a large faction of the younger people, who were politically—they were idealistic—they were expressing this morally important and very valid position about our national ethics, our national behavior and thinking. And now what do you have? You have young people getting rich quick. And if they still have these moral judgments and moral standards, they've kind of given up on them because it's time to make money. I'm afraid (the movie) hasn't affected society very much.

DALE: What was the message of the movie?

DAVE: If it had a message, it was a very simple and very convincing and impressive demonstration of how young people felt. What their moral position was on this Vietnam war thing. And a very interesting demonstration of loyal solidarity on the part of the younger generation. And now I hear things about how young people are completely cynical, selfishly oriented, without-they've retreated from expressing idealistic or moral positions and they're just looking for some bucks.

DALE: What about Wavy Gravy, you said he was important.

DAVE: He was important. He was very important. I met him again recently and he is still charming and amazingly productive and ethical person, but at Woodstock he was a lifesaver, literally to me.

He's an amazing guy and he's still carrying on in his true fashion. He didn't invent himself for Woodstock. He came from some kind of idealistic community that he'd organized in Arizona somewhere. He came to the festival and he's carrying on now. He lives in Berkeley and he has a wonderful summer camp among other things where he gets kids out there and exposes them to things they never saw. He's just a fascinating guy.

DALE: Do you remember filming him at all?

DAVE: Well, yeah. His free lunch, which was something like granola, oatmeal or something-and-milk. And that's what I ate for the time of the festival. I don't think I even got anything solid to eat when I went to the resort. Didn't have to. I was filled up on Wavy Gravy's oatmeal. By the way, his emotional contribution to the festival I thought was important. You remember they sort of put him up as a cool head in the crowd, at times there was a situation that could have gotten more emotional or more destructive and they would just put him up there and he would talk to the crowd. He was just a great influence. He's got a charming and patient way too.

DALE: Do you think the film affected the outcome of the Vietnam war?

DAVE: These generals were doing *mea culpas* in one book after another. Maybe it made them feel a little more guilty.

DALE: I think for the first time the country saw that there was a very large group which did not represent the totality of the people who were that impassioned about these issues as they actually were. These hundreds of thousands of people were a microcosm of the people who felt identically, but couldn't get there. Maybe that's what forced Nixon, eventually, to try to end the damned thing. What about Nixon and Wadleigh?

DAVE: Yeah, Nixon and Wadleigh got along great. I took over on Nixon's second presidential bid. Wadleigh had started shooting with him and Wadleigh with his wildest hippie mode, he and Nixon had a splendid rapport. They got along very well, and when I showed up…

DALE: This had to be 1968.

DAVE: I spent three weeks with him. I don't know where Wadleigh went, but he was sorely missed by Mr. Nixon. We didn't get along too well. All he could ever say to me was, "Oh, I see you've got your longshoreman's cap on today," or something like that. Wadleigh had long hair then. Oh, yeah. He was a wild man. It was very interesting that somehow they had something…Nixon's relationship with Wadleigh was strictly personal friendship!

DAN TURBEVILLE

KEEP FEEDING EACH OTHER!

(ANOTHER MEMBER OF THE Cornell Mafia, Danny was summoned to the site to help translate music to cameramen. His work on the movie would eventually lead to work on the album with Eric Blackstead, producer of the albums.)

It sounded like a great idea. I had just graduated college in June, and was kicking back at home in New Jersey with no immediate plans. Drive upstate and help my college band mate Eric Blackstead work on a film of a music festival? Yeah! Eric had the gig as musical director, the bands were big names. Things were happening fast and I was needed in New York City tomorrow. Sounded like an adventure I wouldn't want to miss!

The next morning we met at Eric's upper West Side apartment and drove the few blocks to Paradigm Films. Michael Wadleigh was there, the director. He was very tall and aloof, like maybe a great person. His eyes said to me that he had seen things far away. The perfect feather standing straight up the side of his tall wide brim black hat must have been a gift from an eagle in one of those high mountain passes. Whew…

My gig was act as liaison between the entertainers and cameramen, helping the latter become quickly familiar with unknown subject matter.

Astounding to think about it amidst today's culture, but no one filmed rock groups then. Only Pennebaker had made a film out of music. My understanding of music and the groups' stage presentations could really make a difference to the quality of the finished film. To boot I would meet some of my heroes. This was a good match.

Our pal Brooksie (Alex Brooks) was flying up from Mexico to take a look at financing the film because to date, no one else had money for this "risky business." At least my expenses were covered. We were leaving tomorrow. My first job was to drive my car to Kennedy Airport, pick up cameramen and drive to a place I'd never been, a town named Woodstock.

David Myers and Don Lenzer got off the plane from California at 9:00 a.m., unshaven and wired. We left the TWA terminal and caught the New York State Thruway North. Everyone was in good spirits, yes, they had paid their own ways and film stock was being bought. David had the same look in his eyes as Wadleigh. Don was cheerful.

We arrived at our motel, the Silver Spur Dude Ranch by noon. Others in the film had come in earlier and were heading out to the site already, seven miles away. I began to meet the pranksters I was to be in cahoots with for the next two years… Larry Johnson, Dale Bell, Jeannie Field, Marty Scorsese, John Binder.

Eric and I were soon back in my Mustang tearing down long dirt back roads through pastures and farmland until we converged with the main stream of pilgrims to the site. We eased into line behind cars, vans, VW buses and people as far as the eye could see in both directions, an "in-odus" of my generation, bare-chested, knap-sacked, long-haired. Smiles, joints, guitars, people hanging out of windows, greeting each other, "Hey man, what's happening?"

The dirt road conveniently flowed directly behind the stage and as we drove through the back gate with our pass, from the air it must have looked as if we were just the tiniest drop left behind as the lengthening living river continued its onward course.

Caribbean weather most certainly had been booked for the weekend (ha!). In the center of the now empty field which a day or so later would hold hundreds of hundreds of people, I listened to the now famous voices of John Morris and the lighting director Chip Monck testing and marveled at the immensity of the stage.

It was so unexpected, that stage in this setting. It seem larger than any barn ever built and so very open, nothing would be hidden. An icon for our generation. Pine flooring stretched in every direction, Bill Graham who never spoke below a shout and never shouted without moving some part of his body (which is how I identified him from a hundred yards out) animating the stage, muscled hippie carpenters everywhere who rippled, hammered and sawed in the afternoon sun, creating special echoes in the woods. Green tree forests dotting the rolling countryside behind and all around them.

The thickening, lengthening mass, stretching, moving in unbroken flow down that long dirt road behind the stage, breaking into rivulets reaching into their own quiet place for the night. Tribal, comforting. Wisps of smoke from early camp fires. Days of music and work before us, no walls. Whatever could be better?

It was the afternoon of the first day and there were several vehicles parked behind the stage. My Mustang was one. Artie Kornfield, one of the main man producers, had his bike and liked to ride it around it seemed in circles much of the time, giggling like he was really high which is how we all know Artie is. Lee Osborne, the recording engineer, had the remote recording truck. So when Sonya Polonsky, our production manager, got sick, it made sense that I would be the one taking her to the makeshift hospital up the dirt road behind the stage. Perhaps she reacted to the first real food we'd had in two days, compliments of Warner/Atlantic who had just picked up the movie and film rights. Or maybe it was the last three days of no sleep.

We drove out the back gate into the "red sea" of people and up the dirt road. Suddenly, a tall fellow thuds onto the hood of the car parallel to the right front wheel and shouts, "you ran over my foot man." It was a very funny moment, like something from Laurel & Hardy...hurt but not really hurt? And the moment wasn't up tight or fearful either because there was an unspoken truth in the air that all of us would look out for each other. "Get in, we're going to the hospital already man," I shouted. "OK" he shouts back and climbs in. Sonya and the guy went different ways when we got there and I stayed with him exchanging the insurance information. Strangely, the doctor couldn't even find a bruise. But it didn't matter because I was feeling magical, like it might have been for those around Gandhi, that we were all part of one family looking out for each other...reverence, good vibes.

Peter Townshend was surly when I interviewed The Who before their set. Although no one said anything, I got the sense it was because they were waiting much too long a time before they played. Thirty years later I read in a newspaper article that he was just coming off drugs at Woodstock and had little patience for all that were around him. Rashomon.

Tim Hardin was so smacked out he had to be physically guided from back to the front of the stage to his microphone to sing. We all used drugs but this was not how anyone I knew wanted it to be. It was the saddest moment of my experience watching this gifted interpreter going down. Tim's wrenching despondent interpretation of "If I Were A Carpenter" was as pure and timeless in his way as was Joan Baez's inspiring and soaring performance of "Swing Low, Sweet Chariot," hours later in the crisp night air. Unscripted and unrehearsed I believe these two artists presented for us the quintessential lows and highs of existence. I believe they unwittingly played out the thought-provoking dilemma of humankind as it is examined in all the great literature. Until this moment I have never mentioned this observation, that the concert and the movie presented us with incredible dramatic theater.

There was nothing in the rock and roll lexicon to describe Crosby, Stills, Nash & Young. I hadn't seen any of their previous bands live but had heard all their records. It seemed as the cool light mist lashed gently through the red, white, and blue stage lights shining down upon David Crosby's fringed jacket in the 4:00 a.m. morning slot that we would listen to their harmonies for a lifetime.

If you had told me, as I jumped up and raised my hands into the air with 500,000 others when Sly and the Family Stone vamped and paraded on stage with the energy of ten USC marching bands, that several years later, I would meet Sly in his experimental West Coast recording studio and be talking to a man descending into drug hell, I would have told you to smoke another one—Jack. But a few years later his miseries were very public. There were no artistic drug-induced insights in his work, no momentary recoveries, and no release to death. This communicative genius, galvanizer of all people across all color lines—a feat few people will ever accomplish in human history and fewer still within their lifetime, looked me straight in the eye with that flash of supreme confidence for which he was famous and answered my question of "how are you doing, man?" with a single cocaine-induced word: "perfect."

Jimi Hendrix changed the way every guitar player reached for their ax and after Woodstock changed the way American kids heard the "Star-Spangled Banner." I was one of those kids. He took psychedelia out of your dreams and put it in your face: "Hey, man, do you think?" How could you not question your government's policies now? He did it all without effort. Swaying turquoise beads dangling from a light buckskin jerkin, fine jewelry and strength, his eyes looked right into your brain, speaking powerful truth after truth if you read the bones.

Amongst those of us who remembered Woodstock—were there, wanted to be there, were in some way touched by it—there is a camaraderie. This was one of the most deliciously productive periods for rock and roll music, a common denominator for youth everywhere. Only a few world events since, such as the destruction of the Berlin Wall and Tienenamin Square have produced the same euphoric "keep feeding each other" utopian sensibility. This total lack of pretense and desire to enjoy living shows itself every now and then in my life through unexpected kindnesses and unsolicited appreciation. It always surprises me, knowing what I know about people today.

We were back in New York without a break. The tempo was exuberant. More new faces in the office now, film editors. Talk of a ten-hour movie—what else do you do with thirty miles of great footage? My job just sort of surfaced as we went along, like everything I'd done to this point, whatever I could do to help. I was assigned to edit the sound, given an old (pre war?) Wollensack reel to reel tape deck and copies of lots of wild footage for cataloguing. I also did the music rough cuts. I tried things which gave Wadleigh and Blackstead a chance to analyze what they had. I had to maintain continuity, all the time looking for the best possible shape to this incredible shifting sculpture.

I had no idea we were making history by writing the first live, full length visual musical essay. Where music had always been a complimentary film element, now it was a pivotal element. It caused the musical director and the film director to disagree vigorously at times, coming as they did from their different disciplines.

I'll give you an example. One Monday, Wadleigh screened Ten Years After's powerful blues number "I'm Going Home." The conventional wisdom was that its twelve minutes length was too long to be considered in its entirety for the film. My task, to be finished that day, was to edit it to about three minutes which was the conventional radio air play time in the 1960s. With my "guess and cut" Wollensack, I spent the whole day trying out hunches and re-hunches. At last I thought my four-minute version had everything: continuity, dynamics, color.... most likely my *tour de force* of music editing on the film.

However, when I slipped into a seat behind Wadleigh in the screening room, I found him mesmerized by the footage…"keep everything" he murmured. The dark velvet of the night wrapped around Alvin Lee's vigorous form and striking red guitar was visually to die for, but we musicians (Blackstead and I) felt the music performance just would not sustain interest for twelve minutes. The finished film piece is about nine minutes long, and I believe it was only Wadleigh's multiple camera, three-split screens and optical effects approach which made that song work well at that length.

Watching it today is like watching a fast paced, exciting MTV clip. It makes me believe our movie was nothing short of the pioneer of the music video.

Woodstock's box office success alerted record company executives to the increasing power of performance to sell product. I bet that for some time after, more record company money went into financing live tours than ever before. Wadleigh's split screen approach conveyed the magnitude of *3 Days of Music and Peace* in a way that a single screen could never have done, if simply for the time

constraints. I don't think many of us had a concept of the technology of the future...
videos, cassettes, CD's. In fact one of the saddest stories of the entire project had to
do with technology within the deal Blackstead, the music album's producer, made
with Atlantic Records.

The way I understood it, the deal gave him a percentage of the record rights
only, which cut him completely out of earnings on cassettes and CDs. And
although it was his first record deal, he didn't deserve to pay those kind of dues.
Can you imagine?

The now famous director Martin Scorsese was editor/assistant director on
the film. He was a generous man with his time and thoughts, a teacher at NYU
and an accomplished film historian. A dozen of us would eat dinner together
at neighborhood restaurants most every night and Marty would tell funny and
interesting stories from Hollywood's great past.

My greatest disappointment was not being selected to go to California for the
opticals and final assembly. I missed the camaraderie of the group. We had a lot of
fun together and from my point of view were collectively dedicated to making the
best movie about the power of music that would ever be made. I was "fed" by my
association with this crew, I was no longer the loner I'd always been. The spirit of
the Woodstock Nation was strong within me. I always recognize it in others.

When the crew returned from California, Eric hired me to help him sort out
material for the first *Woodstock* album. I once again edited, but this time with the
professional equipment at the Record Plant Studios. We worked around the clock
with Tom Flye, our engineer. The documentary audio was fascinating. I collated
heaps of interviews, conversations, and cataloged tons of stage announcements.
Today these would be called sound bites. Back then they were the personalities
of our generation, as resounding for us as anything Walter Cronkite ever covered.
"Please, it is your choice, but we suggest you not use the brown acid." "Please
come down from the towers, we're gonna have to sit out this rain; we don't want
anyone hurt..." "Hey man, the New York State Thruway's closed, isn't that far
out!..." "What you've got now is the biggest freebie concert ever." Hugh Romney's
directive for all time: "...If you have food, give some to the person next to you" and
"Keep feeding each other."

SONYA POLONSKY

ROAD OUT OF THE SILVER SPERM

DALE: The Silver Sperm? [The Silver Spur]

SONYA: Yes, and the owner was Vinnie Sands and he went bankrupt. He made like fifty-six chicken dinners or something. We never got them to the site…

I remember pottering around in the backstage area. And Fern was my boss for the time of the shoot; I don't remember seeing you at all during the shoot. I remember working with Fern and talking to Thelma. I came back before everybody, because my foot had swollen to gigantic proportions. Like a fool I had gone to the clinic Sunday at about 2:00 or 3:00 a.m., because I had a work pass and they promised I could get back to the site; but they were lying. They took me to the hospital in Monticello and x-rayed the wrong foot. And I stayed there all day with some guy from the Lower East Side Motherfuckers or somebody. This guy with a snaggle-tooth.

I remember I called Thelma, I called the site—I didn't know who was going to answer the phone—from the hospital. And Thelma answered the field phone there. I said "look, I don't know what to do…" And, she said, "Just go on home and wait for us," because getting back was ridiculous. So, I went back home.

And, they sent me home; the Monticello Jewish Association gave me seven dollars for the bus and put this bad acid kid in my charge and sent me home. I called my friend Clinton to pick me up because I didn't have my keys, I didn't have my bag with me or anything. I didn't have the keys to my apartment I only had one shoe. He picked me up. I went to his house. The next day I went to work and everybody came back, on Monday.

I remember wearing a short dress because the pain had gone away from my foot, but it had swollen to gigantic proportions. I could not get into a pair of pants, so I had to wear a short skirt. And, I remember everybody came back and Larry

Johnson looked at my leg and he said, "Ugh, how can you expose that? That is disgusting." And I didn't know what it was. After a while it went down, but because of that I didn't experience the end of the festival.

ALEX BROOKS

GOT $100K, WILL TRAVEL!

(IN OUR WILD SCRAMBLE to find money with which to make the film, we contacted everyone we knew, including "Brooksie," also from Cornell's Cayuga Lake, and his trusty trust fund. He was Eric Blackstead's buddy.)

After a crazy year owning a nightclub in Managa, Nicaragua, I was twenty-four, it was August 1969. I was hanging out on the Jardín (plaza) in San Miguel de Allende, Mexico. Just up from the coast of Michoacan, I was only "thinking about" returning to the States.

I was visiting my older brother, who had lived in San Miguel for years. Warm days and cool nights were among the many pleasures of that gringo-friendly town.

About nine, one evening, I was helping some new friends from Iowa City buy some blankets, when my brother came hurrying toward us. The Hidalgo Hotel had received a long distance call with a message to call New York collect. This was a big deal for the little Mexican pensione and the hotel family had all turned out to watch when I returned to the Hidalgo. The phones were fairly primitive in the Guanajuato mountains and there was worry that an eventful call to New York City would not be possible.

Miraculously, the call went through to my Cornell buddy, Black (Eric Blackstead, *Woodstock* album producer-to-be), who was wheeling and dealing in a movie production office on Broadway. An excellent blues guitarist and singer, Black had been hired as Music Director for a documentary film to be made of a gigantic rock concert north of New York City. Although I'd been on the road for several years, he knew I had some money socked away and he wanted me to help them out. The Wadleigh-Maurice production company didn't have enough cash to buy the film for the three-day event. They didn't want to sell out to a big company like Warner Bros. They wanted to have absolute control of the artistic content of the documentary and my investment of one hundred thousand dollars would keep the production "in the family."

I was skeptical in that little hotel lobby with the Hidalgo family milling excitedly about. That one hundred thousand dollars was the grubstake for my next nightclub and this all sounded a bit overwhelming. Black started reeling off the names of the bands that were to appear...Janis Joplin, The Band, Hendricks, Country Joe, Sly, Butterfield, Richie Havens, Joan Baez and so on; Music Heroes, all. Danny (Turbeville) and Doc (Dave Robinson—Cornell pals who had played in my club in St. Thomas, VI, in 1967) were on the team, too. He said, at least come see the show. I was sort of hooked.

Never being one to pass up an adventure, I said Okay, I'll be there. This was Tuesday night and the Festival started on Friday! A third class bus left for Mexico City at 2:00 a.m. I was on my way and started throwing my clothes in my knapsack.

I slept pretty well in the old rattletrap bus and taxied from the North Bus Terminal to the Airport. It was a shock to find there were only two flights left to New York and they were full. I got standby tickets on both and watched the Air France depart without me. Fortunately, the Eastern flight took me and I landed at Kennedy Airport around 6:00 p.m. Customs went smoothly and I arrived at the address on Broadway and there were Black and the production team.

We were in a crummy office building and the rooms of Paradigm Films looked like they belonged to a destitute Mike Hammer. They immediately pitched me the concept for the film...a mammoth documentary (possibly ten hours long) that would define our generation. Their equipment included a German editing machine, which could synchronize up to three different images of the performances for a unique look in documentary history.

A producer, Dale Bell gave a calmer, more practical impression, explaining that they only had enough up-front money to bring film crews from LA or to buy the unexposed film. As of that time, they had no film. Warner Bros. had evidently offered to finance this but then THEY would own the film. I got a subtle feeling that Bell didn't think that would be such a bad idea.

The other producer, Bob Maurice, was pacing around the office, muttering and waving his arms. This guy seemed to be the most uncool and unbalanced executive I'd ever seen. Perhaps he recognized my skepticism and thus unwillingness to invest. It was immediately apparent that this project was much larger than the likes of us could pull off. Also, it seemed that Warner Bros. would have a lot deeper pockets and could get the finished feature into distribution a lot better than I could. I said I'd have to pass on buying onto the film.

They were good sports and put me on Blackstead's team that would work on stage to interview the bands for planning of the shots. On Thursday morning I drove an old panel truck with equipment and a film crew from Manhattan to the site, just past White Lake. On the road, we traded rumors and speculation about the impending event. We heard radio ads for the festival, but were not certain of anything that was to come. These were West Coast MOVIE guys who were anticipating sort of a lark.

Our access to the site was by a dirt road that wove through the now famous resort community and then leafy woods and small fields, until bursting out at the bottom of the hilly field that belonged to Max Yasgur. The first thing I saw was a big old crane, manned by a tie-dyed hippie. He was finishing the light towers astride the stage, which was also in the final stages of construction. Four by eight's of plywood were being passed up by hand for the surface of the sixteen feet high stage. A few desultory hippies were building a plank fence across the front of the stage. This was to be the fence that encircled the site. I could tell, that fence was never going to make it around the site, even if they worked all weekend. Not many tickets were going to be collected at this event.

I checked in at the Butler Sound truck where Black was stationed. Gaffers were not arriving from California, as anticipated, to run the electric and communications lines for the film crews. I was given some tools and wire and a rough map of the stage and towers and I got to work. (I had done some wiring in my nightclubs.) From a central box beneath the stage, I ran Romex cable up both towers and to four points along the front of the stage, using bailing wire to secure it to the risers. The union electrician who was installing the circuit box was shaking his head at the arrangements but was good natured about the half-assedness of the entire proceedings. Once I had installed the receptacle boxes, he turned on the juice and, to our amazement, THEY WORKED! With some helpers we dug a trench out into the middle of the field to the mixing board and left it for the Audio Team to fill. Mission accomplished, I met some of the Hog Farm folks who had been building the fence and we cooled out together.

The rest of the film and sound people arrived early in the morning and we did a lot of unloading and unraveling. Rumors swirled about various aspects of noncompletion of the stage, the fence, the roof and almost everything else. I followed one of the handheld camera crews with extra film, and there was a now historic morrient. When John Morris announced to the show's young promoters that it would have to be a free concert, there was some weeping, which I believe was edited out of the film. It seemed like the end of the world to them and I was glad I'd held onto my one hundred thousand dollars.

Nevertheless, the necessary stuff all came together and Richie Havens started playing to a large group of people sometime that afternoon. And they kept on arriving! It was like a storm tide, building up into a tumultuous sea.

Backstage passes were relegated by the use of colored tunics and T-shirts with the Woodstock bird/guitar on a large white patch. (The film crew was exempt because they had no shirts for us). Black was "security", Red was the off duty NYC cops, Green was stage workers, etc. Security had to learn OUR faces so we had full access. At one point, the crowd rushed the barrier of the stage and many crazed, muddied, individuals made it to our platform. Those off-duty cops were so great in their control…they let the crashers watch a few songs from the platform before they willingly went back to the field. Those cops also specifically looked the other way whenever illegal drugs were used.

My spot was on the platform across the front of the stage where the film crew and photographers operated from. I carried film canisters, Nagra recorders, cameras and duct tape between the trucks in back and the cameramen. After the rain started that evening (during Joan Baez' set?) my ungrounded electrics caused a bit of a buzz to pass through the metal risers but, as far as I know, no one got any bad shocks. Arlo Guthrie and Joan Baez hung out with us on the camera platform to see if the rain would abate but it just kept coming and the show was stopped. That Upstate rain has a different smell and feel than the tropical kind and it made me feel at home, rained out and all. Getting out of the site was now impossible, so that night, I found my four by eight up under the stage and slept in relative dryness.

The morning dawned and the rain had stopped. During the night, a muddy couple of flower children had crawled onto my plywood bunk to sleep. We talked about the amazing scene a while then they split for the Hog Farm breakfast. Fortunately, the film team had coffee and doughnuts, which really hit the spot AND my clothes were almost dry! Looking out on the field was something else again…during the night, their numbers had doubled and it really became an enormous mud party in the milky morning sunshine.

Eavesdropping on John Morris while he was figuring out what to do as various problems and crises arose was a special treat and insight to what really was happening. Decisions were made out there on the deck of our mighty stage-ship cruising in the roiled sea of our audience (there were even flapping tarps, high above, to suggest the galleon illusion). If anyone is responsible for the successful journey of the Sailing Ship Woodstock, it is John. He knew all those band people by their first names and had what they wanted. When the Snafus were piling up, he improvised a way to apply the oil. Chip Monck and John's calm, deep voices had a great influence in keeping everything cool.

We knew WE had a tiger by the tail as the bands were having trouble getting to the site due to highways being clogged. It was known on stage that they had gotten the National Guard to send some helicopters but the crowd did not. The Vietnam War was at it's height and everyone knew the chop-chop-chop of their rotors from movies and the news. From beyond the hills, we heard that sound steadily increasing until three Hueys in phalanx appeared above the crowd, aimed at the stage. Quiet settled over the throng as heads turned to watch those dark machines coming in low and fast. Many of us felt like we were Mekong Villagers for a moment. Were they going to open fire? Quickly, Morris got on the mike and announced to the crowd their purpose, and cheers erupted out of that moment of doubt.

Then the helicopters started arriving with the bands and still the audience swelled as Country Joe McDonald did his impromptu opening for Saturday's entertainment. About this time, Danny, Black and Doc started taking me along to interview the bands before their sets. All of them were both elated and awed by the size and intensity of the audience that was looking down at us.

Canned Heat played one of the greatest sets I've ever seen and the looks on their faces said everything about the power of music. Pins and needles ran up my back as the swelling crowd and bands interacted. What a great time to be HIGH! As the helicopters roared in and out behind the stage, ferrying rock· and roll heroes, someone commented that this was OUR Flower Power L.Z. (landing zone) of the Vietnam War.

We were raving for PEACE!

Mike Wadleigh, the director, did much of the camera work as well. With a handheld camera he moved in and about the performing groups like a member of the band.

Straw-like, long hair under a sweatband, he showed no fear. Sometimes in a white peasant shirt (Mexico!) and sometimes bare-chested, he was a dynamic part of the festival we saw. It took balls to do that and those close shots are a big thing in what makes the movie bold and personal.

At some point, it became an ordeal to turn around and look at the audience. Many people on the camera platform mentioned it. Eight-hundred thousand eyes, all of them SMASHED and looking at You! It gave me this drifty feeling, like I was going to float away; Good stuff all right! I sat for about ten minutes at the back of the stage, drinking with Joe Cocker just before he went on, both of us marveling at the crowd, looking back at us. He said he really needed some fortification to face that throng. As he left to go on, he gave me a wonderfully limp English handshake and said, perhaps he'd fortified a little TOO much. As I watched him sing, he certainly WAS loose, howling and playing his air-guitar.

I got to sit with Janis Joplin and share her bottle of Tequila Crema, talking about Mexico. Like everyone, she was amazed by the crowd. I got the smile of a lifetime from her as she walked out on stage. Tim Hardin was so loaded on downers, he couldn't sing. He started to play but couldn't remember the words to his own songs. We had to help him off the stage before he could even complete one song; a casualty of our quest for Freedom.

Sly and the Family Stone were my favorite performance of the whole show. They were so loose and funny before they went on, I camped out between some cases and stared. They had FUN and steps and routines and blew that soggy crowd away. I think they were one of the best visuals of the movie, too. Melanie played a great set but we missed shooting her. Her song, "Lay down candles in the rain" might have been the most relevant song of the concert; a casualty of not enough film.

I passed out somewhere along there. There was a damp little groupie who slept with me somewhere. I didn't get back to consciousness until I was pushing the Jefferson Airplane's set riser into position. Dawn was breaking and Grace Slick was out there bellowing out "Volunteers". That must have been the highpoint of the 1960s! Every time I hear that song, the hairs rise on my arms and I see that sight: white sunlight bouncing off the wet stage, and the Youth of Our Nation, as far as the eye could see, pulsating, cheering, exploding... "We are Volunteers of America..." with The Airplane out there, egging them on.

Toward the final dawn, Monday Morning, I was running on Autopilot. Coffee and that Smoke were all that were keeping me on my feet. I was hauling coffees and sandwiches up the towers to the camera crews and it's a good thing I was immortal in those days. Jimi Hendrix was to be that last act and we had saved a lot of film for his set.

The sun came up and we were going to take a breakfast break during the next to the last act, called Sha-Na-Na. Nobody knew who they were, except that they had something to do with the Columbia University Glee Club.

WOW! When they hit the stage, coffee cups went flying! Bleary-eyed and amused, the entire film team said, "We'd better get THIS!" The band's brazen energy got us right up to speed and the handheld crews got what is another highpoint of the film.

After a pause, Hendrix arrived at the back of the stage as high as The Himalayas. His eyes were as big as peyote buttons and the call went out for "Valium." Once he settled down a bit, he motored right onto the stage and took off with everyone running to catch him.

Jimi Hendrix was such an imposing figure with his incredible guitar licks, he turned the place to butter. Power, Power, The Bonneville Dam! When his guitar neck moved, the crowd moved. All of us on stage were pushed back to the edge. Even Wadleigh, who had had his handheld camera in the faces of all the greats, that weekend, was pushed off onto the platform. Doc said, "Look at the Crowd," and they were transfixed, wide-eyed, hundreds of thousands of mouths wide open; as if they were chanting to the sun. Finally, it was a time of introspection and contemplation. Relief was also a common emotion on stage. We had been a part of the historic cultural-social event of our time and LIVED!

I had had it! As Hendrix was finishing the "Star-Spangled Banner," Danny and I nipped out of the backstage area and took a car he had stashed there. We zipped over to get our gear from the Dude Ranch then roared up the road to Ithaca, where the beds were warm and dry. I discovered that I was really back in the USA!

Six months later, I visited with Black and Danny while they were working on the mixes and engineering of the soundtrack on Franklin Street in Hollywood. I was never more glad to have not invested my grubstake in the venture, as it often looked like it was on the rocks. Wadleigh still pushed for a six-to-ten hours film that would be the "true documentary"(but perhaps an ordeal of fanny fatigue). Warner Bros. wanted a shorter version for practicality's sake and, I guess, they won. Black and Danny struggled mightily with the music audio as it had all been recorded from two mikes, suspended in front of the stage. There was a lot of muffling and noise to filter out and this was before digital.

The sound track and records did come out well, (as did as the film!) and I'm very proud of them, considering what they had to work from. Black was the first of the Players to make money from *Woodstock*, and he earned it. A few years later, royalties in hand, he visited me in St. Thomas where I had another club. After an afternoon of Pina Coladas, one day, he left a check from Atlantic Records for eighty-two thousand dollars on the Morning Star Beach Bar. When we went back the next day, Bobsie the bartender had it for him. (he didn't think it was real anyway!) It occurs to me that being a Player in the Woodstock Family changed their lives forever. Whatever fame and/or fortune came their way, they couldn't put on The Suit or kiss the corporate butt again.

I was happy to see that they gave me a credit at the end of the film in "Thanks to those at the site" (or something like that). That proves I was there (to me). It was my only film and I stayed behind the cameras like a good movie helper. They did send me to the truck for the movie equivalent of a left-handed monkey wrench but, there I had some nice conversations with Marty Scorsese and T. Schoonmaker, now legends.

All told, *Woodstock* was an organic experience of gigantic proportions. Nothing worked, except the way it HAD to work. Nobody who was there will ever forget it (or be free of it).

HART PERRY

ONE VERY ADDITIONAL CAMERA

(As THE YOUNGEST CAMERAMAN, Hart seized golden opportunities, then and later on in his life. His fascination with the process of motion picture photography led him to create pixilation, one frame at a time, from one of the Woodstock towers.)

Dear Dale,

Here is my *Woodstock* story.

I was a film student at Columbia University when I heard about the Woodstock concert. I was interested in attending the concert as a fan and member of a rock band but had made no actual plans to attend. What held my interest at that time was to develop abstract expressionist ideas in film. I had a Bolex camera and was developing my film, printing it, and animating it. I needed an optical printer to put my film together. As I called around New York filmmakers in pursuit of a cheap optical printer, I was given Michael Wadleigh's number.

I called him up, made my case about an optical printer and he replied that he couldn't help me. He did ask me whether I could shoot for him on the Woodstock concert. Of course I could shoot. If he had asked me whether I wanted to be a musician, painter or filmmaker, I would not have been able to give him an answer. But I could definitely shoot rock and roll. Shooting gave you the best seat in the house. He told me to bring my camera to Bethel New York a day before the concert.

I loaded up my gear into my girlfriend's Dodge Dart and we started to hit heavy traffic en route to Bethel. Something was happening but its significance was still latent. We got to the site and parked the car at the rim of the amphitheater like field. The stage was under construction. I think there was a fence or one was under construction. Tents were going up and some sort of concessions. People were arriving but the crowd was not huge. A lot of people were walking because traffic was backed up and cars were parked haphazardly.

We made our way to the stage and asked about the filming—Michael Wadleigh had sent us. I met Michael, reported for duty. He sent me to Dale Bell to take care of business—the salary was one hundred fifty flat Fine with me (I think it was one hundred twenty-five dollars a day, Hart, with only a one-day guarantee!). There was a meeting scheduled with the camera men at the side of the stage.

As we sat in a circle on the ground, a joint was passed as Michael explained his strategy for covering the concert. At that point his company was producing the film on spec. I quickly realized that I was the youngest and least experienced camera man. So did Wadleigh. My assignment was to get shots of the crowd. There was a tractor trailer where the film equipment was stored and where I could get film. When a huge crowd assembled, we knew that we were recording history. From that point until the festival was over, almost every waking moment I saw through a lens which I tried to keep in focus and at the right F stop.

I took off and got shots of the crowd coming in, and of the stage being constructed. When the concert started, I got the assignment to do shots in the crowd. The coveted stage positions were taken by Wadleigh and the more experienced cameramen. I went through the crowd shooting cutaways, and stopped from time to time to smoke pot with people.

After a while I found that I was bombed and need to chill out. I climbed up on the scaffolding of one of the speaker towers and set my camera up on a tripod. I proceeded to shoot single frames for several hours until my head cleared. The shot appears on one of the screens in the film. The crowd in the back looks as if it were in real time because the people did not move over the time. I was animating the crowd. Avenues of people surfing like a stream appear in the animation. These avenues were not apparent in real time. The people in the front of the crowd were animated. I also did shots with dissolves made in the camera of people in the crowd, including some topless women. From this vantage point I was disappointed in the Grateful Dead's set and became a fan of Santana's.

I found that being the least important cameraman had some artistic advantages aside from being assigned to the crowd shots. When it rained, the cameramen huddled in the truck. I was instructed to go out into the rain to see if anything worth shooting was happening. I got some of the classic mud slide footage. I realized that I could never get a position shooting on stage with a Bolex camera. An Arri-camera was available so I took it up and waited for a shortage of stage cameramen which I figured would occur, when exhaustion overtook them from round-the-clock filming. Let me not exaggerate my role. I was the extra cameraman, doing cutaways.

I caught some sleep during Joan Baez's set in order to be ready. My opportunity occurred with Janis Joplin; there was a minor stage position for me. While waiting for Janis Joplin to start her set, a woman sitting next to me made conversation about how she felt Janis used her sex appeal to cover up a lack of vocal chops. Since I had slept through Joan Baez's set and I did not recognize her as Joplin's critic until, to my chagrin she was pointed out later.

A memorable stage moment was The Who's set. I had a good shot of Abbie Hoffman's acid ranting to the crowd before The Who came on. Suddenly Pete Townshend's guitar came into frame, whacking Abbie in the back of the head. He scampered off the stage and climbed over the barricade which separated the crowd from the stage in disappeared. My negative feelings about this gratuitous violence were mitigated by their powerful performance.

Another moment was Jimi Hendrix's performance as the sun was rising. My shot was a master of the stage from the crowd. At one point I started to run out of film. Here was an historic performance and I would not have the film to record it. My girlfriend had left a while ago to get more stock. She was nowhere to be seen. I zoomed in on the stage to see if I could spot her. I forgot that the camera was rolling. There she was, dancing and sharing a snort with Chip Monck, the guy who built the stage. I didn't realize that I had filmed the scene until I saw the film.

There was a special feel to the production which I have not experienced since then. Wadleigh was directing by example. He was shooting. It was a cameraman's film. We were supposed to figure out the shots and work out who was doing what. There were some terrific cameramen, who I learned from. David Myers recorded the famous Port-O-San scene. We have worked together since then. Other talented cameramen I got to know were Dick Pearce, Ed Lynch, Ted Churchill, and Chuck Levey. Larry Johnson and I have remained friends over the years. I can not think of any other film which started so many friendships continued over the years.

The production people were very supportive. When Warners came in to pay for the film, helicopters ferried in film stock. At one point an Indian doctor appeared to inject cameramen with Vitamin B12 to keep them going. It made little difference to me because the event was an adrenaline rush. I slept for maybe two hours over the duration.

When it was over I went to the trailer to drop off my last rolls of film.

Later I went to the editing room to see my footage. Thelma Schoonmaker did not treat me like the least important cameraman on the film. She offered me a job as an assistant editor. I turned it down because I had found an optical printer and was in the middle of spraying on developer, printing with mattes in an effort to discover abstract expressionism in film.

My only gripe with *Woodstock* is with my credit. I got a "special thanks" rather than "additional camera." A number of my shots were used in the film so a special thanks is an inappropriate credit, even for the youngest and least important cameraman on the *Woodstock* film.

DON LENZER

A VISION FOR ANTONIA

(DON WASN'T IN HIS usual place at the Chelsea Hotel when I found him. Don's peripetatic camerawork had taken him to California just prior to Woodstock. Luckily, I was able to bring him back so he could count this as one of the many seminal events of the 1960s he had participated in and documented for the world.)

We were up high, very high, maybe twelve feet though it felt like twenty— Richard Chew and I—high up in a tractor trailer looking down at the countless sleeping bags that were half submerged in the mud below; in the distance about as far as the eye could see, three hundred or so thousand rain-drenched spectators. But our eyes were drawn at that instant to the mud below. I've often thought of that moment and many others connected to the events of those few days that took place nearly thirty years ago. Lately it's become an exercise in memory and the truth and fantasy of it are not always easy to separate. I'm not sure anymore if it was Richard or I who said it as we stood up there on the second day of the festival, but one of us said, "One day when we look back on this, I guess we'll be happy we were here." How little we imagined then the enormous impact those events would have on our lives.

Thirty years ago. I'm astonished at how fast the time has gone by. It's not such a long time in big historical terms, but it's long in terms of a man's life, my life, and as I say, I'm not always sure the memories are so accurate now. But the exercise of remembering is an interesting one, a little game I sometimes play with myself. There was a period when I think I denied the importance of that moment in my life, in the life of our culture for that matter. And I even felt a little guilty spending as much time as I did reflecting on it. Its importance seemed to pale next to Mississippi Summer and so many other moments of the Civil Rights Movement; next to Vietnam and the way it wrenched our country apart; next to the way a generation of German youth was trying to deal with or deny the legacy of fascism and the Holocaust; next to the events of May 1968 in France that nearly toppled

DeGaulle; next to the coup in Chile that with the help of our government crushed democracy in that country. I realize, though, that Woodstock was both a real and complex event as well as a mythic presence in the narrative of my generation. It was the biggest free gathering ever of peace and music; of sex, drugs and rock and roll; three days of ecstatic community and solidarity. But it was also "hip capitalism", bad trips and a muddy, debris-strewn disaster zone, And no matter what other young people had gone through in other times, this was part of our reality and out myths and finally, I think its not a bad exercise to try to make some sense of it.

I was in California, my native California, on vacation with a girl friend, when I received a call about shooting at Woodstock. I'd just finished producing a film for public TV about student radicals at Stanford University and had never even heard of the festival plans and really wasn't in the mood to return to New York to work on some pop music film. It just didn't mean much to me at the time. I loved the music, particularly the San Francisco and British varieties, and I'd been excited and somewhat influenced by D.A. Pennebaker's *Monterey Pop*. When my girlfriend told me I had to do it, that it was going to be the biggest music festival ever, bigger than Monterey, bigger than the Isle of Wight, I remained unmoved. But I was impressed by the prospect of getting together for a multiple camera shoot with a good many of the heaviest documentary cameramen (and in those days they were all men) in the country. Somehow I was led to believe all the stars, all the people I respected like Leacock and Pennybaker and the Maysles would be there. Although competition was a value on which we didn't place a premium in those days and the feeling of comradery was truly great among those of us who were relative newcomers, I'm sure I wanted to come up against the "top guns."

There's something you have to understand about that time that seems to have no parallel with the present. It's not that we were any more ambitious than young filmmakers are today. But there was something in the air then, something that led us to believe we were part of a great transforming force in the life of our society and culture. And the music, which was new and completely exciting, had a lot to do with it. We were engaged as cinematographers not merely in describing it but in interpreting it. In a matter of speaking, in "playing visual rock and roll". That was terribly important to us. And the images of Janis Joplin and Ravi Shankar at Monterey were the ones that inspired and challenged us. Ironically, none of the star cameramen who had shot that footage showed up at Woodstock.

Except for one, the cameramen who shot at Woodstock were all relative newcomers. The one exception was a man by the name of David Myers with whom

I drove up to the festival from New York. I'm stunned to think that David was only a few years younger then than I am now. It seems like only yesterday that we were driving to Bethel together and that David a couple of days later shot what was arguably the most famous and best scene in the film, the one with the Port-O-San man. David, I understand, is a healthy eighty-five now, which only means that time flies and that you better live it well if you have the good fortune, and from everything I hear, David has. I remember him talking a lot on the drive about his wife, Barbara, who's an artist and was a model for the photographer, Imogene Cunningham. The wonderful black and white image that I later found of Barbara as *Savonarola's Look* in a Cunningham monograph will be etched in my mind forever.

So many of the images I retain in my consciousness of that lived experience of Woodstock are faded now and some no doubt distorted like the ride on the back of a motorcycle (was it Richard Pearce's?) over a dirt road to a dilapidated dude ranch motel where we were supposed to be lodged over the course of the festival. We got through to the motel that first evening, I think, but never again. I don't even remember the when or where of ever sleeping again during the next three days. I must have slept, but I don't remember. In fact all I remember is standing up in the doorway of that tractor trailer looking down at the muddy sleeping bags. After that we were deep inside the experience, full bore inside it.

I remember being on the stage a lot, filming a lot of performers and being connected to what was going on, feeling a part of it, of the music in a way I rarely have since. It started out hot and never let up, right there next to Richie Havens, his foot filling the frame, beating out a rhythm that seemed never to subside. Anyway that's the way I remember it. It was easier for me there on stage than to make forays out into the crowd.

For David Myers, I think, it was just the opposite, and he captured some of the most wonderful moments of the film out there. I remember him telling me that the only performer he really longed to film was Janis Joplin. I wanted to film her too, but when I got the chance, the electric black and white images of her great performance in Pennebaker's Monterey Pop were so lodged in my consciousness that I think I was inhibited from doing anything really original, was trying too hard maybe to compete with someone else's work rather than become fully engaged with what was going on as I most often did when I was filming on stage.

I think I chose to wander most of the time through some of the more bucolic spots during the moments when I was off stage rather than wade into the crowd. I remember in particular floating on a pond in a rowboat with the young soundman, Bruce Pearlman, filming the now famous nude bathing scene. I remember feeling a little uncomfortable with our intrusiveness. And when I heard people call to us to join them in the water, I became really concerned that they wouldn't accept our friendly refusal, but would simply pull us and our camera equipment in with them. But that fear was never visible in the images we captured that day, images that became almost iconic of the spontaneity, naturalness and freedom of a whole generation.

Was it the governor who declared the festival site a disaster area? I'm not sure now, but I remember medevac helicopters flying in on a hill overlooking the festival a little like a scene out of *MASH*. I was up there filming the rock impresario, Bill Graham, watching the choppers bringing in supplies and taking spectators who were probably suffering from bad trips out of the area. I remember how critical he was of the festival promoters, of how little they had prepared for the hundreds of thousands of young people who had inundated the area. It was a long way up there from the peaceful scene of nude bathers in the pond down below. There was nothing intentional about the festival being free.

Everything seemed to coalesce in Jimi Hendrix's performance at the end of the festival. And it also seemed to inspire me to capture some of the most incredible footage I've ever shot. By the time I heard the first few bars of his brilliant, twisted "Star-Spangled Banner," I was totally involved, at one with the music and performer.

I was on automatic pilot. It was the "zen art of cinematography," and I was finding visual equivalents for the music that would surely recreate for future spectators the amazing experience, my experience, of being there, and they'd have the most privileged seats in the house. There was one problem though, and it was a big one. No one would ever see most of the incredible footage I shot of Hendrix's performance because I was so into it that I didn't realize I had run out of film long before he had finished playing.

My seven-and-a-half-year-old daughter, Antonia, loves rock and roll. She hasn't seen *Woodstock* yet, but I think she'll soon be ready for it and I'm looking forward to her response. She's heard about it, though, from my wife, Bettina, who was a sixteen-year-old in Germany at the time it came out. She tells us that seeing the movie as a teenager was one of the things that drew her to America and therefore is partly responsible for our finding each other and is indirectly responsible for Antonia coming into the world. That's a powerful connection between *Woodstock* and the two people I cherish most. I don't know whether it's completely or even partly true, but it makes a good story and I like to believe it and I like to tell it to my daughter.

What I do know for sure, though, is that the idea of *Woodstock*, however much it diverges from the reality of the experience, is very much alive for those of us who were there and even more, perhaps, for many who only heard about it or saw the movie. Even then, thirty years ago, it represented something far greater than the reality we experienced, not that the music and community weren't great highs. Surely it represented a "vision of fulfilled desire" that stood in such contrast to the boredom and flatness and competitive isolation of so many of our parents' lives. It was a vision of something—dare I say it?—snappier, more colorful, more erotic, more generous, more equitable, more morally worthy of us, that I hope—that I'm certain—will animate some future generations, perhaps even Antonia's.

PART IV

OKAY, WHERE'S THE MOVIE?

THELMA SCHOONMAKER

POSTPRODUCTION IN NEW YORK (AUGUST 19— DECEMBER 7, 1969)

DALE: I was thinking of something I could use at the start of postproduction that would be your philosophical view, not the mechanical thing of how to put it all together. What were you and Michael thinking about? What was the process that you went through as you had 120, 130 odd hours of stuff to deal with?

THELMA: I guess after we got over the exhaustion, the first thoughts we had were how to make it all work, how to intersperse the documentary footage with the concert footage. And just the act of finding a way to project all six images from the cameras that were on the stage together at the same time, with six projectors locked together—gave us a feeling right away as to whether the multiple image idea was going to work or not. It was really quite amazing to be able to do that and have everything stay in sync—which it did. And I think we were all a bit overwhelmed, quite frankly, by the enormity of the work that had to be done.

We had people syncing dailies for a long time, since almost everything had to be synced by eye—particularly the footage on the stage because we didn't have any way to sync up all those cameras with each other —we had no common sync signal for all those six cameras on the stage. We had to spend months and months just eye-syncing all of the various cameramen's footage—which was completely nightmarish because the 16mm magazines were jamming all the time because of humidity and rain and other problems.

The cameramen would whip off the jammed magazine and put on another— so you might be in the middle of the Grateful Dead—which was the hardest number we ever had to sync up—very low light level—and a cameraman would have switched camera rolls in the middle of the song and just to even figure out where the hell—which camera roll went with which camera roll, and how much time had elapsed during the change was a nightmare. Even to try and figure out who was singing, since you could barely see them—and get it all hooked up—was a huge job.

I've never in my life ever heard of people syncing dailies twenty-four hours a day, which is what we did. We had three shifts including a midnight-to-dawn shift of people. Scorsese and Wadleigh were the people who were deciding which groups and which numbers to shoot.

Cooperation with the people who were backstage trying to make deals with the performers…who was that, Dale, anyway? Who was back there trying to get them to agree to let us shoot them?

DALE: Well there were, among other people, Eric Blackstead and I don't know who else was doing any of that stuff. Danny Turbeville was there, but he was working for Eric so to speak, just kind of trying to line up the numbers of the groups. And somebody was typing and/or printing out in some arcane fashion, on the Xerox machine that was in the mud in the trailer, the order of the songs and what the groups were going to be singing.

THELMA: That was an incredibly important thing when you imagine that there we were—I mean you'll have to pardon me, I'm going to jump all around when I talk. Is that all right?

DALE: It's okay. I'm putting it in, that's all.

THELMA: It was very critical. First of all, having lived in the Caribbean for most of my young life—until I was fourteen—I was very ignorant about the music that was being performed there. Quite ignorant. So I had no participation in any of that decision-making. It was all being done by Scorsese and Wadleigh, and obviously Eric Blackstead in the back. And the fact that both Scorsese and Wadleigh knew the songs so well and knew where the chorus was going to come or when a particular lyric was going to come—it was amazingly important that they knew all of that and felt the music as deeply as they did.

Wadleigh had an unbelievable ability to move at exactly the right time because he knew a chorus was coming or a special lyric was coming, and he would make a special camera movement at that moment, which was amazingly valuable. If we hadn't had his camera, frankly, I don't think we would have had anything. The film would never have been as powerful as it was, because that up-angle with him bent over that camera for twenty-four hours a day for three days. I don't know how he did it, it was a superhuman feat. That up-angle is what gave us some of our most powerful imagery. He, of course, knew that and positioned himself exactly right.

And it was, as I say, his intense understanding of the music that allowed him to photograph it so beautifully.

But for those of us who were there trying to help out, my job was mainly to make sure that there was film in the cameras, if at all possible, which was difficult enough. And to try to get the people that were doing the lighting on the stage to give us enough light so that we could see what we were filming, I would go over to Chip Monck who was in charge of lighting, and beg him and plead for him to give us more light on someone like Janis Joplin and he would just say, "I don't give a damn about your film. I'm lighting for those people out there."

And so it was a constant battle, and press photographers were constantly trying to get up on the platform we had built for Wadleigh so that he would have that beautiful up-angle, so we were constantly fighting, not fighting with them, but trying to keep them from jostling him.

People were flying over the fence in states of ecstasy, and being handled very beautifully by the security people. And it was like being in Vietnam. For me, at the time, it was a total and complete nightmare. I did not enjoy it, I have to say. Looking over the fence at all the people out there was a bit frightening. The smell of the mud and the garbage and things was a bit frightening. The fact that there was no place to sleep or eat or wash or anything—it was just an amazing ordeal.

And we were, of course, so close to the speakers that we were just being pounded with incredible decibels, and so for me, it was just constant worry. I was terrified that the film wasn't going to be exposed all right and because of the constant rain there were going to be major disasters. We had gone up there with no insurance and all this equipment and all this film and there was a strong possibility that we were going to have a lot of problems when we got back and looked at the footage.

Luckily for us, we didn't. But we didn't know that at that time. So I think, for me, it was just a constant worry while I was up there. Whereas for Marty and Wadleigh, it was more of an exhilarating experience because they had more of a sense of what they were getting than I did.

And as I said many times, when dawn came on that final day and Sha-Na-Na came out, I thought we had all gone mad. I mean, I had never seen that group. I didn't know what the hell was going on. I literally thought that we had just lost it—that we had just been up too long and were beginning to hallucinate. And then, Jimi Hendrix came out and played that incredible set and I'll never forget that. That was just a stunning moment in my life. But I wasn't quite sure that I hadn't completely gone mad either. And then, of course, we were just so exhausted at the end of it and we had to pack up all the equipment, and I went out into the field with—who was it?

DALE: David?

THELMA: David who?

DALE: David Myers?

THELMA: No, Pearce. I think I was out in the field with Pearce for a bit, filming all those battlefield images and coming back and trying to get everything packed up and getting into a something…I don't know what the hell we were in—starting to drive back to New York and stopping at a restaurant to get something to eat for the first time in three days and I'll never forget that Wadleigh was sitting in front of a plate of spaghetti and he suddenly just crashed into his plate of spaghetti. He was just so exhausted that he literally passed out.

And then we were all trying to get the car keys away from him so that we could drive back to the city safely, and he was in such a state that he refused to allow that —even though he had just passed out—he wouldn't allow us to get the keys out of his pocket. It was just a nightmare. I can't tell you. We were all just covered with mud—and so exhausted. Anyway, that was my feeling while we were up there. Later on I came to enjoy it in retrospect, but not while I was there, I have to admit.

Anyway, how we decided to put numbers in or not: whether numbers went in or not had a great deal to do with whether we had gotten good enough footage of them. First of all, whether Wadleigh's great camera work was good, whether he had enough light, because he just used to scream to me, "Get me some light! Get me some light!" as he was looking through the view finder and couldn't see Janis Joplin.

Anyway, if we had good multiple cameras, or if we had just one camera, which is what we had mainly for people like Richie Havens, for example—that would determine what went in the film and what did not. We would have loved to have Janis Joplin in the film, but our footage was too dark, as was the situation with the Grateful Dead.

I mean Marty spent, I can't imagine how long, trying to sync that up and I don't think we ever did get it all synced up.

DALE: And they never made it into even the *Director's Cut*.

THELMA: No. Because it was hopeless. The footage was hopelessly dark and it was a mess; it was just a mess. So that, right away, determined what went in and what didn't. And then as we went on and we saw how long the film was going to be because we had all that good documentary stuff in addition, then we began weeding down and weeding down, so that things like—whateverhisname Sommers?

DALE: Burt Sommers?

THELMA: Right! Burt Sommers went out, even though we all loved him. And Johnny Winter, and then what was the blues band? They never went in either.

DALE: Butterfield Blues?

THELMA: Butterfield Blues—which we had a lovely number on. We had a lot of great footage...

DALE: Melanie.

THELMA: Melanie, right. And then, of course, if we had too many numbers on The Who or whatever, then of course we had to prune down there too. And so it was just gradually a whittling down process and finding out what impacted the most.

There are certain numbers, for example, Joe Cocker—where we had practically no footage at all. We had Wadleigh's beautiful, beautiful camera, and so the power of his performance meant that you didn't really need that much. And so it was rather simply done because it had to be. It wasn't a stylistic decision. But the power of his performance is what makes it work.

Same thing with Richie Havens. We had practically no footage on that either. In fact, the first person who worked on it just kept cutting away, in a newsreel way, to any old thing in order to make up for the fact that we didn't have enough footage to cut him together. And one of my jobs was to go and try to correct that and somehow make it work even though we had very little footage. And so it was just a constant process of trying and screening and whittling down. Where you intersperse certain things was so important, you know. And there was the basic chronology, of course.

DALE: You guys were trying to create the sense of three days. Two nightfalls.

THELMA: Oh, definitely. Of course, we open the film with the building of the stage and we closed with the battlefield images of people walking across this landscape which had been devastated by having half a million people on it for three days, which worked so beautifully with intercuts of the "Star-Spangled

Banner" being destroyed by Jimi Hendrix on stage. So yes, we definitely had a chronological conception.

DALE: Talk about the documentary stuff. When I talked with Tina (Hirsch), for example, she said that when she came up to apply for work, there was never a question in her mind about wanting to work on the performance. She was interested in the people. What fascination did you find in the documentary side?

THELMA: Well, we had working with us some documentary cameramen we didn't know at all, and some that we knew well—David Myers being one that was the most important to me because I had known his work and had admired it for so long. What was important was his ability and others as well, to wander around this amazing thing that was evolving before our eyes and find the right ways to make sure that the world saw it.

Al Wertheimer's decision to interview that lunatic woman in the information booth is perhaps something that not every cameraman would have chosen to do. These guys were completely unsupervised. They would come in at night, and tell us what they had gotten - there were about fifteen teams, right?

DALE: All together, but there were about half a dozen in the field.

THELMA: Well anyway, the decision of what you film and who you decide to talk to at great length is, of course, extremely critical. And David Myers with his wonderful sense of human beings, and of who might potentially turn out to be someone interesting, was a godsend because his choices weren't conventional. He just had an innate sense of who to go to and who to talk to. And David had a wonderful interviewing style which was quite critical. He wouldn't formulate any particularly significant question. He would just open a conversation with people.

For example, when he filmed the Port-O-San Man, he just said, "What are you doing there?" That's how he began, and I'll never forget I thought how brilliant that was of him to do that. Just to ask that question instead of, "What do you feel about being up here at Woodstock?" Then later on, he did ask that question. No, as a matter of fact he did it again in a roundabout way. He said, "It's great of you to be doing this for these kids." And that's when we got the wonderful answer.

DALE: David's initial question was, "Getting a little behind on your work, aren't you?"

THELMA: Oh, was it! Right you're quite right! You know, it's disarming when he would do that. And people would open up and sort of blossom and say the kind of things that you really need, to show what's happening at an event like this. And then when he said, "It's nice of you to do this for the kids..." and the man said, "I'm happy to do it. One of my sons is here and the other is in the DMZ..." I mean you couldn't ask for more than that...because of the resonance of Vietnam throughout the movie.

So it was extremely important that we had such excellent people out there totally unsupervised. And they would come back and tell us what they were getting, but we had no idea. We just knew they were good and we were just praying that we would get what we needed. Then we bought footage from a lot of people that we saw filming. That's how we got the building of the stage, because we weren't even up there then.

DALE: The two Mikes.

THELMA: Right. One of them had a wooden leg, of course.

DALE: Both of whom were British. And both of whom had been hired by another Mike...Lang...and by Porter Bibb and the Maysles.

THELMA: It was a wonderful revelation when we began to see what they had gotten. We were very, very lucky to have had them there.

DALE: In the editing style, the multiple images, how did they all evolve?

THELMA: Well, that's actually a technological thing. The introduction of digital technology to editing films has created certain interesting situations that nobody ever expected. For example, we now do incredibly complicated scratch mixes here in the editing room without having to go to a sound studio before we screen rough cuts. Which is now creating problems when we do go to our final mix because we've been mixing the film in such a complicated way—sometimes with twenty-four tracks—that when we get into the mixing room we sometimes want things the way that we had done them and the mixer feels, in some ways, cut out of the creative process at those moments because he hasn't woven it together. It's quite amazing what we're doing, but we still need something even better for the final mix. So what I mean by that, is that multiple image was a profound change which came about strictly because of a technological revolution. What happened with the flatbed multiple picture head editing machines we used on *Woodstock* is that we had one of the first in the country—do we know this for a fact?

DALE: We know this for a fact.

THELMA: We had the first KEM flatbed editing machine in America—it played three picture heads. Wadleigh had gone to shoot an Aretha Franklin concert in Rhode Island for the Merv Griffin show, and there were three cameras running. We were able to put all three cameras up on the flatbed and were able—for the first time in editing rooms—to be able to see all of the three cameras synced together simultaneously. We were sitting there watching this wonderful performance by Aretha Franklin, and we said to ourselves, "God, that really is great. It really dynamizes her performance, having the three images up there all together." So that was the germ of the idea for the multiple images in WOODSTOCK. But it happened because of a technological development.

Of course we had been deeply in influenced by *Monterey Pop*, a wonderful example of how to capture a music festival—not wanting to duplicate it, but madly in love with the way that the performers were shown. So when the whole idea, the possibility of *Woodstock*, first came up, instantly we decided that it was going to be multiple image as much as possible.

DALE: Were you orchestrating them deliberately?

THELMA: No, I think the number determined how, or if, we used multiple image. The way certain things had been shot obviously lent themselves to flashy uses of it—like in Ten Years After—or more carefully constructed uses like the Who, where it was orchestrated quite a bit more and took a lot of experimenting and juggling around so that we could get this really almost theatrical way of using it. Whereas in Ten Years After, there were just a lot of times where there were two cameras, or we would have one camera and duplicate it on the other side so it was actually the same camera but the image was flipped and we could get very flashy uses of it.

But then there were other performers where you just wanted to have a single image. It depended on the performer and how many cameramen we had on the stage at the time, how good their footage was, how good the lighting was—there were a lot of factors that went into the final decisions.

I think the wonderful use of it by Scorsese who did some of the seminal early editing, particularly on Sha-Na-Na and Santana—the wonderful witty way he used the mulitple image was a great example of his extraordinary editing genius.

DALE: Talk about that a second, would you? Were those the two that Marty essentially…

THELMA: Marty worked the most on those, yes, before he left to go to Hollywood. And I don't think we ever even changed Sha-Na-Na after he left. It was just so incredibly witty and wonderful the way he'd done it. My memory is that we hardly touched Sha-Na-Na.

DALE: While we were in New York in postproduction, do you remember anything that was something you'd like to preserve forever?

THELMA: You mean a memory?

DALE: Well, process. I talked for a couple of pages about the October screenings as being, for me...

THELMA: You have to remind me about the October screenings.

DALE: Well, the October screenings were when—for the first time, after we'd gone through twenty-four hours of syncing for four weeks—that we were then able not just to sync, but to actually look at the material. And we had, by that time, the six projectors locked together. And we had the variable speed silent 16mm projector on which we could look through MOS (silent) footage, and we just sat in the screening rooms for four or five days?

THELMA: Yes, that was a really remarkable experience. I do remember very vividly what that was like. To see all those images working together was, even though it was haphazard, what was on what projector, you still could get a feeling of what you had. And it was an amazing experience.

DALE: To me, that was almost better than the finished film.

THELMA: Well, the dailies always are in a way.

DALE: Because the whole sense of reality, what we were numb to on the site, we could now begin to appreciate because we were the lucky people who had all of these other viewpoints. We only had one pair of eyes while we were there, and now we had fifteen pairs of eyes.

THELMA: And you're right that perhaps nothing ever equals just being able to watch the raw six cameras working together—maybe nothing ever equals the power of that. And of course there's no way you could ever project an image like that for the masses. It's something that can only be done under a controlled situation. But the rawness of it, the accidental way that things happen—maybe one cameraman panning one way and another panning the other way—and it all working together to create a kaleidoscopic effect with incredible energy, yes, you never get that raw feeling again. Once we started to have to lasso it all and get a comprehensible piece of film, perhaps we lost a little bit of it.

DALE: Unfortunately, that was the task at hand. Rather than invent some sort of wide-screen video that would capture all six images at the same time…that would have been ideal.

THELMA: Of course, it didn't always hold up. If one cameraman's camera jammed up we'd be watching black for a while, and it was very very documentary-like and accidental. But, of course, being documentary lovers, that didn't bother us.

DALE: Did you comment on Marty Andrews's tooth?

THELMA: Wait a minute, I don't remember that.

DALE: Well, he reminds me that he was pulling out some insulation from a wire with his tooth and it was in the frame…and part of his front tooth flipped out and it was caught on film, and apparently in the screening, it was run back and forth so many times that you could never find the image again. And he was really pissed that the image didn't make it into the movie.

THELMA: I don't remember that at all. I do remember certain accidental things happening, for example, when we were editing and trying out various multiple image ideas, I remember that I just slapped together Gabe Pressman (of WNBC-TV) on one side of the screen and the couple making love in the grass on the other side—I just sort of slapped it together. I didn't intend for it to stay that way, but when everybody saw it, it was just so funny that it stayed. So there was a great deal of that kind of stuff that went on.

DALE: There were a batch of accidents, of accidental inventions…

THELMA: Well that happens all the time in editing and during the shooting of feature films too. Scorsese is someone who loves accidents, and if he can incorporate it into the film, he will. It's a wonderful thing and it happens all the time in editing because you just sort of put two shots together and something happens that you just never expected. And a third thing is created by this accidental placing of two things together. So accident is very important.

DALE: Talk about freeze framing—from your point of view.

THELMA: Really, Wadleigh had a very strong conception for the Who material. He really wanted to make a very theatrical event out of those numbers because we did have good footage and good light. And those are all his ideas. About the slowing down and freeze framing and the wonderful way that the guitar is destroyed. He had a very, very strong vision for that sequence, as he did for Jimi Hendrix at the end. Well, just because of the way he shot the damned thing, so brilliant the way—at that time, after having been up for three days—to have had the presence of mind and the artistic sense to hold on the frame when Jimi Hendrix went down out of it, and let him come back up into it, just gives you an example of the formidable talent he has. I'll never forget that. At that point in the festival I was probably a vegetable. But he could hold that camera and conceive of that shot with the crane in the background.

DALE: It's the crane in the background and the arching of the structure of the stage…

THELMA: Right. That he could get it together enough at that point in a state of total exhaustion, and lay down such an artistic image. And to have the courage to, instead of following Jimi Hendrix when he went out of frame, to know how wonderful it would be if he went out of frame and came back up again. Well this is real artistic thinking. I don't know how he did it.

DALE: Another point in there is where Jimi stares him down and then starts manipulating his feet to push the pedals—it's a real "watch this, you SOB."

THELMA: It's so beautifully shot. I'm telling you, he really knew how to do it and he had such a sympathy with the material. And the film is filled with those marvelous moments of his; for example, deciding to shoot up, in a sharp up-angle, into Richie Havens' toothless mouth, some cameramen would think, "Oops. I'd better avoid this. Maybe if I move over to the side, maybe people won't notice." Wadleigh knows, "Hey this is great. This guy is the perfect person to be opening this festival. I'm going to shoot right up there and get this dynamite, dynamic up-angle shot and not care about the teeth." I mean, even though you laugh when you first see the teeth, it just doesn't matter after a while and he knew that. He had tremendous courage.

DALE: The courage to put himself so close to the performers and then augment it with a five point nine lens. So, think about the Bob Hite piece, which I think is one of the most brilliant magazines I've ever seen, uncut, to be able to follow and be able to listen and to anticipate the guy with the cigarette pack coming up around him and going to the drummer and then coming back again to Bob, all in one take.

THELMA: You not only have to have great artistic skill, you have to have incredible physical skill and control—which Wadleigh had. It was just extraordinary what he did. I do not know how he could do it. It would be one thing to do on a long shoot day, but to shoot for fifteen or sixteen hours under those terrifying conditions, bent over a camera, bent over—I just don't know how he did it.

DALE: One of the things that Tina was talking about and maybe you have a perspective on this, is the Jimi Hendrix piece at the end, and apparently Wads was putting down, on paper, a series of cuts that he wanted Tina to assemble. That he had done just from memory. And it was an A roll, a B roll, a C roll, and he gave her a list...do you remember this at all?

THELMA: Sort of. I remember how clear his vision was for that sequence.

DALE: But then what he did was, she did it—they laced up three of the six projectors and he converged the three images into one and then played the three projectors. So that you had, in very rough form, the overlapping of the single image that he wanted to create and that eventually became the ending of the film—the "Purple Haze."

THELMA: I was involved with the editing at some point but I think he had already done the basic work. I'm not hundred percent sure of the chronology of that. But he had done the basic work and he probably just asked me to do a little bit of work. But he had a very strong idea on that.

DALE: What else would you like to say?

THELMA: I don't know. You've talked about the whole battle on the lot and all that stuff?

DALE: Well, I have. I've written a piece called "Ping Pong" which is about the ping-pong table.

THELMA: The stealing of the tracks and all that stuff?

DALE: I said that they were gone, but I didn't say that I stole them.

THELMA: And the press screening in New York?

DALE: I didn't talk about the press screening in New York.

THELMA: I can talk generally about the attitude.

DALE: Let's go to the end. I have a wonderful piece—Charlie Cirigliano scurrying through and picking up prints from Technicolor and taking them to Wads at the airport because it is reel 110 of the film. The credits were on the last reel and had to be flown to New York... where the film was being screened for the press, tell me what you feel, what you think at that moment...

THELMA: Just to lead up to it, the executives just didn't seem to understand what we had and they were just encouraging us, they just kept saying "you have to get the film out quickly or people are just going to forget about the event." You don't understand—it's just a news event—what are you fussing about it so much—why are you spending so much effort on this complex editing—we just had to get it out. And we knew that we had something special and that when it came out people would respond to it. So there was a big tug of war that was going on the lot, and we were mixing in a studio environment which was very alien to us. We were long-haired, crazy, documentary filmmakers from New York and for us to be mixing in the same room where *The Jazz Singer* was done—if it was done there, I don't know if it was exactly the same room—was a little odd and it took a great deal of adjustment.

So there we were, we arrive on this studio lot and it was a great deal of adjusting for us. We had never seen four mixers, for example, one doing the dialog, one doing the effects, one doing the music and one swinging the tracks across the wide screen—that was a whole new setup for us. I think they thought we were all completely mad. And gradually, we began to form friendships with some of the people we were working with.

But I'll never forget one time when Joe Cocker was up on the screen and the man who was the head of sound at Warner Bros., I think his name was George Groves... came in the room and he had mixed *The Jazz Singer*, the first sound film. And there he was watching *Woodstock* being mixed and it was a little bit of a shock for him. And he said, "You'll never be able to lay music down that loud on film. It won't stay. It'll jump off the film," meaning it would distort or it would never reproduce in the theater, and we said, "Well, we're going to mix it like this anyway." And he said to me after watching Joe Cocker, "You know you shouldn't make fun of spastics."

But my favorite experience was with the sound editor, Ed Scheid. There were these two wonderful sound editors who had worked on many many many films, ever since they were very young men and they were probably in their early sixties. They were, at first, a little suspicious of us, but then we began to become friends. And they were always saying, "Aw come on, let us put in a little 'Land of the Pharoahs' wind in the storm sequence'", and I said, "Oh, good heavens, no.

We're cinéma vérité documentarians...we never put anything in that isn't actually recorded at the site..." and they'd just say, "Come on, let me show you...let me just put in some lightning bolts from..." and then he would name some other big film. And I would resist and resist and finally he would take me into his little room, which was a concrete cell with a Moviola clattering away, deafening, no carpet on the floor or anything, literally like a row of prison cells where these hardworking guys edited. And with incredible speed he would slap something together for me and show it to me, and I was impressed. And finally we did allow him to put in some stuff and amplify some of the sound. So we became very good friends and I loved him. And then finally he would show a little bit of his... shall we say "not normal" side because they were forced to dress a certain way on the lot during the week, but on the weekends he would wear two different colored socks. Which I was very impressed by and I think it was his way of showing us that he could be a bit of a free spirit too. And so I loved him, they were great guys. And by the end of it we were all having a great time. But at the beginning it was quite stiff.

Anyway, during this whole period, we just kept being warned by studio people that what we were doing was mad, and that they had no intention of releasing a film this long, etc. etc. and so finally when we did go to the press screening in New York, people were dancing in the aisles, there was an amazing reaction going on— and it was very tense between us and the studio executives. Finally, Ted Ashley came up and tapped me on the shoulder and I jumped about six feet because we were all so tense, and he said, "You were right. It is going to work."

TINA
HIRSCH

PEOPLE ARE ALWAYS FASCINATING TO ME

(TINA'S SENSE OF ORGANIZATION and detail placed her squarely at Thelma's right hand, the assistant editor in charge of the "documentary" material and the "room.")

DALE: Okay, good morning. This is Tina, this is Tina…how do you want to be known? H-I-R-S-C-H. Tina Hirsch. The day is January 5, 1999.

TINA: Okay, let's listen just to make sure. Testing, testing.

DALE: Okay, do you remember when you first came into our offices and what happened and how you ended up where you ended up?

TINA: I remember it very well. I got a call from Sonya on a day that my eyes were bandaged because I had left my contact lenses in too long the day before. I was thrilled to hear they were making a movie about the Woodstock Festival. Thrilled to hear that they were interested in interviewing me, but had to tell her that unfortunately, I couldn't be in that day and would tomorrow be alright. Tomorrow was fine with her, so, I went in the next morning and interviewed with Thelma Schoonmaker.

Thelma explained to me that the movie was going to be divided in two parts during the editorial process: one part was the documentary section, which was basically the story of the festival and the people who were there, and the other was the music section which was to be the cut musical acts. She asked me which part I would be interested in and, of course, for me, there was just no question, I was much more interested in the documentary section, the event and the people who were there than the performances. I was much more interested in finding out why the people were there, who they were, what they were like and what they were thinking. People are endlessly fascinating to me.

DALE: Are there things that you remember that passed through your eyes that never made it into the film that you would have loved to have seen in the film? I mean, is there anything like that?

TINA: I can't think of anything off hand. Thelma did a fabulous job of getting in all the goodies, and I actually saw every frame of documentary footage because one of my jobs, probably one of the most important jobs I had, was checking sync on everything; making sure that the sounds coming out of the people's mouths were in sync with the movement of their lips. I should explain that the problem with syncing the film occurred because there was no slating system the way there is now. Now there are these things called smart slates that carry a time code and make syncing automatic. In those days they used a little bloop light or handclaps, if anything, but frequently camera and sound were on the run and they didn't feel they had time to get slates at all. Out in the field nobody ever thinks of the editorial process, so it was kind of sloppy. We had scores of people syncing in three shifts: a day shift, a night shift, and a graveyard shift. Some syncers were better than others and some scenes were easier than others to sync.

Wherever sections of picture and track had not been matched, it was up to me to figure it out. I had a great time trying to sync up things like someone splashing in the water or a dog barking. I had to create the rhythm in my head from seeing the picture and then seek it out on the sound track. I got to be pretty good at it.

DALE: What was your experience prior to this?

TINA: Frankly, I had very little experience prior to this. My first film job was syncing dailies on *Hi Mom*, Brian DePalma's second film. My second job, the one that I had just finished, right before the Woodstock Festival started, was a hyphenate-job: assistant editor-script girl. I had to get up at six in the morning to go out on the set, be on the set all day, come back, have a quick dinner, sync dailies till the wee hours, and then be up at six the next morning. All that for a hundred dollars a week. I had just gotten home from location when I got the call on *Woodstock*. In fact, I didn't go to the festival, even though I'd planned to, because I had just come back from location and I was too tired. Thank God I didn't go, because, in the end, I got to see a lot more than anybody who was there and I didn't have to go through all pain and aggravation everyone there did.

DALE: What was it like working with Thelma? What were you being asked to do?

TINA: It was great working with Thelma. I like Thelma a lot and I have great respect for her work. We're still friends to this day. Thelma gave me a lot of autonomy in the cutting room. My job, in the beginning, was, as I said, to check sync on everything and to figure out a coding system for the documentary footage. Later on my job was to keep things organized and running so that Thelma could concentrate on editing. Basically, that's an assistant's job. Sometimes, you get to sit with an editor, but most frequently, you don't.

DALE: When it came time for the screenings, can you describe the screenings, like say, the October screening?

TINA: Let me go back and describe the first screening I ever witnessed. One morning I came in and found a note on my bench, left by Michael Wadleigh, saying "Please put this film together according to my list." Beneath the note was a yellow legal pad with three columns of numbers. One column was labeled "A", one "B", and one "C". In each column was either a set of code numbers or the word "black". I was to put the footage indicated by the code numbers in either the A, B, or C reel and black leader in the other two. Sometimes the film in the A reel would overlap the film in the B reel, and the B would overlap the C, but basically there was film on one reel at a time as I wound it through the synchronizer.

I had just finished assembling the footage when Michael came in, and said, "Great, let's run it." The screening room was set up with three projectors each pointed to a single square in the center of the wall. Rather than three separate images, you would see the images on the three reels overlap, so that when an image came up on the A roll and ran for a while, the film would come up on the B roll, overlapping it giving you the impression of a dissolve. And then B would dissolve to C. They wouldn't always dissolve; sometimes they'd overlap for quite a while, you know in a long-lap dissolve or a by-pack of some sort. As we watched the Jimi Hendrix sequence, virtually the same as it is today, emerged from those projectors. All figured out on paper by Michael who had never really cut anything before—at least that's what I'd been told. He wasn't able to physically cut the film, but he was able to conceive this wonderful sequence in his head. I was amazed that he could put it down on paper and it would play as a sequence. A wonderful sequence.

DALE: Do you remember what the music was?

TINA: Yes, it was "Purple Haze" and then it went into the "Star-Spangled Banner." It was the end of the movie. He cut the end of the movie—all on paper.

DALE: Do you recall the screenings in the big room with the six projectors, besides this one that you described?

TINA: Yes, I remember seeing what I think must have been a "first cut"—after all the sequences had been cut and assembled together. It was in the second place we worked in New York—just across the street from the location we started working in. The film ran something like a seven hours. It just went on and on forever [laugh]. It was great. I remember the room being full of people and everyone really loving it and I remember feeling very lucky I was able to see that much of it knowing that it wouldn't be that way forever.

DALE: When the time came for decisions about who was going to go to California, did you have any sense then of the fact that the ax might fall and might include you or might not include you?

TINA: No. I just assumed I was going. It never occurred to me to even question it... [laughs]. It never even occurred to me that I wouldn't be asked. I felt like a valued employee [laughs].

DALE: You arrived in California. What was your impression?

TINA: Oh! God, I loved California. I remember everything about the first day. remember the date, December, 7, 1969. I remember coming on the plane. I remember seeing a very early Woody Allen movie, *Take the Money and Run*. I remember it was out of sync and I complained to the stewardess. I remember arriving in LA. It was warm and sunny and just so beautiful. I remember we, "we" meaning Sonya and Miriam Eger and I, drove directly to our house on Genessee, changed into shorts, and drove to Cafe Figaro, which was very hip at the time, very LA. We had a fabulous lunch, paid the bill and then walked outside. We were freezing. By then, it was four o'clock and it was very cold. Coming from the East, we were not used to LA weather. In the middle of winter, it can be eighty degrees at noon or one, and go down to sixty by four, and then forties at night. It was quite a shock. We ran home and got dressed, again. That's what I remember of the first day.

DALE: Describe the work you were doing during this Los Angeles period.

TINA: I remember one day, being in a room with my apprentice, trying to get her to put trims away and instead all she wanted to do was write Christmas cards [laugh]. She wasn't a very motivated worker. I remember that soon after we got here, we started making thirty-five-millimeter blowups of the film. The film had been shot and cut in sixteen millimeters. One of my jobs was to sync up the thirty-five-millimeter picture blow up with a new retransferred thirty-five-millimeter track. And there was this huge rift. Now, sync, you would think, would be a fact; would be finite, would be one-way, either it's in sync or it's not in sync, but there were two factions of us. And I can't remember who was who, but I know that there were two of us who felt sync was one way and two others of us who felt sync was one or two frames different. So there were always these disagreements about what real sync was and distance from the microphone and all sorts of theoretical stuff. It was a constant back and forth. In the end, I don't remember which faction won. But whoever won, it definitely looks in sync to me now.

DALE: Was there any feeling, on your part, as we came to California and brought the first KEMs to California, of the theoretical revolution we were implementing in the movie capital of the world?

TINA: No, I had no sense of that because in order to see that you have to be older, you have to have a sense of history, you have to have experienced change yourself before you can recognize it. In other words, when the digital revolution happened in editing about four years ago, I was well aware that it was going to completely change the way editors worked and thought, but I had no historical context when we brought the KEMs to LA. I started to have an idea that it might change things when an editor I'd worked with the year before in New York, Bud Smith, came to a screening of the film. While he was walking around the cutting rooms, he spotted his first KEM. He asked what it was and I showed him how it worked. I remember him calling me a couple days later and asking, "What do you do with the little trims? Can you run the little pieces?" I said, "No, no. You've got to assemble everything back into the daily reels," and he said, "okay". And then Bud turned out to be one of the first Hollywood film editors to buy a KEM. I think he might have been the first editor to bring one into the studio system and started people noticing it.

DALE: When you started working with us in New York, had you ever worked on a flatbed?

TINA: No, I had only worked on moviolas with arms [to hold the reels]. We even sunk [synced] the dailies on Woodstock on moviolas. But then, once we were in LA, we all worked on flatbeds. Then when I actually made the move to LA as an editor two years later, I had to learn how to cut on a cutter moviola [one without arms], because flatbeds were too expensive for the low-budget productions I was doing.

DALE: In Hollywood here, describe what you felt was your daily life. What was it like being here? What were some of the funny little stories, or were there any?

TINA: Well, let me see. Most of the stories I remember center around eating. We were on per diem for the first time in our lives. So, when we first got here, we made it our business to have breakfast, lunch, and dinner—all three meals. We would get up in the morning and drive to the International House of Pancakes and have these huge breakfasts early in the morning, and then go to work. We'd work for a few hours and then we'd stop and go out for a huge lunch, and then [Laugh], finish in the evening and have huge dinners. Pretty soon, we all realized that we'd gained weight. I remember one day I bent down to pick up a grease pencil and my jeans popped open and I said, "oh, dear. I think I'd better go on a diet." So I went on the first diet I'd ever been on in my life. I think several of us went on it, that Stillman diet. In two weeks I lost the fifteen pounds I'd gained in the first month or so that I was here. So it worked very well.

I remember one day, eight of us went out to lunch to the only good French restaurant in LA, which was called Au Petite Cafe on Vine, just south of where we were working. We were celebrating making some kind of up-all-night deadline. We got the private room and I remember the waiter coming to the door to announce the menu. There was no written menu, it was a verbal menu and as he recited the menu, tears welled up in my eyes. It just sounded so fabulous. [Laugh] I remember going back to work feeling as though I'd had eight hours sleep.

Another thing I remember is the group dinners. Stan Warnow was newly married and his wife Kathy wanted to cook for all of us, so I remember coming home every once in a while to a home-cooked meal. And I remember that when I left early to take an editing job in New York, I threw myself a farewell dinner at the house. I made shrimp curry. It was the first time I'd ever made it and the first time I'd ever tasted it. It's still one of my favorite meals.

I remember that we really had a great time living together, living in "Woodstock." We worked very long hours, but we really were like family.

DALE: Were you a member of the 107th Street Bowling League? What was that about?

TINA: That was about Sonya's birthday party, January 20. We all went to a bowling alley. I guess the joke was, Sonya Polonsky was of Polish ancestry and therefore, must bowl [laugh]. So, her party was held at a bowling alley and we all got these t-shirts that said "The Sonya Polonsky 107th Street Bowling League". I had that t-shirt for a very long time. That was a great party.

DALE: When the film opened, describe your feeling. You saw it, probably in New York, at the Trans Lux. Describe your feeling, or do you remember it?

TINA: I was extremely proud to have worked on that film. It was one of the most wonderful experiences of my life. And I'm glad that it happened at that time in my life because had I been older, I'm not sure that it would have meant as much to me. As it was, it was the equivalent of going to high school or college, in terms of its impact on my life. I mean, the friends I made then, are still, most of them, friends now.

DALE: Anything else?

TINA: Well, I was just remembering another thing about my going back to New York. My last day on the job I was sent over to Warner Bros. Studio, which was the first time I'd been there. Basically, we were nonunion people and really couldn't work on the lot. We'd worked in an office building at Yucca and Vine. So going to the lot was very special to me. And I remember going into this screening room to screen the blow-up of The Who doing Tommy, you know, "See me, feel me, touch me, heal me…," to make sure it was in sync and that the blow-up was okay. I sat in this dark room all by myself with this huge image in front of me. It was the first time I'd ever seen it that big. And heard it that loud. And in stereo. It was fabulous. It was as if the music were inside me. It was probably one of the most exciting moments I've ever experienced in film. All the way home on the plane, I kept wishing I could hear that music. I wanted to be in that music again. It had been such an amazing experience for me.

JANET LAURETANO SWANSON

FROM *WOODSTOCK* TO *GIMME SHELTER*

(JANET WAS SYMBOLIC OF the many people who joined the assembly line of syncers who worked around the clock for weeks, painstakingly marrying picture to its respective piece of sound. Luckily for her and many others, *Woodstock* served as a launching pad for some dynamic careers in documentary filmmaking over the years. And particularly among the very resourceful and patient women in film who dominated our editing team.)

I had a very minor role in the making of *Woodstock*, but on a personal level it was the beginning of my "career path". I was an assistant editor, age twenty-three. I had been working in New York for about a year, had few contacts, and had been working in nonunion not-very-fun places for about onr hundred twenty-five dollars a week. In August (not sure of date) 1969 I got a call, I don't remember who it was that called. I had been referred by Ed Cariati, whom I had worked with on a previous job. I was offered a job syncing dailies on a rock concert film for two hundred fifty dollars a week for a six-day week. I don't remember being interviewed, I think I was just hired over the phone. All of a sudden I would be making twice what I had been earning up to that point!! It was quite a transition.

I had been working all alone in a dingy editing room on the East Side on Friday and on Monday. I entered the chaotic world of the *Woodstock* postproduction offices. I was scared but excited. My job was to sync up dailies on two concert performances, Sly and the Family Stone, and Country Joe and the Fish. I had done syncing before but never anything as challenging. There were shelves full of rolls of film and rolls of magnetic track and the process of getting the two elements together in a cohesive order was daunting. There were virtually no slates. The camera crews were shooting madly but there was no reference to where in the performance they were.

When I got there someone had already organized the rolls of picture and sound into performances. My part was to put the two together. I was in a small room with two other syncers, Mirra Bank and Barney Edmonds. We were working on sixteen-millimeter upright Moviolas with headphones for eight hours a day. It was like a factory assembly line. The process was syncing by eye. I would look at the picture and try to figure out where they were in the song. Sometimes it was obvious, you could tell if it were a beginning or and end. And sometimes the cameraman would shoot straight through. But lots of times there were little short bursts of picture and it was a slow process of trial and error to find where it went with the audio.

Country Joe's performance was in the daytime so at least I could see what was going on, but I recall Sly and the Family Stone performing at night, which made it harder to see. Sometimes flashbulbs and light changes helped syncing one camera to another. There were a new cameras for each performance and they had to all be in sync with each other as well as with the audio. My memory is fuzzy but I must have been working on a double headed moviola now that I think of it. My job lasted three weeks, that's how long it took to sync up multiple cameras of two performances to give you an idea of how painstaking the procedure is.

The most awesome day for me was the first time I had to present "my work" to the editors. I entered the dark screening room and sat on the floor. The creative team was in there, having spent most of their days and nights in that screening room I suspect. I had never been involved in such a large project with so many people before and it was frightening to me. The only person I remember was Thelma Schoonmaker, called "T." The projectors started up and there were all the reels rolling simultaneously. The upshot was that things looked pretty good as far as the syncing went and I got a few notes of where sections were out by a frame or two. I was relieved and simply proceeded to correct the mistakes and that was that for my job.

A few weeks later I got a call from David Maysles, who was looking for an assistant editor. He was part of the Maysles Brothers filmmaking team that were pioneers in the cinéma vérité movement. I had been a huge fan of their groundbreaking film *Salesman* and was blown away when I found myself talking to David on the phone. He had gotten my name from someone on *Woodstock*, I was hired by the Maysles, I ended up being an assistant on *Gimme Shelter*, and the first part of that job was syncing hours of concert footage of the Rolling Stones. My next job after *Gimme Shelter* was as first assistant on *An American Family* for WNET.

Working on *Woodstock* opened my eyes to the world of documentary film and started me on a path of working with some of the best documentary producers and editors in New York.

My friends were very impressed by the fact that I had worked on *Woodstock*. Even today the subject comes up occasionally in my professional life. I am still an editor, working in the "reality TV" niche of documentary in Los Angeles. Once in a while I will mention that I synced dailies on *Woodstock* and the young newcomer to the business will say "wow." My nineteen-year-old son thinks it's pretty cool and he loves the film.

It really is an amazing film and I wish I had been involved more than just as a syncer (although I later got my chance to be part of a mega documentary on *Gimme Shelter*). The concert footage was amazingly shot by some of the most talented people to ever shoot film; Don Lenzer, Chuck Levey, and forgive me for not being conscious of the others but I was a novice when I worked on *Woodstock* and I don't recall who the others were. As I work with footage of the people shooting today I often lament that rarely do I get the quality of "the old days," when camera people had the patience and confidence to hold on an image, the intuition of when to stay with an image or move to another in a fluid way. And of course the editing was phenomenal, making a cohesive document of thousands of feet of film. Even though I had a small part I am grateful to have been part of such a groundbreaking piece of film art.

MUFFIE MEYER

WORKING WITH MARTY SCORSESE

(LIKE SO MANY PEOPLE who entered our world, Muffie, as assistant turned editor, represents those who were able to build on their *Woodstock* discoveries.)

Like many people, my memory seems to call up "snapshots" rather than a coherent narrative. Here are some of them...

Woodstock was my first professional film job after getting out of NYU Graduate School of Film and Television. I was twenty-two. *Woodstock* was a seminal experience for me. It was while working on *Woodstock* that I really learned what editing was.

Brian DePalma, who was a friend, told me that they needed people to sync up (match the film to the sound) on *Woodstock*. After a brief interview, I was hired and began work immediately.

I was handed a small roll of sixteen-millimeter film and a huge roll of sixteen-millimeter sound. When I put the picture up on the Moviola, it turned out to be an interview with the Maharishi. There were no slates, no indication of how to match the several hours of sound with the ten or so minutes of picture. The cameraman had turned the camera off and on numerous times, so there were many takes. One of these little one-minute bits of film would find its sound match somewhere in the hours of sound. This was daunting task under the best of circumstances. It required the ability to lip read. This was a skill for which I somehow had a knack. However, in this case, the Maharishi had a heavy Indian accent, which made his lips very hard to read. But it was far worse than that he sported a bushy mustache that totally covered his top lip, and a beard that pretty much masked his bottom lip! I was tenacious: it took two weeks to sync up about ten minutes of film (a job that under ordinary circumstances might have taken an hour).

At a certain point, I was asked by Thelma to stay and work on the editing of the film. She indicated that I should think about what kind of money I wanted. I spent the weekend debating with myself about whether $150 per week was too audacious. I was still debating on Monday, when Dale pulled me aside, told me that they didn't have a lot of money, and asked if $300 a week would be okay! Okay? It was a fortune! Far more than any of my friends made. A real job and real money: I marveled at my good luck!

At NYU, I loved editing. I edited my own student films and those of several of my classmates. When I began to cut on *Woodstock*, I was assigned to work under Marty Scorsese. (At this time, Marty had directed a few shorts and a feature, *Who's That Knocking*, which I had seen and loved. He was not yet the well-known director that he would become.)

Picture the scene: a large room with shades pulled down to keep the daylight from reflecting off our picture screens. Three huge KEMs in one room, with numerous other editing tables, rewinds, reels, bins etc. Different groups were being worked on by different editors at each of the KEMs. Some people worked with earphones, but mostly we all tried to keep the volume down, attempted to focus on our own tracks, and tried not to go mad.

My first task was to edit Sha-Na-Na, a 1950s revival group. I had never heard of them before. They wore gold lame and sideburns....way before Grease and Happy Days. They were fabulous and very funny. Six cameras "covered" the stage performances. (The KEM editing machines had three picture heads, so we could watch three of the six on-stage cameras at one time.) I picked three cameras, and cut them together, choosing the best angles for any given moment. For example, when one guy was singing the lead, I chose the camera that was on him. Then when two other members of the group did the "do-wahs" I chose the camera that shot a close-up of them. Then I put up the other three cameras, and added in the best angles from those cameras. I showed Marty my cut of the song. He was extremely nice and indicated that it needed a little more work.

For the next two days, he sat next to me and made suggestions: "try it here... what happens if you cut there..." In a gentle, collaborative way, he told me exactly where to make each cut. And all of a sudden, one day, I got it! It was a revelation! In a flash, I understood that editing was about rhythm, not merely finding "the best angle." I understood how you could use the rhythm of editing to create a "build," to create a climax, to create a kind of closure-in short, to create (even in a funny, three-minute, 1950s song) an emotional experience.

Although I only "half-knew" it at the time, it was easily the most important lesson of my professional life...one that has obviously been expanded-upon and grown with experience, but one that lies at the core of everything.

PHYLLIS ALTENHAUS SMITH

THIRTY YEARS AGO! HELP!

(PHYLLIS'S SENSE OF ORDER ensured her a long-term place, keeping track of all those hundreds of boxes over the course of three moves, the last to Hollywood.)

Before my Woodstock experience I worked in the music business with Jimi Hendrix, The Animals, The Soft Machine, Frank Zappa, The Velvet Underground, I had just completed a six month film editing apprenticeship and heard about the filming of Woodstock...I knew immediately I had to work on this film.

I traveled to the festival with friends. Stayed for one day—too much mud...got back to the city and managed to have an interview with Thelma Schoonmaker...I was hired...I was thrilled, this was THE event of the year. I lived in the Village and took the subway uptown.

That first day of work was raining, raining, raining. I arrived in the loft-like cutting room and I remember the hundreds of boxes of film that had to be sunc (or synced, or sunk, or sinked—or sunq!) up. I was confused, excited, scared and completely overwhelmed, this was my first editing job!

The rough cut screenings were fantastic...so exciting...we would all crowd into the small screening room, which had a few couches some chairs and the floor to sit on. It was breathtaking to watch Jimi Hendrix so close-all the acts were fabulous to see this way.

From my film editing experience I always thought that the rough cut was the best version of any film...when I think back and remember working side by side with Marty, Thelma and Michael—how great that was!

Being part of the Woodstock editing crew was a once in a lifetime experience and nothing could compare to it. Imagine being a young woman, living in

Greenwich Village and working on the most famous movie of a generation. What was better than that in the 1960s? After work, going to Max's Kansas City and having a burger with tons of chick peas and then watch Andy Warhol and his group of people; that was a great evening.

Moving to Los Angeles to complete the editing process was "the icing on the cake." I remember so many times after we all finished work going to the house on Orlando Street (rented for the crew) that had this fantastic pool with a slide. The water was hot, the air was freezing and there were lights in the pool and this was being in "Hollywood."

Most of us hung out together…we worked long hours and very hard and had lots of laughs—I'm sure there must have been many disagreements as well but I don't remember those.

After the finish of the film I continued editing and worked with Frank Zappa on *Uncle Meat* his video concert/dramatic film—that was also a great great experience.

I then lived in Europe for a few years and worked in Paris in a postproduction studio—the two-hour lunches at the local café were just one of the wonderful things about being in Paris along with everything else about Paris.

I have been in film since my *Woodstock* days, except for a six-year period in the 1980s when I had a vintage clothing store in the West Village. I now work at Paramount Pictures in Hollywood…it's a beautiful studio and it's lovely driving through those gates every morning. So thats it…for now.

ELEN ORSON

THAT SYNCING FEELING.

(FROM THE YOUNGEST PERSON on site with our crew, Elen then continued her role in the editing room.)

Back in New York, the studio went into a deep Zen mode to prepare for the onslaught ahead. Thelma Schoonmaker had devised a beautiful system for logging and organizing the film, and this became the *Bible*, the template which all syncing editors followed. It took days just to prep the footage for developing, there was so much film. The cans of exposed negative were sorted in huge stacks on the projection room floor by stock type, by performance, and by cameraman, according to the labels, which we assistants had taped to the magazines. All of this information would be crucial to the syncing process, and it followed the numbered rolls as they were printed and distributed to the editors.

As people caught up on their sleep, others were being hired. The call went out to hire all editors in town who could sync documentary dailies. There was a steady stream of eager people arriving at all hours for interviews, because by this time, word was out that this was a massive project, and the concert event had drawn so much attention on the news.

Three shifts worked around the clock. I worked at night. I got to learn all sorts of things from the more experienced editors, in the relative calm of the evening shift. (I remember lots of philosophy with Stan Warnow, Larry Johnson, and Yu Bun Yee over diner breaks. I remember Thelma being everywhere at the same time, but she always had time to stop and say things like, "Brown mascara looks good on you..."). I think there were something like ninety-four people on the crew during the height of the syncing frenzy. Most were young; wild hair on the men, long skirts on the ladies. Professionals, but Hippies, nonetheless. Our boss was the weirdest-looking one of the bunch, with the big Indian hat and ice cream in his beard. The Warner Brother executives would come by for preliminary screenings;

we'd all look out the window at their limos pulling up downstairs. They'd walk in, wearing their three-piece wool suits in August, looking around at all of us, furtively commenting to each other something like "Yeee-eeech" and we tried not to stare at them. This was before the term "Suit" entered the vernacular, but we would have used it if we'd known it. Here they were, on our turf, and they were the ones who looked strange. Mars meets Jupiter.

On the concert site, Hanley Sound had run continuous B-track recordings of every performance, which would become our master tracks in the final mix. Composite dubs of them were made onto sixteen-millimeter mag for us, to sync up with the picture. These became the master work tracks for the performances.

But how to find sync? As in the *Grand Teton Survival* film, there were no slates or sync references of any kind. There was no way to do that while in performance. Not even the miraculous Bic pen could be used here, because in this case the cameras could not "talk" to the recorder. But since the sound and the cameras were plugged into the same power source, the sync, once found, could be maintained without drift.

Once found...the challenge was to find the points of correspondence. And this is known as "eyeballing" the sync. Lucky we knew the songs. With five or six cameras running during the performance, the goal was to find sync at the downbeat in a wideshot, studying the moves and sequence of events. Sync would be maintained until the camera cut. Then you inserted blank film, or leader, in the roll during the time the camera was switched off. You had to reestablish sync when the shooting resumed, hunting around a bit (like, half an hour...) for the new point of correspondence farther down the track. Then you could line up the other cameras by comparing the action to the first camera. And by making your way (plodding...) through all the footage in this way, one could establish all the coverage for the song, building five rolls of synchronous print running with the master track.

Nowadays, these problems do not exist. There are other problems, to be sure, but today a time code signal would be sent to both the camera and the track, and all you would need to do is lock the track and picture on the same minute, second, and frame... the time code tells you where sync is. But time code was in its infancy in those days, for video only. Alas, not for us. (We were fifteen years away from having a reliable system for interlocking sprocketed film and multitrack tape.) This was like slashing your way through the jungle with a machete, blazing new trails. I don't think anyone has ever eyeballed that much footage, before or since. We were inventing new methods as we went along, Necessity Being the Mother of Invention.

All this work was done on the wonderful new Keller editing machine which had caught my eye on my first day. I learned to run it: engaging and disengaging the picture, marking the sync points and slugging the picture out. We started bringing in all the machines Keller could get to New York, even renting some from Canada.

Some sadist in command decided that for my first sync job, I should take Ravi Shankar's material. There were no vocals, no lips to read, no flashy rock and roll moves, nothing to establish a point of correspondence. Just five people sitting calmly making many, many hand movements...oh, and sometimes they would nod to each other. Or smile. I do not know if this was given to me as a test, to see what I could do (or not). Or maybe they knew that because of the rain and the general difficulty of shooting on the first night, the footage would not be complete and it wouldn't matter very much.

Later I got to sync up Tim Hardin, Sweetwater, Crosby Stills and Nash, and more. As an act would be completed, everyone would gather for these monster screenings to see what we'd got, in the screening room where Larry Johnson (inventor of the Bic method) had rigged a synchronizing system for six projectors. We had to check our work, it's true, because you couldn't run all five rolls at the same time on the Keller. And Michael, Thelma, and Marty had to see what they had to work with. But the room was always jammed with interested and curious people sitting on the floor, (who should have been syncing); sometimes rock stars who came in for a visit, sometimes studio executive types, all digging the music and cheering on the great camera work. Toward the end of a number, sometimes, the cameras would all start running out of film at the same time and the leader would come in on one, then two, then three or more of the projectors. Everyone would hold their breath and wait to see if any camera could manage to slap on another magazine in time before the last one ran out...Big cheer for the victorious!

A combination of happy accidents brought us all together, but were they? (Accidents, I mean.) We were hippies, but we were also extremely well-trained and disciplined documentarians. From the director on down to the lowly Hippie Chick, we all had a great desire to get it right, not to leave it to the NBC guys or the Big Studio guys who may or may not understand its value in society. The film had to be made by young hip people who would not interpret, or misinterpret it, but allow it to flow through their hands.

If the festival became an adhoc expression of the political and cultural movement, a sign of the swelling and gathering of powerful youth, the film came together just as organically. It quickened, and expressed the nature of its existence. It took on a life all of its own.

This is not to say that the film made itself...there had been a deliberate effort to shoot it in a certain way. The director made choices: to shoot certain songs, skip others. Some cameras were told to stay wide and some were to move in. I have read other accounts that say the cameramen simply directed themselves; this is not true, except in the case of the roving *cinéma vérité* cameramen out in the field. If direction on-site was shared, it was shared by Michael and Thelma and Marty, almost every step of the way as far as I know. They inspired genius in all of us who did the work, they provided leadership. And we worked our butts off for them.

It is truly boring to write the word "I" over and over—what "I" did, what "I" thought. But I'm still so amazed I was there in the first place, it's almost as though this happened to someone else. And I'm amazed that the endeavor in which I found myself was so complex and so profound, its images are still fresh a full thirty years later. Memories worth cherishing. I hold on to fragments and *souvenirs*. And the lasting friendships.

A TOUGH ACT TO FOLLOW

The day came, eventually, where the crew had to be pared down. Syncing is simply prep work, and the prep work was finished; now the editors had to be alone with the footage. Day by day, lay-off notices were given out and the studio was to be moved, first around the corner, then to California. By November, I was well-into my Junior year, and the move to California would not include me.

So I was laid off, and a month later I went to work on a feature, then on to some other smaller films; but not much could compare to the incredible experience I had just come through. Following soon after that were "The Lost Years," where I rambled around the country looking for new adventure which I could not find. The 1970s took hold. The war dragged on, Nixon took charge, things slowed down and we all retreated, after a fashion, to assimilate our wild experiences. You can only look through a kalidescope for so long.

People react strongly when they learn that I was on the crew of *Woodstock*. The first thing they say is always "Wow!" A part of history. "You were on The Towers?!?" And then they ask if I had any of the Brown Acid...little do they know, there was no time for acid, aspirin, food, or anything; just work, and stand-by to work more. But the romantic notions are firmly implanted, by the film itself.

MIRIAM EGER

I WAS AN OUTSIDER

(MIRIAM BECAME ANOTHER ASSISTANT editor who stayed the distance because of her patience, diligence, and organizational skills.)

The first time I heard of Woodstock was when I arrived in America and began looking for a job. I was born in Hungary in 1944 in a traditional conservative Jewish family, who managed to survive in Budapest through the war into the beginning of the Communist Regime. We immigrated to Israel in 1949 and grew up in the foundling state. I served in the Israeli Air Force and then worked for a degree in construction engineering and drafting. At the age of twenty-five, I decided that I needed a change. I traveled with a friend to Paris to study French but got stuck in the May student revolution of 1968. Everything was on strike so to pass the time I decided to take a trip to London where I decide—because I knew a little bit of English and liked the city a lot—I would try to find an excuse to stay there. I heard about the London Film School where you can apply without having a college degree, decided to go for it and was accepted.

I had just started in London School of Film Technique and met Jeffrey Eger, an American. Jeff was the first hippie I had ever met and with long hair, boots, and beads, he reminded me more of an American Indian. The word "hippie" was not yet a part of my working English vocabulary. We got married in the second semester. We wanted to start working. We got on a boat to New York, hoping we had enough background to get some jobs and continue our studies while working with a hands-on job experience. Arriving in New York, being swept up by my in-laws into highways, tunnels, and turnpikes was my first remembrance of America. I was culture shocked and depressed. I started to go from one independent filmmaker to another looking for jobs, but having no diploma or union card, my prospects looked pretty dim. Then somebody told us about a new film that was looking for assistant editors that could be just about anyone, nonunion, and with little experience.

I remember going into a big main office building in New York and being greeted very warmly, by Sonya Polonsky—the first person I met from the *Woodstock* team and until today my best friend. Then I was interviewed by Thelma Schoonmaker who later joked that she didn't understand anything that I was saying and didn't think I understood anything she said. Amazingly enough, I got the job.

I was put in a dark room and explained how to log rushes, and try to make sense of the different photographers who shot the same pieces. For weeks I was locked in that room. Occasionally, Thelma would pop her head in to check up on me and give me more material. I guess I didn't make too many mistakes because they didn't fire me.

At a later stage, I was assigned (on Eightieth St.) to assist Stan Warnow, one of the editors. The best way to describe Stan was like a big grumbling teddy bear who always appeared a little serious, a little angry at the world but very patient, dedicated, and a great teacher who occasionally let me put my two cents in, whatever it was worth. Also we were experimenting with the new equipment, the KEM editing three screen table, and learned the ins and outs of how to use it. I was taught how to synchronize and spent most of the days rewinding and watching Stan working on the various pieces. My only direct contribution to the film, and I could be wrong, was one day Mike Wadleigh wanted to screen the Joan Baez piece and Stan Warnow wasn't there. I had to put the two edited pieces together, and decided to do a very long fade in and fade out between the two reels. Nobody said anything but I think those pieces stayed in the final cut.

Occasionally, every several days in the beginning, there used to be screenings at the end of the day of the footages. Often there were six sixteen-millimeter projectors in sync with sound for the initial screening where we all got together, passing joints, ordering in food, and staying up late.

The whole hippie scene at the time, as well as the Woodstock festival, was very strange to me. I didn't understand the Vietnam War and anti-war movement because I had been raised in Israel and had just been through the war of 1967. To me, war was a heroic thing. The music was also totally weird to me. Until then, I had only listened to jazz. The first long-haired person I met besides Jeff in London, was the group of people I worked with on *Woodstock* starting with Mike Wadleigh, who to me had the ultimate look of Jesus Christ (Superstar).

There was also gruffy looking Bob Maurice and Dale Bell who was a cleaner cut version, but also with jeans, boots, long hair. It took me a while to become a part of this scene. I was an outsider and everything was new to me—starting with the entire culture, its music, and its cause. I didn't even know how to smoke grass. It was fascinating to me. After spending a lot of time working with Stan on various bands like Santana, Country Joe & The Fish, and Joan Baez (who was the only one I had ever heard of), and also listening to the other pieces of music during the various screenings, I slowly began to appreciate and like the music and the people. I really got into it.

By the time most of the editing was done and they were choosing people to go to California for the final edit, I was quite surprised to be selected. Being newly wed and in the first year of my marriage, the commitment of a long separation was awkward. I went anyway.

The next phase of the project took place just before Christmas time in Hollywood, California. My first observations of LA and Hollywood were the huge numbers of cars, and no people on the streets. We were assigned three rented houses. The one I was in was with Sonya, Tina, and Phyllis. The three rented houses had identical rented furnishings. I thought it was so funny that we went from house to house and saw the same furniture, not to mention the white and pink imitation Christmas trees sold in supermarkets. Since no one drove a stick-shift vehicle, I was the designated driver of a large van, even though I had never driven a van. I managed after taking some pieces off of our fence.

For Christmas, the spouses came for a week, and we planned a big dinner. Jeff and Kathy, Stan's girlfriend, and the rest of the spouses were in charge of the dinner because we were all working. The spaghetti sauce as I understood later was spiced not with oregano or basil but with marijuana. The ceremonial cooking of the spaghetti involved taking numerous strands of spaghetti and whipping them against the wall. By the end of the meal about fifteen of us were sitting on the floor of the living room, listening to music, singing, and falling over each other in hysterical laughter. Some of the people who were there were Jere and Linda Huggins, Eric Blackstead, and Charlie the poster guy who was always there helping everybody out.

The one other party I remember was a party in the "executive" house where Michael, Bob, Dale, and Thelma lived. It had a swimming pool and we all got stoned and I remember we dove off the diving board, some of us without bathing suits.

I stayed on for another month and when the editing was locked in and the sound was ok, I left to go back to New York. When the film opened in New York, my parents happened to be visiting, so I took them to it. At that point, being familiar with all the pieces, it was a very exciting moment for me to show my parents. I think they were totally shocked and deafened by the experience, but put up a good front and said how much they enjoyed it.

For someone who had no experience in the film industry or with American culture at all, the *Woodstock* job introduced me to wonderful people.

After *Woodstock*, I stayed in the film industry for another fifteen years working as an editor and assistant editor. Our first child was born in 1972 in Union City, New Jersey. He was raised in the Woodstock fashion with long hair, tie-dye T-shirts, and overalls.

STAN WARNOW

MUSICAL RHYTHM AND EDITORIAL RHYTHM

(STAN SHARED PERFORMANCE EDITING responsibilities with Jere Huggins and Yeu Bun Yee. The Sha-Na-Na and Santana pieces had been initially roughed out by Martin Scorsese before the move to Hollywood.)

By early September I was back in New York, totally broke and eager to work. Since I was already a reasonably experienced editor (I had actually already edited my first feature film, *The Honeymoon Killers*, the previous autumn and winter), and since the idea of working with all that concert footage on what would clearly be a major film was immensely appealing, I began to make inquiries.

Of course, while I was getting back to nature in the Catskills, Thelma Schoonmaker and Mike had plunged headlong into the monumental task of beginning postproduction and hired a lot of people to help them do it. The first step was naturally to get material out of the lab, which was a slow process as there was so much of it, and then putting all the footage in sync. By the time I called, I was told they had everyone they needed for the time being. I wasn't about to give up, so I began to drop by the editing rooms on an almost daily basis, ostensibly to see if my footage was available for screening, but more importantly to try and become involved in the editing. Finally, after about five or six visits, Thelma finally gave in.

Was I willing to work at night, she asked? I was willing to work on Mars at that point, so I finally had a job...syncing (SINK-ing) up the concert footage, along with four or five other people on the graveyard shift, 9:00 p.m. to 6:00 a.m. Normally syncing up footage is a fairly straightforward mechanical process, referencing "slates" on the picture and sound elements to put the two together in synchronization. Naturally, the *Woodstock* footage was not normal, because the concert footage had been done, out of necessity, totally without slates.

Instead of being able to simply grab the two appropriate elements and mark them up according to the slates, it became a giant musical jigsaw puzzle.

I would be given a pile of film and sound (mag track) for the group in question. Sometimes, but not usually, there were rudimentary notes, like "We think we didn't start shooting till the third song, and shot every other song until near the end, when we shot three in a row, we think." I would then plunge in—could this footage be the beginning of that song? No? Well how about the next song, or maybe the lab printed the camera rolls out of order and what I think is the beginning is really the middle of the set. It was a tedious process, but satisfying in that puzzle-solving kind of way. In addition, as I've always loved music, immersing myself in these classic performances as part of my job was just fine with me.

Some nights I would work for hours, and not get anywhere—and others, I would lock onto the right material almost immediately and be able to sync up an entire act in one night. As time went on I began to learn little tricks…such as using the flash bulbs going off as sync marks to align one camera's footage to another. The silver lining to the graveyard shift was that those of us working all night together formed a special camaraderie that can only be shared by people that have undergone some trying and difficult experience together under adverse conditions.

Finally, around the third week in September, there was enough material that had been sunc up (past tense of sync…OK, OK, I know there is no such word in the dictionary, but almost every film editor uses it) to begin cutting. There must have been twenty people who had been working on the syncing, and naturally all of us wanted a shot at actually cutting the material. I was given mine after a few days. I sat at the KEM editing table and with a fair amount of trepidation that always happens when I start a project.

I began reviewing the footage of the musical act I had been assigned (again after almost thirty years I really can't remember which one it was). I was looking for a way in, a structure, which in many ways is at the heart of editing documentary footage. Of course in some ways editing a performance is easier, because one has the progression of the music as a guide, but nevertheless I felt that it was important to have a concept in mind before I began to actually cut. And in the case of Woodstock there was the additional challenge of editing for three screens.

This was going to be a difficult task, but it was certainly made a lot easier by the KEM Universal editing machines we were working with, because they had the ability to show material on three screens at once. The KEMs (and other systems called Steenbecks) were part of an emerging technology known generically as flatbed editing that was then in its infancy but was to revolutionize much of film editing in short order, as digital nonlinear editing has revolutionized it recently.

Until then films were viewed for editing on machines called Moviolas, which have a transport mechanism similar to projectors in that the film moved through intermittently with an upper and lower reel feeding the mechanism. When the film paused, a shutter revealed the image on a small screen for a brief moment, closed and the film moved up to the next image. The biggest disadvantage of this technique was that it limited the speed the film could move, as the film had to start and stop in order to view each image. Additionally, the editor had to pull the film over to an adjacent table in order to splice it. And it made an industrial clatter while running.

Flat beds worked differently in that the film moved constantly and was viewed through a rotating prism lens which lined up with each frame as it passed through the optical path that led to the display screen. This meant that the film could be viewed and rewound at high speed, which was of great value in documentary editing in particular, as large amounts of footage could be viewed quickly when looking for a particular type of shot or moment Additionally, the reels were laid flat on each side of the system, which allowed for a work area right on the surface of the machine.

(Moviolas have other aspects that made them more viable for continued use in dramatic editing, namely the ability for the film to be broken down in small rolls and fed by hand into the machine. This was and is particularly useful on dramatic films where each scene and take can be meaningfully numbered and kept in those rolls for quick and easy access. And while digital systems such as the Avid and Lightworks have pretty much replaced film editing using film, some feature films (such as *Saving Private Ryan*) are still edited using Moviolas or flat beds.)

But getting back to 1969 and KEMs, this was entirely new technology and it enabled us to approach the editing process in a more modern and streamlined way. The KEMs had the additional ability to allow us to view three screens at once. In fact, this is one of those cases where the technology we were using helped determine the creative content. If it wasn't for the fact that we had these systems, we probably would have ended up with a very different looking final product.

I had never done film editing for three screens before, but fortunately, with my friend to this day, Bob Nickson, I had collaborated on a slide show that coincidentally had many of the same elements that we used in *Woodstock*. Bob had a friend who was associated with the Jefferson Airplane, and through him in fall of

1968 we were able to get press passes and shoot stills during performances of the Airplane at the Fillmore East.

I had worked at the World's Fair in 1964-1965 and therefore had of course seen Francis Thompson's wonderful three screen documentary *To Be Alive* several times. Bob and I had also gone to Montreal and visited Expo 1967 as part of an NYU Film School trip and had seen many multi-screen short films while we were there. So it seemed only natural to incorporate those multi-screen techniques when we decided to put our slides together into an early multimedia show. Inspired by the Francis Thompson film, we decided to use the triptych form as well, (being diligent film students, we were also aware of Abel Gance's three screen *Napoleon* as well as the use of the triptych in various painting contexts). We evolved a show with three synchronized slide projectors with the appropriate recordings playing as the soundtrack. It was primitive, but fun, and thinking about it now, I remember that some techniques (such as mirror imaging on the side screens) that I later used to good effect in *Woodstock* were actually part of those slide shows. What it meant to me is that when starting to edit the three screen material, I wasn't starting from absolute zero.

I must have spent a day or two looking at the footage and then taken the plunge and started cutting. After a few days of work I was ready to show Mike and Thelma (except she generally went by the name T at that time) my first cut. To my immense relief they liked it, I revised it slightly, probably went back to syncing for a while. But as they had liked my first cut they soon gave me another one to try, and I began to feel like I might be on my way to a full time editing job.

There were definitely awkward aspects to the whole process, as clearly everyone wasn't going to get to be an editor. The whole thing was reminiscent of going out for a high school athletic team, where a whole lot of people try out, but only a limited number make the final cut. Well, in high school I wasn't enough of an athlete to even bother trying out, so it was immensely satisfying to me that as time went on and my work continued to be well-received, I began to realize that I was likely to be chosen as a full time editor. It's a fact of life in the free lance world that you have to compete with your friends for jobs, and sometimes you're successful and sometimes not, but I was beginning to feel a sense of destiny about the project, as the film seemed so right for me.

I don't remember if there was a moment of formal designation where I was told I was now an editor on the film, but by mid-October, it was quite clear that I had the job. At around that time I was assigned a full time assistant, Miriam Eger, an Israeli who recently arrived in the US via the London Film School, where she had met her husband Jeff, an American. She was of immense help, in what was a very complicated project on every level.

By late October, I had done rough cuts on most of the acts I would be working on for the rest of the film: Crosby Stills and Nash, Joan Baez, John Sebastian and Santana. At this point we were well into developing our techniques for two and three screen editing. I remember sitting with Thelma, Michael, and the other editors discussing what was the best way to approach the multi screen material. One moment with Thelma stands out where I remember discussing what looked better, making the cuts in multiple image sequences simultaneously or sequentially. At first our instincts had been to cut all the images at the same time, but after some evaluation screenings we came to the conclusion that in general it was better to cut first one image and then another, in order to let the viewer see both transitions and to not overload them with too much at once, especially on the big screen. Naturally, this didn't mean always cutting this way, for there were certainly times when I felt it was more effective to have a concussive change of all images at the same moment.

Similarly, I was refining my own personal approach to editing performance. One evolving idea had to do with the interplay of the musical rhythm and editorial rhythm. In film school it seemed only natural to use the beats in the music as cutting points while working on a music-based sequence. But on Woodstock I realized that while I needed to respect the rhythm of the music while cutting, and use it to help propel the editorial structure along, it wasn't really desirable to make every cut on a beat. When the editing becomes a visual metronome to the music, it becomes predictable and boring.

Another basic principle for me also had to do with respect—respecting the integrity of the musical performance as presented on the stage. While I certainly did my share of flashy quick cut editing, I always tried to make it an integral part of presenting the performance. I felt it was important to never have the audience feel that flashy editing was being done for its own sake—that the presentation was taking precedence over the content

When editing I always had a specific structure in mind for each act. Joan Baez sang "The Ballad of Joe Hill," a story in dialogue form between the singer and the dead labor hero. I consciously cut that song so that it had the feeling of a dialogue dramatic scene, with Joan facing one screen direction when she sang Joe's lines, and the other direction when she sang the narrator's lines. And I was sure to use some really wide shots to emphasize the ethereal nature of her voice and the spiritual aspects of the song. I remember making some of her wide shots even wider by optically blending the black edges of the frame with the black background of the full two point thirty-five aspect ratio frame, to heighten the feeling of her solo performance in the August night.

For Crosby Stills and Nash, who sang "Suite Judy Blue Eyes," I tried to embody the different "movements" of the suite through the way I structured the multi screen layouts, cutting rhythms and shot selection. One satisfying aspect of CSN for me was the opportunity for me to use a fair amount of my own performance footage.

When Thelma suggested intercutting John Sebastian's song "I Had A Dream" with shots of parents and children at the festival, I knew it made perfect sense.

My most satisfying editorial assignment would prove to be the work I did on Santana's "Soul Sacrifice," a dynamic and powerful instrumental. The piece was a natural for a different editorial approach, because it had a classic building opening which added one instrument at a time, an accelerating momentum throughout, several instrumental solos including a spectacular drum solo, and as a special bonus, because it was a daylight performance that had a terrific response from the audience, incredible audience reaction shots.

In designing the opening for "Soul Sacrifice" I was able to use an idea that been on my mind since starting the editing on the film. Most of the editing was composed of one, two, or three screens that more or less used the full aspect ratio of the image as shot by the cameramen, but for "Soul Sacrifice" I was able to use shots that were optically cropped and positioned to pop on as individual smaller elements against the canvas of the full screen. This made perfect sense to me because of the nature of the intro, one instrument at a time being added to the blend. And I found the ideal shot to begin with, with the camera being lifted up over the lip of the stage to reveal the bass player playing the first notes of the intro, (except of course, if memory serves, I "stole" that section from later in the piece).

As the performance developed, I tried to present each soloist effectively while maintaining a sense of the band as a musical unit. After a lot of consideration, I decided not to show any audience reactions till later in the performance. I've always felt that this decision helped significantly in the effectiveness of the edit. I wanted to create in the audience's mind a question of how the crowd was reacting and tease out the answer as long as I could, and then finally explosively reveal an audience totally enraptured with the music, which in fact they were. And of course I had a fair amount of my own camera work where I knew for sure people were dancing to this exact performance, as well as lots of excellent material shot from the stage. I then came back to performance for the *tour de force* drum solo played by Santana's drummer Mike Shrieve.

As the performance wound up there was a moment when the music came to a complete stop for about half a second. What to show then? It took me a little while to figure out that the best thing to present at that moment was the exact analog of the music, which was totally silent: I simply cut to black and brought the images back after the pause. It turned out to be a very effective moment. There was then a quick cut finale and the piece ended with tumultuous applause and Bill Graham coming on stage to shout something in the organist's ear. At a screening in New York I asked Bill what he had said at that moment expecting him to relate how he had told them they had just given an historic performance that would make their career, which was definitely true on some level. But of course instead of having said anything really weighty, he told me he had just told him to get to a mike and thank the crowd.

ED GEORGE

SHORT HAIR AND BUTTONED-DOWN COLLAR

(ED REPRESENTED A BUNCH of young men who literally walked in off the street looking for any kind of work on our movie. Like Ken Glazebrook, Anthony Santacroce, Al Zayat, and Charlie Cirigliano, they discovered their niches and helped us enormously. One of Ed's principal responsibilities was as projectionist.)

I showed up wearing a yellow shirt with a buttoned-down collar, a tie, short hair; Dale Bell hired me as a PA anyway. What followed was a kaleidoscope of long hours, fascinating work, and a musical education. During the frenzied, almost round the clock two weeks or so of syncing up, I was transferring the sound from quarter-inch to sixteen-millimeter mag. I remember the work being interspersed with long dinners at Italian restaurants with Marty sitting at the head of the table, long dinners at Chinese restaurants with Win Tucker ordering in Mandarin. I remember Dale's amazement when I turned in my hours and my amazement when he paid them.

As footage started coming off the five KEM and three Steenbecks, I became the projectionist. We had six projectors and two magnasyncs with synchronous motors, so I'd theoretically flip a switch and all eight (or however many were needed) units would crank up and run in sync. It usually worked.

At Bill Graham's Thanksgiving dinner at the Fillmore, we showed some footage with three projectors with zenon bulbs and during Canned Heat's "Going Up Country" (Wads shot this from low-angle with a five point nine) the projector jammed and Bob Hite melted on-screen. Everyone went wild. They yelled "do it again."

The climax to all this came with the three eight-hour screenings of the rough cut that we gave just before leaving New York. Michael and I would crawl through the maze of equipment in the dark, shifting the projectors to create the proper split-screen effect The film never got any better than those three nights. It was a condensed, exhausting, exhilarating *Woodstock* experience.

I think the first public airing of any of the music came during a big anti-war rally on Broadway just below our office. We set speakers in the large, open bay windows and blasted Country Joe singing "be the first one on your block—". We got busted.

I think it was shortly before we shifted to LA that I dropped the center out of a two thousand feet reel while we were screening the cut for Ted Ashley. Thelma looked at me with intense severity as she frantically put it back together just in time.

The day we flew to LA to start the fine cut was December 7, Pearl Harbor day, and YeuBun Yee, our Japanese editor, showed up at the airport grinning, wearing a leather flying helmet. It was my first trip to California, palm trees and warm December sun. We went to Le Figaro for lunch and right into the LA scene. The work on the West Coast didn't seem to have quite the raw edge that it did in New York. A lot of the exciting stuff was happening at the optical house.

Then came the mix and it was a treat to watch Dan Wallin slide the levers and twist the dials. Sometimes I'd slip into the next mixing stage where Sam Pekinpah was finishing the "Ballad of Cable Hogue."

I remember Alvin Lee watching Ten Years After "Goin Home" on the big mixing studio screen. He was stunned. He finally stammered "...Could I see it again?"

Then in April, as *Woodstock* was just about finished, we received the finished print of *Thirty Days To Survival*, the Time-Life film on the National Outdoor Leadership School in Wyoming that Michael had shot and directed the previous July. It hooked me, and off I went as a student June 1 and wound up teaching there for the next three summers.

HANNAH HEMPSTEAD

ROLLINS COLLEGE ALUM, PRODUCTION SECETARY

I'M NOT SURE YOU remember how I got on the Woodstock team. Ed George, a camera department "wanna be," was a friend. I was living in New York after graduating from Rollins College in Winter Park, Florida, and driving north with sorority sisters. We rented an apartment while I was doing temp work. Ed, dating one of my "sisters," told me about an opening at Wadleigh-Maurice and encouraged me to come apply. I had been to Woodstock (the festival) for the final day (still have my ticket stub). My boyfriend at the time dragged me there telling me that I HAD to go with him—I would regret it if I didn't go. I followed up on Ed George's suggestion and dropped into the W-M office to ask about the job. Someone—probably you, Dale—asked if I could type (Yep, that was me!). I said yes and was given something to type and sent into a room. When I came out the office was empty. "Helloooo?" Nothing. "I finished the test. Helloooo?" I sat down and waited and waited. Finally someone came back (maybe from lunch break), I told them I had completed the test. They laughed and said, "We were just kidding. Who cares if you can type?! You're hired!" The rest is part of my history.

I went on to become a script supervisor, a production manager, a producer and then a commercial director. I won a Cannes Lion for a Heinz commercial I directed. I owe it all to Woodstock.

DALE BELL

THE FIRST SCREENINGS

SOME WILL DISPUTE ME, but I think I remember the very first screenings of the dailies as perhaps the most exciting and thrilling of all. Every image was raw, so full of energy. It was an opportunity to relive those three days in August, but it would take us more than ten fifteen-hour days to see everything we had filmed.

Imagine that you are a fly on our wall uptown where Eighty-First Street meets Broadway. From the second-story, large, arched windows (it is now a Staples Store), you look down on Broadway, and if you skew slightly north and across the avenue, you catch sight of that glorious store, Zabars. You begin to salivate for some of their very special foods and coffees from exotic countries. (It had great take-out!)

For the past four weeks—from mid-September to mid-October—you watch dozens of people scurrying about a two thousand and a half square foot office which, under normal conditions might have housed ten or twelve people with desks and offices. The sun may come up, or set, but the activity rolls on, uninterrupted by normal routines. These people, you must observe to yourself, have a PURPOSE and a DEADLINE!

We grew overnight. Once word was out that we were looking for people, they magically appeared before us. A quick interview, a conversation with Thelma, a cross-check of their references, a salary for a day or week, an inquiry as to whether they would work the midnight to eight in the morning shift, and they might be hired that very night. If they didn't work out in a day or two, they were released. On the other hand, if they could handle the tediousness, the pressure and the complexity of the job, they would be given a week's worth of work, then extended as needed.

Editing tables were constantly being moved about the space as we tried to maximize every inch. So urgent were the editors that even while a table was resting in a space for a few minutes in between a move, two editors would clamour for it.

Sonya and I were always searching for equipment. First, we had to locate multiple-headed, upright Moviolas for the assistants and editors to use in the initial phases. Once we had rented five of them, we then turned to finding more KEMs or Steenbecks. These flat-bed editing tables were much more efficient editing complexes than were the Moviolas. Almost every Friday night, we would be returning gear and releasing people. We were on a loop.

Though Wads was the first to import the KEM into the country more than a year earlier, others had followed his footprints. When the importer revealed who owned them, Sonya and I began our calls. One was in Montreal. Once it was described on the phone, and endorsed by the importer, we flew one of our editors up to inspect it. That day, he rented a truck in Montreal and drove a second KEM to our offices that very night. A second was in someone's garage in Westchester county; another truck retrieved it the same day. The distributor regretted they had told us about a demo machine in California; within a day, we had coerced them into shipping it back to us in New York, threatened as they were by our "bad" publicity machine! In the space of ten days, we multiplied our original one machine into five.

Our luck with other machines was sometimes not so glorious. Wanting to keep the editorial troops happy day and night, Sonya and I explored a coffee machine service. The Demo Man, in suit, white shirt, and tie came in with his gear, not bothering to look around the space. After a short unpacking, he had coffee brewing with its fragrant aroma wafting into the nostrils of some thirty thirsty long-hairs. Silently so as not to disturb his pitch to us, they all stopped their editing for a moment to gather behind him. Oh, how proud he was of its percolating capacity, the varieties of coffee he could bring us, the round-the-clock service! But when he turned around to see who his clientele would be, armed with their very empty mugs, he panicked. As quickly as the one demo pot was emptied, he had fled our space, all equipment under this arm! Probably a scene reenacted in many offices across the country! Examples of culture clashes.

No sooner had he left than the water cooler Demo Man arrived. He offered Bob and me a choice: to lease or to purchase. We looked at each other and came up with the same answer: lease. The Demo Man thrust a standard contract into our hands which Bob hastily signed. When we left for Los Angeles two months later, we discovered we had signed for ten years! They sued!

Recollect: We have been syncing—matching picture to sound—these separate strands of film—350,000 feet of sixteen millimeters—night and day in three eight-hour shifts, and now, finally, we are almost ready to view our handiwork. Up to now, we have been preoccupied with technical issues, organization charts, coding numbers, color coding film reels to individual cameraman and days shot, distinguishing between documentary footage and performance material. Rarely, in this nonstop process with these dozens of people, have we been able to pause, except for a moment, to enjoy the actual footage. Always, it was Press On, we'll look at it later. Only then, during the screenings, would we decide whether it was worthwhile to spend more time on a sequence or abandon it completely.

To view the footage properly, we prepared a special room. Wads had said that because we had six cameramen on stage, we need a corresponding six projectors in our screening room. With three already on hand, we ordered—on Super Rush from their manufacturers in Rochester, New York (Rochester again!)—three Grafflex projectors constructed identically with heavy-duty synchronous motors to match the ones we already owned, so that each strand of performance workprint would run exactly in sync with every other one. Each would also have to be equipped with a lightly pressured gate, to allow the easy passage of film spliced together with tape on only one side. Grafflex said it would take two months to adapt them. We asked: Had they read the newspapers? WE were doing that *Woodstock* film, and they'd better cooperate or Warner Bros. might get back at them! Warners, we assured them, would pay the overtime necessary to get the projectors into our offices within two weeks!

Each projector was positioned on a stand, three at a lower level, three higher, all equi-distant from the screening room wall, so that the projected images were two-tiered, three abreast. Three projectionists, especially hired and trained for this ordeal which would last for days, were assigned to a pair of projectors.

To hear the music, we had modified two Magna Tech sixteen-millimeter playback recorders with the same synchronous motors adapted for the projectors. Though the soundtrack was then only monaural, the playback machines fed four huge speakers, two beneath the images in front, two behind us, the audience, giving us the sense of "surround", a concept we would later implement in the Hollywood mix.

When all eight machines were plugged into one common electrical outlet, and the switch thrown, eight synchronous reels of music and picture would run together, enabling us to view each piece of music, song by song, at one time, in half-hour or one-thousand foot increments. Beneath each image projected onto the freshly painted iridescent wall, we attached the responsible cameraman's name.

Because documentary (nonperformance) material had been organized against an hour-by-hour, day-by-day grid of activities which spanned the original three days of peace and music, we would thread up those reels in and around the respective day's music, changing the lens on the projector to make the images broader. Our goal was to maintain proper and accurate historical context of documentary and music sequences to preserve the actuality and the simultaneity of events as best we could. Later, we would decide how docu and music would fit into the multiple panels we had envisioned from the outset.

Purely silent MOS (Mit Out Sound) documentary reels were threaded onto a variable speed projector where we could speed through some sequences, and dally with others, depending on their quality and relevance.

Sound track without accompanying picture was also played according to its TOD (Time Of Day). Most of this material comprised announcements from the stage. A fast writer was assigned to try to transcribe as much of the essence as possible, then it would be typed up and given to Mike and T.

Put yourself in our place for a moment. Two months have passed since you were on site at Max Yasgur's farm. Your exhilarating yet exhausting experience of three days and nights of filming has been completely supressed by the night-and-day attention to every detail since. Phone calls at night because of the round-the-clock shifts of editors and assistants. Editing room space so crowded you had barely enough room in which to wind your reels on your editing bench without striking someone else's twirling arms. Putting down a splicer for a moment while you went to the bathroom, only to return to your space and find the splicer on another bench, being used. Bins and bins of loose film being wheeled from one area to another. Repairing torn sprocket holes. Running out of white leader on which to write your reel identification information. Checking on the color codes for each performer and each day. Code numbers exhaustively annotated so that they—and the film they represented—could never be lost or misplaced. Saying good morning to the 8:00 a.m. syncing crew as you returned home from your own midnight to eight in the morning shift on their editing bench. Finding a new assistant working on your material and immediately wondering whether that person was going to replace you tomorrow. Negotiating for a three-headed moviola instead of a single-headed one. Detail, detail, DETAIL. And such stress. But was it organized!

There were certain designated shelf areas which were absolutely off bounds to anyone except Mike and T. One infraction required a reprimand; two was good reason for dismissal! Some stuff just couldn't be touched! Particularly after it was synced, coded, color coded, annotated, and run through a six-gang synchronizer as a final check. It was ready for the projectors!

Almost. The Moratorium to End the War in Vietnam was taking place in October on Broadway outside our second-story windows. Hordes of people holding candles against the darkness were marching and milling just below us. We had to participate. But with what and how? Placing two of our biggest speakers in the open windows, we racked up Country Joe McDonald's "Give Me an F. U. C. K." cheer, cranked up the volume and watched the response with amusement. The neighborhood rocked in unison, the words echoing in the canyons of the Upper West Side. Until our speakers blew, that is, and the cops came to tell us to turn them off, whichever came first.

Or, in his eagerness to get performers to sign their contracts, Bob would hold 3:00 a.m. screenings which proved to be disastrous. Not really knowing how to thread up the complicated projectors and sound system, Bob would nevertheless make an attempt. Repeatedly, I would get phone calls in the middle of the night from him, asking how to repair this, or that which he had just broken in an effort to repair the first mishap. Soon we outlawed him from conducting these screenings without a projectionist. Too risky! We were running out of spare parts!

So here we were, looking forward to actually viewing our footage. In a way, it would be a vacation from everything else we had had to endure to arrive at this point. We would relive a collective experience in slow motion, one reel at a time, as though time was standing still. Through the beauty and versatility of film, we would be able to visit places on the farm we had only heard rumors about eight weeks earlier.

At 8:00 a.m. sharp, the screenings began with coffee and donuts. Lunch menus were passed around in the middle of the morning but the screenings did not stop, except for reel changes. Lunch was brought in at breaks, but as soon as a new batch of reels were threaded up, we focused on the film, on into the night until about 9:00 or 10:00 p.m. Then, while some of the editors returned home, others of us went to dinner and then home. It was a chance to catch up on the other activities of the day.

Mike ("Wads") and Thelma ("T") watched everything, taking notes all the while. Marty, Stan, Jere, YeuBen and Larry would always be close at hand. The editor and assistant who were assigned to an individual performer would listen closely to their instructions and suggestions, then return to their editing areas to try to implement the ideas. One editor would generally be assigned more than one performer. All the documentary footage was handled by three assistant editors who worked closely with T.

Assorted people would mill in and out of the screening room, silently. People from the festival, agents and managers representing the musicians, the musicians themselves, cameramen who knew their material would be shown between x and y, technicians who had to deal with the sound, the picture, or the editing machines, journalists who had wangled an invitation from one of us or another, and from time to time, Warner Bros.' executives, very much out of place in these hippie surroundings. Our space was so small and so incredibly crowded, we had to insist that newcomers wait outside until a batch of people left the screening room. Almost everyone was smoking something. Seeing and breathing were difficult tasks.

Some people would show up for the screenings, then call in sick to their regular offices so they could stay hours or days longer. Our own office personnel couldn't resist the tapping of their feet to the music which then drew them to lean on the doorjam to get a peek. The flying images were irresistible. The volume was deafening. Even as we recognized the power of what we were involved in, we had to keep moving the hangers-on out of the room so the editorial part of the postproduction could take place in decent surroundings.

Those who gathered for the night-time screenings would join us all at Max's Kansas City for dinner; sometimes we were twenty strong in five taxis aiming for a raucous dinner downtown, if Tony's Italian Restaurant on Seventy-Ninth Street was already closed for the night.

The screening began slowly at first. A single reel of documentary material led the ten days. Green grass, rolling hills, bright sky, a pristine farm spread out in every direction to distant horizons. Shot by a pair of Englishmen who had the foresight to start filming long before we came on the site, these early images described the Garden of the First Eden. Cattle lowed, flowers bloomed in the field, birds flew, horses romped. Peace and harmony prevailed. We were lucky. When we were first on the site, (that momentous Saturday before the Friday when the music began!) we met these two Brits and asked them whether we would be able to buy their footage, since we presumed, we would be making the film. Of course, they resisted, but as Warner Bros. got into the act, money talked. Hired originally by Mike Lang through the Maysles brothers, the footage quickly found its way into our offices, then into the soup at the lab, and finally, onto the editing benches.

It was good stuff, steady, well composed, and oh, so very green. Max Yasgur's farm would never be the same again. Certain shots just lept out from the screen, crying out for identification. Mike and T furiously took notes, Lightning T capable of typing at a mere hundred words per minute, flawlessly.

When the music sequence began with Richie Havens, all work in the office stopped. Like moths to a candle, we flocked to stand in the doors of the screening room, drawn by the music and the roar of the crowd behind him. "Freedom, Freedom," he chanted, and we thrust our right fists into the air in unison. To Hell with the phones for the time being! In BAM—a time Before Answering Machines—, we assumed they would call back if it was important! The feeling was visceral, deep from within the groin. All our work had been worthwhile.

Entranced, we analyzed each cameraman's work, for this was the first time the on-stage camera team had ever been linked together by Marty Andrews' interconnecting headsets. We had no idea whether they would work, or whether Wads' or Thelma's or Marty Scorsese's off-stage instructions to the rest of the camera team could even be heard by them, let alone adhered to. Or even if they were relevant! Wads' admonitions to everyone were simply to trust your instincts. He "directed" more by example than by instruction. Each of the on-stage team was assigned a particular position; within that perimeter, they had to find the best shots they could for the kind of music, light, and group they were covering.

On Richie, Wads retained the down center stage position. He was flanked on his right and left, while two other guys were up stage, shooting the performers from behind, with the crowd in the background of their shots. On the face of a clock, Wads was at six, while others fanned out to four-thirty and seven-thirty, ten-thirty and one-thirty. A sixth camera roamed while a tripod camera from one of the towers got the "master" shot occasionally.

Thankfully, Wads preferred the wide lenses and would generally mount the 5.9 m/m if he felt he could get his camera close enough to the performer. He never hesitated to push the end of his lens shade within eighteen inches of the musician or the instrument, whichever presented the more engrossing shot. The detail, dimension, structure, and the expanse of the frame from his close proximity was usually the most dynamic angle of the six cameras on the screen. Though all on-stage cameramen handheld their cameras, no one wavered. Their ability to hold this nearly twenty pound amalgamation of steel and raw stock rock steady was a marvel to behold. (All of this is pre-Steadicam, mind you! Yet the cameraman's use of his body and spine on the stage at Woodstock gave rise to the profligate development and use of the Stediam-type shots soon thereafter.)

Strands of film rushed through their respective projector's lenses. By analyzing where black leader had to be inserted by the editors and assistants to keep image and sound in sync, we could easily tell which cameraman had run out of film, when, and how long it took them to slap on a new magazine and continue their shooting. In some instances, the pauses between images were longer. At these point Wads, or Thelma, or Larry or Marty would recall what had happened at that particular moment on stage. Maybe the song was not materializing as they expected and one or more of the cameramen had been asked, through the headset, to rest while the song developed. Maybe this was only a practice run! Maybe one of the cameramen noted a jam in their gate! There were always reasons. For one thing you always notice about a cameraman: when they are shooting, or recounting the story years later, they retain indelible memories of that evolving miracle which transpires within the tiny confines of their eyepieces. The imprint on the brain echoes that of baseball players who even remember the wind velocity when they are at bat!

On the first night of the festival, Friday, August 15, it began to drizzle on the farm. Collecting in the dips of the plywood stage, the water created little puddles where Joan Baez was singing. Though the reflections of the blue and magenta tinted lights on the wet stage looked entrancing to Dick Pearce's upstage ten-thirty camera, we could observe that, from time to time, when the cables connecting the headsets became so loose they trailed in the water, all cameramen would jerk in sync as they received electric jolts from little short circuits along the lines. At the time, it was both painful and disconcerting to those receiving the jolts. Here, in the relative safety and comfort of their directors' chairs, everyone burst into uproarious laughter.

At other times, you could detect the ingenuity and spontaneous response of the cameramen. I remember one instance when Sly and the Family Stone was invoking the sky during "Higher." Gesturing with pointed finger, his fringed sleeve caught the multi-colored light just as the lighting director added enormous shafts of white light onto the audience for the first time. Instantly sensing what was happening, Wads slowly spun around with his camera, maintaining part of Sly in the frame, even as he displayed the vastness of the mesmerized audience, backlit, rocking, transported. I marveled at Wadleigh's instinct. Seeing what other cameramen might be doing at the same time revealed their capability as well.

The projectionists themselves were now under the gun. If one of their strands broke, all projectors would have to be shut down while an instant repair was made. Before they could start up again, a common spot for all eight strands had to be identified in the re-cue. Only then could the switch connecting them all be thrown and the screening continue. When the thousand feet (times the number of projectors being used!) signaling the end of half-an-hour would run out the reels would have to dismounted and new material threaded. Assistants were chained to the two power rewinds during the screenings to keep pace. Pee breaks were scheduled during what we all hoped would amount to only a five minute interval. But sometimes frustrating occurrences prevented that kind of continuity.

All through the day and on into the night, the three days of peace and music unraveled themselves on our wall, thousands of feet at a time. Over an exhilarating period of some ten days, we viewed it all—all 350,000 feet of sixteen-millimeter, all 175 hours, all 875 individual cans of raw stock.

In the course, we began the massive whittling process, the elimination of the chaff from the wheat, the search for the positive space within the mass of negative; pick your own metaphor for what was to become the most massive, complicated, intricate, and organized editing process ever known to documentary filmmaking, none of which could have been accomplished had we not begged, borrowed, or "stolen" (from Francis Ford Coppola's American Zoetrope) our trusty KEMs.

Wads had imported the first KEM into the USA, but Francis was not far behind him. In fact, Francis had designed his entire postproduction facility in San Francisco around the new machines. When we heard through the distributor that the second KEM was on its way to Francis, I called JFK airport to stop it. While it was being loaded off a pallet on the tarmac, I got Francis on the phone to tell him what we were doing and offered to rent it. We had a long and heated discussion about it, but just as we had operated on site, possession was nine-tenths of the law. We ended up paying Francis a monthly fee until our movie cleared Warner Bros. in March. I'm sure he forgave us, for he invited all of us to the gala opening of American Zoetrope just days after we had arrived in Los Angeles in December. What a memorable night! And in the end, what a friend for our film!

From this first "screening of the dailies," our movie would now have to be reduced to about eight hours in length. Safe to say that we could never revisit that initial experience again.

DALE BELL

THE RED NECKS VS. THE LONG HAIRS

(YOU MAY KNOW THIS first paragraph already!)

Here is the interconnecting chain: Merv Griffin was using Teletape Productions in New York as a production facility for his *Sidewalks of New York* and *New England* series. Wanting to get cameras out of the studio into the real world, Teletape encouraged Merv to hire a film production company they were involved with: Paradigm, comprised of John Binder, Mike Wadleigh, Larry Johnson, and later, Jeanne Field, Thelma Schoonmaker, Sonya Polonsky and Bob Maurice. Paradigm was renting space upstairs from the Teletape Studios on Eighty-First Street and Broadway. All very innocent. But watch what happens when the smell of money permeates the premises.

As it appeared obvious that Paradigm Films was evolving into Wadleigh Maurice Productions, Ltd., and John Binder was withdrawing to devote time to his personal work while Bob Maurice advanced, change was in the air. When Wadleigh/Maurice emerged as the likely candidate to be the producer of the documentary to be made about the Woodstock Festival, they quickly offered Teletape an opportunity to invest in the project. Teletape declined. "No, you're a bunch of long-haired creeps and we don't want to be involved with you." A mistake, perhaps, but other companies had been given similar opportunities and had not stepped up to the plate. It was a very tough call.

Warner Bros., coming in, did so with great hesitation, foreboding, fear, suspicion; you name it, they had it, in spite of the fact that they had adequate cash to finance the whole thing. To say *yes* meant would they have to deal with hippies, too!

Once we returned from the site on August 18 and 19, and had safely stored all of our exposed raw stock—hundreds of carefully labeled 400-foot cans—under twenty-four hour watch, we knew we were going to need more space than we had.

But we also felt that we could not move because of our loyalty to Teletape. We decided to stay and adapt. We were oblivious to the cultural division which was brewing between a traditional engineering society and an equally intense, but less prejudiced group of flower children bent on fulfilling their dream.

Over the next days and weeks, we had to add gear and people, install more electricity, lamps, desks, chairs, editing benches, telephones, etc., to bring the space up to working capacity. Trucks would line up on the street, unload onto the elevator, material would be brought to our second floor and then, if we were fortunate, we would find a place for all this stuff we needed. All under the very curious eyes of the Teletape people.

Too curious. When the September rent invoice was presented, it was curiously higher than the August 1 invoice, though we were not renting more space. Elevator usage, the Teletape people mantained. Since the amount was only a couple of hundred dollars, we did not make a big deal. We paid, even though we had been tipping the elevator man deliberately, knowing we had added significantly to his load. And almost every day, one of the Teletape guys would mosey by.

When the October invoice arrived, hand delivered by one of their "Suits," it demanded $20,000 as "key money" plus an increase of two thousand dollars over the previous month. They handed us a lease for five years! (Had they been talking to the Water Cooler Demo Man??) Electricity and the increased elevator usage, we were told. We had people working around the clock for several weeks, they complained. It cost more money! We were getting irked but could do nothing, with Warner Bros. breathing down our necks. Not only were Warners demanding that we produce a single-image film by Christmas, they were also paying our bills. Though the Teletape increase was simply absorbed, their presence in our already crowded space was becoming increasingly more irksome.

But as our October screenings subsided and we began the actual editing process, Teletape began to visit us more than once a day, putting their noses directly in our way. Toward the end of the month, they arrived with another invoice which they demanded be paid, above and beyond the increased rent. A surcharge for two thousand dollars. We said we couldn't do it.

That night, the electricity was shut off at six o'clock. We thought it could have been a power failure in the neighborhood. But when it became apparent that every building surrounding us had juice, we knew it had to be Teletape. We converted to candles, stopped work, broke out some champagne, and plotted.

Tomorrow, we would be prepared. During the day, we would access the base of the outside lamppost where we could tie our electrical needs to the city power supply with our huge alligator clips. Hundreds of feet of Horsecock, the descriptive name given to the diameter of the electric cable necessary to draw the juice from the city, would be strung on pulleys and ropes from the street through our second-story windows where it would be downloaded into a variety of smaller recepticles and then distributed to the editing tables and machines. We would not stop. Nor would we be stopped by a bunch of Red Neck engineering types from downstairs who could not leave we Long-Hairs alone to do our work.

This was a cultural war! Like many before them, and those who would follow, intolerance was their by-word. Bigotry, preconceptions, and sexism weighed heavily in their every action. They could not accept the fact that we, who looked, dressed, and acted differently, were on our way into the history books, right under their noses, by dint of our own ingenuity. It was no doubt a scene acted out in countless workplaces across the country throughout the late 1960s. Acting on behalf of that part of society they symbolized, they had to rub us out if they could.

Promptly at 6:00 p.m. on the next day, the lights went out again. Within five minutes, just as the Teletape Short-Hairs mounted the stairs to observe the results of their rabid sand-box game, we flicked the lights on in their faces. Were they pissed! Not simply Red Necked, they were Red Faced and furious. We told them to get out, we had work to do and they weren't going to stop us!

That night we plotted again. We did not think we had heard the last of them. They would do something worse. We left an armed guard on our premises that night after we went to dinner. Our instructions to him: Let in no one, even if you had to scare them by firing a pistol into the air. We rehearsed him and left.

On the subsequent night, though our electricity remained on after six, we still did not trust the Red Necks from Teletape. Once we were assured that they had left the premises, we put our new plan into action.

Over the course of the day, we had purchased several hundred moving boxes, wrapping tape, rope and color-coded markers; we rented hand dollies, moving dollies, and huge rolling bins. With all of our people fueled by pizza, beer and wine, we carefully packed each roll of film, dismantled all of our equipment, and moved our entire operation from the northeast side of Eighty-First Street and Broadway to the southwest side of Eightieth Street and Broadway. Editing tables, chairs on rollers, desks on dollies, lamps in bins, file cabinets on dollies, barrels on wheels, everything had been shoved downtown one block.

As the traffic on Broadway subsided after the midnight hours, we pushed our editing tables down the avenue, pausing only for pedestrians and the traffic lights. By six o'clock the next morning, forty people had moved everything we owned—this burgeoning documentary which would one day refinance the Hollywood movie industry and serve as an icon for a century—ignominiously through the night, out of the clutches of the Red Necks and into the welcoming arms of another pair of New York filmmakers, Chuck Hirsch and Brian De Palma—responsible for *Greetings!* and *Hi, Mom*—who had graciously agreed to rent us their office space at reasonable rates on a moment's notice.

Such was comraderie!

After breakfast a few of us returned to the Teletape offices to take down some special overhead lamps we had installed. While we were on two ladders reaching for the lamp attachments, the Teletape folks arrived. Immediately, the sight of the very empty offices threw them into a fury! They knew that we had outwitted them. But now, to demonstrate their desperate mentality, they began to grapple with the base of the ladders. We brought in "the fuzz" to try to intercede. We were twenty, Teletape were five. Fisticuffs broke out. Tools were wielded as threatening weapons. They accused us of using their ladders to steal their lamps, but our invoices substantiating our ownership proved otherwise. Finally, with our lamps and ladders in hand, we gleefully rushed downstairs and onto Broadway, free at last, free at last. Their extortion, their jealousies and their prejudices would require new targets elsewhere.

AL ZAYAT

LATE ARRIVAL

(AL ZAYAT JOINED OUR team in New York just as we were moving from our location at Eighty-First Street and Broadway to Eightieth Street and Broadway. He was a Production Assistant.)

Wouldn't you have liked to have been a fly on the wall, in the studio on NYC's westside in 1969, where I say with great affection…a menagerie of creative people spun, twirled, or likely went near blind reviewing the hours and hours of film, yes film not digital, shot by a plethora of handheld cameramen and brought back from Woodstock? Phew. Yes, that's a mouthful. Well, I was a bit more than that fly. I was in fact an employee. A very minor one, I'll add, but a diligent and devoted one at that.

Before I divulge the great secret of how I hornswoggled myself into such a lofty perch, I need to go back in time a brief bit so you understand the running start I had to make that leap.

So, in honor of Dale Bell, my old friend, and mentor, and fool, who offered me the job, I'll digress. Briefly, I promise.

June of '69, I graduated from an all-boys Prep school located in Massachusetts, without cheating too much to accomplish same. Truly, the institution was an amalgam of essences of *Animal House* and *Dead Poet's Society*. I didn't come from a family of privilege. I did come from a family with a mother who knew if I didn't go to this place, she would be visiting me on holidays, etc. More likely the term "visiting hours in cell-block 9" instead, or something like that. My choices were either there or in a military school option. Ummm…no!

Mom knew best, and, as I said, after a few years of whatever you might imagine, I was sprung. Now what? College? Maybe. Remarkably, I had grades sufficient to get me into somewhere notable. But no. I decided I wanted to be a painter. No, not a house painter. A "fine artist," which, at trails end, led me to NYC's School of Visual Arts. A fine school with great teachers and students, for the most part. I was perhaps "the exception" to the fine students. You see, my grandmother was a great artist. Knew a bunch of bohemians way back in the day. With particular emphasis, okay here's the name drop, a suitor named Kahlil Gibran, in fact. So of course I thought, Hey, if she can do it and live the life, why not me?

Here's why not. The issue was this: on my best day, I wasn't half as good as they were on their worst.

Okay, plan A fails! Now what? I'm living NYC's East Village in a quasi-tenement apartment with two other roommates. No visible means of support or particular skills, etc.

Luckily a local air-conditioning company needed someone with a strong back and weak mind. I passed the test. Phew, income. Concurrently, a dear friend who lived directly next door to my apartment was working at the famed concert hall The Fillmore East. He said he could get me hired there to do whatever they needed and wanted. I went inside one afternoon. Someone saw something in me and immediately offered me the position. I was a bit confused because I remember asking, "Do you mean to tell me all I have to do is seat people, etc., etc., and watch all of the great legendary groups and you'll pay me?" "Yes" came back. I extended my hand and announced, "I'm your man!"

Okay, what does this have to do with the price of butter? Well, nothing but it does lead to Woodstock, a concert my buddy and I were headed toward until the "powers that be" closed the highway.

Now, I will tell you I'm also not one to favor sleeping outdoors. Especially in the rain. I had multiple horrible experiences doing so when properly prepared. And properly prepared isn't something most people associate with Woodstock. And since I had already seen most, if not all of the acts, I suggested to my friend who was driving his jeep with canvas flaps for doors, turn west and we'd go to California instead.

So we're back now from a very long and complicated trek. My old preppy look had long succumbed to a new hippie look. A very ungroomed one at that. Factually, from living in the hood, our appearance evolved or devolved, depending on your POV. Worthy of arrest, I'd say.

So, we're back. I'm installing air conditioners. We have a job at a hip ad agency. So I ask, hey, do you know anyone in the film industry looking for help.

You see I still had designs on a creative future…it just morphed from painting to filmmaking. You know where this is going, don't you?

Yes, in fact they did. They said a company of filmmakers just came back from filming Woodstock. Go see them. They gave me the address, and go I did.

I filled out the requisite application, in about three minutes, and met with one Dale Bell. Long story short, like the Fillmore, the great Dale must have seen something in me. Perhaps an entertaining smile. I don't know, but he offered me the lofty position of production assistant. And I thought about it for less than one second before wholeheartedly accepting. I still remember where his desk was.

What does, or shall I say, did I do as a production assistant? Well anything and everything. What does that exactly mean, Al?

This, in stream-of-conscious form:

Build screening rooms where the rough footage was projected over and over.

Be a projectionist where one had the honor of seeing weeks of film, over and over as it was gently whittled to perfection.

Build sound rooms. Yes, sound was very important as one would imagine. The sound engineers were great. I remember when they queued up CSNY's rendition of Joni Mitchell's song for the first time, commemorating the festival before it was ever publically released.

Assemble new flatbed film editing machines called Steenbecks, as I recall. Yes, "Steenbeck," not the great author John Steinbeck.

I took myself with tussled afro, torn tapestry pants, pack of Marlboros to the bank, after hours. There a very nervous bank manager opened the door with a wet forehead and accepted the white envelope I was tasked to deliver. A check of some huge amount, if you were wondering, from the sponsoring company, I forget who. Maybe Warners. I didn't know you could have so many zeros in a number.

Oh yes, let's not forget excusing oneself as I shimmed by visiting rock legends on my way to pick up the Chinese food. This was a very important job as work often went on into the night.

Sharing a cab with one Martin Scorsese well after hours so we could get home. A very nice man who humored my film questions. I did walk the sixty-eight blocks south and many avenues over on occasion when the circumstances were just right. Just right meaning being broke.

And of course, being the witty clown that so many classroom-teachers despised.

All of this I say is gospel. All from today's freeform memory like it was yesterday. Why do I say this? C'mon. You know why!

Because working on Woodstock was the icing on the cake for my years living in the hood. It'll always be a very dear part of my existence, soul I'd say even better. I turned seventy a month ago. I was nineteen then. A lasting memory? A significant part of me? Without any doubt!!

Epilogue…perhaps

I attended the premier when released in NYC.

If I think of anything else I'll let you know, but know this: my experiences living in the hood, working at the Fillmore and the Crown Jewel working on Woodstock resonates with me at all times. I still have my opening night ticket and a few ribbons honoring same all safely put away, for all time, just as my memories are.

But my soul was much fuller……………

Peace.

SONYA POLONKSY

ONE PERSPECTIVE ON POST

(Sonya was the movie's production manager.)

DALE: Michael got the first KEM.

SONYA: Right, but in books it says Francis got the first one. I know that you intercepted it. It was on its way to Yucca Street.

DALE: It was on its way to San Francisco.

SONYA: Oh, you diverted it to Yucca Street.

DALE: To Broadway. Right, I found out from the guys at Keller, whether in New York or somewhere else that there was one on its way to Francis Ford Coppola. It was leaving Hamburg, Germany. When it stopped at JFK, we intercepted it.

SONYA: You kidnapped it.

DALE: We kidnapped it, exactly.

SONYA: How did we kidnap it, though?

DALE: We got a forklift truck, took it off of the pallet. We stole it.

SONYA: We stole it. We didn't tell Francis. We didn't have some negotiations with him, we told him after?

DALE: No, during.

SONYA: Oh, we told him during and he said Okay.

DALE: It was a heated exchange and I asked Francis to write a piece for the book about this. Give me one page of his recollection of the conversation.

SONYA: What did he say?

DALE: He said, "I'm busy in Paris and I'm writing a screenplay. I can't be interrupted, but I remember the incident very well." As I remember it, we intercepted it; he was pissed. We told him we'd pay him. He grumbled and was eternally pissed, but I have to remind everybody that he wasn't so pissed that he ignored us completely when we got to Los Angeles, in early December. Five or six days after we arrived, we were on airplanes to San Francisco to celebrate the opening of his new company, the American Zoetrope. A great party.

Let's go into what do you recollect about the whole postproduction process, in New York. What are the things that come to your mind?

SONYA: The things that come to my mind are sitting in that outside room with the personnel changing everyday. I remember everyday at six o'clock I couldn't bear it. These shifts would change. We had several shifts of people syncing. And, at six o'clock everyday I would try to escape, because it would just become too much for me. But I had to stay. Because at six o'clock everyday, we'd either get more Moviolas or send some of them back. Which I didn't quite understand. You were masterminding that. People would be added on; people would be laid off. I never got it.

I do remember at one point you and Bob Maurice and Mike Wadleigh decided that I should learn bookkeeping. Because I was doing the petty cash and making a mess out of it. And, I was always behind and I actually worried a lot about that for months. I loved doing all the phone calls and emergencies that came up and last-minute things, but there was this growing back log of stuff like petty cash records that had to be reconciled and invoices and stuff that would haunt me.

And, I would think "I can't delegate it to someone else because it's too much of a mess, but I can't do it, I can't do it!" And then, at some point you all decided that I should learn bookkeeping. And, I remember I went home that night to my apartment at 107th Street, and I thought, "What should I do? I should kill myself. I left book publishing so I could work in the movies and they want me to be a bookkeeper! And, I'm really stupid with figures, and not only that, I'm not interested in them…"

So, then the next day I put up a fuss. And the next thing I knew you had hired some lady named Marion. Who was very nice and was a real bookkeeper.

DALE: Probably what was going on was that there was a need. We figured well… but you were smart and you protested.

SONYA: I wasn't smart I was desperate and hysterical and I thought it was the end of my life, as I knew it.

DALE: Right, so you protested and look at what happened.

SONYA: You see, what I do remember also, right before Woodstock, I had said to Mike: "I'm going to move on. I'm going to California because I don't know what I want to do with my life and now is a good time to go." He said, "We're going to shoot this film, it's only four days, won't you stay on?" So, I said sure. He said it will be exciting, it will be an adventure. I said sure.

So, I stayed on and afterward he said "Why don't you stay on and do your job and you can work with one of the editors?" And I never got free, to work with the editors.

DALE BELL

HOLLYWOOD'S LONGEST OPTICAL

IT WAS AN AUSPICIOUS day. The "Suits" were in town. Up to now, they had only caught a little glimpse of our editing. Bob had been masterful about purposefully keeping them at bay. Every time one of them would show up, the "suit" would wonder out loud what we were doing? Why didn't we get the editing done faster? Who were all these people Warners was paying for? Why did we need such exotic gear? Our flat-bed editing tables didn't look at all like those old Moviola editing machines they were used to watching!

The "Suits" were acting like "Suits"—probably doing exactly what they get paid to do!

Get the film out by Christmas! They insisted. We've got Radio City Hall booked. December 17! Every day for the past few weeks, Fred Weintraub had been sending telegrams: "What have you got for us today, Michael?" Bob would respond: "Nothing!" Warners kept reminding us that the kids would just be getting out of school on their vacations, "Hurry up! We've got to make money on this!" (Let the record show that Warners had absolutely nothing else going on that winter, or spring either, for that matter. No wonder they wanted *Woodstock* out early—they had their stockholders to satisfy. To hell with the quality of the film! What did they think: we were the tooth fairy? Which mile of footage from the seventy-five we had filmed would we throw at the audience?)

I remember one "Bob and the money" scene. Bob would call the Warners money man, requesting twenty-five thousand dollars to repay some of the bills which had accumulated over the week. The Warners person would ask what we had been spending the money on? Bob would enumerate the invoices we had prepared. The Warners person would respond: "We won't get that to you for at least a week, if then!" Then he would hang up. Bob would call someone else at

Warners and tell him that we needed fifty thousand dollars and receive a similar response. Bob would turn to us with that twinkle. Then he would pick up the phone again, talk to someone new, presumably higher up, and say we needed one hundred thousand dollars that very afternoon because our creditors were suing us and Warners wouldn't like that kind of press in tomorrow's papers, would they? Fred Weintraub would then call back from Warners to find out about the problem. Bob's reply would be something like: "Do you want to continue to send telegrams or do you want us to stop editing the movie? Send the one hundred thousand dollars this afternoon." In a couple of hours, a meek man with a check for one hundred thousand dollars would arrive. Bob's drop-a-keg-of-nails philosophy had to be invoked. And although it sounds funny now, at the time, it was very painful for all of us, particularly for Bob who had to adopt a different personality in order to succeed on behalf of all of us in this movie-making game.

To get a feel of how young audiences might respond to our "rough cuts", we previewed several single-image sequences one night at the Woodstock "Alma Mater", NYU Film School. These privileged students were the very first outside of our "immediate family" who would see what we had been working on for the past months. Much to our surprise and shock, our pieces were greeted with mild applause and such expressions as "Far out" or "Wow" or "Groovy." Period. We looked at each other incomprehensively. Were we making a big mistake? We wondered out loud. But a subsequent dinner at neighboring Max's Kansas City, with their carafes of wine, restored our sense of purpose.

That experiment being inconclusive, Bill Graham urged us to try another screening at the Filmore East over Thanksgiving. We rented the projectors, projectionists and stands; the plan was to view, then eat turkey dinner with the staff and audience, answering questions as we could. But the turkey arrived earlier than expected: just after we began our half hour sequence on three projectors, one by one the bulbs burned out. Frames of film exploded on the screen while smoke emitted from the projectors. Though many in the audience cheered, thinking, perhaps under stupor, that we had created an extra special effect for their viewing pleasure, Bill and Mike were so embarrassed, we gathered our broken film and went home, tails between our legs.

Now, today, all day, we were finally going to show the "Suits" our work.

After lunch, we stuffed about forty of them into our compact and very makeshift screening room, then turned out the lights. Crammed together expectantly in the darkness were Fred Weintraub, who had helped to bring the film to Warner Bros. through the producers of the festival, and John Calley, producer of *Catch 22* and other movies, as well as various other promotional types. Significantly absent was Chairman of Warner Bros., Ted Ashley, who had let Weintraub shepherd the picture. On cue, three projectionists switched on the five Grafflex projectors and two Magna Tech sixteen-millimeter magnetic playback machines. This day marked the end of just three months of work, most of which was conducted around the clock.

It was early December 1969. For this rough cut screening, we had edited 350,000 feet of sixteen-millimeter film down to approximately 17,000, once you counted all the multiple images. Or to put our historic accomplishment in another context, we had cut 165 hours of original screen time down to eight and a half hours. Or, consider that for every twenty feet of sixteen-millimeter film we had shot over those three days in August, we were throwing out nineteen! There was no physical, practical, mechanical way we could release the picture by this Christmas holiday.

Maybe by the next holiday? Bob suggested with a twinkle in his eye. In the Spring? Regardless, the pressure was on us every day. He and Mike Wadleigh were taking the pulse from within the room. Larry was on sound.

Thelma Schoonmaker, our supervising editor, was still bent over one of our four KEMs, her fingers whirring over her splicer, putting the last touches on one of the latter reels which wouldn't be up for a couple of hours.

The configuration of the screening room, with its five projectors on their stands, was designed to create the effect of multiple images for the audience. Wads and Larry would choreograph the projectionists so that at appropriate times while the film was still running, they would grab a couple of the stands, and move the images on the wall to a different position. Thus, we could create between one and five overlapping images. In that darkness and among the spinning noise of all these machines, Wads, Larry, and others were designing, through trial and error, how the final film would look. When he could, Larry adjusted the pots to even out the sound track.

All along we had known that only the West Coast had the technological know-how to realize Michael and Thelma's creative decisions about postproduction.

Our task, once we got to Hollywood ourselves, would be to translate this on-the-fly technique to thirty-five-millimeter CinemaScope, a term most of us heard simply as moviegoers, not as producer/editors. We had no idea of the problems we were going to bring with us.

This first screening lasted well into the middle of the night. Reel changes, a food interlude, and breakdowns contributed to the delay. Perhaps because we had deliberately served our audience many Alice B. Toklas brownies, perhaps because the room was saturated with smoke of all kind, the retention power of the "Suits" was becoming a little slurred—and blurred!—after midnight.

At one reel break, they were so overwhelmed, they called a halt. The sound of the machines, coupled with the sometimes-deafening sounds of the music, was enough to numb the senses. Monitoring the multiple images dancing on the wall, the lack of fresh air, collective body odor, all contributed to a sensory overload!

It was decided that the screening would continue the following morning at ten. When Wads checked the carefully stacked and numbered reels awaiting their respective projectors, he determined that we still had almost two hours to go! We had aleady spent more than ten hours in the screening room, the "Suits" on chairs, everyone else on mattresses scattered about the floor and among the legs of the projector stands.

The following morning, the "Suits" accumulated again, but this time there was a new arrival. Fred Weintraub had invited his Chairman to view the end of the movie with him. Bob, however, in his brilliance, designed a different opening scenario over coffee and donuts. Wrapping his burly frame around the diminutive Ted Ashley, who had come dressed like a bell-boy in spats, Bob whisked him away from Weintraub. "Hi, Ted, how are ya?" Ted's response: "Understand you got a good picture here!" Out of earshot, Bob told Ashley he would have to see the film from the very beginning. Ashley, Bob insisted, could not rely on Weintraub to interpret the film for him. Weintraub was causing all of the filmmakers too much distress. Masterfully, Bob was excising Weintraub out of the picture forever, even as Weintraub stomped angrily around the office, bemoaning his fate, yelling to me to "Stop him! Stop him!"

Almost alone, Bob walked Ted into the screening room and started the film at its very beginning, with Sidney Westerfeldt's prologue (much to the astonishment of the projectionists who had to hustle to catch up!). I think the Warners' business and legal guru, Sid Kiwitt, was in the room, too. All other tall people, like me, were kept out of the screening room so as not to overpower Ted. It marked the end of Fred and the inception of our relationship with Sid Kiwitt, for better or for worse. (On another project, I was to have my confrontation with Ted months later in Burbank, in an office specifically designed to raise him to eye level of other, much taller participants. The issue was another follow-up movie Warners wanted to make so badly, they commited the hubric mistake of being over eager and not listening. Because of my fluent French, I had been hired to work as line-producer with French director, François Reichenbach, on what was to become *The Great Medicine Ball Caravan*, another glossy attempt by Fred Weintraub to co-opt the long-hairs with a rock and roll road movie. It didn't work. Without an interpreter, the French cameramen and the director could not understand how the Americans they were filming responded to this traveling concert film. Warners took a huge bath on the project!)

The screening of *Woodstock* culminated with the searing rendition of the "Star Bangled Banner" anthem, as reconstructed by Jimi Hendrix. His finale on the Monday morning of the festival would mark the end of our movie, played over the debris and devastation left behind by half a million festival participants on Max Yasgur's hillside. Overwhelmed by the totality of the movie, the "Suits" retired to their downtown offices to reconnoiter. Many of their best-laid plans would have to change. No Christmas at Radio City Music Hall. Yes, they would lose all those kids home for the holidays! Steve McQueen's movie could now get in there. More money to spend to complete the movie. More hemorrhaging, possibly. No quick solution to the irascible hippies they were in bed with. But maybe, they would get a good picture out of it all!

And Bob, who had originally committed to Warner Bros. for a December delivery date to induce them to back the movie, was ultimately relieved that the "Suits" would accept the film later without recriminations. He always admitted it had been a dumb but necessary decision, bred of a combination of *naivete* and negotiation.

Yet at the same time, the press began to visit us, eager to do a story before we fled New York for Hollywood. Warners wanted to get the word out one way or the other. Today, you'd call it "spinning" or putting on the "buzz."

This was only the first of four screenings scheduled before we were to depart for Hollywood. After the "Suits" left, we invited people who had worked on the film to come by, critics, and friends. Some would come by early in the morning, catch a few reels before work, and then return to view the middle of the movie during their lunch break. One screening started in the evening and went through the entire night, finishing early in the morning: this to accomodate those who could not take time off from their normal work. It was like a floating crap game in New York: you could float in and out of the movie on your own schedule! It was on a continuous loop!

During these last few days, we were able to pack up everything not needed specifically for the screening to make it ready for the trek across country. One U-Haul truck would carry the furniture, editing tables and the bulky, uncartonable equipment. The two who drove the truck were told they would have jobs in California, if they arrived safely. Otherwise…

One incident comes to mind. Wads had long ago purchased a motorcycle which never ran. He decided it needed a new home in California. As the truck was being loaded, we decided we would put the cycle in the back of the truck. But there was no key; the cycle was locked. And Wads was asleep by this time. Not to be deterred, we took the cycle down to the street in the elevator. Five of us were carrying it to the truck on Broadway that night when, you guessed it, we were accosted by the fuzz. "Hey you guys, what are you up to? Are you stealing this motorcycle? Whose motorcycle is this?" I answered the last of the questions. "It actually belongs to a guy upstairs who is sleeping and we don't want to disturb him, so…" Of course, the cops wouldn't let me finish. What a line! Herding us together while one of them stayed on the street with the cycle and the truck, the other cops accompanied the rest of us to the fifth floor.

Wads is asleep on the screening room mattresses. Bob tries to mollify the cops: "Michael had bought the cycle in Italy," he began. "We don't have the registration. It has Roma license plates on it, you know." Bob was going no where fast. The cops were getting more frustrated. Wads heard the commotion, emerged sleepy-eyed from the screening room, asking "What's going on?" The cops asked him to identify himself. But then one of them said: "Hey, aren't you the guy in the *Daily News*? Aren't you making a movie? About freaks? Didn't I see your picture in the *Daily News*?" Wads acknowledged, explained that it was his cycle and that it was on its way to California. The cops shook hands all around and helped us complete the loading! A cultural gap had been bridged.

Crates were built to contain the sensitive gear we would ship by air. Some of the edited workprint was copied just in case it got lost or broken in shipment. Special cardboard boxes, filled with insulating material, would transport the gold—the 350,000 feet (seventy miles worth of material spooled around itself!) of sixteen-millimeter negative which would eventually serve as the basis for constructing the multiple images on the West Coast. Nothing was more valuable than the negatives. Even the gear could be replaced, but there was no way to go back and reshoot!

It was also at this time that we completed the whittling down of the staff. At one point during the syncing-up process, we were up to some forty employees, working three eight-hour shifts. As we entered the editing phase, the lack of gear, space, and supervisory people forced us to let more people go. These days were called "Bloody Fridays" when I would have to invite people into my desk area—offices did not exist—and let them know we could not continue them into the next week. When they saw me coming, and heard me announce their name in a mournful tone, they knew their days were numbered. It was sad for both of us.

But now there loomed the Final Cut—the time we would pick those who would accompany us to Hollywood. Bob, Wads, T, and I had determined that we would take only seventeen people. I had the dubious distinction of letting everyone know their destiny. It was not a kind task, but someone had to do it.

To this day, I do not recall exactly what I said to Marty Scorsese who was not part of the "finishing team". I still feel awkward about it. It was difficult for both of us. Thankfully, we overcame it. (When he had *Mean Streets* and *The Italian Americans* to do two years later, he called me both times and I joined him again, absolutely thrilled to be in his creative company. In 1975, I had to regrettably turn down his invitation to join him as assistant director—my *Mean Streets* function—on *Taxi Driver* because the Directors' Guild, which I had recently joined, would not permit me to change category from Production Manager to A.D., infuriating him and me. A couple of years later, we briefly explored my producing *King of Comedy* but couldn't work it out, alas. Talk about the turns of life. Wow!)

We had truly become a very large, devoted, family. The intensity of the work, the historic nature of the project, the symbol we began to represent, our visibility, all had bound us together in a sort of eternal comradery which would extend far beyond the confines of work. Though there were many disappointments and some tears, it was replaced with a great deal of understanding and spirituality over the years. Those who had been designated part of the finishing team in Hollywood were given their first days off in three months. Actual days off they weren't; for everyone had to pack, say good-bye, while preparing themselves mentally for an even more intense period of learning new technology, disseminating information to a new team of professionals, and much reworking of the sequences.

These were our guidelines to those who would come to Hollywood:

1. You are coming for an indefinite period of time. We cannot predict now how long we will need you.

2. We will pay your round trip transportation.

3. Effective Monday, eleven to ten and thereafter, through California, there will be no payments for overtime. Your salary will remain as is.

4. We will pay each individual seventy dollars per week in perdiems (including Saturday and Sunday) which you do not have to account for. This is to cover your food, laundry, etc. (This was 1969 and we would generally pick up a communal dinner! Remember that this money is not taxed.)

5. The housing accomodations present a problem and we would like some answers as soon as possible so that we can firm up our temporary arrangements. There are two options: private houses, seven bedrooms each or the motel route.

From an economic standpoint we cannot afford to provide more than the private house. The cost to the company is forty dollars per week per room. Due to the close proximity of these accomodations, and the fact that seven people will have to share private bathrooms, kitchen, etc., we do not feel we can provide space here for spouses or friends. Therefore, for those of you in the latter category, we would like opinions: if we provide a room at a cost to us of forty dollars per week per person, and you want other kinds of accomodations, will you pay the difference between forty dollars and the price of other accomdoations you may desire in a neighboring motel? Our estimates on motels booking for a length of time comes to about eighty dollars per week per room. If we arrange these kinds of accomodations for those of you desiring them, we feel you should pay the additional cost. Okay?

The truck left at dawn on a Wednesday with an ETA in Hollywood of Saturday. It would take the southern route to avoid possible bad weather across the country. By prearrangement, Ed George and Ken Glazebrook, the two drivers, would call in every night to assure us of their progress.

Finally, Saturday, December 7—Pearl Harbor Day—arrived. In the early morning, just hours after the last screening, we loaded another truck with all the gear, negative, and workprints which would be taken to JFK for air shipment to Los Angeles. So fearful were we of losing something, or of an airplane crash, that we had created a system whereby we would ship only part of the negative of a certain musical group on one airplane. We would put the other portion on a second flight. Nor would we ship the workprint of one group with the negative for that group, just in case we would have to replicate the editing from the workprint. We were paranoid about it. With the gear, we followed the same procedure, shipping only one KEM on a pallet, under a net, per airplane. Four KEMs, two Steenbecks, six Grafflex projectors, two Magnatech playback machines, and more than a hundred separate boxes of negative and workprint, carefully numbered and labelled, were slipping from our primary custody, entrusted into the hands of others for the first time since mid-August. The surrender factor was difficult to grasp! From about ten in the morning until late that evening, we used more than fifteen separate flights to ensure that everything would arrive safely. Cross-checking with Lewis Teague, our newly-hired production manager in LA (and the guy who had originally introduced Bob and Mike) assured us that the flights were arriving with their predetermined loads. Lewis and the two drivers then transported everything to our new offices on Yucca and Vine, in Hollywood. Sunday, they set up the office and the cutting rooms.

The new team flew over the weekend, picked up their cars at the Los Angeles airport, and spread out among the three houses Lewis had rented for the duration of our stay. Wads and I stayed behind for several hours more, checking and cross checking our plan for Hollywood. And finally, as the sun set in New York, we boarded our flight to LA.

Airplane rides are often ethereal experiences. Purchased by Warner Bros.'s travel people, our tickets entitled us to first class seats. But neither Wads nor I ever felt comfortable there. Within a few minutes, we took our drinks and spread out in the relatively empty coach section. It represented our first pause from eighteen-hour days in almost five months. The process had been unforgiving. And here we were floating in space for the first time, very detached from life itself, or so it appeared...

I looked over at him. I had almost killed him on our first major job together outside Chicago. Here, just three years later, with the help of many of our friends, we had created a movie which embodied all we had stood for in those trenches of New York during the 1960s. More than any other place in America, New York represented a thriving cauldron of concern and passion: for civil rights, against the Vietnam War, for education, for the environment, about music, about achieving peace and harmony in spite of, at the expense of, or around the Establishment.

And what allies we had all become: Bob Drew and his associates had started the 1960s with a bang. Their revolutionary use of the new technology astounded television viewers. Add to this mix Al and David Maysles, Ricki Leacock, Don Pennebaker, Fred Wiseman, Amram Nowak and his cohorts David Hoffman and Harry Wiland, Beryl Fox, Bob Elfstrom, Bill Jersey, Al Perlmutter, Irving Gitlin, Arthur Zegart, John O'Toole, Ofra Bikel, Jack Willis, and these were just some of the documentarians. Think of Arthur Penn, Phil D'Antoni, Kenny Utt, Gordon Parks as dramatic filmmakers and you have a sense that New York was precisely—

and only!—where the action was. When Antoine de Saint-Exupery wrote his monumental work, *Night Flight*, he was describing filmmakers bound together by their camaraderie, facing the very uncertain forces at work in society, trying to set them straight. Filmmaking had become confrontational, and in some instances, a life and death struggle. It put you on the front lines between good and evil. We can't even remember what kind of films Hollywood was turning out during this time. And now, here we were, on our way to Tinsel Town with a picture born in that New York City foment.

Even during the festival, Wads and I never had time to think about what we were doing: it was a totally instinctual response to the situation. And training. The people we picked, the strategy we employed. Keeping it all together, reminding the entire team of its mission, there was the baby boomer Larry Johnson, deeply in tune to the needs of the music.

Bob Maurice had been such a logical person to fill the role of barrier between us and the Warner Bros. types. Crafty, wily, cunning, smart, outrageous, a brilliant debater, insensitive and callous when necessary, enormously kind and generous at an instant's provocation, Bob had been successful in holding those "Suits" out of our way in spite of his instincts to be a burly Teddy Bear (he was also a marvelous maker of omelettes!). All he and Wads had argued for with Warner Bros. had been artistic freedom: to make the picture their way. As the plane took off, Wads and I knew we were halfway to the finish line. Soon both of us were asleep.

Our drive into Hollywood from LAX took us down Sunset Boulevard. From our vantage point in the rented white convertible, California did not have truly black nights, even at four in the morning. Grey, hazy, like aurora borealis, a glow glimmered all along the route. The boulevard was empty. What a heady feeling as we wound beneath the swaying palm trees. We were coming to town with the hopes of setting it on its ear. Little did we know what awaited us.

Armed only with the addresses of the three houses which Lewis had rented for us, and minimal knowledge about Hollywood, we targeted the one which theoretically had a swimming pool. One street number loomed out of the darkness. It checked. Yes, one of the houses was on Franklin Avenue. We stopped the car and explored. Lewis had worked wonders! Here, set up against a communal garden just north of Hollywood Boulevard was a huge mansion, separated from Franklin by a wrought iron fence. We tried the gate. It opened. We ventured inside to the vast porch and tried another door. It, too, opened. We were praising Lewis to the heavens. If we had this kind of place, what were the other team members going to have as their accommodations? Hollywood was grand, wasn't it? Now we were inside this mansion. Posh furniture. A pool out back. All this for three hundred dollars per month? Then we were met by someone with a flashlight. No, he was not a member of the team. We were in the wrong house! We apologized and quickly left. Such is what Hollywood dreams are made of. Thankfully, the man was not carrying a gun!

After a little more reconnoitering, we did find the right place on Orlando Street and settled in. Much more mundane than our original stop, it did have a pool with a slide, and a good kitchen. For the next several months, Orlando was our communal home and the center of our team's social life.

Monday morning brought everyone back together again at our new offices. Our color-coded workprints were stacked in the editors' respective rooms. The screening prints were in the newly-designed central screening room, complete with its six projectors, playback machines and speakers. Much of the foam rubber used to line the crates transporting the equipment had been tacked to the walls and ceiling so that the sound would not disturb our neighboring tenants. Our precious negative was carefully delivered to Ed Richards, T's choice as our negative cutter, under contract to us. Everything was accounted for. A miracle of planning, or luck. We were ready to work again and it was only Monday noon. Plans were discussed. Some initial deadlines were set.

The arrival of the ABDick copying machine caused a slight diversion. As soon as we realized that, in addition to paper, it could also copy a hand, for example, everyone decided that we should have a little contest inserting other body parts into the scanning device. The only way to ensure fairness was to sequester the ABDick copying machine in a room of its own. There, in private of course, a particpant could expose whichever body part(s) they wanted, place it—or them—on the cold glass with the help of a nearby chair, if necessary, and push the Print button. Amidst a constant stream of giggles and laughter, each participant would emerge from the ABDick room with their printed results hidden from everyone else. After each had printed everything they wanted to, the black-and-white portraits were discreetly inserted and shuffled in a left-over moving box.

Then, the goal of the contest was to try to determine the owner of a particular private body part! One picture at a time was drawn from the box and held up to view. Guesses were made. Such knurled and matted shapes! More laughter and high-pitched shrieks of delight and horror. But the rules dictated that no one could be forced to acknowledge their own part(s) unless they wanted to. Many actually denied ownership! The individual portraits were pinned to a wall as inducement for future contestants. Group initiation complete. The ABDick copying people were thrilled at our inventive use of their gear. Warner Bros. was aghast! Our new technology work in Hollywood had begun! After all, weren't we in the picture business?

That night, the Orlando group invited everyone else to a cookout around the pool. After the meal, everyone stripped and either jumped or slid into the pool, some naked, some attired in bathing suits. Too late, we learned by the burn marks on our bare backsides that the slide had to be watered down before it could be used! The end result revealed an interesting 1960s' psychological-sociological equation: those who would not acknowledge ownership of their body parts in the office by day wore bathing suits at night. It would be the first of many such parties.

Tuesday morning, we began in earnest the process which would consume us for the next four months: making the longest optical yet devised by man.

Explanation: we had filmed the festival in sixteen-millimeter. To project a movie in theaters, we needed to create a thirty-five-millimeter print from our original. In short, we had to enlarge, or blow up, our original negative or color reversal to another negative, from which we could make a print. "Add a generation" is the correct parlance. But because our original design consisted of multiple images to convey simultaneity of action, we had to enlarge some portions of our original hundred percent, some several gradations less than that. To achieve a CinemaScope look, where the image on the screen is almost twice as wide as it is high (today we would call it "Letterbox") where a black border on top and bottom frame the image, we had to crop the images, even as we were enlarging them. Some images had to be cropped, much as one does at a photo store when you want to obtain a closeup out of a frame which was originally shot wide.

The size of a thirty-five-millimeter frame is more than twice as high as a sixteen-millimeter frame and more than twice as wide. If we were to enlarge each of our original, individual frames to the thirty-five-millimeter frame, or almost three times their size, and then throw that across fifty yards of theater onto an eighty-foot screen, our image quality would break down so disastrously as to make viewing it very uncomfortable and unsatisfying. Grain like dancing golfballs. Thus we had to design a process which would allow us to achieve the CinemaScope look, create the "letterbox" effect, separate the individual frames from each other, crop some of the area from each frame, and permit combinations of images up to five to appear on one thirty-five-millimeter frame. Each image had to run synchronously with one or more other images, and the color balance between the frames had to match exactly.

It was a tall order. Almost impossible, as we were about to experience. No one had ever done it before. Calculate for a moment with me. Assume that our edited film would run about four hours in length. sixteen-millimeter runs at thirty-six feet per minute. At 21,000 feet of sixteen-millimeter film per hour, you have 8,400 feet. At twenty-four frames per second, times sixty minutes, times four hours, you have 345,600 individual frames to which to apply these techniques, IF you are releasing only a single-image, non multiple-image film. We were not. Many of our sequences would contain two, three, four, and sometimes five images on the screen simultaneously. Let's say, for example, that we had at least twice as many images as a single-image picture, or 691,200 frames; maybe we had more. I don't know the answer, even today. Regardless, a helluva lot of frames to deal with!

When a commercial, for example, is submitted to an optical house for this kind of work, it may be thirty seconds long and contain ten to fifteen individual edits. The optical house would complete the job in a week or so.

Compare that to what we were seeking. In a rush.

Pacific Title Company, owned by Shirley and Gordon Hubbard, was one of the optical companies recommended to Bob, Mike, and T on their initial visit to Hollywood. Gordon and his technical wizard, Dick Bond, became our first visitors on Tuesday. Now understand something. No one in Hollywood had ever seen a KEM editing machine up close and personal, unless at a trade show in some distant city. There were NONE in the film capital of the world until we brought our four and set them up in our editing rooms. Consider as well that we were not at all the well-manicured, short-haired people represented by our first visitors. To them, we must have appeared very strange, even though we were able to keep up with them in the vision-and-technology department.

After we screened some of our material for them, they were nothing short of astonished, shocked, overwhelmed, probably fearful, too. So much to deal with: problems, time, capacity, personnel, equipment.

To produce the opticals we described and illustrated with the screening, Dick had recommended that we employ a two-perforation Techniscope process. In an optical camera, loaded with thirty-five-millimeter internegative film, they would photograph our sixteen-millimeter camera original through especially designed stationary mattes that would conform to our desired combinations of images, but instead of using four perforations, they would use only two perforations per thirty-five-millimeter frame. A four-perforation squeezed print would be made from the two-perf negative. Technicolor Labs would handle all the processing. The CinemaScope look we wanted would then be accomplished by equipping the projectors in the theaters with anamorphic lenses which would unsqueeze the image. Complicated, to say the least.

When asked how long it would take them to make one of these, they said they needed to make a test. We selected a five-minute not-very-special sequence, ordered the pulling of the respective original from Ed Richards, and waited for a response from Dick. It was not immediately forthcoming.

In the meanwhile, we met the people from Warner Bros. we would be working with: Rudy Fehr, an emigre from Germany, now the head of postproduction; his associate, Fred Talmadge, an ex-film editor who would be our daily point man; Dan Wallin, a staff music mixer who would be in charge of our mixing board and guide our sound team of Larry Johnson, Eric Blackstead, Lee Osborne, and Danny Turbeville in the processing of the music and production tracks; George Groves, an Englishman now running the WB Sound Department whose claim to fame had been as mixer of the first talkie, *The Jolson Story* in 1927, more than forty years earlier; and Graham Mahin, our jump-suited Dubbing Supervisor, who would work closely with T and the editors in the technical preparation of the edited sequences for the mix. An interesting group!

They had to come to us. We couldn't go to them yet. The screening room was our bastion. And like the Pacific Title group who had preceded them, they were blown away with our mastery of the technology and by the power of the film itself. We didn't, we couldn't show them everything. Too much time. So we cherry-picked our way through some of the sequences, trying to offer them a taste of things to come. One single-panel, a double, a triple, and so forth. Some doc. Some music. A broad palette of senses. None of them had any conception about how we had done it, or indeed, what we would have to do to complete it!

So in spite of the Long-Hair Short-Hair bit, we recognized we had a massive job to do and we'd simply better get down to work.

The next day, we were given a guided tour of the Technicolor Laboratory on Romaine Street. Again, the Short-Hair Long-Hair cropped up but was quickly dispensed with. Walking down their hallways decorated with legendary movie posters everywhere, we felt like time-travelers. Just a few years ago, we had been simply movie-goers, gawking in wonder as our favorite films transported us to other places, allowed us to be other people living in other times, captivated by darkness, music and images. Now, we were filmmakers in our own right. Probably not exactly what the Technicolor folks were used to, but filmmakers, nevertheless. Soon, they might instill our poster along side that of *Gone With The Wind* and others, ensuring our place in the historical annals.

Already, we thought, we could be creating the longest movie ever distributed. And, we knew it would be the longest optical ever made. If we were successful in processing our primitive sound tracks so that our vision of full wraparound sound in the theaters could be achieved, we might be able to make an innovative mark there, as well. Larry, Michael and Thelma had always envisioned that the sound would be passed from speaker to speaker to match the ever-changing picture. Yet these criteria mattered little if we failed to convey the power and symbolism of the actual event. Though only a few people had attended the festival—half a million if you accept the highest estimates—many millions more around the world would get a sense of the 1960s, the music, the sociology, and the festival by our uncommon combination of darkness, music and sound, and the rhythm of our images. Though selected only through the improbability of happenstance and by a willingness to risk everything for a cause, we felt we were speaking for an entire generation of Americans. It was a heavy responsibility.

The Technicolor people readily accepted us as their customer. We signed their papers describing our relationship to them. Forewarned by Warner Bros., they knew this would be a massive project. Yes, they said, they were looking forward to servicing our requests. At one point on the exhaustive tour of the plant, their chief executive told me that, in rare instances, they were even able to move huge pieces of machinery and equipment from floor to floor to accomodate special situations. I silently stored some of these public relations tidbits I was gleaning.

Technicolor's role was simple, relatively. Once the optical house delivered the thirty-five-millimeter optical Techniscope negative to them, with each frame exposed every two perforations, Technicolor would first develop the negative. Balancing the color from one part of the negative frame to another—"timing"— would require a different set of sensitive instruments orchestrated by a "timer's eyes." Then, in another part of their plant, they would make a four-perforation anamorphic, or CinemaScope, print from that negative, running it through what was called a "liquid gate" to eliminate any scratches or other imperfections. The finished print could then be projected through a CinemaScope lens in a theater.

We left their plant confident we would be in good hands once we had created the opticals.

Yet we still had not heard back from Pacific Title as to the results of their preliminary test.

A DAY IN THE DESERT

We hadn't been in Hollywood more than a week or two. Confined to New York City, subways, buses, narrow streets and work around the clock, we felt all of California spreading out before us, beckoning us to explore it. We were young and eager. And above all, adventuresome.

Just before the Christmas holiday season, we decided to spend one day of the weekend in a place we had heard about only through mythology: Palm Springs.

Still in possession of the truck which had transported our equipment across the country in four days, we loaded Wads' motorcycle up its gangplank, climbed into our rented cars, and headed for the desert two-hours-plus away from Tinsel Town. I don't think we numbered more than ten on this holiday.

The drive to Palm Springs wasn't eventful, thankfully, but our arrival was. We had to get out of the vehicles! I can't state it categorically, but I believe that we were the very first hippies ever to be seen on their streets. Now, I can only surmise this. Chiroprators must have been busy in the days following our afternoon visit, for many heads crooked wildly to watch us, to stare at us, and finally, to avoid us, as though we were contaminated with an alien disease. To complete the ironic picture, the holy music of Christmas squeezed out through tinny speakers along the sidewalks. Wasn't this the time for forgiveness, for accepting our neighbor? Not in Palm Springs, apparently.

When we ordered a cup of coffee, or a sandwich, we were treated like infected victims of the plague. Directions were difficult to obtain as the people we were aiming for immediately had other destinations in mind than those to which they were originally aiming themselves. Ah, the Christmas spirit!

All we wanted to do was to play. To play with our motorcycle in their back yard so to speak. As soon as we found the way to the trail we were seeking, we left town.

Unloading the motorcycle for its warm-up run, we noticed that we were being watched. Someone from town had called the fuzz. We became the object of their attention.

Had our Short-Haired friends from Teletape in New York called their kissing cousins in Palm Springs? In how many places, in what numbers, were these similar scenes being played out across the country. We certainly felt the symbolism of our effort in creating this film.

As soon as Wads began a simple run up the trail, we were stopped by the fuzz. They wanted to check license, ownership, insurance…all the rules they could muster. We felt we were playing in *Black Like Me*, a fictional documentary starring James Whitmore in which a white man participates in the daily life of a Black man by coloring his own face. Yes, in California in 1969 in Palm Springs, we were being discriminated against because of the way we looked. Perhaps, it should not have surprised us.

But it did.

Back in our editing rooms, our editors—Thelma, Stan Warnow, Jere Huggins, and Yeu-Bun Yee and their assistants—had to learn a whole new language. We were already designing film mattes for single, double and triple images which would be used throughout the major portion of our material. When special circumstances arose, we would design special mattes.

Four-field sizes were selected for single images. All had a seven-field north and south, but their east-west dimensions increased in half-field sizes, from six through seven and a half.

Double image, north-south dimensions were six and a half. East-west was a full twelve field with a solid black line dividing the two images at the center.

Two formats were designed for triple images. The daytime sequences would conform to five and a half north and south with the three images arranged in a twelve west-four west, four west-four east, four east-twelve east configuration, black lines separating the images. Because of the black background of the nighttime material, we wanted a one field overlap between the images, sometimes with a soft rather than a hard line.

When our editors would lay out a triple image optical, for example, they marked sync at the head and tail of each reel, labeled each "left," "center," and "right" and indicated, on a label, affixed to each roll, the size of the matte to be used. Then, when we wanted to change field position on the sixteen-millimeter image, to have the best part in the finished optical, they wrote in at each sixteen-millimeter cut the desired placement in north, south, east and west dimensions. They also indicated fades or dissolves. There were to be no travelling mattes. On a piece of paper, they wrote out these same dimensions along side the cut-by-cut footage for each sequence. In this way, the optical men would have a cross reference as a guide.

Beyond learning this new language of opticals, the editors also had to reduce the length of some of their sequences while cleaning up all of their edits. After all, we left New York with an eight-and-a-half hour film. Music comprised about five hours, documentary about three-and-a-half. Our target for the optical was four hours, balanced with a comparable ratio of documentary and music so that the true nature of the festival would emerge. While T was concentrating her attention on the many documentary sequences, she and Michael would give guidance and recommendations to each of the editors as they began to hone their music segments. Those that could not be edited quickly were dropped, under pressure of time.

Within a couple of days, absent a sample from Pacific Title, we determined that one single optical house could not possibly handle this movie. Calling on Warner Bros.'s Fred Talmadge to help us, we invited four other houses to our screening room for a "war-room" conference. Dick Bond laid out the technical dilemmas. We then looked at a calendar. Too many sequences, too few days.

We looked down the line. Back-timing our schedule from the day the finished, mixed prints would have to be shipped to theaters in the eight opening cities on March 21, 1970, we calculated—or better, we estimated—how many days the sound mixing would require if we mixed five-day weeks. We estimated how many days Technicolor would need to manufacture sixteen prints of a potential four-hour movie. Because we could not mix without a thirty-five-millimeter print, we spread out the days and filled in the blanks with the projected ETA of individual segments from the optical houses. It appeared as though we would have to start the mix in late January. Unless I'm mistaken, everyone in that room turned sheer white and broke into a cold sweat! It was now early December. Subtract a couple of days for the holidays. Or calculate that Warners would have to ante up extraordinary overtime if they wanted the union members to work those holidays. *Deja vu* all over again: we would have to repeat the twenty-four-hour cycle of September and October.

There was no other course. All five houses would have to work together. Pacific Title would supply the stationary mattes. Although Pacific Title was to be the overall technical coordinator, we, the producers and editors, would work independently with each optical house, supplying them with material, asking only that they communicate with each other, sharing their innovations and problems.

To expedite all these matters we appointed our production manager, Sonya Polonsky, to act as a central communication center. She would keep day-by-day progress charts.

Recorded under very primitive conditions, where the voices and instruments frequently landed on the wrong, competing tracks, the sound processing was going to need a lot of work. Larry and his team spent more than a month at the Record Plant, attempting to cleanse and enhance both music and documentary.

With these procedures agreed upon, we expected good, smooth cooperation. What worried us most was the time. The optical people estimated that each house could turn out a maximum of five minutes each per week, if the material coming from us followed a normal schedule. Calculation: five houses times five minutes per week per house equals twenty-five minutes per week total. We would submit four hours or two-hundred forty minutes. These bastions of technology, these masters of Hollywood-the-movie-captial-of-the-world were telling us they would need ten weeks to complete our task. They couldn't make Warners' opening nights in mid-March simply with the picture-side! Never mind the sound! Never mind the laboratory process, the shipping, the promotion, etc.!

We thought we were presenting the optical people with a simple prescription: we were not asking for wipes, travelling mattes, spinning images or strobes, in short, nothing time-consuming. We would submit to them ten minutes of new material each day, beginning January 5, and we would deliver all the edited footage in a one month's time. We expected that one week later the optical work would be completed by all hands. The schedule we were working on dictated that we have optical prints available to work with in the mix, which had to begin in February.

To meet the deadline, the houses would have to cut their time in half.

Michael and Thelma decided to begin the picture with a single image. The first sequence was a prologue, an overture to the main attraction, necessary to establish the lush green setting for this largest "instant" gathering of young people.

As more activity invaded those once vacant fields, they expanded the image. Unless they cut mercilessly back and forth, chopping from sequence to sequence, they could not present the night-long activities at the site without going to double images. They wanted to create the impression of the simultaneity of the events, not their separateness. When, in the theater, they would add announcements coming from the surround-speakers, while at the same time show on screen the performers arriving by helicopters on double image format, they were creating, in essence, a third area of simultaneous activity.

We wanted the audience to feel that it had experienced more through the medium of film than it could have by being present at the festival itself. A single strand of images was incapable of telling our story in any manageable length of time.

When only a single performer appeared on stage—Richie Havens, Joan Baez, Arlo Guthrie, John Sebastian, Country Joe McDonald or Jimi Hendrix—we used single images. With group performers, we reached for multiple images.

Ten Years After, for example, offered us a simple optical problem, or opportunity. We filmed only one number of this group—that everlasting encore, "Goin' Home"—with three cameras. Mid-way, one of the cameras ran out of film —he had to change his magazine. When we saw the first prints—the rushes— together with the sound, we realized right away we had to show Alvin Lee, the lead musician, in triple image. As the third camera ran out of film, we simply took the continuing image from the right side, flipped it to reshoot it optically, and let it run on the left side as a mirror to continue the triple image optical throughout. It is also a sequence which has very few cuts. When filmed, the sequence ran eleven minutes; in the final edited version, it runs nine.

The keyboardist for the band, Chick Churchill, told me later that he had brought his entire family to the opening of the movie in London to see himself. Anticipation was high. Everyone in his party was blown away when he only appeared for six seconds, the victim who landed on the cutting room floor. Only years later, when I explained to him that we had filmed but one number, and that only with two cameras most of the time, did he forgive us and his vocalist, Alvin Lee, from his thirty-year suspicion of conspiracy theories! I think we had put every frame we had of Chick into the movie to make the sequence work.

Some of the opticals were arrived at by creative accident, such as the stop motion in The Who. Michael was working at the KEM table running the opening shots back and forth through the three viewers. Suddenly, he noticed that if he stopped the motion periodically, the flying fringe of Roger Daltrey's jacket formed fascinating patterns across his face. We ordered a sixteen-millimeter reprint of the sequence, cut out specific frames to create the halting, staccato effect now widely adopted by many television and film editors, and designed the opening. Sly and the Family Stone received similar treatment.

Four days after giving the optical houses our first sequence, new problems popped up. We had seen and approved the color timings before committing the material to the camera. Color was not the problem. Mysteriously, a black speck appeared in the center of the projected image. It was not a spot on the screen. It was not in the projector gate. It was not done in the printing, nor was it in the film we sent to the optical house. It was, we discovered, in the techniscope internegative. In short, it had been photographed as part of the solid matte, the frame around the image.

We messengered a memo (there were no faxes or email then!) to all houses to be sure to clean the mattes. The cameramen checked their mattes under high-powered magnification; they air-cleaned them, they changed them intermittently throughout a given sequence. But the spots returned day after day in sequence after sequence. Sometimes the houses could not even see them; they didn't know exactly what they were looking at, but we did. That was enough. To eliminate them, the material would have to be reshot from the nearest pickup point. In the case of multiple images, this would mean finding a point where both images cut straight across. It was impossible to start a pickup where only one of the multiple images had a cut.

About two weeks after the spots began to appear, Bob Sader of National Screen had an ingenious concept. He would build solid mattes out of razor blades that conformed to the proper field sizes. Because they had no centers, no dirt could come to rest, so now, happily, only unblemished original came through. Sader built special gates to hold his mattes in position in front of the techniscope camera. We had the mattes and gates mass-produced and distributed among our optical houses. It signalled the end of the black specks, but not to our problems.

Proper left-to-right color balancing in multiple image opticals is critical. It wouldn't do, for instance, to have a light sky on one side and dark sky on the other. Nor could you have one skin tone on the left side and a different skin tone on the right. Both sides have to conform as closely as possible. Our first pass on Joan Baez, for example, yielded a glowing yellow face. When we resubmitted her for correction, her yellow face was replaced with a huge speck of dirt which traveled like fly all over her face! And once again, to find a pickup point, you had to go back to the nearest straight-across cut. If the sequence was built with dissolves rather than cuts, the optical houses would have to retreat to a point before the dissolves began to start a pickup, for you couldn't begin a pickup in the middle of a dissolve.

Since some of the performance sequences required as much as twenty five hours on the optical bench the first time they were photographed, the optical men dreaded going back through that material for pickups. Remember, they are doing this frame by frame. First they would photograph the right side, rewind the entire negative without scratching it, then photograph the center section, or the left side onto the negative. It is a mind-blowing procedure requiring much skill and patience. I recall one pass on Alvin Lee and the Ten Years After band; for some reason, they had been squeezed into postage-sized frames surrounded by huge mattes of black.

Early January. I am going over the invoices from Technicolor, preparing them for payment by Warner Bros. I notice Technicolor is billing us for two prints, not the single one I always request when I send in the purchase order. We only receive one print. What happens to the second one if it is delivered? Or where is it delivered?? Bob and I talk about it. I naively ask the Tech people about this apparent mistake, since we only get one copy. They tell me it is not a mistake. It is standard with them to bill for two copies. We get one and Warner Bros. gets one. It is sent overnight to New York for their viewing. I quietly acknowledge that this might be standard operating procedure and hang up. Bob and I talk again.

Warners is watching our movie in New York!!!! Who is? Who ordered it? What right do they have? They are looking at all the mistakes, too. Nothing in the contract between Wadleigh-Maurice Productions, Ltd. and Warner Bros. permits Warners a look-see at our material until we are ready to show it to them ourselves. We are the client of record with Technicolor! We submit our purchase orders, not Warner Bros. If Technicolor is doing stuff without our permission, behind our back, they have a problem! Perhaps a big one.

Bob calls an attorney. Within hours, in New York City and Hollywood, we have slapped an injunction on Warners and Technicolor, the accomplice in this subterfuge. Unless the practice is halted immediately, he tells them, we will stop editing on the movie. We will not submit any more work print to the optical houses. The whole process will stop dead in its tracks!

Technicolor is immediately apologetic though it maintains Warners has always received copies of dailies from other pictures; they don't see why this situation is any different. But Warners is intransigent while Bob argues with them on the phone. They have the right to see what we are doing, they insist. After all, they are paying for the picture. The contract is repeatedly brought out; language is read. Nowhere does Warners have the right to look.

Bob decides he has to go to New York to present our case. He is protecting our right to make the movie our way. Besides, he has not yet agreed on an opening date or cities. The promotion has to be designed. All this has to be dealt with at the same time, he reasons.

A day passes. The clock is ticking toward the deadline: the opening of the movie.

Before Bob departs, we develop a strategy. Very carefully, so as not to cause alarm among the Warners' staff editing people who are helping us, we will pull back one sequence at a time. We will claim that someting is wrong, a segment is out of sync, a new piece has to be reedited, anything to recall our material into our own shop.

We use the same approach with the optical houses. Pull back a piece, request to look at another segment because....

Bob leaves for New York, promising he will only stay three days.

Over these days, we systematically withdraw all our work from Warners and from the optical houses. It is stacked in our offices on Yucca and Vine. We hire a series of armed guards who protect everything at our command. No stranger is allowed in. We continue to work, unbeknownst to everyone on the outside.

Warner Bros. and the optical houses confer, discovering that they are both in the same situation: they have nothing to work on as the hours tick by.

In our screening room, the telephone is connected to the speakers. When Bob calls in from New York to report on his progress, or more specifically, his lack of it, he is piped into the screening room where everyone gathers to hear his rendition of the talks. He is getting nowhere but he receives cheers from all of us for his fortitude. We know he is in a battle fighting for our ability to preserve our artistic control and we love him.

As the days pass unproductively in New York, we continue our editorial work but do not let the Warners' people know of our ongoing progress. On the third day, we take a truck to Ed Richards, our negative matcher, and pull out all of the negative, very carefully. This action triggers another phone call to Warners. They discover that they are paralyzed.

The negotiations, according to Bob on the speaker phone, begin to change. He is beginning to get consessions. We've got this point, he says in the screening room, and we cheer. We've got this, too, and we cheer again. We know we have the upper hand. Piece by piece, the film finds it way back to its original spot, on the Warners lot, in the optical house, inside the negative matcher's vault. Bob has won all his points and then some. The project is resuming its speed. Artistic integrity is restored. He returns from New York triumphant.

Warners has backed down, but in the process, they introduce Sidney Kiwitt, one of their attorneys and business people, to our team. At first he deals only with

Bob and Wads, to finally negotiate Warners out of this snafu of their own making. Soon, all of us immediately befriend Sidney whose sense of fairness, honesty, and ability to forget that he is a "suit" make him unique among the Warners personnel. Without Sidney as our interface, I doubt the movie ever would have been completed.

We resume the preparation of the material for the opticals. In editing the scenes, Michael and Thelma had foreseen the difficulties inherent in doing pickups mid-stream and had, in fact, built in straight across cuts every two or three minutes. But, as luck would have it, they unhappily occurred at the wrong points!

By now, we had five houses working twenty-four-hour days, seven days a week, in two or three shifts, much as we had begun this project in New York during our syncing in September and October. The monster was devouring all of us whole!

The optical house cameramen were beginning to live with the Woodstock footage far more than they wanted to. Because we were asking them to work exceptionally long hours, we would receive material where the image on the left side was out of sync with the material on the right. A bi-product of fatigue. The optical house lineup men would have to go back to their benches, recalculate the footage, have it rephotographed from the nearest pickup point and hope that nothing else would go wrong in the reshooting.

Our original film had by this time gone through a number of passes in the attempts to produce acceptable material. In the rehandling, it acquired hairline scratches which, when enlarged in a CinemaScope image, looked like railroad tracks. We had to use liquid gate. The only type available in the houses we were using was an applicator type. It reduced scratches, eliminating them completely in some of the material. But because of a coating that had been put on our original film by some of the New York labs which did the processing months ago, the liquid from the gate began to build up on the original. Fine for the Rain sequence, perhaps, but!

At Hal Shieb's Cinema Research, one of the five optical houses we were using, we located an immersion type liquid gate. But they didn't have a Techniscope camera. Scouring throughout Hollywood, we found one the next day and put Cinema to work. Supplying all the houses, Jack Glass preshot the mattes we required to proper field sizes and lengths. Because his mattes were to be bi-packed with the negative as it received images from the sixteen-millimeter film, one potentially dirty frame would never be noticed as it would only last one-twenty-fourth of a second on screen. Jack's invention virtually eliminated all spots and saved the entire process. We kissed a final goodbye to the awkward but inventive razor-blade mattes.

Four weeks into opticals, it became clear that we would not meet our deadline. Material had to be resubmitted as many as eight times to get an acceptable negative we could cut for Technicolor. We waited impatiently for that negative and also for material we could use in the sound mix. After we asked the optical people to work twenty-four-hour shifts, we then demanded that they find more Techniscope cameras.

When optical equipment would breakdown in the middle of the night, no repair man was available—until we hired one to stand by for emergencies. As it happened, he saved us a full day in the very next week. After all, we had required that a German engineer, Herr Schneider, reside at the Sunset Marquis to be available to service and repair the KEMs whenever they were not being used.

Because we were under such pressure, we couldn't spare daily sequences for viewing by the optical people or others. As soon as Technicolor gave us a print we rushed it out to Warners Bros. for the mix. Now we did order two copies of every daily—one for the mix and the other for us to look at. Warners still received nothing.

It was not infrequent that one of us would get a call in the middle of the night from an optical cameraman, questioning a particular piece of information or instruction. On occasion, one of us would have to get dressed, drive to the house, and work with the technician to sort out the problem.

Infrequently were we bouyed by hope and optimism. We did not think we were going to make it. The pressure was deadly.

We had begun to submit material to the optical houses the first week of January. It was now late in February.

Allowing for two passes for each sequence, opticals ideally should have been finished four weeks later, by mid-February. Eight weeks later we still did not have all the material to cut for Technicolor. We had all grossly underestimated our prospects. Or did we overestimate them?

It was like plugging up a dike with your finger. One problem was solved, but another, unpredicted and unrelated, took its place. It was not the fault of the optical houses. No one had ever conceived of an optical four hours long. No producer had ever before worked with five optical houses simultaneously. We were asking them to stop everything else, delay their regular clients, turn themselves inside out for us. The problems we encountered and set before them were unorthodox;

way off the beaten path of film making practices. It was a very trying experience for all of us.

Even as Technicolor supplied us with sufficient prints with which to conduct the mix, they were still making repairs and corrections on the opticals to eliminate the errors.

Every time we thought we had a decent enough picture and its respective sound track even roughly mixed, we would put out the word to the artists to see whether they wanted to come by the screening room to take a look at themselves. Because now they could. We would explain that corrections were constantly being made to both picture and sound; not to worry.

In some instances, we wanted the artists to "approve" their sequence so that they would sign their contract with Warner Bros. allowing us to include their segment in the movie. For some mysterious reason, for example, the Jefferson Airplane refused to sign, citing creative differences between what they envisioned and what they saw. Or maybe they wanted more money. On the other hand, Alvin Lee, vocalist for Ten Years After, dropped by Warner Bros. and plunked himself down in the darkened theater.

ALVIN LEE

PLAY IT AGAIN!

(ALVIN WAS THE VOCALIST for Ten Years After.)

DALE: I was there and I remember what you said. Because I think you were almost alone in the screening room, maybe you brought somebody else...I don't quite remember, tell me what you remember.

AL: I was hoping you would remember. You tell me first because I...[laughs] I only remember a little bit. But how I got there or who I was with...I just remember being there. And Bob Maurice and Michael Wadleigh were there. Where's Michael these days? What's he up to?

DALE: He's up in New Hampshire, he's living on a farm with a woman named Cleo. It's a several hundred year old farm, and I was up there in September. They've got about two hundred acres that have been in her family, not in his, for some two hundred years.

AL: Oh he's a father now, is he?

DALE: He's not a father...no no no, he is a father, but he was a father long ago.

AL: No, I meant a farmer!

DALE: No, he's not a farmer. He is a motorcycle rider...

AL: Hey. Good man!

DALE: He did something like six thousand miles in India alone, back in August...

AL: All right! ok...

DALE: ...and took a batch of pictures on Digicam, I think he said fifteen thousand pictures. And between the two of them, he and Cleo his ladyfriend, they design and write CD-ROM's. But that's as much as I know.

AL: So what did I say then...

DALE: Well I remember what you said because I was sitting right behind you. And what you said was, something like "Oh my God, that's absolutely so pretty"(or so stunning, or something else). But then you said, "If that weren't me up there on that screen, I'd bloody well wish it would have been!"

AL: [laughs hard] That's a good one!

DALE: …and then you said, "Could we play it again please?"

AL: Huh, yeah!

DALE: And of course we did and we played it and we played it of course.

AL: Oh, yeah, I was really knocked out with it, that it came out so well. I was quite nervous, wondering of course what it'd be like. But, it was great I remember that.

DALE: Had you heard anything in advance of getting to the screening room, about what it might look like?

AL: Not at all, I think Michael had told me it was really good, but that's a very relative kind of thing to say. I really didn't know what to expect. Yeah, I was really pleased. I don't think I said it was stunning, I might have said it was great [laughs].

DALE: That's my interpolation.

AL: [Laughs, says something inaudible like yeah, breathtaking.]

DALE: When I talked to Chick Churchill, your keyboardist, he said…do you remember what he said?

AL: No.

DALE: Well, and I didn't know either, but he said when he went to see it, at Leicester Square or some other place like that in the UK, he said, "you know I was so pissed because there I'd taken my whole family and my girlfriend and everybody, and I was on the screen for six seconds! And I was so pissed at Al!"

AL: [He laughs]

DALE: …And I explained to him that the reason that he was on for only six seconds was, as you can tell from the editing of the piece, that one or two of the camera guys ran out of film. And the reason that we put you side by side in that kind of mirror image was because there was only one camera still running!

AL: That's right. yeah, it was something they tried out and it worked really good, didn't it?

DALE: Yeah, it, it was marvelous actually. I mean it was so sensational, it was the only time that we ever used that technique.

AL: Well. Let me tell you my story of this because it kinda happened after that screening. Michael then told me all the problems he'd had with Warner Bros., said they'd wanted it to be an hour and a half long. And I think he showed me a telegram he'd got saying that "if you don't cut it we'll cut it." And there was a big hoorah going on and they'd had guards on the film cans. And I remember one night Michael took a car out with loads of empty film cans in the back so that the guards would stop him, just to be a nuisance, you know? I think they threw them all on the guards. But what he told me was that all the artists, Janis and Jimi and all those guys were all getting together and sending telegrams to Warner Bros., saying "You're not allowed to cut this movie, it's got to be left as it is."

So I got on to my manager, at the time it was Dee Anthony, and I was very enthused by this "artists all pulling together" business, and I told him this, and I said we've got to send a telegram. And so he composed the telegrams saying "you're not allowed to cut any of this, any of our music out." And I think he signed it "Long Live Artistic Integrity." And the next morning he got a call from Warner Bros. and the first thing they said was, "You're out of the movie!" But they got the hump about that (meaning they were sullen). And we were the only band that sent the telegram!...

[Big laughs]

...But I don't know if it was a kind of perverted joke of Michael's, but I don't think so...I think he was serious, I think everyone else just chickened out, you know?

DALE: I think everybody was serious, and I know damn well he was, because we were having to pull that kind of a ploy with Warner Bros. every other day.

AL: That's right. Yeah. Anyhow, we sent the telegram and the first thing they said was "you're out the movie," but as it happened, Dee Anthony was also managing Joe Cocker. And they got down to that "well, okay, if they're out the movie, then Joe Cocker's out the movie too," and they managed to come to some compromise. But it wasn't a compromise, I think we were really lucky to have such a long jam without being cut. I mean it's long, wasn't it?

DALE: Well, you were about eleven minutes, I think, and you know, we were all... there were a couple of times in the editing when we tried to make a music cut, you know in order to shorten you down, because that "Going Home" still went going on, and going on, and going on.

AL: Yeah, it could've lost a couple of minutes without...but the trouble is it's very difficult to cut Ten Years After because the tempos change all the while. And once you cut a bit out, you got to find another bit the same tempo to get back in, that's tricky.

DALE: Well that's exactly what happened, I mean we tried. We had a couple of, you know, quote "expert music editors," trying to make an incision here and there in order to get it down to around eight minutes. And we took you know, in the end, we capitulated to the music itself.

AL: Great! I'm glad you failed. [Laughs all around.] Give everybody my regards.

DALE: Of course I will.

AL: But that was a funny thing though with that telegram. Because Dee Anthony said, "You nearly got us thrown out the movie." But it wasn't really, I think it was, uh, it was all done in good faith.

DALE: Did you get a chance to see the *Director's Cut*, the longer version?

AL: Yeah, I did, yeah, I was grooved about that because there was a picture of me and my girlfriend arriving that I hadn't seen before. Of course Johnny Winter was just great.

DALE: Wasn't he fantastic?

AL: Fantastic. Yeah. Should never have been left out the first time, should have been four hours long, shouldn't it?

DALE: Well, that was a big problem, I mean I'm writing about that in the book of course, but at the time, a lot of artists had not signed; secondly, some who didn't sign like the Airplane had said, "Oh, you've made an edit in ours, and we don't really like that edit." Or something else...third was they, Warner Bros. couldn't come to terms, fourth was with all the music in, everybody seemed to feel at the time (and I think this is probably the pressure of sociology) that there was an imbalance on the side of the music, against the sociological stuff, you know, the documentary stuff. And it would have heavily weighted it as a "just plain music film" rather than as an overall document of what it symbolized. And the fifth reason, which of course was a valid reason from the Warner Bros. side, was they couldn't convince, they didn't want to be able to convince their exhibitors that the movie would turn around only twice in one day. You know, because the exhibitors would be losing money fist over hand and so they wanted a three-hour version. And the other thing was, they didn't want Jimi Hendrix's "Purple Haze" riff to go on as long as it did. Because they thought that it was a little bit down, at the end. So all those came in to…

AL: Yeah, I know, but I mean it turned out great in the end, I think the balance was great. It's just I mean, somebody had to get left out and that Johnny Winter, that's good. It's good to put it into the *Director's Cut*, I'm pleased with that.

DALE: Alvin, how did it affect your career?

AL: Well, it…I suppose it put Ten Years After into the stadiums when the movie came out. In fact that wasn't particularly that good in the end…But it gave the career a tremendous boost. Because I think up until that time we were playing, apart from festivals, we were playing, kind of, Winterland and Boston Tea Party and Kinetic Playground…they're all 4 or 5,000 seaters. And then as soon as the movie came out, then we were playing Madison Square Garden and those 20,000 seaters.

DALE: How many times have you sung "I'm Goin' Home"?

AL: …Um, 17,346,928…

DALE: I figured the answer would be something like that. How do you think the movie, and the distribution of the movie, changed the music business from what it had been before to what it became immediately thereafter?

AL: Well I don't know, I have never really looked at the music business side of it. I mostly stayed out of that. I know one thing, it suddenly became very fashionable to have concerts where the ticket holders got burnt and the people came in free. There were a couple of festivals in England where they did exactly the same thing and I thought to myself, "sooner or later someone's going to not get away with this! It's getting too good."

But no, at the time, at the time of Woodstock it was the young people's world and we were all taking over, and that's what was great about Woodstock, the fact that it was an accident, basically; it was just one of those great accidents. And you could never plan that, I mean all the attempts to plan another Woodstock…I mean to have another Woodstock you'd have to organize the festival for two million people and have six million people turn up, to have another Woodstock these days.

DALE: Al, where are you living? You're in Barcelona, one of my favorite cities…

Al: It is rather nice here, yeah. Yeah, I spend a lot of time here.

DALE: And do you speak Barcelonese?

AL: I get by, I get by in the supermarket.

DALE: What is the name of that language?

AL: Catalonian.

DALE: That's right, that's right…and I assume you've been up to the Gaudi Cathedral twenty times?

AL: I'm a big Salvador Dali fan, I go up to Figueres and he's got a museum there. It's pretty amazing…and I do a bit of painting myself these days.

DALE: Good for you. Good for you.

AL: Anyway, it's great talking to you, I wish I could remember more, but I actually remember you. I remember sitting in the seat; I've got a kind of mental picture of that moment when…well, I say a moment, it was about ten minutes, wasn't it? That whole little period, I've got a mental picture of it; I can almost run it frame by frame in my mind. And I was a bit embarrassed at the time, and a bit sort of apprehensive, wondering if it was going to turn out all right and then, tremendous relief when I realized it was a cracker.

DALE: Well what was amazing too was, whoever your second guitarist was, there…I mean, luckily you can see in the editing, when we got another camera loaded and shooting, because that's when we go from the double image mirror to the triple image, with the mirror on either side. And we all, when we were editing this thing, and of course screening it, we were just jumping up and down because we knew…

AL: Ha, that was no other guitarist, that was two of me.

DALE: No. The dark guy with the mustache. He's slapping away at his…

AL: The bass player. Yes, Leo Lions. He's very active, he looks like he's riding a bucking bronco, doesn't he?

DALE: And the other thing is all the women were swooning at him when he came on because he has that sort of darkish, swarthyish, look, you know? Not to say they weren't swooning when you were on…

AL: They was swooning days, weren't they?

DALE: They, they've…they've gone, Alvin, they've gone.

AL: I know, I know.

DALE: Luckily.

AL: Okay my friend…

DALE: Goodnight.

STAN WARNOW

FROM STUDENT TO THE WARNER BROS. LOT

(STAN WAS ONE OF our three performance sequence editors.)

In early November, we heard that the postproduction would be moving to the West Coast after Thanksgiving for the remainder of the process. But once again there was the question of who would be making the trip, as the editing staff would have to be further streamlined. My anxiety quotient went up again for a few days, but I was finally told I would be going. Naturally the prospect of working in LA was immensely appealing and exciting. When it came to dramatic films, my personal orientation was more toward what is now known as Independent Film, and was then known as underground or art film (with European cinema being a prime element). However, Hollywood certainly had a mystique and glamour all it's own, and besides, I had never been there. Plans were made to leave just after Thanksgiving. But once again, my fast car fixation was about to get me in trouble.

Ever since the mini had been totaled, I had been without a car that I could really enjoy driving. I decided to buy a car that I could drive out to LA and then sell out there at a profit, as I believed that used sports cars were worth more on the West Coast. Full of youthful foolhardiness, I set out to find the perfect LA sports car. In my delirium I ended up spending every penny I had saved since the job started, borrowing the rest and buying a modified Porsche 911. It had an even more powerful engine than normal, a beautiful maroon lacquer job, and dark tinted windows. I was totally confident that this car would sell itself in Hollywood, and before that I would have a great time on all those curvy roads in the Hollywood Hills. Or so I thought. There was, of course, one little problem—I now had to drive from New York to LA over a single weekend so I wouldn't miss any work. I quickly realized this was not really feasible, but I figured I could make it in three days, leaving Thursday after work, if I had someone to share the driving. Mike and

Thelma generously agreed to give me a day off, and I set about finding someone to drive with me.

Dan Turbeville, the assistant music supervisor, knew of someone, an acquaintance from college. I should have known there would be a problem when Danny said that while he knew this fellow, he couldn't really vouch for him. But time was getting short, so I agreed to let him be my codriver. We started out and this guy turned out to be a real 1960s nut case. Somewhere before the Pennsylvania Turnpike, he informed me he had dropped acid just before we left and that while he was enjoying the trip, he wasn't ready to take the wheel just yet, and yes, I suddenly decided that I really wasn't so tired after all. I ended up driving almost all the way, fearing for my life every time he was at the wheel, as he couldn't really drive a stick shift, on acid or not. The car broke down in Ohio, he was snorting heroin in New Mexico, but somehow, after driving myself to the point of exhaustion and beyond, as the sun was setting on Sunday, I finally saw the magic words "Hollywood Freeway" against the setting sun. I felt like a pilgrim who had finally reached Mecca.

As I found my way to our new offices and edit rooms on Yucca Street, I had the slightly surreal feeling of running into several of my crewmates from New York who were outside the office enjoying magic hour in Hollywood. There was a feeling of irrational dislocation caused I guess by all those grueling hours on the road and then seeing the very same people I had left behind in New York. While rationally I knew they had flown out the previous day, emotionally I couldn't reconcile the fact that I had been driving nonstop for three days when they weren't with me and yet they had somehow magically arrived. Within a few minutes I had taken a brief look at the editing rooms, said a relieved good bye to my passenger and was on my way to the house on Genesee Street in Hollywood where most of the editors were going to live communally for the duration of our West Coast stay. This was one aspect of the experience that I liked a whole lot, as it seemed right to me that in working on the film together it was only fitting in the spirit of the 1960s for us to have our own little commune, especially as we were on per diem!

Monday morning I awoke reasonably refreshed and we all went to the Yucca Street offices to begin our adventure as working citizens of the film capital of the world. At first I was naively impressed that our offices and editing rooms were located right in Hollywood only two blocks from the legendary intersection of Hollywood and Vine. But it only took me about half a day to realize that Hollywood and Vine had gone the way of Times Square and was now the center of the sleazy part of Hollywood.

Still, there was a certain satisfying symmetry, as the film district back in New York (at that time) was in fact centered around Times Square. And the edit rooms were really comfortable with the windows that almost every editor wants as a feature of the work environment. Within a few days we had settled into our house on Genesee, and fallen into a comfortable familial rhythm. We would usually all breakfast together and then drive to work, go out for lunch together, work till late in the evening, go out for dinner, and go home exhausted to sleep the sleep of the just. While at work it seemed that every day brought a visit by at least one famous or infamous member of young, hip Hollywood.

Our film was definitely a high profile project among Hollywood's young elite. There was a subtle satisfaction in knowing that a group of documentary oriented outsiders were working on what was clearly a major project of the season in the film capital. I doubt that a documentary has had such a profile there before or since…

After a week or so in Hollywood I began to realize that however much I enjoyed the Porsche as a fine performance automobile, I was uncomfortable driving it daily while all my peers were using the rented Volkswagen Beetles supplied by the production. For me fast cars have never been about the status, just about speed and handling (which was one reason I loved the unassuming mini). The sleek Porsche, however much fun it was to drive, didn't really fit in with the counter-cultural image of the *Woodstock* film, and it mostly sat in the garage. Our VW beetles were much more appropriate means of transportation. What I would do occasionally was take the Porsche out late at night on thrill rides in the Hollywood Hills or on the misting roads in the canyons near Malibu.

As Christmas neared, it became time for me to return to New York for one weekend, because I had a preexisting engagement—my wedding to Cathy. Once again I got a Friday off, flew to New York, had two frantic days of wedding preproduction, and we were married on a Sunday, December 21, 1969. Monday morning we were on a plane back to LA and by Monday afternoon I was back at work. The honeymoon would have to wait.

Once the Christmas holidays were over, I became totally immersed again in the musical performances of the Woodstock festival. Although the material was roughed out, there was still a lot to be done. This was due to two major factors, one common to all editing, and one unique to *Woodstock*. The more normal one is the issue of having enough time to get things right. One of the best things for me about the postproduction on *Woodstock* was that enough time was allotted so the editing process could run its natural course.

As in writing, the first cut is often more of a draft subject to radical revision than something close to a finished product. I often feel when I'm editing that the real work begins after I can sit down and view a complete first cut. It is only then that a full picture of the strengths and weaknesses of the work begin to emerge. Or to put it succinctly, a sense of what works and what doesn't. All too often because of the constraints of deadlines and budget editors don't get the time necessary to feel fully satisfied with their work, to do the best work they can, but on *Woodstock* I was fortunate to have all the time I needed for which I will be eternally grateful to Mike, Thelma and Bob Maurice for insuring that we had the time we needed.

I particularly remember screening my much-revised version of "Soul Sacrifice" for Mike just before we finally locked, and him telling me "It just keeps getting better and better," which I naturally found very satisfying.

I was reminded of that moment years later while watching *All That Jazz*, Bob Fosse's autobiographical film. It contained several sequences set in the editing room, with Fosse's real life editing collaborator, Alan Heim more or less playing himself as Eddie the Editor to Roy Scheider's Fosse alter ego. The fictional producer comes in to view a much revised cut and after screening it exclaims "It is better" in an astonished voice. I found that moment very satisfying, although of course Mike's comment was made in a much different spirit; that of a collaborator who is himself a gifted editor among his other talents. Editing is one of those processes that can keep on going forever...the old saw is "Films aren't finished, they're abandoned." I've had that feeling on many projects in my career, but *Woodstock* was definitely not one of them.

The factor unique to *Woodstock* was having extensive multi-screen sequences and the additional complications they engendered, both in the editing itself (as I've written about earlier) and in the preparation of sequences for final printing. As we began to lock up the final versions of our cuts, we were faced with the reality of transforming them from up to three individual strips of film to one combined version that would exist on a single anamorphic thirty-five-millimeter print for theatrical projection. This was done by optically transferring the images to that single strip of film, using a layout grid on which each editor would sketch the locations of each image in each sequence exactly as he or she wanted them, then working very closely with the optical house personnel to insure that the opticals came out as planned. As the details of that process are explained elsewhere in this book, I'll just say that it was an extremely detailed and exacting procedure, involving many hours of preparation before submission to the optical house and additional hours in reviewing and revising the material that came back.

Around the time that we were locking picture, we moved the offices and editing rooms from the Yucca Street location to the Warner Bros. lot in Burbank. This was another milestone for me as I suddenly found myself working inside of a major studio. Eighteen months earlier I had been a film student, and now I was working at Warner Bros. For the first several days there was a definite thrill just driving through the security gate and knowing I was part of a privileged group of industry insiders. As we were a group of nonunion kids from New York, we had to have union standbys for every one of us who was actually editing, and I got to meet and work alongside Hollywood veteran editors, and see how they did things, which was certainly revealing. Our main liaison to the whole editing infrastructure at Warners was Fred Talmage, who seemed to always be there to expedite matters in every way possible and was always a cheerful source of information. Even though he may have thought we were a bunch of wild-eyed radicals on some level, he was unfailingly supportive and friendly.

I particularly enjoyed the proximity to the Warner's backlot, and began to see it on a certain level as my own personal theme park. On my lunch breaks I would often pick up a sandwich from the commissary and go exploring among the various unused standing outdoor sets. One day I might eat lunch in Victorian New York, on another in Dodge City in 1870 and so on. It was an intriguing combination of the fanciful and mundane.

As we continued to tighten and finalize the cutting, it was becoming clear that we were forging a film that would be worthy of the historic nature of the festival itself. We were getting almost universally positive reactions from our screening audiences, and this was of course enormously satisfying. Eventually the day came when all my sequences were complete in their final form.

The next and last big stage was the final mixing process. Though I was not directly responsible for the sound, it was great fun to sit in the giant mixing theater as the sound track for the sequences I had edited was forged from the original multi-track master tapes augmented by sound effects and dialogue.

There were a few major disappointments, however. I remember one day in particular, when all the members of the Jefferson Airplane, (a personal favorite group of mine) showed up to screen a completed version of their sequence. They had been on stage at dawn on Sunday morning, and their sequence, edited marvelously by Yeu-Bun Yee, had a wonderful surreal quality due to the early morning light. When the lights went up after the screening, we waited with bated breath for their reaction, which was unfortunately negative. While they admitted that they liked "our part," the look of the performance and the way it was edited, they were unhappy with "their part," the sound of the group in our mix. They wanted to remix it in their own studio in San Francisco, but this would have been a Pandora's Box, because if they had been allowed to mix their own performance, the word would have gotten out and every group would have wanted that privilege. While I could understand their point of view, I could also understand why Mike couldn't agree to it. Neither side would give, and they were dropped from the film.

But we forged ahead, and then one day there was really no more for me to do, everything had been checked and rechecked, the mixes were done, opticals complete, and it was time to call it a wrap. It was a moment tinged with sadness, as there could be no doubt that this would be a tough job experience to top. But it was time to move on, we packed up our stuff, and drove back East in the Porsche.

A few months later the film opened to universal acclaim, which was of course very satisfying. Then came our Academy Award nominations, another gratifying moment. The film was nominated for Best Documentary, Best Sound, and Best Film Editing. But this was a bittersweet moment because despite all my work on the film, I was not personally nominated, nor were Yeu-Bun Yee and Jere Huggins who were of course equally deserving. At the time, I didn't think that much of it, having a "1960s" attitude that it was really only the work that was important, and the establishment recognition in the form of awards and such really didn't mean much on the cosmic level. So I didn't object.

Now I know better, that an Academy Award nomination may not mean much cosmically but it means a hell of a lot in building a career. If I found myself in that situation today, I'd make damn sure my work was recognized, because those things do count; like it or not *Woodstock* will always remain as a wonderful work experience for me, but if I had to list a regret it would be my failure to fight for what I deserved. Nevertheless, over the next few years my *Woodstock* experience did help me get a variety of jobs on music oriented films, such as *Hair* and *No Nukes*. And the *Woodstock* experience was invaluable when I coproduced another anti-nuclear film. *In Our Hands*, the chronicle of the June 12, 1982 anti-nuclear rally in New York, which, with it's interwoven documentary and performance sequences, had many similarities to *Woodstock*.

DALE BELL

PING PONG ON THE DUBBING STAGE

EVER WATCH A TRULY silent film? Barely, rarely makes an impression. That's because we see with our ears. I think technicians have measured that the sound contributes about seventy-five percent of how we perceive and feel about movies.

Walk into any old time mixing studio. They're generally drab, nondescript looking places. Motion picture sound tracks get "mixed" together on a dubbing stage. In a way, it is a misnomer, for there is no actual stage. The room is generally quite large, for it needs to accommodate a screen at one end where the moving image is projected. All the sound technicians orient themselves to this image. It is the moving image which provides the "bed" for the sound which is synced to this picture which rolls back and forth on the command of one of the three mixers on the board, who face the image. Each of the mixers has his/her own responsibility: one for music, one for dialogue, one for sound effects. All the remaining three walls are soundproofed or baffled so that the speakers distributing the sound represent a true acoustic of a motion picture theater.

Yet it is in this room that the magic is created which captivates us with its inuendo, its music, its sound effects, its dialogue, and its orchestration of all these sounds, and silences. In the darkness of the theater, the combination of image and sound transports us out of our own world and into that of the movie.

One of the goals of our movie was to let the audience feel that they had become the actual center of all the activity. Sound would be our tool. Larry Johnson, Dan Wallin and their team would be the guides.

We had the First Dubbing Stage at Warners. Why not? Nothing else was happening on the lot. In fact I don't think any renovations had been implemented in this particular room since the head of Warners' sound, George Groves, won an Oscar for the sound he mixed in this very room for *The Al Jolson Story* more than forty years earlier. Let's just say, it appeared—and performed—that way.

George had to be in his sixties, or beyond. White haired, clipped mustache, British upper crust tongue. "Dyed in the wool" one might say. George has his way of doing things in his studio. Apparently everyone listened very carefully. Some were actually intimidated. Once he accepted our looks, (he never got over them!) he had one basic word for us: "Don't!" Early on, I lost count of the number of ways he told us we were foolish, time-wasters, unorthodox. We rebutted each of his arguments. He had most difficulty with our proposed use of the surround speakers. Time and again, he would deny us access to them by scolding us in front of his own men. Though they might have been deterred, we were not. "No," he kept saying, "you can't put primary information into those surrounds. They're just for background noise."

The men who were assigned to help us through this arduous task of cleansing and manipulating the dozens of sound tracks we had accumulated in our production were kind and helpful enough, but the gear itself seemed out of an earlier era. Unresponsive. Daunted by their inability to have an effect on old George, they tried to fulfill their functions as we asked them, always running into equipment problems.

What took eternities was the patching. To create a passage for a sound from one track to end up in a new place, a technician had to "repatch" the channels, creating an electrical current between two or more hitherto unconnected modules. Once, this sound board with its myriad of dials and pots might have been able to accomplish innovations beyond compare, but that time had long since passed. Repatching became a nightmare.

One option: We could have abandoned our dream. George was trying to encourage us to do just that every day. Whenever we asked that a sound or group of sounds be patched into the surround speakers behind the audience, for example, George would protest then rush off to complain to Ted Ashley that we didn't know what we were doing, or conversely, that it would require too much time for us to achieve our effects.

All we asked was the ability to make the movie our way. George was intruding.

Bored by the delay of patching. repairing, and repatching our cables, I bought, had delivered, and then installed a full-size ping-pong table on the dubbing stage one evening. When everyone arrived the following morning, there we were with paddles in hand, playing a rip-roaring game as George came in for his morning visit. In clipped tones, he asked "What the hell is that doing here? Is that for sound effects?" I guess I hadn't thought that the pinging and the ponging might have a practical use, so his question took me a little aback. "Well, George," I said, "we plan to play ping-pong in between the roll backs and the takes." He said: "What do you mean? Our men are working terribly fast!" "Well, George," I replied, "apparently they're not working fast enough because they want to play ping pong with us. They are waiting for the men to come to make repairs on the gear." George was extremely frustrated, and flustered. "Well," he said, "we've never done this before. You long-haired freaks come out here and you're the only people who mess up our stage. Don't you know, we try to run this as a very tough business. We're going to have to reconstitute everything after you've left! All this repactching!"

George stalked out to tell Ted Ashley again about how we were disrupting his mixing stage.

We discovered quickly that the technical people on our dubbing stage were fast becoming our friends. No one had ever treated them as we were. We called them by their first name, instead of "Hey you!" Mostly Short-Hairs from some of the more conservative parts of Los Angeles, they addressed us as Mr. this and Mr. that. "Mr. Bell, we would like an additional ten minutes for lunch today. Would that be all right?" We had never been treated that way before either. It was entirely out of character. We agreed to no "Misters"; we all agreed to first names; and we granted them longer lunches as they needed so long as the work got done on schedule. Of course, we discovered that our management style received instant rewards. Gone were the days of "Hey, you, get that outta here!" or screams at editors for the sake of grandstanding. Respect, camaraderie, and friendliness bound us all together much closer. And as a symbol of our new personal and business relationship, we shared our ping-pong table.

It was not long before we brought the table outdoors to get some rays. On one vacant patch of green lay our green table, not far from the croquet court we had also installed onto the lot for diversion. Everything was taking a good deal longer than we had ever expected from a Hollywood that was far from the technological capital of moviemaking. When equipment was down, or we were simply waiting for a take to resume on the dubbing stage, we would take turns exploring the vacant lot on the electric golf cart assigned to our team. Birthday parties were celebrated on the dubbing stage with birthday cakes for all, even the projectionists and security people. If nothing else was happening on the lot, we would change that.

Our journey to this stage had been "a long time coming," so to speak. By virtue of the deal between Atlantic Records and the festival producers, delivery of the tracks was the producers' responsibilities. They hired Bill Hanley. The original music tracks recorded on the site by Bill and his team were not exactly perfect examples of location sound, not due to his inabilities, but attributable primarily to the changing situations governing the event itself. His team could have microphones set on stage to record one group when an entirely different group would appear. Where one mike might have been positioned for drums, it might now be in the right place for vocals. Or where another mike was to be for bass, it might record drums and vocal, a lethal combination of sounds. Mix-ups were the norm, unfortunately.

Of the eight tracks available for recording on site, one had to be reserved to take the crystal sync pulse from the 110 volts running the Éclair cameras, thereby ensuring that cameras and sound recorders were operating at exactly the same speed. Thus only seven other tracks could be used for the music. At any one time, with a possible dozen mikes opened on stage, impossible sound combinations required a great deal of time, energy, and of course money to be clarified.

The lethal combination of one of the seven tracks would have to be recorded onto a virgin track where efforts would be invoked to split its combinations into separate instruments. The track would have to be filtered, equalized, squeezed, expanded—processed, in other words, so as to obtain the cleanest track with one set of instruments or vocals on it. As a result, the seven tracks were split into some twenty separate tracks before they were brought into the dubbing stage in Warners.

Larry and I had this "foxtail" joke going: he was buying foxtails for his sound tracks simply as embellishment or as enhancement, not as necessary adornments to the music. His instant response was conveyed in these two words, or sounds: "humma humma" which soon assumed universal meaning for the entire sound team when referencing anything at all! "Humma humma" was verb, noun, adjective, an all inclusive code word. I simply could not believe that he could spend so much time—at hundreds of dollars an hour even from dusk to dawn, the cheapest time period—with his pals at the Record Plant on Santa Monica Boulevard. It was endless.

But as I was later to learn, it was also very necessary. The original tracks were a den of snakes, each trying to consume the other. Larry and his team had to straighten them all out so they were proceeding in the same direction.

After more than a month of playing with his foxtails, Larry brought his multiple, remixed twenty-four tracks into the dubbing stage. Of course, they were accompanied by the original eight tracks. When the new processing did not seem as successful as the original, in spite of the reprocessing, Danny Wallin would make a decision to try to clean up the originals by using the many pots and tweeks available on the mixing console. Comparison between the two would be made by A-ing and B-ing the two sounds. A vote conducted between Dan, Larry, Michael and Thelma would determine which source would eventually be used.

To clean up the "noise" which had accumulated on the reprocessed twenty-four tracks, we discovered a new process—or foxtail—which might cleanse and eliminate some if not all of the noise build up. Standard today in movie theaters throughout the world, Dolby sound was in its infancy in 1970. The concept was that a Dolby noise reduction processor would be added to the sound just before it was rerecorded onto the four-tracks used on the theater release prints. Just before the final moment, Larry had convinced all of us that this was absolutely necessary. We believed him. So I ordered four from Wally Heider who was running a sound equipment rental house in Hollywood at the time.

I thought Larry meant that this little filter thing would fit on the end of a patch cord somewhere. But when the truck pulled into the loading bay at the back of the dubbing stage, I knew I had miscalculated Larry's foxtails again. A forklift unloaded these huge black-box processors and positioned them on the floor of the stage. I couldn't believe what we were getting into, particularly when Wally, who spoke loudly and stammered mercilessly, brought me the invoices for the rental of these little boxes. To my mind, Larry had won again. And I was the dupe.

Probably the least technical member of the team, I nevertheless had to admit that my lay ears noticed a perceptible difference between the sound pre-Wally and post-Wally. Larry was crafting a very complex tapestry of sound.

Gradually, inexorably, we were loading all the tracks—music, dialogue, effects, sometimes sixty individual tracks—on sprocketed thirty-five-millimeter magnetic film in sync with each other in two rooms far from the actual dubbing stage. The sound from one track would be filtered through the pots and dials on the mixing board, then funneled down to one track or more tracks, whether it was emerging from beneath the center of the image, or from the right, or from the left, or onto the fourth which fed into a series of smaller speakers in a U-shaped surround pattern behind and on the backsides of the audience. All in all, pretty complicated. And very necessary to put the audience in the center of the action. No wonder Larry and Dan would later be nominated by the Academy of Motion Picture Arts and Sciencesfor Best Sound! And Larry still wasn't shaving!

Music mixer Dan Wallin celebrated his birthday during our mix. Since nothing we were doing was ordinary, the singing of "Happy Birthday" required some extraordinary effort. In one idle moment we had quickly edited together a sequence which featured John Wayne (who had visited our dubbing stage a week or two earlier and laced through us with comments about our looks!), Sly and the Family Stone, and the traditional "Happy Birthday" song. I think the editors were able to make Sly sing "Happy Birthday," topped off by John Wayne's sardonic remarks! What ever happened was hilarious, I recall, probably because it was accompanied by cake and champagne for one of the more brilliant Warner Bros. staff people who really got our film.

On another occasion, we became actors in our own film. When we arrived at that point in the mix when the Rain Sequence arose, everyone said it was very flat. Where were our original production tracks that we had recorded on site? We explained that it was raining—couldn't they see it??—and that we could barely get motion picture, let alone sound. The mixers felt it had to be more lively. All the sound was too general, too distant, wallpaper!

Everyone was summoned into the large, adjacent studio, where engineers set up some microphones on the floor. Danny divided us into groups. We devised lines that each of us had to yell. Separate microphones would pick up our antics, then feed them into the mix.

DAN WALLIN:

AS TOLD BY JOHN ROTONDI

THE MAKING OF THE SOUNDTRACK

THE MAKING OF THE soundtrack for the documentary concert film *Woodstock* posed numerous technical and logistical challenges to the staff of the Warner Bros. sound department. Its completion marked a turning point in the development of sound-for-picture. Up until this time, feature film postproduction was a staid and proper affair. The sound director of Warner Bros. was a formal English gentleman by the name of George Groves. Mr. Groves did not know what to make of the "hippie" film crew, so he gladly turned the project over to the department's youngest mixer—the forty-year-old Dan Wallin. Dan's experience as a music scoring mixer, along with his big band and rock and roll mixing background, made him the most qualified person in the department to handle the sound for such a production, both in abilities and temperament. As Dan reflects, "The film's director, Michael Wadleigh, and supervising picture editor, T. Schoonmaker, drove the department mercilessly, dragging them into the twentieth century, in search of perfection." For Dan Wallin, this would be a great experience, and a welcome advance in the state of the art as it stood at Warner Bros.

My first viewing of the partially edited and assembled film took place in Hollywood. The screening room was at Ivar and Vine, not far from the famous Capitol Records Building. The production was filmed with up to fifteen cameras running almost simultaneously, full-time. This first screening utilized three sixteen-millimeter projectors running in sync on a splitscreen. This was very exciting and impressive new technology for 1969. The screening gave me a glimpse of what Director Michael Wadleigh was striving for, to capture on film the energy and scope of this one-time happening, this amazing experience. The whole spectacle, the music, hippies, and various "characters" involved, proved to be an amazing revelation to a me, a guy from the big band era. The scope of the event—cars locked in for miles, and the mountains of garbage in the fields afterward—was beyond belief! I was now eager to become involved, and knew that this would also prove to be a big challenge.

When the editing crew moved onto the Warner's lot, they brought with them four KEM flatbed editing tables. This was my first time seeing such a device, as all editing was done on upright Moviolas at that time. Ed Shied, Warner Bros.'s senior effects editor, seeing these editing tables for the first time, stood there with his hands on his hips saying, "What the hell is THAT? It'll never take the place of a Moviola!" And of course today, both are in declining usage, as digital workstations have superceded mechanical editorial systems for cutting of both picture and sound elements.

The first part of the process undertaken was the mixing of the location music tracks. These were recorded on eight-track one inch analog audio tape, possibly on a Stephens or 3M machine, as there was no capstan. Sync to picture was maintained by resolving the sixty hertz pilot sync tone recorded on track eight, the remaining seven tracks containing the music. Larry Johnson, the location sound supervisor, was very helpful in providing information on the recorded tracks, and insight into the sound of the actual venue, so this could be recreated during the dub.

Artistically, the music and performances were great; Sly Stone's set was particularly exciting, as was Richie Havens. Unfortunately, some performers did not make it into the film due to usage issues—the permission to use their segments may not have been given by the record companies they were signed to. Those great performances that were being used were often plagued with technical problems. I knew it would be a hell of a job to attain the standards sought by the Director, and I hoped I was up to it.

The music mixdown was made from an Ampex MM1000, and made to four-track magnetic sound film in the CinemaScope format—three front channels and one rear (surround) channel. In this format, the release print itself was striped with magnetic tracks, which allowed a full fidelity, discrete sound track to be presented—a welcome improvement over the mono optical sound tracks of the time. An important note was that, for the first time ever in the production of a feature film sound track, Dolby Type-A noise reduction was utilized on the magnetic sound elements to reduce the magnetic oxide noise build-up that accumulates with successive generations of transfers and mixing. The mixes made were based on the cut of the film. When the recordings were evaluated, it was found that there were some problems in various tracks.

In the case of the tracks for Alvin Lee and Ten Years After, the drums were not picked up on tape, so these tracks could not be used. I enlisted studio percussionist Larry Bunker to "foley" in the drums. This was done on the Warner Bros. scoring stage. The good location tracks were mixed to magnetic sound film, so they could be played back as a guide track. An interlocked three-track mag recorder was used for recording the new drum track. Mr. Bunker played along with these tracks while watching the picture, maintaining sync with the visuals. The recording was done through an RCA tube console, with twelve rotary pots, plus an additional six outboard faders. Alvin Lee personally approved of the final music mix, being very pleased with the results obtained by this method.

During Joan Baez's rendition of the hymnal "Swing Low, Sweet Chariot," the tracks were played out through the scoring stage playback speakers, and picked up with Neumann U67 tube microphones. This use of the large stage as a live acoustic chamber added great warmth and dimension to this poignant moment.

Jimi Hendrix's now-historic rendition of the "Star-Spangled Banner" was much too long to be presented in its entirety in the context of the current cut of the film. His improvisational virtuosity was quite complex, and posed a challenge to edit down.

Composer Dominic Frontieri, who was working on the Warner's lot at the time, was brought in to help edit the piece, and was able to do so while maintaining its musical integrity.

The film was dubbed (final mixed) on an RCA tube console. This console consisled of groups of rotary Daven "tri-pots"—each pot being linked mechanically to three channels (left, center, and right) of audio signals. I was joined in this process by Dialogue Mixer Gordon Davis, and Effects Mixer Fran Shied. Generally, the tracks were balanced and equalized for proper perspective to the action on the screen. Vocal dynamics were sometimes controlled using an RCA tube compressor to smooth things out. During the dub, Senior Effects Editor Ed Shied suggested adding rolling thunder to the big rain sequences, but the production team rejected this, wanting to maintain accuracy in the manner of cinéma vérité. However, upon revisiting this scene, it was decided that the addition of thunder would add life to a scene which might have played weakly otherwise.

During the screening of the completed film, Sound Director George Groves was very puzzled by the wonderful performance of Joe Cocker, asking "Is he spastic or something?" and "What's wrong with his voice?" Mr. Groves' limit of tolerance was reached during Country Joe McDonald's "Fish Cheer" sequence! Upon hearing the chant, "Give me an F! Give me a U!", Mr. Groves turned a ghostly white, and left the screening in a speechless flabbergast, never to return!

This ground-breaking project's sound track was done in about eighteen weeks (Less than that Dan!), and was ultimately honored by being nominated for an Academy Award for Best Sound. The passion of its production team in striving for excellence shows, as this film is regarded as a classic of its genre. I was honored to be able to participate in this creative endeavor.

COUNTRY JOE MCDONALD

THE LEGACY OF "GIMME AN F!"

DALE: Joe?

JOE: Yeah?

DALE: Good morning!

JOE: Good morning!

DALE: Thanks for calling back.

JOE: Thanks. You're welcome, let's do it.

DALE: When you first saw yourself in the movie, what was your reaction, please?

JOE: I was…Awed, I would say. Stunned. Stunned. I was totally unprepared to see it. You mean my solo performance?

DALE: Your solo performance.

JOE: Yeah. I don't think I even saw the band performance before the film came out. But the solo performance, yeah, I was there by myself, in a viewing room with Michael (Wadleigh). And I was blown away. Blown away.

DALE: Did we have the titles on at the time we showed you that?

JOE: Yes, and he told me he wanted to put the FUCK on the screen and they had said no, but they had the bouncing ball and the whole thing. Yeah, that's what I saw, yeah.

I don't think I realized that there was even a movie, you know, that I was going to be in the movie. And Michael didn't really tell me anything. He said, "I want to show you something. And when I saw it, it was just like, "Fuck!" I didn't even make a rational decision, now when I look with hindsight. Because that appearance totally changed my life. And it changed…well it had an unbelievable effect upon Joe Mc Donald's musical career. But that never occurred to me at the time. We never had a discussion...I think he might have said, "Well, do you like it?" and I said, like, "Wh-huhhh!". I mean I don't remember saying I liked it or I didn't like it. I just was like, just blown away. Because of course I was...large. You know? Larger than life.

DALE: That was a big screen.

JOE: Yeah, I saw it on a pretty big screen. Yeah. I wasn't prepared, to see myself that way. And then the bouncing ball was just so cute and clever; I realized also that my harangue in the middle, because of the audience not singing, was untrue. I could see their mouths moving and I heard them; when I saw the movie, it was obvious to me that they were all singing along and they knew the song very well.

DALE: As well as you did.

JOE: That's right. The vast majority of the audience knew the song as well as I did, and the cheer in front of it too. And I wasn't aware of that because the sound was going up, you see, and outside it goes up and you can't hear it; inside, it bounces around, you hear it on stage; but outside, you have to learn from experience that the audience is singing and, you know, don't yell at them!

But I didn't know this so I just said, "...You fuckers out there, I want to hear you singing!" And then, from the film, I actually learned that they did even try to sing a little bit louder, but they were sure singing from the very first moment. That was obvious. You don't see in the film that I had been onstage twenty-five minutes before that, and no one paid any attention to me. I walked off stage even and no one even noticed I walked off stage. I had a conference about doing the cheer and the song. And it was decided that it didn't matter, because no one was even paying any attention.

So, what the hell. I mean, up to that point I was a little bit scared, needless to say, performing in front of that many people, solo acoustic. But when I actually realized that no one was paying any attention, and they were all having a good time talking to each other, then I came back on stage and I went, y'know, "Gimme an F!" And then, it seemed to me as though every single person in that audience stopped talking, looked at me and yelled, "F!"

And you know, in show biz parlance, I thought to myself, "It's too late to stop now, fuck! Here we go, here we go..." And I completely forgot that there was cameras around, I don't remember cameras being around me when I was doing that solo thing at all. That's why, when Michael said he wanted to show me something, I had no idea what he was going to show me.

DALE: How did it change your life?

JOE: There are many, many, many reasons. First off, it established me as being Country Joe McDonald, a solo act, which I never was before. There was a group called Country Joe and the Fish, and I guess I was Country Joe; but with the release of that film, and that image of me singing that song, I was definitely Country Joe McDonald. A solo act singing that song. I wrote the song in 1965, and this was 1969; so the song was an underground smash global hit. Even Pete Seeger recorded it in 1972 and no one would sell it. It was so controversial, just the lyrics themselves, not with the cheer in front of it at all. But when I put the Fuck cheer in front of it, which we had invented, the band had invented months before and we were used to doing it then, it guaranteed that it was unplayable. Absolutely unplayable. Absolutely unplayable.

So you combine this lyric, which was blasphemous because it was, from a military point of view, essentially demanding the right to be empowered and make a decision on whether you're going to lose your life or not, and it dissed everybody that was important—Wall Street, the Commander-in-Chief, the generals, everybody, just in general all the fuckin' leaders, it dissed in the song, and not the rank and file at all—and so it made all the leaders mad, right, of course?

It made the left wing mad as hell; they didn't really know what to do with this song because of the satire in it anyway. The Anti-War Movement, they loved it, the rank and file, but the leaders, the left-wing leaders themselves who were very puritanical actually, in a left-wing way...when I put the Fuck Cheer in front of it and it came out, and millions of people saw it, I mean, that just guaranteed that I would never be a left-wing darling in my life. Never. Never. Which means that the Right Wing hated me now, and the Left Wing also hated me.

The Establishment didn't know what the fuck to do. Like, I saw Bowser from Sha Na Na like ten, fifteen years after the film came out, and he came up to interview me for some Rock and Roll thing he was doing. And he said that Sha Na Na, the whole group, thought that I was nonexistent. That someone had created a Country Joe McDonald, and it was an act. You see? It was like a Tiny Tim act or something, like a shocking kind of a "Country Joe" suit that I put on and I came out there and did that...but that isn't what happened at all, so, it made Country Joe like, I don't know...like a living legend but also an asshole as far as the business was concerned. So it made me unbelievably famous. I mean I had the number one hit song, for the Vietnam War era. The number one hit song as far as the Woodstock Festival was concerned. People have now said, most people have said that one of the greatest highlights of the film was yelling "FUCK!" And singing that song, you know, which was not apparent at all.

So to this day I haven't sold quadruple-platinum copies of "Fixing To Die Rag." Today you don't hear it. So it just stuck me in a larger-than-life weird place, that forced me in the long run to deal with my role in the Vietnam War and my military background and my political background, in a way that no one else from the Festival or the Generation has had to cope with. I have become a living symbol of the Vietnam War, and now I'm a living symbol of not only the resistance to the Vietnam War, but of the veterans themselves. And almost all the veterans have come to love that song.

And so it's still today. Here we are, it's 1999, and the song is really not...the *Woodstock* version of that song is really not playable. In an era of Dr. Dre and Snoop Doggy Dog...(laughs from both) it's unbelievable that Country Joe still strikes fear into the heart of program directors. Many who are thirty-something now and have never even heard the Fuck Cheer. Maybe. But they just know the reputation of Country Joe McDonald. And well, I can laugh about it now but at times, it was a real albatross around my neck, and that's why I said that if I had thought about it from a boxoffice point of view...

Well, I tell a story sometimes that I was touring around Germany, because I had to work a lot in Germany after the Fuck Cheer came out because, well, I worked in non-English speaking countries...[laughs] I was banned in every municipal hall in the country...from the Hall Managers Union, you know, this organization they have.

I was touring in the 1980s in Germany. It just went on and on and on, the reputation of this thing, and we would go everywhere, and on government radio and government TV and we would always talk about the *Woodstock* film and the Fuck Cheer. And the person I was talking to on television or on the radio would always talk in German except for the part where they'd go to say *Woodstock*. And then in German they would say something like "F.U.C.K. " and then they would go on, and speak in German. I couldn't stand it after two weeks of this. I said to the tour guide, "Now what the hell is going on?" This is the most progressive country I've ever encountered in my life, in the States I can't...I got dissed big-time for saying fuck and all that and people got fired from radio stations for playing the

Woodstock track and he said "No, no, you don't understand; In German, the verb is fichken, and they don't know what fuck means at all!" They have no idea. And then I thought Christ if I had done the FICH Cheer at Woodstock I could still work in the States big time; I probably couldn't work in Germany, you know? But I mean, Jeeze, there's a fine line between fich and fuck I don't know.

DALE: (laughing) Wonderful, wonderful…We gave you a premiere on Broadway at Eightieth Street when we were editing. We put two big huge speakers out the windows of the second floor, on Eighty-First and Broadway, just down the road from Zabars, and put on the Fuck Cheer outside…There was a march going on.

JOE: End the War march. Probably.

DALE: Yeah, probably. And we had pande-fuckin-monium for about three blocks, from about Seventy-Ninth Street up to Eighty-First Street. 'Cause we kept replaying and replaying and replaying the song. Finally we were busted.

JOE: Oh, really?

DALE: It was sensational. Just classic.

JOE: Well, see, I told you the whole thing is a miracle. That it turned out the way it did, that you put the bouncing ball in, because the sound was all muddy, and whatever. The end result was, just miraculous. Unstounding (sic). And to this day, it's cutting edge. Even to this day, I mean, it makes people nervous. That performance, that little excerpt there you know? There's some parts of the film that just make people nervous as hell, and it's the prefrontal nudity (sic) is one of them, and Country Joe, I mean, singing that thing.

I always thought, "Well listen…" (it was Richard Nixon in office, right?) and he must have said "What the hell is going on up in New York?" you know? And they said, "Oh, well, there's like…they closed the freeway down…" (This is stuff I imagine in my mind, because the FBI had been watching my family and they were watching me, and I know they were really aware of what the fuck I was doing, anti-war and all that). There must have been a point where they said, (voice Nixon-esque) "W-hell, what happened? Tell me." "Well Mr. President the whole audience just yelled FUCK!" And sang a song that essentially said, "fuck you, we're not going to Vietnam."

And I just always thought "Whoa, what did he say, 'Get that guy!'" Or something 'cause it must have made him really pissed. It must have made a lot of people really, really pissed off. You know? That was in there. And even to this day, like I said, it doesn't get played as much as "Give Peace A Chance" I'll tell you that.

DALE: Well, listen, you're marvelous, I thank you, I thank you, I thank you, we thank you.

JOE: The other thing that's funny, is that: you know when they had the twenty-fifth Anniversary (of Woodstock…) Michael Lang has written a book and he gave me a copy of the book proudly and he said, "Here's my book about Woodstock." And I came back to him and I said, "I'm not in the book!" and he said, "What?!"… (laughter from both)…right? Like he didn't even know I wasn't in the book. But then at the twenty-fifth anniversary I muscled my way onto his stages, and I had my press agent, and we were constantly harassing him about, "How can you have Woodstock without Country Joe and the Fish?" Without Country Joe and the Fuck Cheer and whatever…And I know he's thinking to himself, "God damn, can't I shake this shit?" (you know?) "It just follows me around, all I want to do is make a pile of money and put on a show, you know? But these fuckin' hippies, an' shit; they're following me around, harassing me."

And next year the same thing's gonna happen. Several people are gonna put on Woodstock thirtieth Anniversary shows, and Country Joe is going to be ringing their phone, going like you know, "Hey, how can you have a thirtieth Anniversary of Woodstock without a Fuck Cheer in it, you know? And 'Fixing to Die Rag'?" And they all want to forget the Vietnam War, and they want to forget Fuck, too, actually…

Oh, I remember: when I saw *Network* and Faye Dunaway, remember *Network*? When was that, fifteen years ago or something? I couldn't believe it; I was in a big theater, the theater was packed out, and there was Faye Dunaway, and she was saying "fuck" every five minutes. And I thought, "What a rip! I can't believe it." I kicked down the fucking door so she could say fuck every five minutes in a Hollywood film and make a million bucks! And I still can't get played on the radio. Unbelievable! Unbelievable that they say, "AW, Country Joe. He's the guy that invented the word fuck and made everybody say it." No, no, no, it's not my fault, man.

DALE: I don't know whether you can license that or not, Joe…

JOE: Well, we've licensed it from the "Gimme an F…" I have coffee mugs now that say, "1, 2, 3, What are we fighting for?" I was thinking of sleepwear that said "Gimme an F…" maybe on it, you know.

DALE: That's a great idea! For the Boomers? Come on!

JOE: I can get Disney interested! They seem to be very hip lately...

DALE: Right! Sam's Club and Walmart!

JOE: Yeah, yeah, "Gimme an F..." Woodstock Commemoration Sleepwear, you know? Little shortie nighties, and Teddies, you know those Teddy things? "Hey, Hunny, gimme an F..."

DALE: Right now!

JOE: Put a little dissing Michael Lang in there, you can use my words and I...

DALE: I will only use your words!

JOE: He already knows he's afraid of me...I can't believe in all the years, didn't Warners or anybody ever say anything to you about the Fuck Cheer? Didn't they ever have a commercial conversation (sic) with you where they said, "You know, Jeeze, this maybe wasn't a good idea," or "was a good idea" or what I mean, you know...

DALE: Well, what I'll do is I'll ask Wads to comment on that, I don't remember it myself...

JOE: And on the record didn't they know that they had this monster hit on the record that couldn't be played on the air? Because, you know it just...I was with DJ's when we were on the air, and we were on the radio live, and we used to play a joke on them, you know, they'd say, "What do you want us to play?" you know? And we'd say, "Oh, why don't you play this track." And we wouldn't tell 'em, right, and they'd just put the, drop the needle on there and they'd turn the volume down 'cause we'd engage them in a conversation so they wouldn't hear that they were pumping the Fuck Cheer out over the airwaves, and then we'd leave, you know? And then the shit would hit the fan, you know? General Manager call in and say, "What the hell's going on?" You know? And the guy'd get fired, he never knew what happened. Right?

DALE: Good for you...important stuff. Well, I think maybe I'll see you in August of next year somewhere.

JOE: God I hope so, Will it be Austria or New York?

DALE: Both. There'll be a Concord between the two.

JOE: Shuttle back and forth? The Shuttle Service, Austria...what? Michael's nuts. That's going to be stark mania. Ok. Bye Bye.

DALE: Thanks, Joe. Bye.

RICHARD
CHEW

UNDER COUNTRY JOE

(RICHARD CHEW WAS LIVING in Seattle at the time, and a friend recommended by Don Lenzer, joined us as a cameraman. Richard had to postpone his wedding and pay his own way to get to JFK. Richard would go on to become an editor for some twenty-five dramatic films, working for Francis Ford Coppola and George Lucas, among many others.)

"Gimme an F!" commands Country Joe McDonald over the sound system. A sunburned, mud-caked crowd—numbering 300,000, give or take 50,000—responds in unison, "E-f-f-f!" It's August 1969. The cheer awakens me from my nap underneath a wooden stage.

I'm hearing the familiar Country Joe and the Fish cheer from "Fixin' to Die Rag," an anti-Vietnam War song, which is a favorite of the sixties generation. One of mine too. Several years before, when it first hit the streets, I played it over and over on my stereo. I loved its audaciousness, its irreverence. Now I'm underneath the stage where he's performing it live.

I am working at a three-day rock festival, an event billed as a "celebration of peace and love." To document it, director Michael Wadleigh assembles a dozen cameras and sound teams to capture the entire weekend on film.

As one of the cameramen, I could have been assigned to shoot ancillary stuff, like frolicking skinny-dippers, festival vendors, befuddled townspeople, or local workmen cleaning port-o-potties.

Instead I get to film the acts close-up, on stage, framing them through the viewfinder of a 16mm handheld Eclair NPR, a sync-sound camera capable of shooting eleven minutes of film without reloading.

A day earlier, on a late Friday afternoon, the F belonged to "Freedom," a song that Richie Havens improvises to open the festival. This crowd, initially more like 100,000, many having arrived the night before to pitch tents in surrounding woods, is restless for the music to start. Havens, scheduled to come on later that night, is urged by festival organizers to go on first. He takes the stage reluctantly. Perched on a stool, wearing a loose dashiki and sandals, he rips energetically into strumming his acoustic guitar, singing,"Fre-e-e-dom...free-dom; Fre-e-e-dom... free-dom..."

I start as one of five cameramen filming the very first notes of the Festival Heard 'Round the World. Eventually I would become one of 300,000 participants in the phenomenon known as Woodstock.

"Gimme a U!" continues Country Joe. The crowd roars back, "U-u-u-u!" This is the U of "unprepared." By Saturday, as the festival's momentum builds, steadily growing traffic creates massive jams, forcing unprepared authorities to close down the New York Expressway. Essential supplies of food, water, and medicine stall on the ground. State officials declare the site a Disaster Area.

Helpless to control the incoming crush of non-ticket holders, unprepared festival promoters declare it a "free concert."

Helicopters are recruited to fly in the bands and medical supplies. We're burning up so much film that even additional film stock is flown in, along with whiskey and Nathan's Famous Hot Dogs—both of which I down before a short nap under the stage. All quite contrary to my earlier plans to take High Tea in Canada on this Saturday afternoon.

Only two days before, on a Thursday morning in Seattle, I am preparing to leave on a four-day trip to British Columbia. After three phone calls, instead of taking a ferry to Vancouver, I'm flying to New York's JFK, then picking up a rental car to drive to Bethel, a hamlet near Woodstock, to work a weekend rock concert where it's rumored that Bob Dylan and maybe The Band would play. I'm a fill-in for a cameraman who withdrew unexpectedly.

Following directions to Upstate New York, I find myself on unfamiliar two-lane country roads. Even though it's 2 am, traffic slows. Cars, pick-ups, and vans begin to clog the road ahead so that both shoulders carry the traffic in only one direction--toward the festival. I finally reach the crew motel a little before dawn.

"Gimme a C!" shouts Country Joe. "C-e-e-e!" comes the reply. This is the C of cinema. We're not merely documenting a rock festival like *Monterey Pop*, but chronicling a watershed cultural event, where a developing generational consciousness revealed itself through its music. And 300,000 show their support in person.

What does a crowd that size look like? From my position onstage, all I see are dots of faces merging into a multicolor blanket stretching to the horizon. Too large for me to comprehend. My task at hand was to gather raw material for the filmmakers to use in the editing room.

With my Eclair, I film Credence Clearwater Revival, The Who, Jefferson Airplane, Janis Joplin, Joe Cocker, Canned Heat, Crosby, Stills, Nash & Young, Joan Baez—all the greats. I'm witnessing history unfolding, but I don't realize it because I'm busy composing shots, finding focus, keeping the camera rolling. Rolling, rolling, rolling.

Night falls. Sly and the Family Stone take the stage under color spotlights. I'm stationed to his right, with a three-quarter frontal of him. There are four other cameramen placed at strategic angles. As usual, Sly is resplendent, this time in white fringed suede, sheepskin knee-length boots and wraparound aviator sunglasses. He's taking all of us heads "high-yer...I'm gonna take yah high-yer... high-yer."

I become a shootin' fool. Panning up his boots, zooming into his hands on the keyboard, tilting up to his glasses. When his all-women horn section takes over, I pan to a three-shot of trombonist, saxophonist, trumpet player. Again, panning, tilting, zooming...into camera heaven. Yeah, this is the coolest!

The song ends, the applause is deafening. As it fades, I realize that instead I may be in camera hell. I hear my camera magazine flapping, meaning only one thing. My load of film has run out.

But how long ago? When the song ended and I panned to the crowd?

Or earlier, when Sly blasted his keyboard solo? Or even before that, when the horn section was workin' it? Oh, man...

I see later they used some brief cuts of my loosely-framed horn blowers from early in the song—nothing exciting, nothing memorable. Only then do I realize my best images are imprinted only in my memory.

"Gimme a K-a-y!" goes Country Joe. "K-a-a-a-y..." goes the crowd. "Wazzat spell?" asks Joe. Three hundred thousand voices, give or take fifty thousand, give their answer in unison. "Wazzat spell?" Joe repeats, "Wazzat spell?" And reminiscent of the climactic scene in "Spartacus," everyone rises to his feet to be part of the conspiracy and announce his answer.

This is the K of Okay. It's Monday morning, a few hours after Jimi Hendrix closed the Festival with his dazzling, mesmerizing "Star Spangled Banner" guitar solo. I put down my camera on the plywood stage while crews dismantle scaffolding, move lighting and audio equipment, roll up cable. I am standing there with my buddy Don Lenzer, the ace cameraman who got me this gig. After filming all night, we're zonked, but relieved.

"That was far out," says a voice behind us. We turn. It's Black Maria, a woman I once met at Ken Kesey's farm in Oregon. She traveled crosscountry to Woodstock with the Merry Pranksters on Go Further, their psychedelically-painted bus. Notwithstanding her name, Black Maria is a sunny soul.

We look out to the fields around the stage. Early morning sun picks up shiny surfaces in the litter strewn about. Only hours ago, hundreds of thousands were here. Over the years, that number grew with the legend. Initial reports said 300,000 attended. In the eighties, it became 500,000. By its twenty-fifth anniversary, memories upped it to 750,000.

No matter the number, those present were celebrating the birth of a new community. A community desiring peaceful coexistence with neighbors, freedom to explore meaningful lives, and elimination of social injustice. A community some call the Woodstock Nation, of which many still declare themselves to be citizens.

The sun is now higher. Cleaning crews move in. We watch them work. Too overcome by this weekend, we are quiet. Finally Black Maria says, "That was oh-h-kay, wasn't that? That was oh-h-kay."

We turn to each other. Yes, it was. And I was there.

DALE BELL

THE FINAL BATTLE

EARLY MARCH. THREE WEEKS to go before we were to open in eight cities: Los Angeles, New York, Washington, Boston, Chicago, San Francisco, Dallas, and Toronto. Bob Maurice had been so successful in keeping the "Suits" at bay that no one from Warners, except Sid Kiwitt, the sound mixing people, the staff editors, and the projectionists, had seen anything of the movie, with or without sound. Even we had not seen the entire movie strung together, only individual pieces out of order as they came from the dubbing stage and Technicolor. But that would soon change.

Warners wanted a screening. What did we think, they were going to promote this movie without having seen it through even once? Only twenty five of their executives would see the film, they promised, Chairman Ted Ashley, John Calley, Fred Weintraub among them. Use the big screening room where the screen and speakers had already been adapted to our movie. They wanted their way in two days.

Bob protested. What would you expect? Only their executives? Of course not. How could their "Suits" get a true sense of our movie, sitting in the back row, talking among themselves? We wanted to invite some of our friends from LA. How many? they asked. Twice as many people as they brought, we countered. Warners wouldn't have it. If the Warners "Suits" couldn't watch the movie with other young people who would be in a normal audience, what good would the preview accomplish? No, said Warners. They wanted to look at it by themselves, come to their own judgment. We wanted to invite some members from UCLA, USC, and other neighboring universities who were studying film; they would be good samples. We wanted a theater-type atmosphere. Warners bristled at the idea. We countered. We had already invited them. "Come sit on the floor and watch the picture." More than a hundred would show up. At the appointed time on March 15, they would be appearing at the guard gate, demanding entrance. What would Warners do then? Risk the bad publicity? We would alert TV cameras.

Warners maintained that the screening room wouldn't hold more than a hundred people. We asked for the building specs, then checked them out with an attorney and a building inspector. According to some Warners staffers, the screening room had received large crowds before. We argued some more. Finally, they relented. I'm sure Sid Kiwitt intervened. Only one hundred, they insisted.

Larry and Dan finished our sound mix on Saturday night, just in time to prepare the tracks for the screening.

At the designated time, 1:00 p.m. on Sunday, March 15, the film students lined up at the gates. Long-Hairs almost exclusively. Clearly, there were more than a hundred but the guards, sympathetic to our cause, let them in. In a very orderly fashion, they climbed the stairs to the screening room on the second floor. Other Warners personnel had located extra chairs for us to use. As the students and friends spread out, seating space for the "Suits" remained near the back of the room.

When the Warners people arrived, they were astonished. They had to step over all the seated and sprawling bodies that littered the chairs and the floor. Students were leaning up against the walls, against each other's knees. Those way down front had to lie down to get a view of the screen. Already, smoke was in the air. As soon as the "Suits" were seated, we began to roll. And rock and roll we did!

Even though repairs were still being made on all aspects of the picture and sound track, and reel-change-overs were still in an embryonic stage, there was sufficient material here to get a true sense of what we had actually accomplished.

First, the screening would last four hours without intermission. Second, there were acts and documentary footage in this cut which would never again be seen, not even in the Director's Cut issued at the twenty-fifth anniversary. Third, the atmosphere in that room was so vibrant, so electric as a result of the "sardine" effect, that its pulse rate could never be measured or duplicated. Fourth, it was the very first time anyone of us had ever seen—experienced—the overwhelming power of what we had wrought almost nine months earlier. Superlatives are inadequate to describe the synergy that bound everyone together for those four hours. It was a once in a lifetime experience, very similar to what we had witnessed and provoked in New York in early December, or in those first multiple-day screenings of the dailies in mid-October, before the move from the Teletape offices.

Little snickers curled to full laughter and cheers. When the students knew the words to a tune, they sang along. As the stereo sound traveled around and around the screening room, behind and in front of them, their heads turned to follow it. As the music modulated on the visual change from a single panel to the twin nighttime panels heralding the beginning of the arrival of the crowds, there was an audible sigh emanating from our audience. After each act, they were applauding and shouting. When Country Joe McDonald asked for an "F" in the "F.U.C.K. Cheer," the students obliged in unison, adding their voices to those they witnessed on screen in front of them and those they heard behind them. The bouncing ball was greeted with hilarious cheers. Even the Port-O-San Man received an almost standing ovation from our audience, the first of many he would motivate with his compassion for young people, around the globe.

Our vision was paying off. More so through the medium of this captivating art called film—the marriage of darkness, light and sound—they were experiencing far more about the festival than they could have, had they actually been there themselves.

Even some of the "Suits" began to get into the mood, irresistibily drawn there by their peer group pressure. Not to tap your foot, not to cheer, not to laugh at the little jokes and innuendos, not to marvel at the editing, the visual panels dancing in front of you, all meant you were not responsive to the work we had put into capturing the essence of the festival and translating it into a symbol.

I frankly think the "Suits" were very pleased, though perhaps quietly so, that we had invited the students. How sterile it might have been to watch alone! The screening went off without a hitch. But still, there were no credits on the movie.

As the "Suits" left, we agreed to a meeting in Ted Ashley's office the following morning at 9:00 a.m. He had been named the head of the studio just a year or so earlier. We met in his "Alice in Wonderland" world where furniture and platforms were designed to increase his height to the level of other normal-sized people. Specific chairs were designated for specific people; I couldn't sit in several of the chairs, for example. Some of the chairs actually had names on them. We were about five people: Wads, Bob, Thelma, Larry, and me. They presented an equal number.

It would be a lie not to say that the atmosphere was extremely tense. The movie was to open ten days hence, on March 26. One day was needed for the shipping of the prints to the respective theaters. Calculate eight days in which to take their "notes," translate them into action if we agreed, remix and/or reopticalize, make prints in Technicolor, pack and ship. Very frightening.

We want a movie which is only two hours and forty five minutes long, Ted began. Not accomodating, we thought. We began our discussion at the end, with the Jimi Hendrix sequence which had played at almost 15 minutes in length. Bob opened by saying we were not going to cut it. Ted said they were going to cut it for us. Bob said they couldn't do it by contract. Ted: "Yes, we can and we will. We want it cut to three and a half minutes. At its present length, it makes the ending of the movie too dark."

Now, Wads thought he had addressed this issue himself back in October. The first Hendrix cut, to close the movie, had been edited to about twenty minutes. Wads and Thelma thought it was the appropriate way to end, an instrumental way to put all that had happened before in proper perspective. It involved a lot of super imposition, double exposures, images of the cleaning up at the festival site on Monday morning after the rain, a sort of purple haze in keeping with the title of the tune Jimi was playing with his band. For this final screening, then, he had cut more than five minutes from that original cut, satisfying his artistic vision. He felt strongly that it played at this current length.

It was a short meeting. Amid much anger, name-calling, and frustration, we got up and left and went back to work. During and after the screening, we had made our own "notes" and had many of them to implement to meet the deadline. We had much to do not to contend with this silliness. But we were scared.

In another cutting room, sequestered somewhere on the Warners lot, we felt there was another editing team, headed by John Calley, who had really not been very much involved in our picture. Unbeknown to us, we feared, Calley was reediting—or truncating, or whittling, or chopping—our film down to the size Ted Ashley dictated. Representing the demands of their exhibitors, they wanted the movie to turn around at !east four times per day in each theater. At its current length, their income would be reduced by one-fourth. Money, stockholders, greed; this was their motivation. They didn't care about our film. Vision be damned! Exhibitors were more important. Ignore what the film represented to us and to the world we felt we were representing. If Calley was at work behind our backs, where did he get his prints from, and his sound tracks?

The next day, we had a second early meeting with Ted Ashley and his people. Apparently, some critical picture and sound elements were missing from the editing and the mixing rooms. The Warners editors could not continue their work. Did we know anything about it? he demanded. "No," we said, "we knew nothing about the missing elements." "What about Hendrix?" Ted Ashley asked. "We're not going to cut it down to three and a half minutes," Bob said. Ted repeated that we would or that they would cut it for us. We reminded him that nothing could be cut without the sound, and they (Warners) apparently couldn't find it. Had they looked everywhere? How irresponsible were their editors if they had lost it at this critical time? Why were they blaming us? Didn't they know their own deadlines?

We talked some more, but the renegotiation did not work.

On Wednesday, we held our third meeting since the Sunday afternoon screening. Ted wasn't there at this one. More accusations were thrown at us about material missing from the lot. Now none of the editors could work. Everything had stalled with the opening dates just days away. We were told that we should edit the Hendrix sequence "down to a size that we think is manageable but make it a maximum of around five minutes." We replied that we would do so, but that it's length would be longer than five. Warners would have to live with it. They said: "In other words, we are going to have to chop it."

Returning to our editing rooms, Michael and Thelma edited Jimi down to eight and a half minutes. The next day, as though miraculously, all the missing material reappeared on the lot again as though nothing had happened. Warners accepted the new length.

Throughout these frantic days, we had other "notes" to implement. Though we liked the Canned Heat uncut sequence Wads had filmed with Bob Hite and his unannounced on-stage visitor with the pack of cigarettes, its boogie-woogie music did not wield a huge effect on the students. We decided to drop it. (Twenty-five years later, it resurfaced thankfully in the *Director's Cut*. Watch it carefully. There is not a cut in it for eleven minutes, the entire length of a sixteen-millimeter magazine, frame to frame. Wads' camera work weaving in and out of the performers with his 5.9 lens [wide angle] sometimes only inches away from the performers is nothing short of astounding in its spontaneity, responsiveness and ingenuity. Listen to the sound, too. As Wads weaves in and out of the performers, the perspective of the sound changes through three sets of front speakers and a surround track to conform with the audience. Credit Danny Wallin, Larry Johnson and the sound mixing team, but it did take a great deal of time and patience to achieve such revolutionary effects for the time.)

Even though the Jefferson Airplane were not enthusiastic about the mix in their sequence at their private screening a month or so earlier, we included it anyway in hopes that Warners would ante up more money to the group so we could include them. Warners didn't want to, so we dropped Grace Slick and the Airplane.

Johnny Winter and Leslie ("Mountain") West succumbed to Warners' request for a shorter film. I guess they fell because of the harange over Jimi. Tim Hardin's, the Greatful Dead's and Janis Joplin's performances were so inebriated, we felt we could save them embarassment by not subjecting them to further, eternal visibility. Coupled with these "notes" were certain short documentary sequences which did not seem to work in their present context. Overall, we wanted to preserve a comfortable ratio between music and documentary. (Much of this original four-hour cut was restored in the *Director's Cut* issued in 1994 under Larry Johnson and Michael's supervision.)

Now we were at length, plus or minus three hours, without credits. But how to manufacture the prints, imprint on them all the technical information theater projectionists would need to play the movie, and get them out to their cities?

And where was Charlie Cirigliano and the credits?? He had begun creating his template weeks ago! Or was it just days ago??? Warners and the optical houses were looking for us to create some fancy titles and credits to accompany what-they-viewed-as-the-fancy opticals. Pablo Ferro, a title man who had just designed the opening for *Bullitt*, was ushered in with great fanfare. After looking at some of our movie, he returned from his drawing boards with another batch of very fancy moving panels and shutters for the opening. It didn't take us long to reject them. Too much competition with our own work. All along, we had been trying to reinforce the simplicity of the event and of the intent of the festival. Pablo's opticals would have taken more time, while taking away from the verdant Garden of Eden we recalled in our opening sequences.

What to do? Remember Charlie? The refrigeration guy brought to our New York offices by his editor friend, Winn Tucker? Son of an artist, brother to a cameraman, this Einstein look-alike Charlie could build, repair, draw, design almost anything in any medium. Extraordinary eye-hand coordination. One of this prime responsibilities throughout our picture was to repair the KEM editing machines. He used to say: He'd take care of the mechanics, let someone else deal with the electronics. Through this peanut-and-butter-relationship, the KEMS remained mostly healthy most of the time. Now continuing his tasks in California where the deadlines were ever more demanding, Charlie was whisked off all of his other duties and pressed into service as the designer of the titles. He had eight days to go!

Already, we had determined who would get what credit and the order in which they would appear. Yet many other people had helped us throughout the movie; we wanted to thank all of them. (If we inadvertently left someone off, please forgive us!) Pablo's overblown designs for the opening titles immediately confirmed another simple concept: No opening title at all. Let Stephen Westerfeld, the man standing on the stairs of the inn in White Lake, invite the people in to the Garden. But what type face, what font to use on the names at the end? Charlie took a look at the poster designed for the festival and suggested that all our names be created in that font. Fine idea, but the poster used only a few letters of the alphabet! Charlie would have to create a template from those letters which would accommodate all others. Then by hand, he would have to draw all the letters, spell the names correctly, get them photographed, opticalized (of course!), developed, printed and attached to the end of the movie in time for the screenings in the eight cities. Eight days!

CHARLES CIRIGLIANO

FINAL CREDITS

I SPENT THE SUMMER of '69 with my brother Michael, who is a cinematographer, and another filmmaker named Winston Tucker, documenting the Huns Motorcycle Club in Bridgeport, Connecticut, and Laconia, New Hampshire. I heard about the Woodstock concert mid-summer, and I knew that it would be large. Winn shared my thoughts and enthusiasm and on the Thursday before the concert, we hitchhiked from Manhattan to White Lake, NY with no tickets and no money.

I think it was the title, "The First Celebration of the Aquarian Age", that led me to believe in its import. There was so much happening at the time: the War, the Moon, and now this. I had to go; and I actually felt that somehow, I could become involved with the documentation of the event. Winn felt the same way, and I knew he had the perspicacity to search out and meet the principal players in the recording of this event, which he did on-site. Winn met Larry Johnson and Jeannie Field, and two days after the concert, he was syncing sound in the Broadway offices of Wadleigh-Maurice. Listening to Winn's nightly reviews of the day's events just added to my thirst for a piece of this job: Mike Wadleigh receiving Warner Bros. first check for $80,000, Joe Cocker's reaction to viewing his act in rough cut.

Not quite knowing which piece of the job was mine puzzled me, until I got a call from Winn to get my ass up to Eightieth Street and Broadway ASAP and ask to see Dale Bell. Upon completing my job interview with Dale, I was hired, and two things were made clear to me: number one, predictably, were the things he deemed most important in an employee, and number two, that Dale Bell was a *he* not a *she*; having seen too many Roy Rogers movies I had asked to see *Miss Dale Bell*.

After this auspicious start, my next meeting was with Thelma Schoonmaker who, hugging her ever-present clipboard, succinctly informed me of my duties: "Fix anything mechanical that breaks, get anything the editors request and give the editors no creative input."

It was from that moment that I knew I had a shot in putting my mark on this film.

Just how I might make my mark would unfold during the next six months of continuous work that we all participated in. I think we took Christmas Day off. (I must note here that I would have paid them to have the job I had, but the company treated me, the "gofer-in-training," as an important member of the team. Their regard for me was also reflected in how they paid me, which was by the hour, with time and a half after forty. I was taking home between four and five hundred dollars a week, which was great pay at the time. Any production assistant reading this will find these numbers familiar thirty years later.)

The unfolding of this episode in my life actually started four years previously while attending the University of Bridgeport in Connecticut. Twelve students including myself organized the "Cinema Guild" there. Pursuing graphic design and fascinated by the magic of transfer, I easily fell into film and frequented the MOMA film program there. Films like "Scorpio Rising" "Ode to Artifice" and a film called "The Sins of the Fleshpods" gave me a glimpse of the future of film making and the future itself. It was from this guild the film department at UB developed, so to speak, through the vision of a fellow guild member, one Warren Bass. It's interesting to note that on a visit to the film department several years ago, I was astonished to see the editing department equipment without a Moviola in sight—Kellers and Steenbecks all over the place. The very models I had trucked onto the Warner Bros. Burbank lot in 1970. The very models so instrumental in producing the film.

At any rate, these machines were to guarantee my tenure on this project. I learned the mechanics of them inside and out. Literally, they were all mine; well, me and Wolfgang, the world head of KEM. With Wolfgang at my ear on the phone, guiding me from West Germany, only I was allowed to open the beast, the automaton with three heads that consumed film. "Consumed" means that the machines' torque motors were so powerful and the tolerances were so sensitive and the machine ran through film so fast that if the splices were off-kilter or the editor was working in too much of a hurry, the gears would "eat" all the sprocket-holes, or slit the print right down the middle, for forty or fifty feet. This could really mess up your day.

Electrics were relegated to Mr. Lee Osborne, our electric wiz in company. But lenses, mirrors and mechanics were mine. The first models were belt driven. The second and third heads on the two attached wings were actuated with gears and belts from a main drive deep within the main deck. Of the eight Kellers (KEMs) and Steenbecks we had, I think only two were belt driven, six were automatic and all were ours. Wadleigh-Maurice were the first importers of these machines into this country. Francis Ford Coppola rented to us, as did Frank Zappa. (He used the machine left at our Yucca-Vine offices to cut *Uncle Meat*). I understand all of our machines are still servicing the industry in Hollywood, and all have their own personalities.

The Steenbecks were fully automatic and had only one head. They hardly ever jammed so long as I kept them clean. Cleaning these things was most important in keeping them up. Grease pencil being the culprit, as I remember.

Keeping them up was one thing, moving them was another, and that I did. Kellers are big, and bulky, and heavy, and they will not easily fit through doorways unless you take them completely apart. Three times we changed location, from Eighty-First Street and Broadway to Eightieth Street and Broadway; from Eightieth Streetto Yucca and Vine in Hollywood; from there to Dupe Three at Warner Bros. in Burbank, California. All the moves were logistically planned out, except the time we were evicted from Eighty-First Street, having to move the show across the street to Eightieth and Broadway, in winter, overnight.

It is my impression that we were the first nonunion crew ever to work on the Warner Bros. lot, and the editors that were left there (finishing up John Wayne's *True Grit*) would not even go near our editing machines. And we were not even to touch their Moviolas. Old Timers, they knew nothing of these new electronic editing machines, nor did they want to. Moviolas were the hammers, we were bringing in the air guns. (Pardon the wood analogy, I've now been building sets and props for the industry as an IA 52 shop craftsman for over twenty years and have seen my department go through similar changes.)

Getting back to Hollywood thirty years ago, it was pretty much dead. They were auctioning off MGM, Paramount was idle, and we were the only thing happening at Warners. We made an eight-hour version and ultimately, Warner Bros. chopped it into the more commercial three-hour version you see as the final release. Looking back, perhaps three episodes of 120 minutes each would have been more profitable and more fair to the creators.

Looking back on all this, many images flash by: the jammed workprint burning in the gates of the three Xenon projectors, rented for the "progress-to-date" Thanksgiving Day Private Screening at the Filmore East; or the numerous conversations I had with Martin Scorcese in New York; or lying to Ted Ashley, the then-President of WB, when he asked me in his office what I had done with the purloined 150 hours of original footage, and the realization that I wouldn't be working for Warner Bros. soon; or the installation of the first twelve track mixing board in Hollywood at the Record Plant to accommodate our sound requirements; at the mix, I remember walking down this long, long hallway, and John Wayne himself comes walking toward me, approaching for a long, long time; when we finally meet up to pass each other he says, "Hiya, Hippie!" smoking hash from Jim Morrison's eagle-clawed pipe in his girlfriend's house months after his death; viewing the rough cut of The Who's performance with Keith Moon, John Entwhistle and Roger Daltrey, as they watched it for the first time. It was a wild six months.

But the climax of this endeavor for me was crafting the logo and the end title sequence. Having done all Bob Maurice's graphics for his film distribution company, Paradigm, and having just completed the four by eight chart monitoring all the end tabs (clips of shots) circulating around all the processors in town, (there were hundreds of them if not thousands), Bob came to me with another favor: make a "W" for the logo because the Warner Bros. designer couldn't get past the "Woody Woodpecker" look.

So all I did was to create a "W" that logically looked like Arnold Skolnick's famous dove on a guitar with the inscription "3 Days of Peace and Music." Bob liked my "W" and now he wanted the whole word, "Woodstock," which was easy. Then he loved the "Woodstock" I came up with, and wanted me to do all the titles. Now the work began.

From those twelve letter-specimens, the numeral "3," and the ampersand, I designed twenty-six upper-case and twenty-six lower case, and nine numerals. I had seven more days to go through all the out-takes and movie footage, selecting those shots that most went with the group or situation, and choosing the sound to overlay on it. Getting shots of groups that fit the parameters of the sixteen millimeters to 35 Anamorphic Panavision was the only tricky part, as one of the titles actually extended off the screen.

Counting from the day Bob Maurice asked me to make a "W," to me handing Mike the finished Main Tide and End-Credit reels at the door of the jet that was to propel him to the NYC premier, eight days had passed. Well, those titles were first viewed sight-unseen at the premier, to rousing applause. My denouement was hearing this news. This final act of mine took eight twenty-hour days, preceded by the six months of continuous work.

Wow, that was film making!

DALE
BELL

THE FINISH LINE

THE FINAL BURDEN FOR meeting the deadline set by Warners fell on Technicolor. Five days to go before opening nights; three days to go before press screenings. Already Bob and Mike were approving newspaper, radio and television advertisements. There was no turning back. Tech said they couldn't do it. I remember saying to them: change! You've got to do things differently! They told me that one piece of gear was on the tenth floor, the other on the third. Remembering what I had heard in our original tour with their chief executive, I reminded them that the gear could be moved closer together in order to obtain greater efficiency. Twice as fast, I remember hearing. But it will cost you twenty thousand dollars to make that move, they replied. Make the move, I said. Do it. This whole deadline business had just cost another seventy-five thousand dollars in the course of one telephone conversation. But in light of the embarassment of not having prints at theaters on time, this was small price to pay.

At the very last possible moment, Charlie Cirgliano's hand-drawn credits, which would appear only at the end of the movie, arrived from the optical house and into the waiting hands of the Technicolor people. The credits would become a separate, last reel to the picture bringing its opening night length to three hours and about four minutes. Certainly the longest optical then known to man!

As the hours ticked away Saturday and Sunday, and more overtime began to aggregate, the weekend bill at Technicolor mounted to one hundred fifty thousand dollars to produce ten full-length prints with wrap-around sound tracks. On Monday, March 23, Warner Bros. executives hand-carried one print to the major cities, except New York and Los Angeles, where we were playing in two theaters, not one.

On Monday evening, I took one print as hand-carry on a plane to New York, just in time for the press screening on Tuesday at the Trans-Lux East.

Other press screenings were held in Los Angeles at the Academy of Motion Picture Arts and Sciences, then on Melrose Avenue, at 7:00 p.m.

DALE
BELL

WHAT IF?

THESE ARE STORIES ABOUT *Woodstock*—The Movie Which Almost Didn't Get Made. Al Maysles thought it was an "Impossible" task: all movies like *Woodstock* or *Gimme Shelter* are impossible to do, he believes.

Think back on it. Ahmet Ertegun was offered movie rights to the festival by the entertainment attorney Paul Marshall; he first turned it down in April. Who, he said, would ever watch a movie? Monterey Pop hadn't made any money. Why believe that another movie about another rock festival would? The Atlanta Speedway music gathering in May 1969 had attracted one hundred thousand spectators but no movie was made. No, Ahmet said, he would save twenty-five thousand dollars and rest solely on the record rights for seventy-five thousand dollars Invisible music was to be listened to, not seen.

Yet a month later, he changed his mind when Marshall again knocked on his door. For one hundred thousand dollars all in, Ahmet-Atlantic Records, division of Warner Bros.-Seven Arts—would control album and movie rights. But then, did he tell Warners Chairman, Ted Ashley, presumably his boss in the scheme of things, that he had the rights?

Porter Bibb, acting on behalf of Al and David Maysles, was negotiating with Ted Ashley to finance the documentary. Apparently neither knew that Atlantic controlled the rights. Although Porter and Ted had recently returned from a scouting trip in Africa together on another project, their discussions relating to the Woodstock Festival broke down when Ashley, very unfamiliar with documentary filmmaking, insisted that the Maysles would have to purchase a completion bond, assuring Warners' investment in the event of rain at the festival site. As Porter tried desperately to explain, the cost of the completion bond would have doubled the cost of shooting and editing the film. No insurer in their right mind would even put up a bond. Too risky. End of discussion. Deal breaker.

As the Warners' talks were proceeding and breaking down, Bob Maurice, Mike Wadleigh, others and I were in preproduction on another music project: the September staging at Columbia Univeristy's stadium of a music festival to celebrate 1950s music so that Mike would have an experimental venue to display his multiple-screen shooting and editing visions. While Mike took a well-paid month in the Wind River Canyons of Wyoming to shoot *30 Days to Survival* with Paul Petzoldt's National Outdoor Leadership School, Bob and I, among others, were trying to entice investors to the 1950s concert. Filming in the rugged backcountry of Wyoming, *Woodstock* was no doubt the furthest thing from Mike's mind. Or was it?

When he returned to New York City at the very end of July, his only thought was to buy some good tickets to this music festival in upstate New York he had heard about. Larry and Jeanne inspired that idea. Larry was far more into the music than anyone else. Accompanied by his friends, they would lie on the grass and hang out! After all, he needed a rest from the rigors of backpacking the past thirty days.

Meanwhile, the festival producers were grappling with insurmountable problems of moving their site from its original Woodstock to White Lake, New York, anticipating that a crowd of fifty thousand would turn them a profit. Yet in all their turmoil, Mike Lang had the presence of mind to hire two British cameramen (Mike Margetts and Mike?) to get some footage of the new site construction. They arrived just prior to August 1, thankfully. (Warners later bought their footage for us.) Others from the festival tried vainly in New York City to get a movie deal together but nothing was happening in early August, maybe because the fate of the actual festival was so much in the air.

I don't believe Bob Maurice or Mike Wadeigh even began to take the notion seriously until the Maysles brothers and Porter Bibb came to our Broadway offices during that first week in August to try to build a coaltion: they, the Maysles, would shoot the documentary portions, they proposed, but they needed someone to shoot the music. On the street, they had heard about our three-screen technique; could they see it? We displayed our demo, the legendary Aretha multiple screen rendition of "We Shall Overcome," Paul Revere and the Raiders, and James Brown, all "godfathered" by Merv Griffin. Richie Havens was in the screening room, as well. So blown away were the Maysles by this rendering, they stormed out of the offices, frustrated, angry, exhanging epithets, and some say fisticuffs, on their exit. They had not tied up anything: not Warners, not another financing studio, not the festival, not the musicians, and apparently, they did not have enough money in their own bank to finance the project independently. The dark abyss was opened. The Ten Days of August began.

No film would be made unless we did it.

Into this power vacuum we plunged, relying solely on adrenaline and our own skills. Carpe Diem. Only then, ten days before the actual event, did we put our heads together in earnest. Michael may have had only $10,000 in his account but his vision and Bob's labyrinthian mind coupled with legendary tenacity easily surmounted that deficit. What did they see?

A challenge of immense proportions. The lure of the unknown...

Though no one knew then that this historic concert would attract tens upon tens of thousands of young people seeking community, it did promise to be the greatest assemblage of musicians ever gathered in one place. Both Bob and Mike pulsated with music, though Bob's love for jazz was very dissimilar from Mike's connection with folk and rock. Larry was pushing, too. He understood the lyric.

Mike had just set records climbing mountains; the ordeals had taught him a good deal about himself as a human being. Bob had other records to his credit: for devouring more courses in psychology, philosophy and religion at CCNY without receiving a diploma. Mike had given up medicine to conquer film; Bob financed his religious and philosophical purSuits by balancing as close to heaven as steel construction girders would allow. Both men were daring beyond compare, though both had their respective afflictions which they were able to hold in check: Mike's was epilepsy, Bob's paranoia. Both disorders, as in Dostoevsky's *The Idiot*, forced them into a clarity of thought, and manipulation, not to be duplicated.

Both men saw an opportunity to accelerate the date and the venue for Mike's experiments with multi-screen filming of music concerts; the proposed September concert of 1950's music at Columbia University could now be accomplished on a farm in upstate New York, produced by others than themselves.

Both felt passionately that the war in Vietnam was wrong. Preserving this concert on film might at least let the message carried in the music and the lyric of the 1960s reverberate more than once. Serving as director on some Richard Nixon presidential spots in 1968 allowed Mike to flirt with an eerie sense of power, but he also was able to turn his back on it. Both were rebels with a cause. Consorting with authority, to learn from it only to defy it was standard operating procedure for both of them, just as scaling heights to defy Newton was also common.

When they began their exploration of the abyss, and brought others of us along, no one knew where the journey would take us, let alone where the end might be. Yet all of us were intensely aware of the yawning chasm before us.

What happened? Documentary filmmaking is so entirely different from dramatic movie making. With a documentary, you cannot control the events; by every rule, silent or carved in stone, you are forbidden to even try. Your job is to be prepared to go with the flow, to film what interests you and to turn off when you lose interest. For comparison, you have to be prepared to run a hundred yard dash or a marathon, depending upon the speed of the subject. You have to be in shape, physically, mentally, and psychologically, and to be armed with the right equipment so you can follow your subject wherever he/she/it takes you.

Sort it all out in the editing room, later!

By contrast, when filming a dramatic film, you schedule everyone and everything for maximum efficiency. Sequences are shot completely out of order to accomodate schedules and money. Control.

The dates of the Woodstock Festival were breathing down upon us. They would not change. Whatever had to be done had to be leveraged within the remaining time vacancy. Staring at a clock and a calendar, you had to be willing to grasp the implications—and the risk—of commitment. Live television all over again. Much like climbing mountains without a rope, free-style, you had to be willing to fall or to climb. Within the last twelve months, Mike had done nothing but climb to great altitudes.

Bob had tiptoed across girders suspended over city streets. Neither was about to fall here, in the man-made canyons of New York.

John Roberts turned down Bob's offer to own the movie rights hundred percent if Michael and all of us would be allowed to make the movie with full editorial control, on spec. Though this decision changed John's life forever, he simply didn't have the cash. His "Just Say No!" forced Grappling Bob Maurice to search out a way to make the movie, because no one else was going to. Pounding on every New York/Hollywood studio door: Columbia, Paramount, and Warner Bros., produced only echoes of negativism. No one got it!

Within those frenetic couple of days in August, Bob scoured about, trying to put a deal together. That's when Artie Kornfeld worked over Fred Weintraub. That's when I called Jules Winarick. That's when Eric Blackstead called Alex Brooks. Others threw out bottles with notes as well. Full press scramble. A Hail Mary. And Bob brought home the bacon; his reward? He then had to deal with all those

Warner's people and keep them away from us so the original vision could be fulfilled. Thank you, Bob. THANK YOU! It was a role you didn't want but it was a job only you could do.

Why? What lessons? If Everest is there, climb it. "When in doubt, go up hill!" is, today, a runner's credo. One person can make a difference. Ask what you can do for your country. Trust your friends; let them help you. Nothing can be done alone. Be prepared to respond to your instinct instantly. Trust your gut. Lash yourself to the mast and keep going forward. Work at a solution piece by piece. Break it down, preferably on paper. Do not allow yourself to be overwhelmed by the totality of your undertaking for it will intimidate you. Break it down into manageable parts. Determine what you can say Yes to, and implement those as you move on to others. Rely on your training. Fight for what you believe in, even if it means you appear to be negating earlier lessons. Don't be distracted by peripheral matters. Focus on your goal or goals, your individual actions which will drag you along your way to your ultimate target. Don't do tomorrow's work today. Envision other role models who have done something comparable; match your actions to those they might do in similar situations.

"Impossible?" Yes. Looking back, very much so. Yet there it is, brought to this point by ordinary, caring, very funny, creative and ingenious people whose collective actions contributed to the entirety. But it required vision and steel guts.

Los Angeles Times critic Charles Champlin, writing from the movie capital of the world in March 1970, would say: "The unifying characteristic of the Hollywood films of the 1970s was boldness. Sometimes, oftentimes, it was a boldness with a cynical eye to profits. In other and more enduring instances, it was artistic boldness—daring to do what had not been done before on the same scale or with the same candor and depth. *Woodstock* with its twenty cameramen [a couple too many, Chuck!] deployed to record an epic musical gathering, became itself an epic.

"The Woodstock Rock Festival of August 1969, started out to be a nice, simple, king-sized money-making weekend. It ended up as an historic togetherness of crisis proportions…The Woodstock gathering has now been recorded in what I think is an historic piece of film, *Woodstock: 3 Days of Peace and Music*. Wadleigh and his platoon of film editors have made superb use of the split screen, have in fact made clear that the split screen is an urgent part of the grammar of film and not an amusing gimmick. The reverberations of the electronically driven music find their shimmering images on the screen. Sound and images echo. Sometimes there are two disparate but related images; a song of children and children in the crowd. It is all ebullient and astonishing.

"The use of film technique is conscious and artful, but there is no sense of technique for its own sake, as a plaything. The multiple images, the wild sound tracks, the faces gone lavender or green under the flood lights in the dark night, the sometimes deafening music, all come as close as film can to recapture the essence of a unique and remarkable moment in time.

"Woodstock" is a record, not an analysis. There is no narration and no real attempt to examine society or a generation of musical history or of American affluence, to learn how it was that nearly a half-million young people showed up, stayed through three cloudbursts in three days and cheerfully endured hardships that would have evoked instant mutiny in any army camp on earth.

"Let the analysis come later. This is source material, brilliantly compiled, It is aimed primarily at the audience that was there—or would have been there if it had been humanly possible to get there.

"Michael Wadleigh's stunning film, produced by Bob Maurice and financed by Warner Bros. to the tune of a reported $600,000 [actually closer to a million, Chuck!] raises true concerns about how responsive our society is to this generation. Yet in its affable optimism, Woodstock also suggests that we're not without a considerable and defiant hope."

New York film critic, Judith Crist, would write, "Woodstock's distinction is in its camera work and editing. Rock groups and personalities lend themselves to theatricality and this film's gifted makers have used split screens, stop motion and freezes to brilliant and striking effect, with subtle variations in the size and shape of the frame. The Richie Havens sequence for starters is joltingly beautiful, and toward the end the freeze of Sly is a work of art in itself."

Time magazine: "It is happening all over again. Woodstock, last summer's 'three days of love and peace' has just been recreated in a joyous, volcanic new film that will make those who missed the fesitval feel as if they were there…But Woodstock is far more than a sound-and-light souvenir of a long weekend concert. Purely as a piece of cinema, it is one of the finest documentaries ever made in the United States."

What might have happened had there been no movie?

At the twenty-third Cannes Film Festival in May 1970 (the movie had played in the States for six weeks to packed and passionate audiences), Warner Bros. scheduled our three-hour movie as one of the five American films in the main festival. One day earlier, as Bob, Mike, Larry, Thelma and I were having lunch at a restaurant on the beach opposite the Carlton Hotel, I noticed a newspaper headline at an adjoining table. In French, it screamed that several students had been killed by militia at Kent State University in Ohio, Mike's home state.

Shocked by the news, we immediately bought papers in French and English and began to figure out what we might have to do to symbolize this horror at the festival. Indeed, had the passions aroused by our movie contributed even indirectly to these traumatic events? Certainly there were red-necked short-hairs in the National Guard in Ohio! Among the many plans we discussed emerged one: find some black cloth, create black arms bands in the hundreds, and distribute them among those who would come to screen our film. It would take us most of the night and the next day.

Rumors surfaced that Yves Montand, the world-renown French actor once linked to Marilyn Monroe, who had recently depicted a French rebel in "Z," would attend our 6:30 p.m. Saturday screening. My assignment, because of my French fluency, was to try to persuade him to wear a band in protest. As the audience crushed into the old Palais, I spied him going up the grand staircase. Once I reached him, he was very sympathetic to our cause, took one of the bands, but explained that he could not wear one there among his countrymen until he had more information about the events in Ohio. I thanked him, then rushed down to the stage where I was to meet Bob and Mike.

We had written a short speech, which I had translated into French, that we would deliver in both languages before the running of the movie. In part it said: "We filmmakers want to dedicate this film to the four American students killed by the militia in the United States, these students who were demonstrating against the war in Vietnam and Cambodia. We also dedicate this film to all those who will die for the cause of peace throughout the world and the struggle against domestic oppression. We completely oppose the wars in Vietnam and Cambodia. We support completely the struggle of students and the efforts of blacks and other minorities to overcome their oppression.

"At the end of this film, if you also oppose the wars in Vietnam and Cambodia, please join us and wear the black arm-band throughout the remainder of the festival."

Vincent Canby of the *New York Times* would comment that, though the film was well received as a "political" film, Warners' high-pressure publicity created a lot of unfavorable comment.

But neither shared our deep sense of purpose or responsibility.

ELEN ORSON

GO GRAB YOUR OWN MOVEMENT!

(ELEN WAS OUR YOUNGEST assistant on-site and in the editing room.)

Woodstock went on to win the Oscar, and The Film Industry discovered what a huge market there could be for films about the counter culture. The next wave brought such films as *Midight Cowboy, Joe, Butch Cassidy, M.A.S.H* and *Little Big Man*. Then TV gave us *The Brady Bunch, The Partrige Family,* and *Mod Squad*, and America ate it up; everyone wanted to be regarded as hip. Not like the angry hip demonstrators in Chicago, but like the beautiful hip people they had seen in *Woodstock*. Bankers and stockbrokers began to wear bell-bottoms and wear their hair "long" and search for inner meaning. And that was pretty much it, for the youth movement as it had been. You're no longer unique when everyone is trying to look just like you.

There is almost no way to trace the million and one imprints that the film has made on society and film culture. When you watch a drama on TV now, and it's shot with a handheld camera panning and swinging around, that's *Woodstock* invading the cultural subconscious. When you watch the beautiful nature documentaries of National Geographic, that's *Woodstock* too; many of the crew members went on to work at WQED Pittsburgh and brought their sensibilities with them, along with their sense of adventure. No retrospective of the 1960s would be complete without footage from the Festival. Our film is the dominant popular image of the Festival, and gave it its place it in history.

The youth movement finally grew up. We now find ourselves trying to lend sage advice to teenagers who roll their eyes as the Old Ones speak. I'd like to think that we did change the world, for the better, and I am secretly pleased when I see kids in bell-bottoms and tie-dye shirts. (Ah, the classics.) I never get offended by outrageous hair. I guess it's a phase everyone should go through. But I don't want them to be just like us, they should go find their own movement and grab it. Run with it. Don't imitate us, or especially our mistakes!

We got clobbered and tear-gassed and arrested, to admit self-expression into the culture. And I get upset when I see it wasted on self-indulgent bull, and I get upset when I see teens leaning on their parents, expecting everything to be handed over to them for free. We blew open many doors, we gifted them with a world where at last they could have their own power, go after their dreams, and make it on their own. And when I see kids going into the military just to get free college, I lose my mind. Sometimes I think these kids don't appreciate the sacrifices we made!

STAN WARNOW

A REVOLUTIONARY EFFECT

(STAN WAS BOTH CAMERAMAN and editor on the movie.)

As the years have passed, the culture that *Woodstock* portrayed has come to be accepted as one of the strands of American life. While the political revolution we hoped was going to happen didn't, our actions and lives have had a revolutionary effect on our society. Compared to the 1950s, we now have a society that has changed profoundly, from women's and minority rights to informality in the workplace. These changes have their roots in the values of the 1960s, the values that coalesced at Woodstock and were represented in the film.

And as far as the film's specific impact, it has been truly monumental. The success of *Woodstock* was an obvious major factor in the evolution of music videos and music television. The artists at the festival who were included in the film reaped huge career benefits, and conversely, the lesser known performers who were not included in the film have mostly faded to obscurity. Ten Years After was only moderately well known before Woodstock, but after the film was released they were huge. In a very real sense the film has become the festival in the public mind. I heard someone say once, "What's happened is that if a performer was in the festival, but not in the film, then they as far as the public is concerned, they weren't at the festival." While that may not be fair, it is true, and another real indication of the film's significance.

Many projects have come and gone since *Woodstock*, but it will always be one of the central events in my life and career. Many of the friendships forged during that span of about nine months (is it just coincidental that films so often chronologically parallel the human gestation cycle?) have lasted for thirty years now and are going strong. I'm still editing and still loving the process, even if it's now all digital and my KEM is gathering dust in storage. But on every job, or when I'm between jobs, there are those moments when a song or a shot brings back my memories and I think: "the event that named a generation and I was there." I was fortunate enough to experience it twice, once at the festival and all over again during months of editing. And those are fine memories indeed.

THELMA SCHOONMAKER

AFTERMATH

DALE: In the aftermath of the release of the movie, you traveled to several places. Describe what that was like.

THELMA: First I went to Cannes, which was quite an event. It was very exciting going around some countries in Europe with the film because it was connecting so deeply with young people. It was very exciting to see that. Not for the press screenings, because a lot of the press didn't quite know what to make of it—didn't respond to it. But to see young people respond to it was wonderful.

But one of the worst things that happened to me was that I went to Cannes with it and it seemed that Warner Bros. had had one of the secretaries on the lot—I don't know how big the department that does subtitles was in those days— but some woman had transcribed *Woodstock* in the way that she thought she understood what people were saying. And it turned out that she hadn't a clue what a lot of the rock lyrics were or what people were saying in just some of the normal interviews. I realized the enormity of it all, when Sly and the Family Stone came up and Sly was singing, "I want to take you higher," and in the French subtitles it was saying, "I have to have a Honda, I have to have a Honda!" And I was saying, my God, what is that?

And then I realized a tremendous number of the subtitles were completely incorrectly translated. First of all, incorrectly transcribed by somebody who had not a clue about this sort of culture, and secondly translated horribly. So all over the world, in Czechoslovakia and Indonesia and wherever, Sly and the Family Stone were singing, "I have to have a Honda; I have to have a Honda."

And from that point on, I have always supervised heavily the transcribing of all of Scorsese's films and I then follow through on the final version before it's sent to the translators. Because even the best transcriber—the most skilled—sometimes don't really understand the director's intent or they get something wrong.

Not as bad as *Woodstock*, but it's made me understand the importance of following through right to the bitter end to make sure translations are done correctly.

Oh, by the way, one of the things that should be noted is that *Woodstock* is one of the last films to be printed in the old Technicolor process. *Woodstock* and *Godfather II*, before they knocked down the Technicolor plant. It doesn't mean it was filmed in Technicolor, but they were doing Technicolor prints using the matrix process up until a certain point when someone, in their infinite wisdom, decided to knock down the plant.

DALE: There is a place, I've written about the end of this whole thing…the technical aspect of all that I think is well enough covered. But I didn't mention the YCM.

THELMA: No, not YCM. It's Technicolor, or just say imbibition.

DALE: Spell that, please.

SONYA POLONSKY

IS OPTIMISM GONE?

(SONYA WAS THE MOVIE's production manager.)

SONYA: There was the world that we reached out to, which we used to call the straight world. (And there was the inside world of the people who supposedly were a part of that generation. I think the people who were on the inside didn't feel like it was that representative of them. Especially the political people.) And the people in the straight world liked *Woodstock*. Like the people who were interviewed in the movie. They expected to see some sort of horrible, decadent stuff. And they didn't. They saw these lovely kids having a good time. So they liked that and many people say that it was supposed to be the beginning of a generation. It was really the end. So I don't know what it meant to people. I know what it meant to some people. That it was a great documentary.

And there was a whole spate of music performance documentaries afterward, for almost ten years, that I believe imitated it and badly. I think they thought it was an easy formula to success. And they missed the wonderfulness of the film itself. And the painstaking care that was taken with the performances and the way they were optically presented. And I think also a lot of television music was shot for several generations and possibly still is, in an imitation of the form that was probably basically developed on *Woodstock*: the three cameras moving a lot and jumping around, which they do very mechanistically and sort of perfunctorily on television. But which in *Woodstock* was really beautiful and really meant something.

So I see a huge impact on filmmaking, just from what has followed. The different kinds of documentary-making about music that I think was imitative of *Woodstock*. But there I might be ignorant. It might have been going on before and I don't know.

DALE: You teach, and you teach film history and film editing to younger people. What do they say, when they find out that you were one of the principal people who helped make the film?

SONYA: Some of them have asked me if it was the recent *Woodstock*.

DALE: You mean 1994?

SONYA: Not because I look so young, but because they can't really believe—I think—that anyone that they know who's living and that they call by their first name is actually old enough to be associated with that movie. And for all they know, I was twenty when I was associated with it. They don't know that I was almost thirty. I showed them the opening of *Woodstock* because I had a documentary class; we were talking about openings, and I wanted to show them Sidney Westerfelt. I was talking to them about prologue openings and as far as I'm concerned that's the prologue opening to end all prologue openings. I think it's great. Some of them surprised me by knowing all about it. Which heartened me, because I thought they might not even have heard of it.

DALE : And what kind of reaction?

SONYA: When I was watching the opening with my class, first of all I felt that it was a lot slower than I remembered. I think it was the reedited version. And I think it is slightly different in the beginning. But it might be me. I mean, these kids are a hundred times faster than me, but maybe even I've speeded up since thirty years ago.

But I also felt very sad. It felt very optimistic to me. I think that it makes me feel sad and possibly—but maybe I'm just imagining—it might make people my students' age feel bored; that kind of optimism, they think it's sappy, I think. They're about twenty-nineteen, twenty.

DALE: Optimism is sappy?

SONYA: I think so. 'Cause they're into irony and being cool. And they only like things that are obviously satirical. They don't like displays of emotion, they think it's sentimental. There wasn't any emotional display in that opening of *Woodstock* it was just that it was all these beautiful young people riding around, and everything kind of golden and nice, and this nice country blues song. So it made me sad, because I felt like it was a feeling of optimism that seems to be gone.

DALE: Gone in the present generation.

SONYA: And gone in life. Gone from me.

LISA
LAW

THE HOG FARM LIVES

(LISA'S PERCEPTIONS AS A Hog Farmer with Wavy Gravy are a part of her *Flashing on The Sixties* book and video.)

Woodstock was the first music festival I attended where there were more of us than them. (Not forgetting the smaller Fantasy Fair and Monterey Pop festivals preceeding it.) We (the Hog Farm) were in charge for awhile, with the blessings of Michael Lang, and it was heaven. We knew what to do because our communal experiences had taught us how to share and care and feed large numbers. Only this time, there were four hundred thousand on the grounds and two million trying to get there. The cops collaborated with us and the result was three days of peace and music. We set up trip tents for those who'd taken too many drugs, helped in the medical tents, and fed one hundred sixty thousand hungry people. I know that's how many people we fed because that's how many plates, cups, spoons and forks we bought with the six thousand dollars I got from the promoters to go into town for supplies. (The food concessions had sold out on the first day.)

Although I documented the events as they unfolded with my trusty Nikon camera, I also captured many magical moments using my Super 8 camera. With my two-year-old daughter Pilar on one hip, six months pregnant with my first son Solar, and my camera in hand, I shot whatever I was doing and the myriad of activities happening behind the scenes. I documented moments both on the ground and in the air that have been used in over fifty films, including my own documentary, *Flashing On The Sixties*, which is dedicated to the memory of that special time on the rolling fields of Yasgur's farm.

The participants of the concert know what went on in those fields in Bethel, New York because they were there…experiencing the rain, the music, the mud and the oneness of it all. But the film, Woodstock, documented by over fifty dedicated camera men and women, brought those harrowing moments to the screen so hundreds of thousands of people could share in the joy, the passion, the one mind, and the birth of a nation.

Woodstock was a concert of young people looking for something real to relate to in a country that was engaged in a senseless war, with its soldiers being brought home in body bags. It was the soul of the1960s defining itself, a point in time that will live forever as a cultural milestone and one of humanity's more blissful moments.

The spirit of that weekend, the vibe that created the Woodstock Nation, still lives today in people all over the world. It's the elevated consciousness that drives us to save the planet, to make things right for native cultures, and to revere all species of animals and plants. These concepts weren't born there but they came together there, and dispersed from there to all parts of the world, spawning a new generation of mindful youth.

JONATHAN DALE BELL

WOODSTOCK THROUGH THE MILK GLASS

(AT THE TIME OF the festival, Jonathan was eight years old.)

Dale: Saturday, August 9, 1969. As a film team, we had just concluded our first rekki of the site. Could we ever pull it off?

As I was driving down the New York State Thruway back to Grand View on Hudson where my family lived, I was astonished at the number of people who were not going my way. Laden with backpacks, dressed in floppy clothes, driving old cars, they were trekking toward Max Yasgur's farm. Within days, they would become so numerous, they would clog the Thruway for a hundred miles, forcing it to shut down for the first time in its young history.

I was reveling in another world. I couldn't wait to tell my wife, Anne, about the camp grounds. Huts had been made with branches. Stones were gathered to create fireplaces. Tipis stretched skyward. Wood chips were scattered beneath pine boughs. Paths led from one hamlet to another through the woods and over the fields. Swings on ropes dangled from tree branches high above the ground. (Wouldn't our oldest son, Jonathan, love climbing up there!) Kids are skinny-dipping in pools. Domes are made with bent branches. Smoke from a fire curls upward through a hole in the center. A sand box as big as our house is there for the playing. Slides beckon children and their parents. The dress of the first arrivals is bright; weird, colorful. Long beards and long hair as men and women, with their children hand in hand, cavort about the landscape. Music is everywhere. This is going to be heaven on earth! A veritable Eden with green meadows, stone fences, and empty vistas as far as the eye could see. All enveloped in music.

Of course, it never crossed my mind that drugs existed. Or that they would be a part of this scene. I was much too innocent.

Oh, how I wanted my family to enjoy this outing. Maybe, I thought, all three of the kids might be able to come up. Maybe the film team would not be working too hard. We couldn't film everything after all; just a little here and there, right?

Maybe we will all just have a fun picnic!

But another part of me did know better....

Jonathan: It was spring 1969 and my parents were having more than their usual amount of Almaden wine parties on the sun-soaked porch of our Victorian home overlooking the Hudson. Laughing guests with hands holding cigarettes gestured in attempts to define the space needed to accompany their grand visions of what was going to take place. They randomly took turns participating while others sipped and listened. Participating in what, I didn't know, but I knew it was a "project"; a "film project." The topic was a recurring theme for the next couple of weeks.

While the grown-ups talked, my brothers David, Andrew and I continued playing G.I. Joe; battle of the driveway and search and rescue missions in the pachysandra ground cover, oblivious to one of the central anthems of Woodstock: to stop the Vietnam war.

Weeks churned into months and the bills began piling up. I remember Da, my father, spending a lot of time at his big desk in his worn leather chair with the phone on his shoulder as he typed furiously into the worn out ribbons of his father's Smith Corona. There were many moments of elation and disappointment which often ended up in the form of arguments between my parents. To my knowledge all of them seemed to be about money, burnt coffee or burnt bacon, which caused my mother to go food shopping often. I always wanted to go on these trips. I think it gave my brothers and me control over some of the food we'd get to eat, especially breakfast cereals, since you can't burn cereal. My brothers and I lived off that stuff and, of course, PB&J sandwiches.

Life was good as I knew it to be, playing with my Bro's and friends. Da was always photographing us with the Leica or the Bolex. I know I'm one of the few kids to have home movies of myself in sixteen millimeter. My mother took those pictures and turned them into portraits. She often painted outside on the driveway as we played in the trees or pretended to help Da with the yard work. Ah, summer life was good.

About a week before my parents left for Woodstock they sat us down to have a talk with us, explaining that they were going away for awhile and that Grandmother was going to come and take care of us. I think we were all a little worried and bewildered as to the reasons for our beloved parents leaving on an adventure without us.

Of course, having Grandmother come to stay meant getting more G.I. Joe stuff, a trip to the toy hobby shop, unlimited television, and very late bed times. After considering these benefits my brothers and I wished Mommy and Da good luck on their trip and worked on tactics, figuring out what new equipment our Joe's would need.

The first action figure I got was a Sean Connery doll—yes, as in Bond, James Bond. He lasted quite a long time even after most of his accessories were lost. However he was never the same after our Dalmatian Sparkle got a hold of him. From that moment on he was destined to forever be one of the walking wounded. Half of his head was gone, similar to what happened to the President Jack Kennedy, my father's fallen hero. Sean had also lost part of his foot and an arm, which I thought was unfortunate, but I saw no reason why he shouldn't become the enemy in our many sorties to come.

As I think back and remember these images I can't help seeing the similarities between my Bond doll and the fallen soldiers of Vietnam. I remember the first time I saw Da cry, it was when Bobby Kennedy was assassinated. He was watching a huge wood television we had when we were living in Washington DC. His face was practically in the black and white screen with tears crawling down his cheeks. I looked at him for a couple of moments to make sure of what I was seeing, then asked him why he was so sad. He explained that our next President of the United States had been killed. We marched in Bobby's funeral procession down the streets of Washington singing "Glory Glory Hallelujah" and I felt sad with a sense of loss because my parents felt so lost; walking with hundreds of other people, souls drained, their eyes drenched and scanning the night sky for answers.

This was my first real taste of death on a human scale. Of course I'd seen death, in war and monster movies and the occasional animal smushed in the road. I guess that's one of the reasons I got a severe whipping for crossing the street without permission because my father knew the cause and effect of an unforgivable road or river. I'd seen his pain once before and I know he'd be damned and devastated if he lost one of us. He wasn't going to let that happen even if he had to hurt us. We weren't allowed to play in or around the river either without some guardian watching. Anyway, we promised to be good and obey these basic rules of survival and mind our Grandmother, which was pretty easy to do. They kissed us good-bye and left for WOODSTOCK.

The morning of the journey started early. Da woke me up by taking the bottom mattress off my bunkbed. I saw the red ball of sun stitching pink light around the rims of purple clouds that stretch across the sky and reflect in the river. That sun beam finds your window no matter where you are on the west bank of the Hudson valley and that still holds true today. Mommy was already downstairs making coffee carefully (no need to start the day on the wrong foot) and peanut butter and jelly sandwiches. Those sandwiches must have been at least two inches thick. We all still make them that way but you gotta have a lotta milk. Da was in the process of stuffing the mattress into our almost new blue and white VW micro bus complete with dome hubcaps, split panel windshield and rubber bumpers all around to prevent the doors from banging into each other.

When I think about it now my parents really didn't take that much stuff: a couple of sheets, two blankets, some jeans and flowered shirts, a leather jacket, some fringed belts and some food, water and coffee. That's a fraction of what my wife and I take when we're going away for three days. We bring food, pillows, reading material, lumbar support, pagers, a phone, schedules, several suit cases (one just for toiletries), golf clubs, video camera, laundry bag, plastic bags and of course the Bank Card.

The Alpha and Beta wolves were gone for about five days while the rest of the pack played and played all the live long day. I think that's what my parents were doing, too, only in a different way. They didn't know until after they got back that they were part of something so monumental that the full impact would not be realized for some time to come.

We were so happy when Da and Mommy returned, since an eight years old kid can only go so long without his Mommy. She was smiles, hugs and kisses and we all ran to her at once, holding on, not wanting to let go. I think she was wearing some different clothes that I'd never seen before. Pretty soon after that there were a lot of new or "different" clothes added to the wardrobe.

The guise that comes to mind was a pair of bells as in bellbottom jeans tied with a leather fringed belt with beads woven into it and a white tank top with a black silk screen peace sign in the middle of it and her head topped with a macrame head band. Now this sounds too stereotypical to be true and I'm not sure this was the exact attire my mother arrived home in, but this ensemble did exist, and I do remember the head band the belt and the jeans.

My father's entrance was also dramatic in that he too had changed in some way in less than a week's time. The one item I remember particularly he wore around his neck: a set of beads made from wood, some in the shape of skinny black thread spools with tan cylinders in between them. I asked him about them and he said they were "Love Beads." To complete the package was his beard and denim shirt and pants that were held up with a leather fringe belt that had no buckle— that was the new Da that had returned.

Although there were some new facets to my parental units, there were a lot of things that stayed the same. For instance all the old rules still held fast—whatever happened to free love or just freedom? We actually did have a leash that was way longer than today's standards.

Sometimes we were gone all day up on the mountain with our dog team pulling our wagons to the latest "lean two" or "wigwam" we'd built; we were totally into Indian lore and bush craft. But some new things that were introduced into my life began with music.

We always had the hippest new music, or so I thought and I started with playing the drums, then moved on to piano lessons in the third grade. Da would always buy the latest Beatles album and we'd play it and sing it and dance to it on his shoulders, or be dragged around the floor interspersed with faux gymnastics and a round of "army frosse" which was really pronounced Army Horse. This game let the pups, my brothers Andrew, David and myself, test our strength in bringing down our father or letting him carry us off the playing field (which was the living room rug) while the music was the driving force that accompanied these activities.

Suddenly a whole new slyle of music began to infiltrate the Bell household. Some of the most notable new bands for me were The Who, Crosby Stills Nash & Young, Santana, Jefferson Airplane, Jimi Hendrix, ShaNaNa and Sly and the Family Stone. One thing I didn't understand was why the Beatles weren't in on this adventure. That question still remains unanswered to this day. I didn't know very much about the Rolling Stones at that time, but I remember the first time I saw the Rolling Stones on Don Kirshner's Rock Concert and my Grandmother called Mick Jagger a simpleton. He was wearing blue eye shadow and a sequined blue jumpsuit.

Just when I thought things were settling down I learned about the cutting process of film. Up until now I thought that the "project" was done and we were getting back to our normal way of life with a couple of added perks, give or take a few.

Now it's November and we are planning to go to California, not just anywhere in California but Hollywood. To be more specific Sunset Blvd. and Orlando Ave where Michael Wadleigh, the director of the "film project" had a production company set up to do all the editing.

We arrived sometime in December to Michael's lair, which consisted of one main house and two other buildings that were more like guest houses or cottages. One of the guest houses had living quarters, two cots and a small kitchen. The living room had editing tables with milk glass to view frames of film at a glance, complete with hand crank reels, viewers, and cloth hampers with racks attached to hold to the film clips. The pool house was converted to the main editing suite that held the Steenbecks, which ran the edited footage in sync with the sound track so they could watch complete sections to determine how to assemble and shape the film.

I considered anything on the cutting room floor fair game for my own editing experiments and I was soon given a small corner with my own reels, splicing block and viewer to cut my scraps together. I think the editors did this to keep me busy and quell my endless questions. They even made me an honorary assistant editor, or so I thought they did.

When I became tired of my little scraps of film—this was after running them forward and backward faster then slower numerous times over—my brothers David, Andrew and I turned to the empty shipping cases for amusement. We had discovered a crawlspace below the main house and thought it would be an excellent place for a fort or our own secret production company. Using a hammer, nails and a saw and the wood and foam from the packing crates, we made a sofa, a chair, and a table lo set up shop. The only trouble was that our clients had to be eight years old or younger because they wouldn't be able to fit in our waiting room without getting their knees dirty.

Another place to play was the foam room which was adjacent to the swimming pool separated by glass sliding doors. This was where all the excess packing material was stored which had to be used again to reship when the rental was up on a particular machine. We'd bounce off the walls, dig tunnels and get all hot and sweaty before jumping into the pool, a great perk since we had never had the pleasure of a private pool. I remember that we all went swimming in the nude on Christmas day and except for the waterslide being kinda dry it was a totally free experience. So natural and fun without any inhibitions. Most everyone participated in swimming, giving gifts and having breakfast. It was the closest I ever came to living on a commune, and I think it was for my parents, too. One day Michael drove his motorcycle through the house and into the backyard. LA was cool back then.

When winter vacation was over we had to go back to school in New York. I think we were all glad to be back home again, especially with our friends, because we basically had to play with and amuse each other in California since we didn't know any other kids.

The wonderful life we lived continued in Grand View. That's where I still live today, with my adoring wife Anita and baby Bell daughter Belinda and frisky Dalmatian Bluebell. Almost all of my childhood friends are still here or in the next town over and they, too, had their lives influenced by the Woodstock movement.

Most of them knew about Woodstock from me, or from their older brothers and sisters. I would play the three LPs constantly, and knew how to sing all the songs and all of the dialogue including the stage announcements: "Alan Fay, Alan Fay…would you please come to the information booth please your friend is very ill…please come to the information booth man it's a bummer please…" When I was in High School some of my friends and I made up a fictitious student named Alan Fay and had one of our buddies from another school enroll as him, so we could enjoy the announcements over the school PA system searching for him when he failed to show up for class. "Alan Fay please report to the principal's office." "Oh yeah we just saw him at lunch time." We kept that joke going for a long time. I think he almost graduated with us.

When the movie came out I was still in grade school and had already seen a private screening with my parents and most of the production team. I don't think I made it all the way through the first time because it was mighty long and wore on into the night. But what I did see was an eyeful and man was it powerful and loud. The fat sounds of the Sha-Na-Na all flash and 1950s rockabilly, mixed with intensity of Richie Havens singing about freedom while he dug ditch with his pick into the side of his guitar while sweat poured off his face, into soulfulness of Joan Baez's piece "I dreamed I saw Joe Hill Last Night" about a man who had died, then reappeared in a dream. Then came the rich but delicate whispered harmonies of Crosby Stills Nash & Young with Stephen Stills singing about the break up of marriage in "Suite Judy Blue Eyes." After that the power chords of the Who rocked the world with "Listening to You" and Hendrix amazed us with technique and sounds that had never been seen or heard before. And no one had ever seen fro and funk like Sly and the Family Stone. All of this auditory and sensory stimulus was then split into multiple screens. There was no way to take all of this in, but it was done in such a way with measured doses that the audience could experience sensory overload, but was then brought back down with the testimonials and interviews and activities that were interspersed between the music acts. Brilliant. I've since seen the film at least a dozen times and listened to the albums well over a hundred times. I still get that visceral feeling of being there, even though I wasn't.

I grew up and had my rock band in high school play many of my favorite songs so I could perform these songs myself and bask in the glory of it all. I went on to study music through high school and college and graduated with a Bachelor of Arts in Music. Today I write music for myself and for films, but work most of the time as a Director of Photography on films and videos. My father told me it was damn difficult to make a living as a musician and said I'd better become a cameraman. I said, "No, Da, I'm a composer, not just a musician," but I took some of his advice anyway and decided to do both.

Not long after the film came out I put away the G.I. Joes and became interested in girls and music and found that love not war should make the world go around. I want to thank my Mommy and Da for making me the person I am today and teaching me to feel and be passionate about the things I believe in. I love you both so much.

Your number one pup,

Jonathan

Grand View, New York

October, 1998

MARTY ANDREWS

THE MEANING OF WOODSTOCK

(MARTY WAS ON SITE as the movie's technical wizard.)

After all that was done at Woodstock, and all that has been said about it in thirty years, what does it all mean?

Woodstock was clearly the apotheosis of the hippie culture. Those revolutionaries, who "dropped out, turned on and tuned in" to do their own thing, manifested their antipathy to the moribund eslablishment through their style of dress, speech, drugs and music with an emphasis on peace and love. Woodstock embodied and epitomized all of this.

The pendulum of history perpetually swings movements in and out of vogue. After some very bad economic times at the end of the nineteenth Century, World War I and the lifting of the stupid Prohibition, our fathers (swells) cut loose and boozed it up to hot jazz with our mothers (flappers) in the Roaring 1920s. Fashion, style, language and music were revolutionary quantum leaps away from the Stephen Foster, square dance, and Church socials that had preceded them. Their party was suddenly shattered by the Crash of 1929 and the Great Depression.

For us, the energetic American accomplishments (settling the land, industrialization, transportation, communication, winning two World Wars) engendered by free private enterprise, had been perverted into the free private avarice of mindless consumerism and the military/industrial complex. It was time to have some fun, and we "kicked out the jams." It couldn't last—and it didn't. Nixon's criminality, the killing of King and his dream for the Blacks, and the killing of Bobby Kennedy, buried the white dreams. Our party was ended as definitively and as abruptly as the Depression had ended our parents' party.

Ironically, the consumerism we ridiculed and despised backfired on us, as, through *Woodstock* specifically, the schlockmeisters discovered the Youth Market;

and Walt Disney, a movie company, makes more annually than half the nations of the world.

Our parents' party had no agenda. Ours did. We were politically savvy: we got our country out of a war in which it did not belong. If that wasn't a historical first, it's certainly the greatest example of one.

If you are hip (a hippie), then, by definition, you can see through the shams imposed upon you by the Establishment. Once you're hip you can't become unhip. You can sell out to the establishment to support your family in the Reagan (ray gun) years, but you don't become unhip. You are just completing the forgotten part of Timothy Leary's dictum: "Drop out, turn on, tune in, drop back in."

Watch out! Here comes that pendulum again. At the beginning of this century, the United States was eighty-five percent literate. We are now less than fifty percent literate. We are "luded out" on polarized, partisan politics. The Fourth Estate is completely out of control with the Bill & Monica thing, while the big corporate conglomerates (who now have more rights than us individuals) keep merging and increasing their power. We do not have the ability to outmaneuver the fast-moving, changing viruses (Sub-Saharan Africa is lost to AIDS, which is now assaulting Asia as well), and we face global economic collapse. Worst of all, the consequences of our petro-chemically caused global warming are becoming ever more apparent in the devastating weather disasters and the debilitating economic meltdowns that follow.

With the inevitable insanity attending the century changes exponentially raised by the Millennium factor, there might just be enough time for one more self-indulgent party. After that we will have to get serious and see if our kids can teach us that our survival instincts are sufficient to make the human intelligence experiment a success here on this planet I'm telling my sons (twenty-two, eighteen and twelve) that only Bucky Fuller had the right answers. His philosophy was simple: if you don't bring the bottom up, the bottom will bring the top down, take heed, mega-corporate greed-freaks! Bucky lucidly explains how we can bring the bottom up and make the world work by doing more with less, by advantaging everybody at the expense of nobody.

Perhaps our kids will hate us for the mess we're leaving them. But they can discover the wealth of Bucky's wisdom and wise us up with a Woodstock of their own.

If not, well, at least we'll have had…our Woodstock.

MIKE LANG

SO LARGE, SO STRONG, SO POSITIVE

(MIKE WAS THE EXECUTIVE producer of the Woodstock festival.)

DALE: When you saw the film, where were you?

MIKE: I thought, it was the premier here on...(at) theTrans-Lux. And I remember Steve Ross (Chairman of Warners-Seven Arts) came up to me, (stops to laugh)... and I hadn't met him till then. And he shook my hand and said, "You know, you and Freddy could do anything together." [laughs]. The sky is the limit. And I thought "Yeah." (More laughs). But it was great to see it in that environment. Again, the theater was smoke-filled. All these Warners execs sitting around. And it was an amazing experience. Seeing it on a big screen. After having been removed for eight months. It just impressed me that you felt the presence of the event so well.

DALE: And now that it's out there, analyze for me from the music business side, two things. Two areas: One, how did the release of this movie change how the establishment dealt with young people? With music business, with the record business; was this a watershed? How was it?

MIKE: Well, I'll tell you one thing: that every place that we go in the world and the reason we're doing this thing in Europe in 1999 is because that film brought the festival to the rest of the world in a very real sense. I mean it really...whatever happened in the microcosm up there was brought very viscerally to the rest of the world, and it became almost a generational high point for every country on the planet because of the film.

I've worked in Europe a lot over the years ever since the mid-1970s. It's so well known everywhere. The experience of Woodstock, and you take a poll in America and you ask how many people came, were at the event, and probably five million people will say that they were there. A similar phenomenon happens around the world, they felt so close to the event and it brought it so much into their reality that they felt that they'd experienced it, through the film. And so I think: beyond it becoming an American phenomenon, it became a world-wide phenomenon because of the movie.

DALE: You've used the two words, thank goodness, that I would use. There were only 350 or 500 thousand people there. They served as a microcosm.

MIKE: Yes, absolutely.

DALE: With the film, we symbolized what the festival was all about. For everybody who wanted to touch it, feel it be there, and couldn't.

MIKE: And it did that extremely well, uncannily well, really. And, I don't know if you remember but, we had very little prepress, 'cause nobody knew really what we were up to. But not until the film came out did it really hammer it home to America and the rest of the world.

DALE: What did it hammer home?

MIKE: The power of… music. That culture. The fact that there was this community that existed in America, that was tied together, and that was so large and so strong and so positive. I don't think anybody before the film was actually released—I don't think anybody realized the extent of all of that. And I think it brought home to people that it was not just these sort of radical groups that were spread around here and there in the East Village and Haight-Ashbury, but this was everybody's son and daughter who was involved here.

You look at that crowd, you don't see half a million long-haired Freaks, you see kid with crew-cuts, you see kids from every walk of life. I've always looked at Woodstock as a way for anybody who was a young person during that whole era who didn't smoke pot and wasn't interested in politics and wasn't, you know, a music fanatic and sort of missed the ride through the 1960s? And it's instant access to that generation. You came, you were in, you had it all. It was an open door for everybody, and I think that the film spread that even further. And I think that that may have been its, the festival's biggest cultural impact, at that point.

DALE: How did it change business?

MIKE: (rapidly, assertively,) It changed the music business radically. Because I don't think anybody'd realized the potential, and the power of bands to bring people into a concert. And it went from I think, right after Woodstock, it went from a cottage industry to a real industry. The amount of money that bands demanded from their performance [laughs] skyrocketed! Instantly! I think the day after! I paid Hendrix fifteen thousand dollars, which was the top, I think we paid him two shows. But the top fee was fifteen thousand dollars an act, and three weeks later I think he was getting one hundred and fifty thousand dollars at the Isle of Wight. It just instantly skyrocketed the price of bands and events, at concerts. 'Cause they realized that the bands were really capable of generating that kind of draw and that kind of income.

DALE: How did it change culture? How did it change, let's say, communications? What was spawned as a result of it? VH1, MTV, The way commercials were shot, the style…

MIKE: I think it changed the way America viewed the power of Youth, and their style, their attitudes, their interests. And their commercial viability, for industry. Because suddenly you saw this huge marketplace out there, that was a lot bigger than anybody had previously thought. And so the thinking from Madison Avenue, which was the first thing I saw, suddenly it came out of the 1950s, [laughs] and into the 1960s and 1970s, realizing that this was their future. And things had to start appealing to this culture and these kids, or they weren't going to survive through the 1970s. And I think that was true pretty much across the boards, y'know?

DALE: Yeah. The music. The Establishment coopted it. You know we designed the movie so that it would never be seen on television and kids, audiences would be required to go to a theater and Warner Bros.would then be required to distribute it in theaters. We never thought that you'd be able to scan this wide-screen format, and collapse it to your TV back home. We didn't want that to happen, that was one of the big reasons for making it anamorphic. It's so frustrating, you know, to try and keep it isolated, to keep it away from all that corruption.

MIKE: I'll tell you, the strongest impact that I saw was traveling through the rest of the world, even East Germany; we were in 1987, the twentieth anniversary was coming up and I really, for a lot of years, didn't want to have anything to do with thinking about another Woodstock…because of the film, the impact that it had on me personally for some reason those images of me have just stuck in people's minds so clearly that, you know, it was hard to go anywhere without people saying, "'Aren't you…" kind of thing, but, traveling around through the rest of the world and seeing the impact that the film had on everybody there, and as I said in East Germany, when Mel Lawrence and I—who is someone else you should probably speak with, the Motor-Mouth? Mel was in charge of Site Operations, and was probably involved with a lot of the problems you had [laughs]...

Mel and I were trying to put together a twentieth Anniversary event that would connect East and West Berlin, and my idea was to put a stage over the Wall. I spent two years working with the East German Government, trying to convince them that this was a good idea. And we got pretty close, actually; they had agreed finally. I did two festivals in East Germany, between 1987 and 1989. And funnily enough Warners was the one that screwed it up, because they refused to give the electronic rights up.

But, even behind the Iron Curtain, as it was then, Woodstock was such a legend, because of the film, that everybody identified with it. Even some of these guys who were very hard-liners in the Government warmed to it, because of the film. So the effect that it had politically as well as emotionally around the world was amazingly strong.

It was...there's a guy in? Yansovka? who was a Polish artist, and told me that he...he related some story of the soundtrack being played. And he was listening to it in a Russian tank. [laughs] I mean, if you talk to some of the people from Eastern Europe or Western Europe, and get their impressions of what the film brought them then, I think you'd be amazed to hear the stories.

We're going to do some of this by the way, in one of the docs; we're going to be interviewing people from around the world, people especially behind the Iron Curtain because for them it really became their link to freedom in that way, and connected them with the Youth Culture and here, which was sort of the core of it during the 1960s. And they became bonded, through the film. And through rumors of the film, and through the record that came out of the film.

DALE: Talk about *Gimme Shelter* [the movie made by Al and David Maysles about the Rolling Stones tour in the fall of 1969 and early 1970.]

MIKE: I think that *Gimme Shelter* kind of shows the dark side of what can happen within...given the same group of people. And for me it maybe showed something different than it showed to anybody else. Because Altamont did not have to be the horror that it was. It was because of a lack of preparation; and something that I always believed and in preparing Woodstock I went to every festival that year where there were a lot of problems. I mean I don't know if you recall that summer but...

DALE: Even Atlanta. One hundred thousand people?

MIKE: Yeah, Atlanta had less problems, it was mostly caused by…different kinds of problems, I shouldn't say less, cause they weren't prepared for the heat on that field and didn't really think through what they had to do for that crowd…But in Denver and other places there were riots and people crashing gates and confrontations with police, a lot of tear gas at some, and it occurred to me that they were always caused by the attitude of the planners, which is, you know, let's confront these things, rather than trying to dispel them or cure the problems before they occur.

Which is why when we planned Woodstock, we planned free kitchens, free campgrounds, we had a free stage, we had speakers set up in the free camping areas so that if people came, (and had we had gates which of course was a moot point at the festival,) but had we had gates people who hadn't had tickets weren't just pushed out of the way and they weren't confronted, they were taken in, and taken care of.

And Altamont, was…the problems at Altamont were caused by little or no planning, and bad decisions. Having the Hells Angels as security for example was a monumental…fuck up. And it comes out of the fact that the people who planned this were from London, didn't really understand what the Angels were, or how that functioned and so you placed a group who was pretty paranoid anyway 'cause of the attitudes of the public toward them, between the stage and 100,000 people, and they're there to defend it, that's what they're going to do. There was more acid eaten that day, than anyplace else that I've ever seen in my life. And…had it gone any other way it would have truly been a miracle.

So to me, as I say, it just means that you have a huge responsibility when you put a crowd like that together, you can't just expect it to work and function on its own and think its way through this. You have to at least provide an environment that lets it happen, the right way. And I know that it is kind of Christ/Anti-Christ stuff that the way people refer to those two events as bookends. And in a way maybe there is some of that element but I think you know, if you look at that film, I don't know if you can see through the film but having been there, this became very clear that a hundred feet out from the stage, none of that was going on. This was all stuff that happened tight-in, lot of pressure; it was transferred to the crowd by the artists who were very involved in all of the insanity that was going on in front of the stage, but the crowd itself was very peaceful beyond that. Initially. Hundred foot parameter.

In terms of the lasting effect, I think that Altamont was looked at as a local phenomenon, you know, a California kind of madness. It did not have the penetration that Woodstock had, anywhere in the world and didn't really represent a dark side of that culture, so much as just a bad incident.

DALE: What of *Gimme Shelter* still remains? How do we still see the remains of that kind of dark side in our culture today? Where do we see it?

MIKE: I think that we relate it to the madness that we see when it comes up. To the Mansons and the serial killings and the horrors that come up in the news every now and then, and that probably occur on a daily basis in this country. But I don't think that's a fair analysis of it. I think that it may be, you know, shows what excesses can do; excesses of drugs and alcohol can do to a person. But I don't think that is a fair analysis of what happened at Altamont.

DALE: You don't think the skinheads and the tattoos and the swastikas and the burnings and the...that's not a reflection of that, years later?

MIKE: I think that's a reflection of some of the elements that were involved at Altamont, but I don't think that's what the event was about at all, I don't think that's what the experience of the audience was, or is why they were there. For the most part I'm sure there was some of that but I think that...I mean I spent that whole day on the stage, a lot of it on top of a truck. Some of it being carried off stage by this guy named Animal, who was one of the Angels wearing this wolf's head. And, it was circumstance, it was...you know, there were some very strange people there who were very stoned, and there was a group of Hell's Angels who were put in a very difficult spot and were given the responsibility to respond to this crowd. I mean it wasn't that they came and decided to do this on their own, they were hired to do this. Wrong people wrong place wrong time.

So I don't think that it's indicative of the nature of everybody who came, or even that, the general nature of the crowd. And I don't think it carries over to the skinheads and...I mean you got to remember that the Angels were involved in dozens of concerts in California, they were very peaceful, had nothing to do with this kind of violence or this kind of outcome. And it's because they weren't put in that position. This was just, as I say, bad planning and bad timing. No planning, really.

DALE: In Woodstock did we glorify the drugs too much?

MIKE: I think it would have been hard not to because a lot of it was so humorous and so charming, in a way. And so much a part of the culture anyway. I think maybe we highlighted it a bit too much, uh, and so it became sort of the overriding theme, in a way, with everybody being high; but I don't think that was even the case at Woodstock it was just the idea, that if you were getting high and sharing it with people that was the essence of it. I don't think that the drug culture per se is what that was all about. I think it was youth culture, not drug culture.

DALE: When you say, well, what about nakedness, but the overriding thing was peaceful.

MIKE: Absolutely. It was peace and it was a coming together of people in very much a real community spirit. And people opening up to each other, I think that was the essence of it that everybody came and found each other. And opened up to each other in a positive way, I really think it's beyond any of the specific drug thing or the nudeness or the music or anything else, it was just how people interacted with each other. That given the right environment and the right chance and the opportunity, people will act that way.

The same thing happened in 1994. I mean I can't tell you how weird it was for me to be pitching this idea to Saugerties New York, a community that went... it's very similar to Bethel or any other small town, same kind of attitudes, every conservative in a lot of ways, people went, the first reaction was "How are we going to defend our homes? These people are going to come and rape our wives and our daughters." Same kind...it was the beyond belief, to me that in this day and age the same kind of things would happen, 'cause I remember very well being in Walkill and being in front of a town meeting and people were voicing the same kinds of things, and they were whistling at me because I had long hair and I said "Listen, these are your kids you're talking about. This is not, these kids are no different. The kids who are coming here are the same as your kids." They just didn't get it.

And the same kind of attitudes existed, and when the kids came, the same thing happened in the town. Go see *Barbara* (Kopple's film about the 1994 festival), you'll see that we didn't have...we had a huge hospital set up. There was nothing in that, there wasn't one case of a person who was sent to the medics because of violence. Not one. We talked to the cops: the same kind of reaction. We talked to the people in the town: (who by the way want us BACK. Amazingly enough.) The same kind of thing happened, and I think that the lesson is that when you give people the opportunity and the environment where they can come together and not be confronted by things that are negative or at all confrontational, people tend to act toward each other with a lot of humanity.

And you know, my thrust, the thrust of my argument to the town in 1994 was that that's why people were coming. They were not coming from the city to stab somebody in the audience, and they weren't coming to Saugerties a hundred miles away to find a house with a woman in it to rape, they were coming to come together and have a great, great experience, and to re live a little bit of all the things they've been hearing about Woodstock from their parents for the last twenty-five years. And that's what happened.

And the truth of the matter is, no matter how much security you have, you cannot control a crowd of half a million people, or 400,000 or 300,000, people who are living in an area for three, four, five days, with security. They have to do that themselves. And you have to create the attitude and the environment for them to do that And to be able to do that. That's the trick.

DALE: Very wise, very wise. Thank you.

AL
MAYSLES

UNCONTROLLED CINEMA VERITE

(AFTER LOSING THE RIGHTS to the Woodstock Festival in August 1969, Al and his brother David went on to make *Gimme Shelter* with Porter Bibb producing.)

DALE: This is December 11, Friday 1998 interview with Al Maysles. I'm in LA and he is in New York. Okay, you're going. Okay, let's talk about *Gimme Shelter*—

AL: By the way, I think that *Gimme Shelter* is being considered for the Library of Congress award. Are you familiar with that?

DALE: Vaguely.

AL: For historical, aesthetic, and cultural acclaim, whatever you want to call it. They come out with a list of some twenty-five films that they honor each year and I think they're considering *Gimme Shelter*. They gave it to *Salesman* several years back.

DALE: Two already. Great. You went to the opening of *Woodstock* the movie?

AL: That's right.

DALE: What was your reaction when you saw this film you might have made?

AL: We were put off. I didn't know how much of the film we saw. We were put off by the fact that there were interviews. And especially the way the interviews were constructed. All the questions seemed to be designed to answer the "well isn't this wonderful?"; we've got the flower generation and everything is just hunky dory, and, instead of even if they had to use interviews, which we felt already a compromise that they shouldn't have in terms of filmmaking technique and in philosophy. If they had to, at least, it would be to open the answers. You know so it would be more revealing and less point of view. So, that put us off and I can't say we stormed out, but we slipped out from the audience.

DALE: When you talk about a tehnique, elaborate a little bit on what you mean.

AL: Well, I guess as most people know from the films we've made, there's probably not many people making documentary films that are as purist as we are about music and narration and script and research. I mean, all that stuff is pretty much thrown away when we make a film. Well, the research is a special thing, when I say research it's not an endless process where there's so much research that by the time you get to make the film you've lost the spontaneous elements of the idea that you've come up with in your research. But, we don't use narration in our films; we don't script it. We don't get people to repeat things; we forego interviewing people. Just as you go to church and God is your guide, in documentary filmmaking the controlling element—the guiding hand, if you will,—is reality and we leave that powerful force to give us what we get so we don't ask anything of anybody and certainly don't interview them. In a word, it's totally uncontrolled cinema.

Now, of course, when you get into the editing room you have to put it together into some sort of structure. That's something else that you can't avoid. In a way ideally, it's just from the point of view of trying to achieve total honesty and authenticity. I suppose if you follow the philosophy to it's brural end, then all you do is show the forty hours of footage, but no one has the patience to see that.

DALE: As we witnessed with Andy Warhol.

AL: Right, boringly so. So, you have to sacrifice some of that spontaneity, but the way I film and the way the stuff is edited, the inclination is for the shot to go on longer because the one thing the reaction shot is usually a part of the shot itself for example. So, this tendency for things or for shots to run a little longer... now I wouldn't expect that one could criticize *Woodstock* the way I mean it happened. *Woodstock* was made long ago so it wasn't effected by the present day kind of cinematographic stylistic nonsense of fast cutting and lop-sided hand held cameras and goofy MTV stuff. I know people can criticize the *Woodstock* use of multiple screens; so far as I saw, I thought it was terrific. Recently I saw pieces from the film at a film festival and I thought that was nifty. And, that's the philosophy.

DALE: Now, carry that technique, that philosophy into *Gimme Shelter*. How did you get involved, what were you trying to do with it and did you succeed?

AL: We wouldn't have made the film if we hadn't had the expectation that it would evolve into something more than just a concert film. The talent (The Rolling Stones) was so great, it might have been easy to do that sort of thing. But, we wanted to go beyond that. We didn't want to control the nature of the story that might go along with the concert. It turned out that just as we were expecting things to go along smoothly it turned out that they didn't, but as it turned out, it was what we got and what we filmed and what we ended up with in the film. It could have been edited differently, could have been shot differently.

I react strongly against the so called "point of view" documentary and because I think that it limits the outcome to the point of view that you start out with, no matter what that is. Maybe you can agree with the politics of the one point of view over the politics of another, but I feel that in a documentary film, which has one obligation above all, it has to be factual. For me, it has a second obligation, that is, to be fair so if there's a judgment to be made, it should come from the viewer. And, the viewer should have a good deal of information from which to make that judgment.

DALE: Well you found yourself in a quandary there when you discovered what had happened right in front of your stage.

AL: Well, what you mean, in that, the question of people being beaten up and so forth. Maybe to drop a camera and take and defend those that are being hurt or something, is that what you mean?

DALE: Isn't that or doesn't that enigma pass through you at some point?

AL: It didn't happen to me, in my case, because I was on the stage, and getting off the stage and getting into the thick of the battle, so to speak, I would of lost what I think we really needed. Which was the point of view from the stage and; of course, we had other cameramen as well. The killing itself I didn't get that. My brother, at that point, was above me on the scaffolding above the stage. Brian, who was the cameraman with him, got it, and in fact, they weren't even quite sure having gotten it because of the quickness with which everything happened. But of course, we discovered later on that it was. There are instances, I'm sure, where something is happening where a moral decision has to be made as to whether it's more important to intercede when someone is being hurt and stop filming even though what you're filming is an essential or nearly essential part of the story. But I wasn't faced with that.

DALE: It's funny because when I did both of my National Geographic specials out of WQED, both of them were on the water. My discussions with the principles in both instances was exactly this: The cameraman is there to record everything. If the boat goes down, hopefully, he will shoot the boat going down. Only in the event that someone is going to be consumed by a shark or where, without his camera, he alone might be able to save that person will he put his camera down. Everybody looked at me like I was crazed. I said I am sorry but that's the rules of the game.

AL: Those would be exactly the rules that I would lay down.

DALE: This was my first encounter with Thor Heyerdahl who had been my absolute idol, you know, since I was twelve years old and saw *Kon Tiki*. He just said "Now I understand."

Al: But you know when you make a film like *Woodstock* or *Gimme Shelter* you know you do achieve the impossible.

DALE: I think so.

AL: If you could look forward or backward on it you say, "My God how can that be done" and there it is-it's done.

DALE: Exactly. I was talking to Porter about this and I discussed it at length, now that I'm doing this book with all the people who helped us make the movie. 1960s in New York, everybody was golden. We were the untouchables. We who were filmmakers—it was a chevron that no one could take off our shoulders. We fought, we were thinking people, we were committed people, we were passionate people, we were urban guerillas. We had a camera, we were honest, we were objective. It all began, I think our godfather was Bobby Drew. He and Mitch Bogdonovich and Kudelski, those two guys designed for us the gear which enabled us to be on our feet making instant judgments about life and death situations in arenas that no one had ever thought people could. We were like gladiators you know.

AL: But, you know without that experience that I had with Drew and Leacock, it would have taken me forever to have reached that understanding of how to do it. That experience making *Primary*, I learned how to do uncontrolled cinema, I built my own camera, you know.

DALE: Right the sawed-off Cine-Voice.

AL: And, but you know having met the right people at the right time and then, of course, the coincidence of having met The Stones and the coincidence of all those things coming together. The Stones' music company, the events of that time, my god, you couldn't possibly have orchestrated those events any more aesthetically appropriated than that.

DALE: What do you think the *Gimme Shelter* factor is still at work in our society today; and how does it compare with a *Woodstock* factor?

AL: Let's see, we have different demons I guess. For most of all these years, and even now, if I look at *Gimme Shelter,* I walk away from that film, there's one impression that I have-most of all that is, oh my god, look at these kids with all that promise, with all that idealism that's lurching somewhere in there. You know, drugs, and whatever else, the energy just can't seem to express itself. I think also that the elements of repression in our society were there then, but it's shifted now. Let's not use the word shift; let's use the word diverted. The energy has been diverted into diversion.

Whereas that music and the kids of that time, the music was a very engaging kind of music. There's a lot of history behind it. If you take the word "entertainment" there was entertainment going on, but it was an engaging kind. Whereas now the entertainment is all diversion and actually it expresses itself in the very way movies are made now and television is constructed now. It's all little pieces of five minutes here and twenty seconds there. Commercials are made up of maybe thirty shots instead of three or four, and it's all dumbing America. Those kids weren't dumb at that time. They were being dumbed by drugs, but the process hadn't been so complete as to dumb them completely.

Now with all of the fact, that people watch kids and older people too watch six, eight, ten, fifteen hours of this stuff a day; all of it diversionary. None of it inspired insight, or to give you pause to contribute to your meditative, contemplative faculties. It's the dumbing of America and I think it's quite a different scene. I'm very disappointed in what's going on right now. It's reaching a point where it's practically prohibited to show anything good.

DALE: You mean anything "positive."

AL: Yeah, "positive" that contributes to those adjectives that I used before.

DALE: When you walk around the streets and you see skinheads and tattoo people and outrageous garb or decoration or body piercing or denigration of body; which of course, also must have some effect on soul and spirit—do you think that comes out or that is symbolic of, let's say, *Gimme Shelter* or *Woodstock* or films?

AL: Those things are so severe that I'm hopeful that kids who do that, it's a rite of passage, but these other elements the cutting down of our attention span through the way the media forms itself now without any content and all style. That's the danger that I see which is so pervasive and so destructive.

DALE: Do you think we as filmmakers bear responsibility and should feel guilty about this?

AL: I don't do that stuff. To help pay for the good stuff, I used to make commercials and I don't make them anymore nor am I called on to make commercials the way I used to. Commercials—they've taken one aspect of advertising that's always been there. They dehumanize the people who are in the commercials in order, I suppose, to highlight the product. When we made the commercials years ago, we used the human factor to help communicate whatever distinguishing the product from another, but now it has nothing to do with a product it's all just—

DALE:. ...the dehumanization, the Ortegay Gassett syndrome. Remember his frightening book, I mean this is the depersonalization and the dehumanization of society.

AL: Well, you know another aspect of that is there's a new book that just came out. I haven't read it but Neil Gabbier just reviewed in the *New York Times*, I think only yesterday. He claims that we all are becoming what we see in, other words, the movie characters and what happens in the movies are who we are and what we do. That's a dangerous trend you consider that there are practically no acts of kindness on television or in the other mass media. Am I not correct about that?

DALE: I'm standing right by your side pointing in the same direction. Oh absolutely, I think the denigration of race, the humiliation of race, the ridicule that ethnic people are subjected to by dint of some Hollywood screenwriter's idea of what a joke is or what a put down is. We are a "put down" society; we're not a positive society.

AL: But, see now taking what I just said now there were practically as I recall I don't know of any acts of kindness particularly in *Gimme Shelter* and yet because it is so authentic a film, it is so correct as to what happened. I have a strong belief that when presented with that stuff in *Gimme Shelter*, you know exactly what it is society is at this point. At that point right, so that by the same token, knowing honestly, authentically how things are and were at Altamont, you're in a better position to know what might otherwise be. So in that way, you're not seeing acts of kindness but to put them into such a film would be fake. There were no acts of kindness when you come to think of it.

DALE: If an act of kindness had occurred at Altamont, you would have included it wouldn't you?

AL: Oh, yeah absolutely. We had heard that there was somebody having a baby and we chased all over the place trying to find it, and it was there, I would suppose, but we couldn't find it.

DALE: Well, we did the same thing at Woodstock. There was one baby born I think, at least one maybe two and by the time we heard of it the baby was born. Yeah you know and basically nothing to film but no I mean we chased those kinds of things down too.

AL: One thing we didn't get into that might be of interest is there were many people when the film came out—

DALE: When *Gimme Shelter* came out?

AL: Yeah. When the event took place, we said, of course, the Stones are there playing this Sympathy for the Devil and that would inspire any group to a riot. My feeling then and now is they just ran parallel to one another. There was not a causal relationship. When you get Stan Goldstein's piece which I'll send it to you, I don't know if this guess is that specifically, but that runs in and out of what he's talking about because he talks about exactly how it is the Hell's Angels got there, and what inspired them to behave the way they did, and so forth. Which all may be very interesting to you.

DALE: Absolutely I'd really enjoy reading it.

AL: The odd thing is that I did more with Michael after the project (*Woodstock*) than before or during. I wasn't involved in the filmmaking, but later on Michael had this dream of doing a film about the American Revolution. So, he hired me to come out with him to Concord and Lexington and we did some filming for his film.

DALE: Well, I remember that I was there with you then with the April nineteenth Society 1975. You may remember we were there, and I think Dick Pearce was there and David Myers was there and Larry Johnson was there. Yeah, we made a very conscious decision then as we were putting that project together to make sure that we got you involved.

AL: Well, he hasn't made use of it?

DALE: Nothing has ever happened with that. It was edited and reedited or assembled and recut and; whatever, but financing was never put together to complete it.

Can you remember what your feelings were in July and August when you were trying to put the Woodstock together and it was slipping away from you? Anything that comes up.

AL: I don't remember, you know; we made an effort, also by the way, to launch the second Woodstock which Barbara Kopple ended up doing. Did you know that?

DALE: Do you have a good batting average now?

AL: We scored zero on that one too.

DALE: How interesting. Well maybe the third time's a charm.

AL: What is the law? Three strikes and you're out.

DALE: Well, you don't have to go that far! There is still time; we can still carry a camera.

AL: We can still score a homerun or even something at first base.

DALE: Absolutely, but you know Mike Lang and John Roberts are planning to put something together for next August.

AL: Are they really?

DALE: Oh absolutely, I've been in touch with them. When I did my interview with Mike and with John Roberts, when I was in New York in September, they were outlining plans. They've got stuff cooking in Vienna, of all places, for August 15,16, and 17.

AL: Now, do you have a filmmaker?

DALE: I think more of this is in the hands of Mike Lang.

AL: But, you might mention that we might want to talk about it.

DALE: Oh, why of course. I mean it would be very funny to ultimately put it together again the way it might have been in the first place. Is that zany or not?

AL: No, it's great.

MARTY ANDREWS

DEATH OF A REVOLUTIONARY FILM

(IN APRIL 1975, THE "April 19 1975 Society Film Team" reconvened in Concord, Massachussetts. It represented the last time some members of the *Woodstock* crew reunited to try to create a film about the earliest known revolutionary event in the nation's history. Al Maysles joined Mike Wadleigh, Larry Johnson, Marty Andrews, Bob Elfstrom, David Myers, and me, among others. Alas, this younger sibling of *Woodstock* was never released.)

I really have to mourn the shelving of Wadleigh's Bicentennial project, because this may be the only resurrection it will ever enjoy. Here was a project with real meat to it, filmed by the *Woodstock* crew plus some newcomers. Boston was celebrating its two-hundredth anniversary a year in advance of the country as a whole, a jump start to get the nation examining itself in the present from a historical perspective. You don't get any more heavy-duty than that.

As usual, I urged Wadleigh to let me shoot. "No way, Marty, I got shooters. You're too valuable to me as a Yankee who knows Yankees and knows how to get these laconic folks to tell their stories. I'm giving you Bob Elfstrom and his soundman to cover Concord. The Maysles are doing Lexington; David Myers is doing Boston with Larry Johnson. Go dig out the stories and make it happen."

Wow! All of a sudden I'm a producer!

Like Merv on the *Sidewalks* shows, Wadleigh was the perfect dinner host to all the crews at the Concord Inn. While the fun of being back in the saddle with the old technical superstars was intense, we also recognized that for feedback purposes we had to recap our days in order to get a sense of the direction in which we were all going.

The political quagmire of the present was being set in the foil of our historical archaeology. Nixon had been deposed after his bloody firing of his attorney general;

Agnew had been cast down in petty, venal disgrace. Jerry Ford, having pardoned Nixon, was parading out his "WIN" (Whip Inflation Now) buttons, along with his Vice-Presiden Nelson Rockefeller. The nation still rankled from the Vietnam War and the assassinations that sounded the death-knell for the hippie fun and love-ins apotheosized by Woodstock.

Paranoia and politicization were running rampant within the government establishment. We interviewed the local police, state police and National Guard, who were generous in revealing the draconian plans they had devised to quell the anticipated second revolution that was to be initiated by the bicentennial we were covering. The government mandated that all official references to the original revolution be prefixed by the word "American" so as not to glorify or in any way validate the concept of revolution. Compare this to Jefferson's dictate that every generation should have its own revolution! They were in every way preparing for full-scale combat with the body politic. They were convinced that the Symbionese Liberation Army was going to blow up the minuteman statue.

They were dead wrong. The people came out to celebrate the first 200 years of America's extraordinary achievements. The Woodstock Nation had generalized their proclivity for public celebration to the general populace. We documented Greater Boston, with its incredible preponderance of highly educated people who either worked for or were products of the fantastic number of institutions of higher education. These folks exhibited their profound understanding of the event in an appropriate sense of upbeat pride.

Once a hippie, always a hippie—as grotesque as that sometimes appears (i.e., not just long-haired motorcycle bums but long-white-haired motorcycle bums). We still had our fun. Elfstrom and I staged a retaliatory Port-O-San sequence. Playing off Concord's "first shot heard around the world," Elfstrom's camera pried its way through a Port-O-San door to find me on the throne, where I announced that the Russians had just launched some sheep into orbit so they could claim to have fired "the first herd shot around the world."

After most of the crew was sent home, Wadleigh, Larry, and I stayed on to crank out bursts of handheld energy, keeping up with Frank Shorter, inter alia, and Erich Segal at the Boston Marathon to ascertain what they thought of the bicentennial.

Those were the post-*Woodstock* days. What a film! Bill Gates, Ted Turner, Richard Branson, Merv Griffin, do your patriotic duty! Don't let this masterpiece "rest in peace." Rain your bucks down and reincarnate *Woodstock*'s younger sibling to the level of historical relevance it unquestionably deserves!

MICHAEL WADLEIGH

FROM COUNTERCULTURE TO COMMERCE CULTURE

(THIS INTERVIEW WAS CONDUCTED in the Spring of 1994 while Mike, Larry Johnson, Jere Huggins, and others were completing the reprocessing of the images and the remixing of the soundtrack in the expanded version of the original movie, which would eventually become the *Director's Cut*.)

Q: Twenty-fifth Anniversary—big thing? Why not fifteenth anniversary?

MIKE: Timing. That's the secret to great comedy. I had no interest in doing this maybe until Polygram started all this shit, where there became a need to remind people what the real Woodstock was really all about. Because in the absence of this movie, what are they going to think? They're going to think it's all about the Pepsi generation.

Q: Did you realize, when you started this, that the other was going to be so commercial?

MIKE: Yes. They only called me about three months ago. And the pitch was—by Billy Gerber and Warren Lieberfarb (of Warners Home Video)—Hey, Wadleigh. Why don't we show them what the good guys are all about? Why don't we do this? Obviously in the hopes of making some money from Warner Bros. point of view. By the way, I've got paid nothing by Warner Bros. at this point. My motivation isn't financial. I truly got hooked by the idea that our movie is the main visual and auditory record of what the whole thing was all about. So why not have the real thing while these fakes are being put on?

Q: So obviously you had already called around and found out what was going on and that was disturbing to you.

MIKE: Yeah. When I first heard about the plans—the moving it from counterculture to commerce culture—I was very upset. Because I know how powerful the media is. And MTV is giving it live coverage, and it's pay-per-view, and it's going to be seen all over the world and I thought, well wait a minute, this is really radically changing what counterculture is all about. You're going to have a situation where it's so formula-ized and corporatized and cutting away to commercials, one could hardly think about it. Can you imagine? We wouldn't have permitted it. If pay-per-view were possible then, with commercial interruptions, I can guarantee you that none of us would have allowed it. That would have been making us cannon fodder—dollar fodder for the mill. That's why I thought it was important to make a clear distinction—have this product out there—so you can see what the real thing is.

Q: What was comforting to see again and what was unsettling? The people who are gone now, for instance.

MIKE: Yeah. That was the single most dismaying thing. It's still dismaying. You hear Janis sing, and as my daughter says, you don't hear people sing like that anymore. You just don't. What a loss. That's the starter. There's Janis, there's Jimi Hendrix, there's Bob Hite in Canned Heat, Adam Wilson, Canned Heat, Keith Moon from The Who, Richard Manual from The Band. Abbie Hoffman is gone, Pigpen is gone, Bill Graham is gone—these people were my friends. They weren't good friends, but I knew them all. It wasn't just that they were in the movie. We hung out sometimes together. Then you kick into selfish gear, and you say, these are some of the greatest musicians there ever were, and now I tune in MTV and what do I get? *Arrested Development*, give me a break. Are these the people who are really upholding this kind of incredible performing ability and songwriting ability and interpreting ability that these Woodstock performers represent?

Q: More and more old timers seem to be signing on Santana, Joe Cocker, Bob Dylan—

MIKE: I even think they're missing the point on that score. If you're recreating the spirit of Woodstock, why on earth are you putting on all these old people? At that time, we didn't have people in their fifties and their sixties in the festival. Why aren't they putting on the best musicians of this generation? That would be in the true tradition of Woodstock. Remember Woodstock, the original one, was content, content, content. The bands were expressive in their lyrics and their music about what was happening in the social issues and politics of the day—the left-wing politics of the day. I would argue that to do a real Woodstock, you would go to the bands of today that are really the kickass speakout bands, whether they're Rap or Latin bands or white and put together that kind of musical statement.

Q: Is there something different about those times, those people that allowed that to happen?

MIKE: I definitely think so. There's a generalized loss of innocence, a generalized instant communication and also a general feeling that the '60s have been lost. That altruism didn't work, that alternativism doesn't work. That it's the end of history. There's one ideology left—free market democracy and a kind of central conservatism. If you're in that kind of atmosphere—like we are today—as opposed to question everything, let's look at all the alternatives, then of course the atmosphere isn't conducive to putting on an event like the original Woodstock. It's more conducive to putting on a Polystock.

Q: Some people might say, "Oh, he's just an old fart. This is the 1990s. We do things differently. Who's he to say?"

MIKE: It's not "we" doing it. "We" don't do things differently. Who's doing it is Polygram and John Sher, who's almost my age. Don't tell me that it's "our" Woodstock. Show me that it's "their" Woodstock. They may have some token teens and twenty-year-olds involved, but I would argue to you that it's not this generation's Woodstock.

Q: Do you think this generation is looking for their Woodstock?

MIKE: I think so. I think they're afraid they're never gonna have it. They're never gonna find it. And that's what I meant about cynicism, pragmatism and a sense of hypocrisy. I think they feel that opportunities are so closed on them that the possibility of getting something on that is theirs and that has a real decency just ain't gonna happen. And they protect themselves with cynicism.

Q: You have a daughter of that generation—what do you kind of see and hear?

MIKE: My daughter's an interesting case in point because she left college and went into marketing. She went to work for BUM Sporting Goods—whereas she said in Taiwan we make the sweatshirts for three dollars and sell them here for sixty dollars. And she found the whole rag trade and marketing to be exhausting and debilitating. She said she came home from work at the end of the day and she didn't feel good about herself. She felt dirty. She felt that she was constantly exploiting people. She made a lot of money, but then she'd try to spend the money by going out on the Upper East Side of New York so she'd feel better compensating. In the end, it didn't work. She said she got more and more cynical, and finally she said, "Okay. Lend me money. I want to go back to school and get my master's degree in education." Because she loves kids and she thinks that education is really important to society. And ever since she's done this, she's never been so happy. The pay is less, but you feel better about yourself. Now she's going to move to Colorado. Why? Because she wants clean air, she wants to go back to the garden. Now if that isn't Woodstockian, I don't know what is.

Q: What has Woodstock evolved to be in their minds, do you think?

MIKE: I think kids are confused about what it was. I think the more spectacular elements stand out in their minds. Like drugs, like nudity, mud, stuff like that. I think they also feel that it's something that could only happen then and could never happen now. That that was an age where there was more freedom. I also think they think it was an age where there were clear enemies. When there was a war going on. When there was definitely segregation left in the world. Fundamental problems. When there was the birth of the ecology movement. Blacks and whites. The shades of gray didn't muddy things up so badly.

Well, here we are in this age where we have nothing but shades of gray. When we have the famous sex, drugs, and rock and roll. Sex, you can't do it without having three or four body condoms on. The innocence is lost with that Drugs—we've now seen that marijuana may be great but heroin and crack and all the other stuff that's going on is just a nightmare. And then rock and roll has gone from rock and roll to Rock and Roll, Inc. So no more can you get these great bands with these great sounds. You get people who have programmed music to get to the chart positions.

Q: Do you think funny little remnants coming out—little fragments, some of the rap groups—

MIKE: I think the Seattle bands have proved that you can be a successful band and not really sell out. That you can talk about fundamental ideas. A lot of their ideas are about getting yourself together, which is very important But I think it's absolutely true that a lot of the 1960s legacy is being an individual, going your own way, not listening, not conforming, and having integrity about whatever the issues are today. Don't go back to those issues, let's deal with the issues we have today.

Q: Does this idealism set this generation up to be marketed and exploited?

MIKE: I think anything today is set up to be easily exploited and marketed because Madison Avenue and this town are so powerful and are so capable of saying, "Right, I see that that's been successful on the news so let's make a buck off of it." The mentality today, much more than then, and the mechanism for it and the money for it is already in place to jump on the next thing that comes along and capitalize on it. And therefore increase the cynicism. Isn't that a lot of what Kurt Cobain talked about in his own angst? That here he wrote this music, and here he was a person and expressed ideals that the kids that he went to school with ridiculed. They were right-wingers. Then he becomes famous and then it wigged him out that they'd buy his records, that they wouldn't even listen to the sentiments. They'd buy it because he was famous, not because of what he was saying.

Q: What about the idea that all the people that were at Woodstock are the population that has ended up on Madison Avenue?

MIKE: Are they selling out? I have mixed feelings about it. I think the 1970s were very hard on people and the 1980s weren't much better. Hard meaning economic realities, facing earning a living. Country Joe told me, Wadleigh, I've got five kids and you know what I've been averaging in income since Woodstock? About $50,000 a year. He said, "I made this Pepsi commercial and you have no idea how much money they offered me. But I did it because hey, if we can't laugh at ourselves …but also if I can't raise my own kids…I'm a working musician."

So of course, since some people didn't have the economic luxury that I did—I don't spend a lot of money so it's easy for me to give up advertising, I used to do commercials. But I just didn't want to do it anymore. I didn't respect that medium anymore. A lot of people will criticize me and say, well, you didn't need the money, but I would point out that a lot of the Madison Avenue executives can buy and sell me in a minute, but they think they need more and more and more.

Maybe what I've retained of the 1960s ideal is that this is about all I need to wear. I don't equate materialism with happiness. It doesn't make me happy. You know what makes me happy? Making a CD-Rom, writing something, making a good film. Making things. Creating things. Bringing things to life. But consuming things is destruction basically. I don't think people are really made happy by destruction. I think they're really made happy whether they're gardening, whether they're making a little toy, writing a poem for their girlfriend, whatever—honestly I think those are the highest forms of happiness. All of which are antithetical to Madison Avenue's, "Hey, buy it and you'll be happy."

Q: Have you ever been approached by Madison Avenue, as Mr. *Woodstock*?

MIKE: Of course, right afterward and over the years I've been approached because all these other famous directors do commercials, and they rediscover—or even *Wolfen*, that I did because it's highly experimental—they call up and say, Wow, we'll pay you a fortune to do a Chevy commercial or some beauty product and I always turn them down. I haven't done a single commercial since *Woodstock*, and I wouldn't do it. I don't have a need for a lot of money, and I simply don't approve of creating dissatisfaction in human beings—which is what advertising is all about. You are unhappy unless you buy our product. As a director and writer for ads, that's what your job is—that's what all advertising says.

My general take on this is that in the future there will be no videotape, this is the future. No videotape, there will be no books, there will be no CDs, there will only be CD-Rom. And what you can do is look at the CD-Rom, just as if it were a video cassette—you can just watch it. Or you can listen to it just as if it were a CD, just listen to the music and it will come in any order you want. Or you can read it as if it were a book, the lyrics, the description of the shots, appended material, bios of the groups—all of that will be available. So this CD-Rom is a step in that direction. To see my movie, you can only see it in a linear way. But this way, you can go into it and access the performers, for example. You can cruise through and look at the music you want to see. You can select any of these songs, you'd get the music, you'd see full video, or you can get the audio or you can get the lyrics.

Q: Who surprised you the most at the festival?

MIKE: Well, I'd never heard Joe Cocker in person before and I couldn't believe how good he was. I'd never seen Santana play.

I would actually enjoy making another concert film. But it's hard to—how do you top this one. Incredible pressure. Dig up Jimi, dig up Janis…all of them.

ARLO GUTHRIE

IT ENDED ONE ERA, AND BEGAN ANOTHER: THIS IS OF BIBLICAL PROPORTION

DALE: Yeah, right! How do you think the movie affected the music business? I mean, up to that point, I'm not sure that the record companies, the music business really understood what kind of an audience they might have.

ARLO: No, I think you're absolutely right, and I think that was the end of it, in terms of the fun we were having and the free-for-all and the fact that nobody up until that moment really thought that this was marketable. And I think after Woodstock everything became part of the market economy. The next day, we were...there was soap named after *Woodstock*, you know what I mean? Blue jeans named after *Woodstock*, I mean, the next day.

I think corporate America realized, "We can sell this." And so we started seeing pictures of sort of natural women washing their hair in streams, you know what I mean? And it has not gone back, I mean, since that day. We have sort of wrapped it up and been buying it and selling the image in various ways for the last thirty years. Which is a shame.

DALE: How does that affect our society?

ARLO: Well, in the long run I don't think it will mean much, it's only in the short run right now that people have bought into it, because frankly, it was only a minority, a very small minority of people who did anything in the 1960s. And yet everyone who was alive gets the credit for it. So, you know, I think that's just the way it works out historically. In the same sense that the American Revolution was probably endorsed by only a few people actually living here, and yet the whole country gets the credit for having thought it up.

DALE: Absolutely, right on. Where do you think it's going?

ARLO: Well, you know in fact, it is still going on, because Woodstock was not a single, unique moment in and of itself. In the context of the times, it was maybe the highlight, but there were a lot of other things going on simultaneously around the world in those few years. And some of it is still going on in places around the world.

I would suggest that the things that made Woodstock so important is that it ended an era. And it began another one. People now would have no concept of the idea that we were living in a country where anytime more than fifty people with hair over their ears were gathered was cause for a police action. There were people actually shot and killed on the streets. Simply for having, for expressing ideas, whether it was about a war, or it was about civil rights, or it was about one thing or another thing.

And we were being told that the people who were participating in all of these were revolutionary, they were dangerous, they were anarchists, they didn't know what they were talking about; and yet, and to this day, when we think of those times, we still fail to realize that the same people who were at Woodstock were in Selma. And the same people who were involved in the Civil Rights Movement were involved in the Environmental Movement and the Anti-War Movement and the Ban the Bomb Movement, and the Educational Movement, and the Power to the People Movement; this whole world is different because it was the same people involved in all of these movements, which we tend to separate in terms of what it was actually about, instead of who participated. And it probably is just a footnote in the history of what was going on, but these people changed the entire world.

And it wasn't just the people that went to Woodstock, because there were people overseas in Holland, in Amsterdam and in Denmark, in Krisitiania and other places where some of the communities and some of the people who were involved in these things are still there, their descendants are carrying on some of the traditions of free thought.

And I tend to view this...I don't want to get too long-winded on you here, but I view this as the Woodstock Generation being the first generation in the history of the world who had the occasion of dealing with instant global annihilation. And that's not to say that the Aztecs or the Greeks or the Romans or the Incas or the Chinese or the Egyptians or the Atlantians or the Vikings or the all these people didn't have great cultures, didn't have a lot of fun, you know, raping and pillaging and partying; but no one of them, and as a matter of fact, even all together, none of them had the destructive power available that was not only in front of us in the years of the Woodstock Generation but had actually already been used.

So it wasn't a question of whether we were going to use this destructive power, the question was were we going to continue historically in the same way that our ancestors had gone, or were we going to do some thing differently, and stop what we saw as an inevitable race toward the destruction of human kind? And maybe other kinds. And we did that.

We changed the course of history. I want to take full credit [laughs] for the fact that we are still here; for the end of not just the Cold War but of all the sort of major difficulties, and I think some of the struggles we've been seeing overseas even now recently are kids who are caught up in the same spirit that we were caught up in Woodstock thirty years ago, are trying to change their own cultures whether in China or Tibet or Jakarta or in Bosnia or in…I can name all the conflict flash-points around the world, and there are generally some kids out on the streets somewhere, reminiscent of what we were going through thirty years ago, who are trying to do things differently so that they can enjoy life.

And that's what we were doing. Thirty years in global time is nothing. So in historic time I think we're still living in that moment, it's just that we're through with it over here and we're on to the next thing, because that's how we're being sort of manipulated by our own buying and selling of what's important.

DALE: Arlo, I think you have made up for "the fuzz, and the New York State Thruway."

ARLO: (Hearty laugh) Well, I have had fun with them, you know, and telling the story of my being there for thirty years onstage, so I'm not…

DALE: I mean, I couldn't agree with you more. When we had an opportunity to do this movie, and we seized the opportunity, I mean it was carpe diem, and we seized the day, only the Saturday before the Friday of the festival where you sang…

ARLO: Wow! Because no one knew. I mean I didn't even know until the day I went that it was going to be the event that…it became in front of our very eyes. It was the last great moment when we were all in the same boat. It was after that we all decided it would be better off to be in separate boats, so that we could get our act together or reevaluate our own uniqueness, or any of the fancy words they use today; but that was the last time we were all in the same boat. Didn't matter if you were black, white, yellow, red, or tan; didn't matter if you were man, woman, clothed, naked, rich, poor, this or that, everybody was in the same boat at Woodstock.

And the fact that we all not only got along, but had a hell of a party, it disproved beyond a shadow of a doubt the theories by the same idiots who proposed the Domino Theory: who told us that if we didn't go over to Vietnam, there were going to be Chinese Communists in New Jersey within two weeks. As if they could have found their way around New Jersey! And we were told by these same people that if those hippies get in control of things, there's going to be stealing, and murder, and injustice, and the American way of life is going to fall apart.

And everybody bought into it! And all of a sudden, when you have a half a million, that's the least number by the way, you have a half a million people all not only getting along, but getting along under the worst conditions imaginable, and everybody going home smiling anyway, this is not just historic. This is of Biblical proportion. And I don't mean that lightly, I think there was a great spirit that moved everything, at that time, and really not only protected us but gave us the right attitude to deal with it.

I'm so pleased to have been a part of that; yeah, it would have been nice to have been able to have been more eloquent, you know, or something like that; or take advantage of the moment; but I've had years to do that now, so I'm not complaining too much.

DALE: Good. Good for you.

ARLO: Adios!

DALE: Arlo, thank you.

ARLO: Sure, man, bye bye.

MIKE SHRIEVE

RECAP: THE POWER OF MUSIC

(MIKE WAS THE DRUMMER for the Santana band, the youngest musician on the Woodstock stage.)

There's no getting around the fact that the power of music is great, and truly, I think that music has the power to heal. I believe to change, to take hate out of people's hearts, and contribute, in a way, to turning negative situations into positive situations.

The power of music is like no other power. What I call it is invisible architecture. Music is invisible, but what other forms are there that affect you so much emotionally that as soon as you walk into it, you can't see it, you can't touch it, you can't smell it, or anything? But it creates this place. Depending on what the music is, it can transport you into different areas emotionally. It can change your life.

Every musician and every artist has their own personal approach to it. I think if you see the power of music then you have a responsibility to use the music in a way that is uplifting and unifying. That's just the way that I feel about it. If you realize the power of it, then I think that you would want to do that.

MARTIN ANDREWS

IN MEMORIAM: TED CHURCHILL

(EDIOTR'S NOTE: TED'S WORK on the Woodstock stage was one factor that propelled him into his innovative work with the SteadiCam. Years later, on the stage of the Opera House at the John F. Kennedy Center in Washington, DC, Ted [accompanied by his SteadiCam] and I worked over the Dance Theater of Harlem's ballet troupe performing Stravinsky's "Firebird." It was the first time formal dance had availed itself of this new technology. Proudly, the one-hour special triggered the Peabody Award for my "Kennedy Center Tonight" series.)

My relationship with Ted Churchill goes back to before he was born. His uncle (mother's brother), Chippy Chase, was a celebrated woodcarver of bird statuary who grew up with my father in Wiscasset. Chippy "met" my mother on a transatlantic crossing when he was thrown through a porthole and landed on my mother's lap. They thereupon became fast friends. Chippy subsequently introduced my mother to my father. They became even "faster" friends as the marriage and children ensued. My mother was Ted's godmother, just as he became the godfather of my first son, Hilary Buckminster.

I had grown up with Ted and his dominant twin brother, Jack (also in the business but not on Wadleigh's team because he was ducking the draft in Sweden), during summers in Wiscasset, Maine. Wiscasset was small enough to force kids within a ten-to-twelve-year age range to play together, dress up in old clothes from the attic for birthday parties, and be driven around in my parents' 1930 Ford Roadster.

I also observed the twins in their active competition in the many events and activities offered by Camp Chewonki, though they were several cabins (years) behind me. I left the camp when they were in their mid-teens and actually lost track of them for a decade until Ted resurfaced in the New York film scene, and Jack had fled to Sweden to avoid the draft.

As youngsters, the identical twins were considered as a unit: the twins. They looked alike and they acted alike; they were always together. They were nonstop fireballs of enthusiasm, energy, competition, and noisy activity. To the discerning, Jack had a huskier voice and was more dominant in initiating their incessant antics of fierce competition. To those who only knew Ted, it was inconceivable that he could be dominated by anyone or anything. He took the competitive compulsion and administered it to everyone and everything with the same exuberant frenzy he had developed with his brother.

Ted and I took part in Ed Lynch's (another Woodstock veteran) foundation of FIVF—the Foundation for Independent Video and Film. Those initial meetings at Ed's place featured our realization that we were onto something radical and new, in contrast to the moribund and exclusive union scene. Ted's enthusiasm and intelligence helped shape our vision of bringing something new, technically and aesthetically, to East Coast filmmaking.

The only job I ever walked off in medias res was a promo for a kids' show featuring a couple of chimpanzees. The trainers were routinely zapping them with cattle prods to the clear agony of the beasts. Ed Lynch, Ted, and I discussed the situation at lunch and then told the producers that they would have to conduct their animal torture and abuse with another crew. Work was hard to come by in those days. It was unheard of, and unprofessional, to turn work down—especially what was to become a series—but we had to draw the line somewhere!

When we weren't being fairly rational and sober at Ed Lynch's, we were freaking out and actively courting "substance abuse" induced insanity (innovation) at my place. I possessed the camera, projection (eight, sixteen, thirty-five millimeters), and quadraphonic audio equipment. My lovely Lizzie supplied the nutrition with style and panache. The Big B was prepared to flip out on command. But it was really Ted, with his bottomless energy and overall readiness for anything, who proved to be the dynamo that drove our antics on a nightly basis.

I was experimenting with what I called four-square filming. I would take an 8mm camera and shoot one side of the film in variable speed bursts on New York City street scenes (Forty-Second Street Be-Ins, etc.), interspersed (with very little editorial intercutting) with similar shots off a television screen. Having finished the roll, I would turn it over and shoot the other half with the camera upside-down to maintain an upright image on both sides of the film. Contrary to normal practice,

I would instruct the lab not to slit the (sixteen-millimeter double-perforated) film after processing. I would then project the film on my sixteen-millimeter projector, giving me four images at once: two similar 8mm images one over the other on the left, showing the subject in forward motion, and two similar images on the right showing the subject/camera in reverse. I would frequently double-, triple-, and quadruple-expose the film. I would also run it through my sixteen-millimeter Eumig camera so that there was a sixteen-millimeter image superimposed over the four 8mm images. I would constantly be opening and closing the aperture so that all these variegated images were fading in and out in organic, fluid dissolves that seemed to sync up perfectly to any music (classical, Hendrix, Stones, Janis, Chambers Bros., Animals, Doors, Byrds, etc.). Multiple exposure was my way of not having to pay for excessive film stock and processing. Two of my notorious quotes (implying my need for thrift) were "it doesn't cost any more to shoot it again," and "keep shooting till the battery runs down!"

The Big B was baking the film pre-exposure and postexposure in Lizzie's oven and shooting stock that had been preexposed to zoom in and outs on a dead bat. Charlie Peck was taking exposed original and unexposed processed film and dragging it along the sidewalk to purposely scratch it! Charlie was the butcher, B the baker, and I became the peripatetic optical bench-maker.

Ah, the halcyon days of the hippie young buck, the avant-garde youth in serendipity run amok!

Ed Lynch was founding FIVF and fantasizing about a pastiche of historical vignettes from eccentric points of view (my favorite being a scene of the Indians skulking away from the Dutch settlers in New York, chortling over having ripped them off for land that was free for everyone!).

While Ted lent his enthusiastic support to all of our "trips" he was pursuing a handheld and fluidly mobile trip of his own. In contrast to our out-of-control wackiness, Ted, though not always exactly sober, exhibited a characteristic, intelligent, self-aware coherence that was unique. He was destined to be and very conscientiously developed himself as the ultimate human fluid "head" camera bi-ped/pod. We were all into hand-holding the camera in order to give it unrestricted mobility. The inherent instability of hand-holding was a problem. I tried to solve this with multiple exposures and the fluidity of the fades and dissolves.

Ted really worked on his technique to keep the camera steady no matter what direction a shot might take. He was much more thoughtful and disciplined than we.

He would really think about a shot before executing it. The rest of us were more likely to just "go with the flow." Ted saw the virtue of this flow and was able to fold it into his obsession for control by becoming the king of single-frame shooting. He would take one frame at a time with his Bolex and choreograph the most elaborate and jazzy studies of stop signs, stop lights, unusual cars, etc. He would circle and move in and out on his subject with a phenomenal sense of control, varying the rhythm of his move by how many shots he would take, ever mindful of the exact effect he was after and fully cognizant of how to achieve it.

Ted was very mechanical. He made a gadget to clamp his Bolex to his bicycle frame. He then fired off his shots with a shutter-release cable led up to the handlebars. He shot the most extraordinary scenes of his travels around New York. The background was ever changing and you could see the front wheel steering the bike in the foreground. What really made the shots, though, was a constant, which was the part of the bike that held the front wheel fork. This bike frame element provided an unchanging frame of reference that aesthetically legitimizes the pixilated wildness of the shot. Ted was fully aware of this and I was there as he made adjustments to maximize the effect.

Later in his career, his design modifications to his Steadicam and firearms became so complex that he had to hire a machinist to execute them. Similarly, he hired a researcher to help him with scientific and psychological studies on the subject of voyeurism, with which he became obsessed. He changed his apartment at Westbeth to face Greenwich Village windows which he could automatically envigilate and record on an elaborate computer system triggered by light and motion sensors.

Ted made a thirty-minute documentary portrait of me called *Hoboken*. The film, shown on PBS, was a portrait of a Greenwich Village hippie and how gaffer tape held my apartment and my life together. It is something of a masterpiece in its bravura, camerawork, and highly intelligent editing. It is a tribute to his integrity that, unsatisfied with his first editing approach, he had the whole negative reprinted and undertook a total recut of the film, at considerable expense—in time, money and effort—to himself. He was a major cameraman on *Woodstock* as well on *Sidewalks of New England*. Ted became king of the single-frame symphony of animated reality.

Ted took a classic backlit shot of me at Woodstock stripping a piece of insulation off the end of a wire with my teeth, with the result that a piece of my tooth broke off and flew across the screen in dazzling backlit glory out of the frame. This shot was such a favorite at screenings that the projector had to be run in reverse and back again so many times that the workprint got totally chewed up. Somehow the original could not be found and the shot couldn't be used in the film.

Ted took up roller skating and dance to perfect his mobile handheld technique. Later he moved up to the Steadicam, developed many custom modifications, and was second only to Garret Brown (its inventor) as its greatest master. His distinguished career was cut short by his tragic suicide in 1997, induced by many factors, not least of which was his being betrayed by some whom he had really loved and trusted. This is my (our) tribute to a unique and fabulous person, an outstanding humorist whose vision extended into the highest technological realization of voyeurism, a key cameraman on the Wadleigh team—a true legend in his own lifetime. Thank you, Ted. May God bless and keep you.

WHERE WE ARE TODAY

ALPHABETICAL

MARTY ANDREWS

LIFE AFTER WOODSTOCK

WOODSTOCK AND I PARTED company when the gang moved out West. I stayed behind to be writer, DP, and editor of a $20,000 (big budget) skin flick. I'd dreamed up the title *Free, White and Uptight* in a cab with Nick Lyme, with whom I had completed a film entitled *Matinee Mistress*. He loved the title, got the $20,000 commitment from one Murray Meadow (a shoe salesman), and we were off. Casting was done at the Executive Hotel in midtown, over the "Quiet Little Table in the Corner" lounge, where married people went to cheat on their spouses and where we had a tab. Two people applying for positions on the crew got the leading roles as actors. Charlie Peck was doing sound. We auditioned a French actress, Louise Lavertue, who turned us on to Pachelbel's Canon, which was popular in France but unknown here at the time. We used it on the soundtrack.

We got further backing from an executive at Columbia Records, which opened up their music library to us, enabling us to use Blood, Sweat & Tears's, Sly Stone's, and Janis Joplin's music. Her "Try (a little harder)" and Vivaldi's "Spring" from The Four Seasons were used behind quick-cut shots of four ski-racers racing head-to-head down Vermont's Magic Mountain resort. This $20,000 skin flick bungled its way (due to fabulous music and production values) to being a $200,000 feature film called *The Ski God* that would have followed *Downhill Racer*—had our lab, Deluxe, not lost our entire negative after we'd spent a year of our lives shooting and editing it. My big chance as writer/DP/editor turned into a seventeen-year-long lawsuit. We taught our lawyers how to bust the disclaimer printed on every roll of film that liability is limited to replacement of raw stock.

We had to produce witnesses, receipts, depositions, etc...We beat a heavily financed consortium of the world's biggest labs. The lawyers then told us to back off for the appeal, which they then proceeded to lose! Instead of getting seventeen years' worth of interest on a puffed-up "investment," I wound up with $10,000 in late wages. I was able to spend $3,000 of this on a thirty-foot trimaran and $600 on a used Volvo. My partner's wife took off with the rest when she left him, taking with her a (perfectly legal) check drawn on their joint account.

I've gone into detail on this because it took seventeen years, and is typical of the catastrophic career I have pursued—or that has pursued me! I've made every mistake in the book that I'd like to write (with this piece as impetus). My upbringing and genetic makeup prevent me from being a hustler in a hustler's game.

Every summer, when the work action heats up, I have taken my three sons to Maine to get them and myself off the mean city streets. I've left the business three times. It started with my packaging film shelter deals (negative pickup of a dozen European films). When film tax shelters got knocked out, we used the same shelter structure on tertiary oil deals. Crazy partners ended this, and we shifted over to solar energy installations in Colorado motels and resorts, in partnership with Exxon, and me as president of the company. When Reagan knocked those out, we moved on to gas deals in Kansas, with an investor (the old shoe salesman) suing us out of business.

Between these attempts at getting rich quick, I managed to dip in and out of the business as a technician. I'd produced a couple of industrials when Bucky Fuller died. I was asked to shoot his office in Philadelphia. The backer I found pulled out the night before. I bankrolled it myself and got Chuck Levey to shoot. He was flawless. Thanks again, Chuck.

Slowly I resigned myself to the fact that my three sons were my real "motion picture productions."

During these hiatuses from the film business I would get my news by watching PBS (Channel 13). I would frequently see pieces done by Chucky Levey and Charlie Peck (Charlie Company). Occasionally their voices would be on the track—and I'd get *Woodstock* flashbacks.

Chuck Hirsch got me on Brian de Palma's *Sisters* as gaffer to some hotshot cameraman from the West Coast who, it turned out, required light readings every minute we were shooting on a ferryboat against a cloudless sky! This was the baddest-vibe film I've ever worked on. De Palma fired everyone, including his best friend Chuck. Marty Scorcese visited the set and started to talk to me. Brian felt slighted. He had some funny friends on the set and filled the limos up with them to go off and screen the rushes. He pulled me out of a limo to make room for one of them, telling me that if I wanted to see the rushes, I could walk to the ferry and then take a subway. He didn't realize that I had the key to the screening room, was to be the projectionist, and had made the deal to transfer the sound and get the syncing done at my old mentor Amin Chaudhri's facility. When I finally arrived, Brian was livid. He didn't even get the chance to fire me because NABET took over the production and I was bounced, in spite of the Taft-Hartley Act (mandating that we be given union cards and kept on the job).

I'd had my completed NABET application on my desk in a stamped envelope for years, but hadn't quite been able to stomach the idea of going union. But *Sisters* forced me to "see the light." I put the extra postage on the envelope (postage had been increased twice while the envelope sat on my desk), swallowed hard, and mailed it.

Once in NABET I got turned on by the members, who were clearly not the swine that peopled IATSE (committed to keeping the effete, educated likes of us out of their cesspool of bigoted brotherhood). I attended electric department meetings, became active on the testing committees, and eventually became head of the department from 1986—1990. I stepped down when my father died and I had to take care of my mother in Maine.

MIRIAM EGER

AFTER WOODSTOCK, I STAYED in the film industry for another fifteen years working as an editor and assistant editor. Our first child was born in 1972 in Union City, New Jersey. He was raised in the Woodstock fashion with long hair, tie-dye T-shirts, and overalls. Five years after being in the States, Jeff and I moved to Israel where we had our own production company. On December 5, 1974, we moved to our house in Ruth Street in Israel, where exactly a year later, our second child was born. At that time in Israel my husband might have been the only hippie there. I think the move and children changed our life dramatically. We were nonconformists in Israel. Our house was always open to guests and we were very laid-back. Our long and involved dinner parties and movie-watching was not a typical Israeli social activity at the time. Probably if I would have never gone and worked on the movie I would have never been introduced to the music and culture that so much helped shape my views and philosophies on life. After seven years, we moved back to America for economic reasons. Three decades later and a world away, I am now a successful real-estate agent.

The twentieth *Woodstock* Reunion in LA made me realize that as painful as it was to leave the film industry, I felt strangely glad that I could look back on those times and reminisce without knowing they would happen again. The other people around me almost seemed like they were locked in a time warp, as if they had somehow taken the environment of the film and the 1960s culture with them wherever they went. It was the first time I realized it was time to move on and that I was not sorry. It was a great experience and a good memory. Whatever the experience gave me, it definitely changed my outlook on life. Looking back it was the best possible way to be welcomed in a new country by this wonderful and welcoming group of people whose values and outlooks on life were so different by their total disregard for social constraints. I was so out of place there and yet in that little cinematic sphere piecing together bits of history, I felt the love and freedom fueled by Woodstock.

ED
GEORGE

SOMEWHERE ALONG THE WAY my 1952 MG wound up parked at Dale's house in Grandview, New York. He refers to it as "The Car That Came to Dinner" and stayed for five years. Yeah, but Dale, it was a pretty funky plaything for your three boys. Then in 1975, I received a fellowship for a MFA in film (thanks for writing my letter of recommendation, Dale) from Carnegie-Mellon University, which mainly consisted of working at PBS station WQED where I was reunited with Dale and briefly with Thelma. I finished in 1976, moved to Jackson, Wyoming, then to a small town in rural Virginia and on to Flagstaff, Arizona, where my wife, son, and daughter and I live in our handmade house in the woods.

Along the way I worked on commercials, TV movies, and features as diverse as *Dune* and *A River Runs Through It*. I think I've finally found my niche shooting documentaries from South America to Mongolia to Italy celebrating diversity, our interaction with the natural world, and hopefully, along the way, cajoling some to be more caring stewards of the Earth. So much of this throws back to *Woodstock* where I saw firsthand what a powerful force a film can be.

CHUCK LEVEY

I DON'T KNOW HOW MUCH PERSONAL LIFE YOU WANT SO HERE'S A QUICKY

A FEW YEARS AFTER *Woodstock* I got divorced from Karen, whom you must have met. I tried to remain as close to our two girls as I could. I think I did. Brooke is thirty-two and lives in Lincoln, Nebraska. She's the head of curiculum for environmental studies at the University of Nebraska. Jessie will be thirty-one. She is married, living in Brooklyn with her husband and little girl, two. She teaches dance and is an Artist in Residence in a teaching program run by Lincoln Center.

In 1973 I met Carla Bauer. In 1977 I found out that I had a brain tumor. Great news! I was operated on by a neurosurgeon I met while shooting a segment for the CBS show *The Body Human*. I came through the operation pretty well, only deaf in my left ear, and six weeks later was on maneuvers with the army in Germany shooting a film about the all volunteer army for ABC. Four years later I met the doctor again. The tumor had grown back. Not so easy that time. I lost most of the sight in my left eye, the left side of my face was paralyzed, and balance was something that I had to learn again. So while other forty-year-old men were buying Porsches and trying to score with young women I had a genuine mid-life crisis. I was out of work for over two years and then I had to start all over again. Fortunately, I had some friends.

Carla was the best of them. We got married in 1987. We have two kids: Nicholas, eight, and Annie, five and a half. We live in Manhattan, have a house in the country, a car to get back and forth, and like most other freelancers are owed money. Sometimes even more than we owe. Ah, *Woodstock*.

Charlie Peck and I had already been good friends and remained so. We formed Charlie Company. Together we got projects to do and tried to do them in the Paradigm/*Woodstock* tradition.

Since the beginning of my career as a director of photography I've shot for both the big and the little screen. National commercials for Ford, Sears, IBM, DuPont, Sony, the YMCA. Major documentaries for theatrical release, public television, ABC, NBC, CBS, and more recently, cable. Industrial and corporate films and tapes for DuPont, Ciba-Geigy, Bristol Myers Squibb, Trinity Church, UJA, and many others. I work, primarily, in the "documentary" style. My interest is shooting in practical locations with real people or actors in more or less real situations.

I shot two films that have been nominated for Academy Awards. One won. Four TV shows that won Emmys. And I've personally been nominated for an Emmy in Cinematography nine times. Won four times.

MUFFIE MEYERS

SINCE WOODSTOCK

As I EXPLAIN TO all the aspiring young filmmakers who ask me how I got jobs in the beginning: "After *Woodstock* it was easy." With *Woodstock* on my résumé, I had a fairly easy time getting editing jobs. I cut a number of music films and documentaries, followed by a couple of feature films, including *Groove Tube* (thank you, Dale!) and *The Lords of Flatbush* (echos of Sha-Na-Na). I worked with David and Albert Maysles on several films, and in 1976 directed (with the Maysles and Ellen Hovde) the theatrically released documentary *Grey Gardens*.

Ellen and I then formed Middlemarch Films, and together have produced and directed over 150 documentaries, series and specials for television (and a couple of dramas). Our most recent work, a six-hour series for Public Television about the American Revolution, *LIBERTY!*, just won a Peabody. And on many of these films, I have continued to work with people that I met during the making of *Woodstock*!

ELEN
ORSON

SINCE *WOODSTOCK*, I'VE WORKED in motion picture, music recording, and live theater production; working with Hal Prince; John Houseman; Quincy Jones; Frank Sinatra; Crosby, Stills & Nash; the Julliard School of Music; the Brooklyn Academy of Music; and lots of wonderful, gifted people. My work is my life and *Woodstock* had a profound effect on my work relationships: my coworkers usually become like family to me, and I'm kind of picky about "redeeming social values" in the projects I choose. This makes me a pain in the ass.

I have been writer, editor, or associate producer (and grunt) on over 650 productions, and involved in many award-winning films and television series including Disney's *New Adventures of Winnie the Pooh*. I was managing editor for Walt Disney TV Animation's Editorial Department for six years, I work on an Avid (a digital Moviola of sorts) now, and I never want to splice film for a living again. Well, not unless it's something special.

In 1994, with my husband Christopher Carysfort, I cofounded a nonprofit organization, Foundation of the Arts for Cultures and the Environment (F.A.C.E.), which has the goal of promoting and publicizing successful solutions to environmental problems.

Still in the Garden...

CHARLIE PECK

CHARLES PECK GRADUATED THE Rhode Island School of Design in 1965 and was a staff designer at New York's public broadcasting station when Binder and Wadleigh lured him away to the cinéma vérité lifestyle.

In the year prior to Woodstock, he worked as Wadleigh's assistant cameraman and soundman. In the decades that followed, he teamed up with Woodstock cameraman Chuck Levey as a partner in a successful documentary production company.

Now in his fifties, he prefers the art direction and design work he left thirty years ago. He says, "It's a less glamorous career, but it's always nice and warm in here. I guess I'm getting old."

HART
PERRY

PRODUCER/DIRECTOR

No ONE HIRED ME as an abstract filmmaker. I did get hired as a cinéma vérité cameraman. I filmed *Harlan County: USA* for my former wife, Barbara Kopple, and then *American Dream*. Both films won Academy Awards. I stopped working as a cameraman fifteen years ago and concentrated on directing, although I continue to shoot my own films and films for friends. This year I directed *Motown 40*, which was a four-hour ABC special, and I am currently directing two one-hour documentaries on paramedics.

DANIEL TURBEVILLE

AFTER FINISHING THE ALBUM, I started a career as a sound engineer at the Record Plant in New York. My career stalled four years later after having, amongst other things, sung the background on *American Pie* as a member of the W. Forty-Fourth St. Rhythm & Noise Choir. I took any work I could find then, mostly in sales, which taught me communications skills. Ten years later, I walked out onto a carnival midway and was hooked. Hi hi hee hee, the carny life for me...! And so in 1982 I became Captain Tattoo, painting temporary body art in fairs in the US and Canada. In 1993 I married the artist Joyce Kingsbury. She, her daughter Rio, now thirteen, and son Logan, now nine, came to live with me and a year later, Raska! Jack Turbeville was born. We live in Ojai, California, and New York City now. Two years ago, we responded to the popularity of henna arts in America and created a small company of friends that sends high quality temporary body art henna products to all parts of the world. We think the thing to do is to "keep feeding each other."

EPILOGUE

DALE BELL, NOVEMBER 2020, SANTA MONICA

AFTER THE MOVIE OPENED March 26, 1970, all of us scattered, urgently looking for our next gig. Wadleigh and Maurice split, went their separate ways, yet for the rest of their lives, they shared a piece of the profits from the movie and the record. Wadleigh became a climate change scientist/activist spanning the globe, Maurice ran a bookshop in Santa Fe where he succumbed to brain cancer in 2008. The grosses from the most widely seen documentary in history would refuel the once-mighty Warner Brothers, pay off the several millions of debts from the Woodstock Ventures festival producing team over the next years, and catalyze the music/youth marketing/technology/performance companies over the next decades.

Almost everyone else who was a part of the *Woodstock* family went on to become greater cameramen, assistants, sound people, editors, directors, writers, and producers—storytellers and entrepreneurs—winning satisfaction, awards, while changing society in the process. Some of their stories are in this book. One story of camaraderie isn't. Here is its brief overture....

Thelma Schoonmaker, our supervising editor, had been trained in part by director Martin Scorsese at NYU Film School, and then as editor of Marty's first feature *Who's That Knocking at My Door?* in 1967. After *Woodstock,* she was sent around the world by Warner Brothers for about a year or so, all expenses paid. But no salary. Part of her work was to ensure that movie theatres were reconfigured technologically to be able to support our innovative "sound and picture immersive experience." Speakers might have to be installed, projectors retuned, all redesigned to heighten the *Woodstock* exhibition experience in major theatres globally.

In March 1974, working in New York City, I was introduced to Rocky Aoki, founder of Benihana Restaurants, who had partnered in a movie project with

Takeshi Kitano, the famed Japanese actor who played the Blind Beggar Swordsman *Zatoichi*. Together they had filmed Muhammed Ali touring Japan for several months in exhibition boxing events. Rocky didn't know what to do with all of this footage. He wanted to make a film about Ali. Could I help? After all, I had helped to make *Woodstock*! I knew I could not do it myself, so I called Thelma, then in the Bay Area of California. Not only was she available, but she could also get on the next plane. It would be a six-week project, I guesstimated. She agreed. When she arrived the next week, we surveyed the situation. It would take more than six weeks. Maybe six months, there was so much footage, and still some being shot. Yes, the Aoki team could afford a picture of this size; Thelma could be available, and so we began.

Meanwhile, Ed George, our chief projectionist for *Woodstock*, was in Pittsburgh, earning a master's degree in cinema at Carnegie Mellon University. For his day job, Ed was working as an intern in the basement of the nearby PBS station, WQED. (Remember, he had left his car, a 1958 MG, in my driveway in Grand View-on-Hudson, NY two years earlier.) He told me that WQED was establishing a relationship with the National Geographic Society. The NGS Specials, originally produced for ABC-TV, might migrate to PBS. Might I be interested in working on them, he asked innocently? Yes, I said, not yet knowing the implications; I was always looking for work. A week later, Ed called with "new news." WQED was creating another alliance with NGS that would lead to the joint production of a series of dramatic films about the 1776 bicentennial. The project would soon need a chief editor. Did I know one?

Yes, I did. When I learned that their start timetable would exactly coincide with the completion of the Muhammed Ali film, I recommended Thelma for the job. WQED accepted her, sight unseen. In early October, she was in Pittsburgh, in the editing rooms in the basement, setting up a team that would edit *Decades of Decisions*. Several weeks later, she told me she had spoken with the "powers that be" at WQED who confirmed the creation of the NGS/WQED alliance. Now, the two heads of WQED wanted to talk with me about helping them to create a larger production/post-production entity to handle the prestige Geographic one-hour series on PBS. Hmmm….my consultancy began….

Then Marty Scorsese called to invite me to work as Assistant Director on his new movie, *Taxi Driver* with Robert De Niro, to start production in April or May. I had worked as his AD on *Mean Streets* (1972) for the New York City filming, as well as his producer on *The Italian Americans* (1973), a short film about his family roots in Little Italy. I said Yes to Marty. *Taxi Driver* would be filmed in NYC. But the Directors Guild, that had recently accepted me as a Production Manager, would not allow me to switch categories of employment to Assistant Director, in spite of pleas from Arthur Penn and others. The DGA ultimately prevented me from accepting Marty's offer. In limbo again....

In our parting phone call, Marty asked me, by the way, if I knew where Thelma was. He told me he was writing a new script with Mardik Martin, his collaborating writer on *Mean Streets*, about Jake LaMotta, the 1949 middleweight boxing champion of the world. They were tentatively calling the project *Raging Bull*. I told him I knew exactly where Thelma was—in Pittsburgh, editing, and that she had just finished an editing project with me called *Muhammed Ali—The Man*. "Boxing???" asked Marty. "Unbelievable!!"

I connected Thelma, from the basement of WQED, to Marty Scorsese in New York, for the second phase of their relationship, begun in 1966. Except for the period between 1970–77, they have worked together on a total of twenty-five films—twenty features, two documentaries, three shorts, creating the longest-running director/editor collaboration in the history of the motion picture business...more than half a century. Fortunately for all of us who love their films, there is no end in sight.

WQED/Pittsburgh hired me in May 1975 to supervise the production of the first twelve National Geographic Specials. My work began in New York, then in Hollywood, setting up a postproduction complex to handle all of the specials, one block away from our 1969 *Woodstock* offices. I would produce and direct two specials: *Voyage of the Hokule'a* that catalyzed the burgeoning Polynesian Renaissance of civil and human rights; one with my boyhood hero, Thor Heyerdahl of *KON-TIKI* fame, called *The TIGRIS Expedition*, retracing early man and the oceans. Thelma would coproduce and edit yet a third special, *Karakorum*, with two other "Woodstockers," before she rejoined Marty on *Raging Bull*.

ACKNOWLEDGEMENTS

THE TRAIL OF BREADCRUMBS toward the publication of this book begin with Peter Pilafian. His introduction to Michael Tobias led me to publisher Michael Wiese and his encouraging staff of Ken Lee, Michele Chong, and Parthena Simone. Thank you all immensely for the opportunity. It represents the fulfillment of a dream born thirty years ago.

Of course, nothing could have been written at all had there not been a movie. For his perseverance, I/we have to thank Bob Maurice, producer; for his encompassing vision, I/we have to thank Mike Wadleigh, director. But as they have readily admitted, the making of this historic movie was nothing but a group effort, requiring the superhuman involvement of so many people from exhausted and hungry assistants ankle deep in mud at the site to optical house, laboratory, and dubbing stage technicians working round the clock in Hollywood months later. As we now know, each person's hands and ingenuity forged an icon for generations to come. Our extended family is vast. Each member is deserving.

Many people helped me in the writing and editing of this collection of remembrances. All of the contributors and their respective spouses (Liz Andrews and Liz George) can now relax; I will not bug you anymore. Thank you all for your efforts on behalf of our tiny piece of history. Our on-paper reunion is complete for this anniversary.

Others who helped include Chick Churchill and Andy Godfrey, who coaxed Alvin Lee to the telephone from Barcelona; Lela Logan and Anne Weldon at Atlantic ensured Ahmet Ertegun's participation; Jackie and Annie Guthrie, who found time in Arlo Guthrie's busy schedule; Ray Neapolitan for Joe Cocker; Kitsaun King for Michael Shrieve; Bill Belmont for Country Joe McDonald; Jerry Hughes for Charles Champlin; Julie Brennan and Gretchen Campbell for Martin Scorsese and Thelma Schoonmaker; Bob Kosberg and Charlie Mercer for Merv

Griffin; and Patti in Richie Havens's office for her persistence, which almost led to Richie becoming a part of the book.

Patti Fela may still be looking through the Port-O-San personnel records with a flashlight, trying to find Tom Taggart, the Port-O-San Man. Thank you.

Without the eager gifts of transcribing services provided through Pi Ware and the Filmmakers's Alliance, the insights and stories obtained through interview would never have left the can. I thank Robin Rindner (who traded her bowling shoes for two tickets to the original Woodstock Festival), Larry Oliver of Post Scripts, and Nancy Williams (who attended Altamont, not Woodstock). In Pittsburgh, Dorothy Hanna and her niece, Cinda Perla, transcribed some of my own recollections from 1970. All gave willingly of their time and skill.

Elen Orson, from our original crew, answered the call for "all hands on deck" just as she had in August 1969. Many thanks to her husband Christopher for letting me kidnap her for the duration. After transcribing many of the first interviews, she then lent her considerable editorial skills to reading and commenting on possible items to improve the work in progress. The combination of her moral and technical support was both necessary and invaluable.

Photographs leaped out at me from Henry Diltz, Amalie Rothschild, Larry Johnson, Marty Andrews, Charlie Peck, Chuck Levey, Steve Colter, and finally, from my summer stock friend who appeared on site thirty years ago, Bill Pierce. Thank you, Marcy Gensic, for getting Larry's photos to me.

Larry Johnson's vital spirit is reflected in every aspect of the original movie as well as in the *Director's Cut* twenty-five years later. I hope that some of his vision emerges from this book.

David Frank, my partner from San Rafael, believed so much in the project that he and his partner, Margaret Wendt, offered to try to sell it as television.

Jeanne Field and her husband, John Binder, listened attentively to my progress, and provided encouragement even as we were trying to develop a series on Los Angeles Jazz and Cultural History with Branden Chapman of Vista Vision Entertainment.

John Andrews, my colleague on The Shakespeare Guild, offered advice in the early stages of organization.

My niece, Holly Scribner, solved many computer problems as my laptop became over-saturated with Woodstockiana.

For providing musical and spiritual fellowship, as well as shelter during the last months of my work, I want to thank Larry and Virigina Keene, Bill Thomas,

David Loeb, Irving and Gladys Cousino, and the Church of the Valley choir and congregation.

For their understanding and patience, I thank Linda Reavely and Brandette Anderson at Campbell Hall School.

To Di Nelson, my then-life partner who grew up distanced from these tumultuous events, I offer this book as a bridge to another culture that contributed mightily to who I have become. My warm thanks to you for standing by me throughout every phase of this, my first book project.

To my first three sons, Jonathan, David, and Andrew, to Anne, your ever-compassionate Mom, and to your respective spouses and children, I offer my thanks for your continuing love and my apologies for any pain I have caused you as a result of my being caught up in this fervor.

To my fourth son, Reave, I offer the hope that, through this book and other media, you will come to understand the impact the 1960s had on us as individuals, compelling us to set down our recollections and perceptions for generations to come—you and yours!

Perhaps you as well as all of our extended families of children can "Keep Feeding Each Other!" Perhaps you can heed Martin Scorsese's vision in the foreword that there may yet be another Woodstock, imbued with the same passion and spirit. It, and the healing power of music, can maintain the Woodstock factor in all of our lives. There is still much to be done! Find your own Woodstock.

Lastly, the errors are mine.

A special thank you to Sharon Weil who led me to Rare Bird publishing, Tyson Cornell, Julia Callahan, and Hailie Johnson.

Now, in July 2020, mid-COVID, I am confined in Santa Monica where my wife, Lizbeth McDannel Bell, and I have lived since our wedding in 2008. "Ticket gods" sat us next to each other at the LA Opera's production of Puccini's *The Girl of the Golden West*. Providential happenstance. My six grandchildren—Julian, Belinda, Joshua, Libby, Christopher, and Katherine—all "Bells," are now firmly planting their roots and planning their futures from bases in three continents. I still hear Jimi Hendrix's wail, Wavy Gravy's admonition ("We've got to keep feeding each other!"), and Aretha Franklin's R.E.S.P.E.C.T. as I continue to produce—and film—media for social justice to build communities with my business partner of twenty years, Harry Wiland, at the Media Policy Center.

APPENDIX

1. Wadleigh, Michael, "The TakeOne Challenge of Filming Woodstock," reprinted by courtesy of American Cinematographer.

2. Garfinkel, Steve, *A Day in the Garden*, 1998.

Early in June of 1998, I had happened across a copy of the *Director's Cut: Woodstock* in a video store. Since it had been nearly thirty years since, as thirteen-year-old summer campers, we snuck into the movies in Hancock, New York, not so very far from the festival site, to witness the film in its first week of release. My mind began to wander...

I didn't quite make it to Woodstock that weekend in 1969. There had been rumblings among the camp counselors about a huge rock festival a few dozen miles from camp. My bunkmates and I were scheduled to attend a basketball game at a borscht-belt hotel that August Sunday. Already a filmmaker, I took my little Super 8 camera and a few carts of film. The stories of traffic are legendary. Our bus was one little part of the procession until, that is, it overheated outside of Monticello Raceway. My old movie footage doesn't reveal much of anything beyond a parade of painted-up vans and carloads of kids passing behind our disabled vehicle. Not quite award material. We got to the game in time for the fourth quarter, and had to settle for listening to stories of Woodstock, courtesy of the counselors who made it there on their day off.

Twenty-nine years later...I brought the movie home. And there it sat, next to the VCR, unwatched for several days. That weekend, I had to travel to the Jersey Shore to open up our summer home, and took the tapes with me, hoping to find some time.

Perhaps my interest in *Woodstock* was largely techincal; I wanted to see how the old Ektachrome movie film looked—something I myself had shot extensively as a film student in the 1970s. Then again, I had always loved the music; Crosby, Stills, Nash & Young; Joe Cocker; Jimi Hendrix; Richie Havens; The Who; Janis; Jefferson Airplane; Sly Stone; Santana; Ten Years After...I had practically worn out the soundtrack LP within days of buying it.

I found the time to watch "just a few minutes," late one night.

The "few minutes" led to a few hours, so captivating was Michael Wadleigh's masterpiece—so well photographed and well recorded. A stunning document of the last great party of the 1960s, and indeed a generation, to which I belong.

The following Monday, I telephoned Peter Abel, President of Abel CineTech, a leading motion picture camera agency and friend, and fellow docu-phile, too.

"Sometimes I need to watch a little *Woodstock* myself," said he. "Just to put things in perspective. Then Pete mentioned that Chuck Levey, the noted documentary filmmaker (and someone that I had recently met at a conference at Abel CineTech), had been one of the shooters at Woodstock. I wasted no time.

I telephoned Chuck, inviting him to lunch. I brought my tape recorder.

"That was long ago," said Chuck. "I have actually taken it off my résumé, rather than have people think I'm an old fart." I was amazed that perhaps the coolest assignment of a lifetime would be exorcised from his résumé, although after nine Emmy nominations and four Emmy Awards, after his work was purchased as part of the permanent collection of the Museum of Modern Art, and twenty years of shooting film worldwide for shows like "60 Minutes," I could maybe understand. For about two seconds.

I was unprepared for the ultimate consequences of that luncheon.

Chuck is an unusual artist; a gifted painter and still photographer, he maintains an understated demeanor yet is one of those magical people that one cannot help but feel comfortable with—and indeed, want to be around. Not a "local hero"—a hero that happens to be local!

The more Chuck talked that day, the more he remembered about that time in the little farm town of Bethel, New York. The story began long before, with Chuck and Michael Wadleigh working together on musical "Promo Films" of contemporary 1960s rock stars.

And through Chuck, I met Michael Wadleigh, whose name I had remembered since seeing it on the big screen in 1970. But how to begin making up for lost time as a both a filmmaker and historian? Fortunately for me, Michael was as generous with his time and spirit as was Chuck Levey. I started learning about the technical side of *Woodstock*. Chuck and Michael's stories and guidance were invaluable, especially as they related to film and camera technology then versus now.

Mike and company had to use AC-powered cameras to maintain sync with the sound track. Red hot camera motors required towels on shoulders to keep the operators from getting burned. AC and rain didn't mix, and occasionally there were electrical shocks to be had. The Ektachrome had a speed of twenty-five Tungsten, sixteen Daylight. And this film was ultimately blown up to seventy millimeters!

Based upon what Chuck said, this is the kind of situation he personally revels in; solving problems as he shoots. To me, this is the essence of being a filmmaker.

An article celebrating the art of these filmmakers was in order. It was a big story, especially in light of the 1999 thirtieth anniversary, and the load of NYC people involved from the start.

About a week after our luncheon and a few more calls to Chuck, I read with interest that some new promoters had decided to do another event at the original Woodstock site. It would be the first sanctioned event since the original. I had visions of stadium seating 1990's commercialism. I was determined to get to the site before "they" ruined it. Further, The *New York Daily News* mumbled something about the Day in the Garden Festival "not being a Kodak Moment" because cameras and camcorders would not be allowed. What kind of people were these?

We drove up to the site later that week, "still" cameras in hand, just for inspiration. As we walked from the Jeep, we found ourselves face-to-face with the new promoters. So I asked who was doing the film of A Day in the Garden.

"Oh. We haven't made any provisions for that this year."

So I made the offer: Let us shoot film here and they get a copy of the greatest home movie of all time. Jonathan Quitt, the festival director, agreed. We shook hands.

Over the next few weeks, the deal got bigger and bigger. What had started as Chuck and I with our Aaton Cameras had snowballed. A Mr. Chip Rachlin called me. He was acting on behalf of the promoters, looking to find out what we had in mind. As it turned out, Chip's sister and I were friends in college. Small world. Chip would be our link between GF Entertainment, the company owned by Mr. Alan Gerry (the legendary cable television visionary and industrialist, who also owned the festival site); the promoter of the festival; and the performers. (Wow. We originally weren't even sure that we'd get to shoot any performers!) Suddenly, doors began to open. Back to Peter Abel, this time to see about getting cameras. A bunch of them.

In that timeframe, I spoke with Messrs. Randy Sparrazza and Mark Gaul, both of the Television Segment of Kodak Professional Motion Imaging. These gentlemen agreed to give us the financial support to get the film shot, and in doing so, broke new "corporate ground." They became our Executive Producers and helped provide us with direction, especially with regard to deliverables from the Kodak standpoint.

Back on the phones, looking for more cinematographers. Richard Dooley, the Line Producer of the television program, *Remember WENN*, had just finished his season, and was available. A mutual friend told him that we needed a line producer. With him came Mary Cesar, the production coordinator, and her associate, Amy Baker. Richard also brought award-winning cinematographer David Sperling, also from *Remember WENN*. Peter Abel suggested Mr. Peter Mullett, a Baltimore-based filmmaker, who was interested in shooting with us. I brought Mr. Roman Vinoly, a gifted young cinematographer already making a name for himself. Chuck Levey would shoot and act as director/DP. I would produce and be the fourth cinematographer. J.T. Takagi was a top-notch sound recordist, and she agreed to spend the week traveling and working with us.

Through Kodak's PR film, I found Ms. Vicki Kasala, who would be our still photographer. Additional stills would be shot for us by the legendary Elliott Landy, who was the official Woodstock Photographer in 1969, and Chester Whitlock, a freelence concert-shooter and thirty-year friend.

All of this came into being the final week prior to the event.

Ms. Robyn Gerry of GF, offered to be our local production coordinator, and worked with Chuck Levey and Richard lining up interviews for the documentary part of the film, to be shot the "week of." Our "centerpiece" would be Mr. Duke Devlin, a man who came to Bethel in 1969 for the Woodstock Festival and never left. Duke would be our friend, unofficial photographer, and spiritual guide throughout. A real-life story that would tie together the last twenty-nine years.

Richard Dooley, Chuck, JT, and I arrived the Sunday before the festival's Friday start, ready to shoot Monday morning. That week, I worked as Chuck's camera assistant. I was fortunate…Chuck demonstrated extreme patience with his new AC! Our schedule was hectic but productive. Our days began at 6:00 a.m. and ended often around midnight.

Thursday around dusk, two vans pulled into the compound. One, a fifteen-passenger model, was jammed with DPs and assistants. The second was driven by Peter Abel, and carried two of his men, ready to work with the crews. Peter also brought about a million dollars worth of cameras and related gear. I counted our crew as they disembarked. Twenty-four souls. Many had never met. Most would become friends and work together again after the festival, under less crazy conditions. We unloaded the gear into a van next to the stage. Another truck would be our film-loading station, a few feet away. Two loaders would do nothing else for three days straight.

A quick production meeting, dinner, and off to our cabins at the little inn Dooley had found for us. Our call was for 6:00 a.m.; the concert started at 10:00 a.m. I slept about an hour that night.

I paused just for a moment. I would actually be shooting, and indeed producing, a film at the site I had only dreamed about…With Pete Townsend, Joni Mitchell, singing "Woodstock," the anthem of a generation, Ten Years After, Melanie, who was only seventeen at the first festival, Lou Reed, Donovan, and a full additional day of new 1990s bands! And working with Chuck Levey! Holy shit, life is good. Back to reality…

Until minutes before each artist began to play, we knew not what we would be allowed to shoot. Chip Rachlin and Dooley kept in touch with the crews by walkie-talkie. Some deals were, out of necessity, made with artists as their helicopter touched down in the field adjacent to the festival site. Song lists were kept on scraps of paper and cardboard by the camera assistants. From a technological standpoint we were fully three decades beyond the 1969 team. As a result, we let the technology serve us. Early on, we decided that we would use the new Aaton XTR Prod Cameras. Equipped with Aaton time-code, these cameras are a virtually foolproof way to do a multicam shoot The same code was fed to our forty-eight-track sound truck, Stereo DAT Recorder. The Aaton Cameras would "burn-in" man and machine-readable code along the perforation edge of the film, making syncing virtually automatic. For years, the issue of sound sync has been a disadvantage for the film user. Videotape shooters using the single-system of a camcorder always had sound on tape. And of course, videotape was never an consideration. The event was too important, and quality was too much of an issue to have something that looks like the evening news or a soap opera.

Contemporary filmmakers had to go through the labors associated with lining up sound tracks in or prior to telecine transfer or film cutting. Aaton's system would all but eliminate this job. Peter Abel brought with him Mr. Jesse Rosen, who would serve as our Aaton/InDaw Digital Sync expert.

The final link in the film sound system is Aaton's InDaw computer. The InDaw allowed us to automatically post-sync our audio literally in a storage room, instantly and without the need to encumber the film colorist in a session. In full bandwidth Digital. Peter loaned this system to us following the concert. It worked. Perfectly.

Chuck chose Kodak's new VISION 200T film for the concert proper. This film's extremely fine grain and superior sharpness coupled with medium speed versatility made it a natural choice. It was three times "faster" then the film of 1969.

In all, some 75,000 feet were shot that week, with laboratory developing and selected roll printing done at Colorlab, of Rockville, Maryland. Postproduction Telecine and editing is in progress at SMA Video, in New York City.

Looking back several months, I still find it difficult to believe that I was "there," albeit twenty-nine years later, shooting my heroes performing onstage—alongside my heroes behind the cameras.